HARD DYING MEN

The Story of
General W. H. L. Wallace,
General T. E. G. Ransom, and
Their "Old Eleventh" Illinois Infantry
in the American Civil War
(1861-1865)

By
Jim Huffstodt

HERITAGE BOOKS
2007

HERITAGE BOOKS
AN IMPRINT OF HERITAGE BOOKS, INC.

Books, CDs, and more—Worldwide

For our listing of thousands of titles see our website at
www.HeritageBooks.com

Published 2007 by
HERITAGE BOOKS, INC.
Publishing Division
65 East Main Street
Westminster, Maryland 21157-5026

Copyright © 1991 Jim Huffstodt

The cover illustration is of General T. E. G. Ransom, from a photograph by Mathew Brady. The drawing appeared in the May 14, 1864 edition of Harper's Weekly. (Photo courtesy of the Illinois State Historical Library.)

All rights reserved. No part of this book may be reproduced or transmitted in any form or by any means, electronic or mechanical, including photocopying, recording or by any information storage and retrieval system without written permission from the author, except for the inclusion of brief quotations in a review.

International Standard Book Number: 978-1-55613-510-1

"The men who fought there were the tried fighters, the hammered, the weather-beaten, the very hard-dying men..."

John Brown's Body

by Stephen Vincent Benet

Contents

Preface: Echoes from the Past vii
Acknowledgments xi
Chapter One
    A Ceaseless Roll of Drums 1
Chapter Two
    A Rash, Brave Fellow 27
Chapter Three
    Lost All But Honor 53
Chapter Four
    Hideous Night 79
Chapter Five
    A Thousand Ties of Affection 103
Chapter Six
    Blaze of Musketry 127
Chapter Seven
    Lightning in the Evening Sky 147
Chapter Eight
    Dying Is No Easy Thing 169
Chapter Nine
    Don't Scare a God Damn! 193
Chapter Ten
    Each In His Own Heart Wondering 215
Chapter Eleven
    The Spirit of Killing 237
Photographs 239
Notes 279
Sources 333
Index 345

This book is dedicated to my wife, Judy,
who has kept the faith through a long march.

Echoes from the Past

Even now, twenty-five years after her death, I can visualize my grandmother with undiminished clarity. By the early 1960's, she was fast approaching ninety; the weathered, creased face was still proud though worn by bitter toil, hidden sorrows, and private tragedies. Celia Sykes was a unique woman whose kindly hands seemed always to be dipping into secret hiding places in a great brown bureau drawer, emerging to display crinkled, many times folded, dollar bills for birthdays or hard candy forbidden by parents. I can see her now, her diminutive frame perched on the green wicker rocker on the wide, wooden porch. Blue-veined, bony hands gestured with animation, and the bright hazel eyes told of a facile mind that mocked the furrowed exterior. Urged onward by an inquisitive child one spring day, she recalled with vivid detail stories heard from her own father gone more than six decades before.

She seemed puzzled and curious that anyone really cared to know about a rather common man who had died in 1902. They had buried him up on the hill whose forested slopes looked down on the riverside hamlet of Utica, Illinois. He was interred in the shelter of the great stone sentinel, a stern Union rifleman who leaned massive granite arms atop a grounded long-barrelled rifle. He was buried with other forgotten men under nondescript white tombstones clustered in bivouac around the stolid soldier's monument. There in oblivion he was to rest, to be remembered only fitfully each Memorial Day when a faltering bugle and staccato rifle salute signals another year has passed.

On one particular Memorial Day the ritual awakened in me a curiosity about this long-buried, faceless man who had been my grandmother's father. And so, on that day, I listened with growing intensity when this faded woman talked of days gone past and retold tales first spoken by her soldier father home from the war. It was a story unvarnished by romance. Grandmother evoked savage images populated by flesh-and-blood beings whose minds were clouded with doubts, fears, and petty thoughts; men, not very unlike us, who yearned for clean beds and undisturbed sleep, detested certain officers and adored a few, ran in fright on occasion but usually fought it through. Remembered again were her father's vibrant recollections repeated with an obvious fidelity. These were harsh memories uncolored by myth: crystal-clear visions of frozen feet and the maggotty horrors of unburied men and horses.

Grandmother's words painted a dreary tableau of a tragic war as described by my great-grandfather, a simple laborer who had marched south in the spring of 1861. This man, Private Martin Baker of Company K, Eleventh Illinois Infantry, was one who had endured. Ravaged by exposure, and with Rebel lead imbedded in his shoulder, he trudged homeward stripped of illusions. At least for this man the recollections would be devoid of the 19th century romanticism that obscured reality. When Baker spoke of those terrible days it was to recall sadness and fright and the names of dimly remembered comrades: one shot through the head at bloody Shiloh, another strangled by disease, or others swallowed up by the Rebel prisons.

Private Baker's saga is a part of the grand epoch of the "Western Soldier," those self-reliant souls from Illinois, Ohio, Indiana, Iowa, Wisconsin, Minnesota, and the rest of what came to be called the "Old Northwest." These men were the nuts-and-bolts of the war machine manufactured by General Ulysses S. Grant: that great iron hammer destined to shatter Confederate dreams at Fort Donelson, Shiloh, Vicksburg, and Mobile. His regiment was the "Old Eleventh," a unit whose history reflects in microcosm the great Army of the West.

The Eleventh's achievements have not been forgotten, only buried in musty libraries in a dozen small Illinois towns and lying dormant in the cavernous archives in Washington D.C. and Springfield, Illinois. Scrawled in diaries, recorded on the pages of rural newspapers, enscribed on parchment-like official reports, are the impressions of battle, the often primitive conceptions of political struggles, and everywhere the mundane, but, for the modern reader, fascinating detail of camp life. Grandmother's reminiscences served as the driving force behind a search for these fragile pieces of the puzzle which, once fitted together, provide a bloody but heroic mosiac. This is a history of the Eleventh Illinois Regiment, dedicated to Private Baker and the other "little men" who stood all that savage war could offer, those who endured the greatest of American tragedies.

Poet-historian Stephen Vincent Benet was motivated fifty years ago to articulate in passionate rhyme that national agony. The present work, in a modest way, may perhaps provide the reader with some insight into the minds and hearts of those who suffered the price of greatness. And, as Benet wrote so well, we invite the reader to hear "the thin, forgotten voices of men forgotten. Crying out of torn scraps of paper, notes scribbled and smudged. On aces, on envelopebacks, on gilt-edged cards stolen out of a dead man's haversack...."

Acknowledgments

My debt to countless individuals is large indeed. Without their assistance and encouragement, this manuscript would have remained unwritten. Three ladies were particularly instrumental in editing the early drafts of *Hard Dying Men*. Mrs. Margie Bearss of Arlington, Virginia, the wife of the noted Civil War historian, Edwin C. Bearss, and a scholar in her own right, provided invaluable help. Her voluminous background knowledge, particularly in regard to the Mississippi campaigns of the 11th Illinois, lent her criticisms, astuteness and comprehensiveness. Mrs. Mary Jane Tonozzi, history and English instructor at St. Bede Academy in Peru, was equally helpful, providing insightful commentary on nearly every phase of the work. Another key advisor was Miss Elizabeth Cummings, retired Director of Learning Resources at Illinois Valley Community College, Oglesby. She brought to her reading of the manuscript the sharp, discriminating eye of the natural editor. Each of these women contributed immeasurably to the quality of the end product.

Primary sources are crucial requirements for writing history. My appreciation in this regard goes to the following individuals: Mrs. Howard Kenyon of Washington, D.C., who provided copies of Lieutenant Colonel Nathaniel C. Kenyon's war diary and related correspondence; Mrs. Gladys C. Todd of Scotch Plains, New Jersey for copies of correspondence by and dealing with Brigadier General T.E.G. Ransom, first cousin to her late mother; Mr. Winfield D. Nevius of Pleasantville, New York, for a collection of letters written by Colonel Garrett Nevius (1861-1863) to his brother in Lodi, New York; Mrs. Warner Whipple of Waltham, Illinois, for providing a letter collection written by Sergeant Major Frank Whipple during the war, and related documents; Steven Adolphson of Salem, Massachusetts, for sharing his magnificent collection relating to Colonel Douglas Hapeman who served in the 11th Illinois and in the 104th Illinois Infantry; and Mrs. June Slater of La Salle, Illinois who volunteered the diary of Private Lemuel Burke, 119th Illinois Infantry.

Many Civil War scholars throughout the nation responded to my requests for information and assistance. Despite the pressing demands of their own research and study, they devoted valuable time and effort to advise me on countless occasions. Many thanks to Michael P. Musick, archivist with the National Archives; Earl Hess, archivist, the Institute of Civil War Studies, Clayton, Missouri; Dr. Gary T. Lord, history instructor at Norwich University, Northfield, Vermont; Marie Gecik, assistant, Special Collections, Chicago Public Library; the late Paul Spence, archivist, Illinois State Historical Library, Springfield; Mrs. Clair Maxwell of Long Beach, California; Mrs. Edward Cahill of Ransom, Illinois; Edwin C. Bearss, author and administrator with the U.S. Department of the Interior, Washington, D.C.; Robert Moulder of Boulder, Colorado, the current owner of a pistol once used by Lieutenant James Vernay of the 11th Illinois; Edward Murphy, associate director of the Medal of Honor History Roundtable, Lombard, Illinois; James Gerrety, chief administrator, Illinois Military Historical Society, Auburn, Illinois; and George E. Parks of Anna, Illinois, an authority on the 109th Illinois Infantry Regiment which was later incorporated into the 11th Illinois.

Numerous institutions, museums, and libraries were gracious in proferring their professional expertise. I remain indebted to the following: the U.S. Army Military History Research Collection, Carlisle Barracks, Pennsylvania; the War Library and Museum of the Military Order of the Loyal Legion of the United States, Philadelphia; the Norwich Vermont Historical Society, Norwich, Vermont; the National Archives, Washington, D.C.; the Starved Rock Library System, Ottawa, Illinois; the Vicksburg Courthouse Museum, Vicksburg, Mississippi; the Mississippi Historical Society, Jackson, Mississippi; the State Historical Society of Wisconsin, Madison; the Missouri Historical Society, St. Louis; and the State Library Commission of Iowa, Des Moines.

Equally sincere thanks are extended to the Stephenson Historical Society, Freeport, Illinois; the Effingham Regional Historical Society, Effingham, Illinois; the La Salle County Historical Society Museum, Utica, Illinois; the Lacon Public Library, Lacon, Illinois; the Reddick Library, Ottawa, Illinois; the Rockford Public Library, Rockford, Illinois; the La Salle Public Library, La Salle, Illinois; the Peru Public Library, Peru, Illinois; and the Morris Public Library, Morris, Illinois. Special appreciation is reserved for Miss Evelyn Moyle, librarian at the Federal and State Depository

Library, Illinois Valley Community College; and Miss Patricia Connolly, librarian at the Jacobs Memorial Library, Illinois Valley Community College. Other individuals who provided their support were: Dr. C.R. Jasiek, Chairman of the Board of Illinois Valley Community College; and Dr. Alfred Wisgoski, president of Illinois Valley Community College.

The author is also deeply indebted to his parents, the late Robert W. Huffstodt and Helen Sykes Huffstodt. His appreciation also goes to Wendy Karppi of Heritage Books, Inc., for her contribution to the work and her patience with the author.

Jim Huffstodt
May, 1991
West Palm Beach, Florida

Chapter One

Ceaseless Roll of Drums

Bursts of jagged white lightning drew back the early winter morning's blackness to reveal, in flickering half-light, the long, ragged Union column. There were more than 2,500 men in all, drenched by a relentless, frigid January rain. Rumor had it that the Rebel General Jeff Thompson was ahead somewhere near the Missouri town of Charleston, bivouacked on the Swank farm with 1,000 cavalry.[1] By 5 a.m., January 8, 1862, the Federals had been lurching about in the wet darkness for nine hours. Many, if not all, must have yearned for the dry warmth left behind at Bird's Point, or Camp Lyon as it was called, which lay ten miles southeast on a bluff above the great Mississippi River. The Tenth Iowa Infantry was on the point, followed by the Eleventh Illinois where Private George D. Carrington of Company B shivered and speculated on whether the uncertain guide was not a Rebel. His doubts were founded on the fact that the column had wandered for hours in apparent circles. Carrington could barely discern the column in the rainy gloom except for the dim outline of an officer's white horse just ahead. At intervals the horse and rider would leap into sharp definition illuminated by the lightning's trembling glare. It was nearly dawn. The column moved "through a lane with corn fields on each side and a house with a blur of trees ahead." Haunted by fatigue, the men shambled along like uniformed sleepwalkers until the trance was abruptly shattered by the sound and flame of gun fire:

> There rang out on the morning air the clear, sharp report of a rifle, followed by a flash of fire and the reports of a volley of musketry. The Iowa boys returned the fire; we halted, some confusion, only temporary for Colonel Ransom sang out "Eleventh forward on double quick," and soon had the regiment in line...we moved forward in the darkness, but

the enemy knew the woods and skededled. No more shots were fired. We remained quiet until daylight. Well! We had smelled powder...[2]

Gray morning light revealed five of the Iowa soldiers sprawled dead, and seven more nursing wounds. Their ambushers had made clean their escape, leaving behind no evidence that the return fire had inflicted any damage whatsoever. Months of futile pursuit had culminated in this brief, bloody interlude lasting not more than a few minutes, conducted in total ignorance in the pitch black night. "I looked at the men killed, lying there dead with the rain beating down on their faces; it did look so hard," Private Carrington wrote. "We felt much depressed at the sight of those poor fellows lying there dead alongside the road, all wet and uniforms all splashed with mud..."[3] There was anger too on that January 8, 1862. The column had been ambushed only 150 yards from the Rodan farm, whose occupants had sworn that, except for a solitary soldier, there had been no rebels in the area for two weeks. Colonel N. Perczel, the expedition commander, was seething. He immediately ordered Rodan's arrest. "The man...willfully and damnably denied all knowledge of the presence of the rebels, while in all probability the ambush proceeded from his house," Perczel reported. "He is at all events guilty of a capital crime, having misled us by his feigned ignorance and caused by this our severe loss."[4]

Captain Nevius of Company D from the Eleventh was convinced that, judging by the "flashes from their guns", the Rebels had fired on the column from no more than twenty-five feet away. He wrote his brother, Will, in New York state how the men had dragged themselves back to the Point that day, "tired and wet to the skin." Tongue-in-cheek, Nevius added:

These little skirmishes are getting to be a nuisance...But I presume that it is all right, a part of a soldier's life, obey orders, let them be what they may be.

Well, I shall try to do my best, and am ready to take the consequences, let them come in any shape. Yet amidst all the trials of such a life, there occasionally breaks into some fun, and good times that we will never forget.[5]

Such a tolerant philosophy was not evident in other circles as the bitter guerrilla campaign wore on. Frustration, coupled with the growing casualty list, bred an environment of hate and vengeance. The emotional climate intensified on January 11 when four more men were shot while on picket at the Point itself. Brigadier General U.S. Grant promptly ordered the entire civilian populace for six miles in all directions from Camp Lyon to be removed. He instructed that

> word (be) given that all citizens making their appearance within those limits are liable to be shot. To execute this, patrols should be sent out, in all directions, and bring into camp at Bird's Point all citizens, together with their subsistence, and require them to remain, under pain of death and destruction of their property until properly relieved... The intention is not to make political prisoners of these people, but to cut off a dangerous class of spies.[6]

This surely wasn't war as envisioned by the Union recruits who had joined the colors with an exuberant gaiety. This was a bleak, inglorious guerrilla hunt climaxed on rare occasion by furtive night ambuscades. How different from those dreamlike days eight months previous when the volunteers rendezvoused at the Illinois state capitol in Springfield...

Fort Sumter's cannon had been clearly heard on the Illinois prairie. The roar was transmitted, at least in the abstract sense, by the telegraph lines whose chattered messages were soon translated into printer's ink from Chicago to Cairo. Even the least perceptive dirt farmer became dimly aware that the stark, black headlines marked the end of something--and a beginning. A few realized how the news shouted out the death of compromise, of debate, of rationality itself. The time for talk had departed; now it was a time for violence. On April 25, 1861, Springfield, Illinois was a magnet for the men drawn by the sound of Sumter's cannon. Thousands slogged into the muddy confines of the Illinois state fairgrounds, christened Camp Yates in honor of incumbent Governor Richard Yates. Volunteers came by rail and by wagon, on foot and on horseback. Attorneys intermingled with newspaper editors; railroad men fraternized with former school masters. Every segment of this frontier society gathered here and listened to hours of bloody rhetoric, laced with ample doses of maudlin patriotic sentiment.

Few weapons were evident except for a motley assortment of antiquated muskets and private arms, which often posed a greater threat to the user than to the intended victim. The scene was rendered even more ludicrous by the attire. The more affluent paraded in a bizarre mix of militia uniforms from past eras. One could dismiss it as a great charade except for the very serious expressions the participants wore as they floundered about, bellowed at and pleaded with by their officers. Hardly anyone had even a grasp of rudimentary military maneuvers, manners, tactics, or strategy. It was to be an amateur's war in the best Minuteman tradition. Nineteen-year-old George D. Carrington of Lacon, Illinois, soon to be mustered in the Eleventh Illinois Infantry, was entranced.

    We were without arms or equipments of any kind. In "citizens" clothes of all kinds and colors, some carrying carpet sacks, other bundles of clothing; I had nothing but the suit I was then wearing. As we marched through the gates I shall never forget the sights that met our gaze, the impressions of that moment. It was night and very dark, at the gate on either side were sentries armed with musket and bayonet. There were probably 10,000 men in camp, standing around the camp fires with red three-point Mackinac blankets over their shoulder. The darkness, the glare of the camp fires, the red-blanketed men passing to and fro...the glimmer of an occasional bayonet; all made up a scene never to be forgotten.[7]

    George was a rover. In 1854, the Connecticut-born boy, at the age of twelve, arrived in Chicago with a rifle cradled in his arms and a desire for new sights and adventures. Before he reached twenty, he had traveled the Great Mississippi River in search of all types of work. Perhaps there was a bit of his grandfather in the lad. His father's father was a prominent "Captain of Ships" in New England at the turn of the 18th century. It was a trade he plied with zeal and apparent success except on occasion, as in 1805, when the British seized his craft, the "*Vigilant.*" They searched her at Plymouth for contraband bound for Napoleon's armies. Less romantic was George's uncle, Edwin, who also held a floating command. He was captain and part owner of a river steamboat.[8]

    The Carringtons, like so many other clans in that raw era, were searching for something better. Maybe they couldn't even define it for themselves, but there was a need for change, for challenge, and possibly for adventure. Political motives aside, young George must have glimpsed opportunities galore to be gained on the battlefield. In the spring of 1861 he promptly joined the Marshall County Guards raised in Lacon, Illinois by Captain Fred Shaw. The recruit brought with him a reputation as a "crack shot" and a fascination with literature. From the very first this perceptive, keenly aware youth jotted down in diaries, on envelopes, and on scraps of paper, his impressions of the infinite details of the life in his regiment: the Eleventh Illinois Volunteer Infantry.

As with the other volunteer companies, the Marshall County Guards were issued the distinctive red blanket and assigned to a long cattle shed filled with fresh straw. Bread, beans, and coffee were distributed as the men divided up into various "messes" striving with all their ingenuity to concoct something edible from the ingredients. Private Carrington would remark that "many never fully recovered from eating of this awful cooking." Burned beef, uncooked beans, and coffee "strong enough to bear up an iron wedge and black as a hat" made for what he described as extremely "outlandish grub." What with fixing the daily meals, the constant drill, and guard duty, the rank and file were in a constant motion while the officers caucused in attempts to determine which companies would join which regiment.

Lieutenant Greenbury Fort of the Guards noted that the camp "presents a lively scene--martial and parade, fife and drum, from daylight till dark...." Lieutenant Fort was an attorney turned warrior. He, too, was dazzled by the prospect of what lay ahead, as well as by the hustle and excitement of the present. Sunday church service even took on new meaning when thousands in camp strained to hear Southern-born Reverend McNeal of Mt. Morris preach an iron-hard war sermon. On hand was Governor Yates of Illinois, surrounded by a stately collection of legislators, judges, and the finest Springfield citizenry. Lieutenant Fort related how the minister dismissed qualms about Christians engaged in the slaughter of fellow-creatures. Instead, his message was that "a man was not a Christian unless he would fight now...he prayed God to have mercy on Jeff Davis, if there be mercy for such traitors." The obvious implication was that the Reverend McNeal would much prefer "Old Testament" wrath. Whatever their own thoughts, the men were at least entertained by such oratorical demonstrations. Anything was preferable to the monotonous camp life that grew tedious after a few days. Lieutenant Fort wrote how it was "...drill, drum, parade, and cheer, same as any other day."[9]

Even more dramatic than the Sunday service was a visit to camp by Senator Steven Douglas, the famed "Little Giant" whose power in the Democratic party had been close to absolute until the recent split drove members into Northern and Southern factions. Douglas responded to the present crisis with a cry for Union, swinging his still considerable prestige and power behind Abraham Lincoln, the president-elect. Only recently Douglas had spoken before the Illinois legislature exhorting that body to protect the government and the flag from enemy assailants. This devotion to the greater good endeared the Senator to the volunteers gathered at the fairgrounds. And, now they glimpsed his familiar squat figure riding in an open carriage about to enter the main gate. Lieutenant Fort recalled:

> A little before sundown on Sunday a tumultuous cheering commenced near the portal of the campground, and it was soon found that Senator Douglas and Lady had entered, riding in an open barouche, which was the signal for a rally. The soldiers rushed out and swung their hats, and cheer after cheer rolled around the camp until he made the whole circuit and passed out. Republicans as well as Democrats joined in the cheer, thus showing their good feeling for all who will support the government.[10]

Jostling among the soldier audience were the distinctive members of the Rockford Zouaves, organized by Captain Garrett Nevius, a photographer by trade who had been extremely active in Republican circles. He was instrumental in forming a brigade of Lincoln "Wide-A-Wakes" who had marched in the recent presidential campaign brandishing their distinctive symbols. They presented a militant, aggressive profile that certainly supported the Southern conviction that this man Lincoln was a radical incendiary bent on the destruction of their way of life. From this organization, Nevius had, with the assistance of young Elmer Ellsworth, formed the Rockford Zouaves trained in the French drill and outfitted in a colorful garb consisting of red pantaloons and ballooned sleeves.[11] One of his key junior officers, Lieutenant Robert Bird, regaled the folks back home with lengthy essays on the activity at Camp Yates, a place he said was inhabited by "a thousand and one contradictory rumors." Bird's letters described the frivolous picnic air that dominated the scene at Camp Yates. For many, if not most of these mostly adolescent recruits, the activity in camp was much like a country revival or a rather rambunctious town meeting. In many ways there could be seen aspects of the county fair as well. All in all, it was an exciting place for boys fresh from the apron strings, and they made the most of it. Lieutenant Bird wrote home, not of grisly preparations for war, but rather the jocular incidents and anecdotes one might encounter at a particularly boisterous sales convention:

Camp duty and camp fun I can give you but faint idea of. Words are inadequate to the task; it must be seen to be appreciated. Among our men we have a right sharp genius from Pecatonica, and withal a capital good fellow he is. He is a genius and keeps the boys in capital good humor. He is a poet, phrenologist, anatomist, and the Lord only knows what...He has examined the heads of a number of the members of neighboring companies, and given them a chart, which I don't know whether they will feel flattered by or not but which forever remain as monuments of the Professor's comical erudition in the noble science... He improvises doggeral rhyme on anything which transpires before him, and always has something humorous in it. He mourns comically over his want of early educational opportunities, and says that all the education he has, he has picked up by the way where smart men had dropped it. He has certainly made good use of such opportunities....[12]

Within days a semblance of order emerged from chaos. The companies amalgamated into regiments and elected their own officers. Both the Marshall County Guards and the Rockford Zouaves were mustered in as a part of the Eleventh Illinois Volunteer Infantry Regiment, an extremely representative unit drawing recruits from all sections of the Prairie State. Freeport and Rockford provided companies from the far north near the Wisconsin border, while Illinois River communities stretching from Morris southwest through Ottawa, La Salle, and Lacon provided five more companies. From further south, in what was called "Egypt," came the men of Effingham, Marion, and Centralia. The latter volunteers were a strong-minded lot, having formulated loyal Union sentiments in an area strongly sympathetic to Southern values and ambitions.

William Henry Lamb Wallace, a prominent figure in northern Illinois Republican politics, was elected colonel. He was a man of property, prestige, and a personal acquaintance of the incumbent president. Above all else he was as romantic a man as any who were drawn that spring by the sound of the guns. Defined by his illusions and a complex mythical heritage, Colonel Wallace was a man certain about the course ahead. He was unfettered by the doubts that so often leave men awash in oceans of moral grays. For forty-year-old "Will" Wallace it was a world of absolutes dominated by a rigid conviction that the national honor was inextricably bound up with his own life. His photographs reveal a sensitive face fashionably framed with curly brown hair of moderate length.

His features remind one of a bookish preacher or solitary scholar, as opposed to the reality that this was a man whose life had been devoted to law, politics, and war. Like many interesting men, Wallace was a contradiction for which there are no easy answers. One aspect was reflected in the dreamy love prose directed to his beloved wife, Ann; yet the face concealed the other man, the aggressive and violent man committed to action. Even as a student at Rock River Seminary in Mount Morris in northern Illinois, the youthful Wallace temporarily abandoned literature and history in order that he might lead a vigilante gang in pursuit of horse thieves and alleged murderers. Once these predators were executed, he returned and debated the moral desirability of vigilante action before the student body. With extreme vigor, he spoke of "higher law" than those embodied in the statutes and won the applause and admiration of his audience.[13]

Wallace was of Scotch ancestry tempered by the American frontier. He was born July 8, 1821 in Urbana, Ohio, and, as a young man, migrated west to La Salle County, Illinois. There he wandered and played amidst the canyons and glens near towering Starve Rock, whose 200-foot heights dominated the nearby Illinois River. In 1839, the family moved north so he might attend the Rock River Seminary, which at that early time offered the only real opportunity for higher education in what was a raw frontier country. Upon graduation, Wallace traveled on the jolting stage south to Springfield. His goal was to join the law firm headed by a gangling attorney named Abraham Lincoln. These plans evaporated, however, when Wallace engaged in an absorbing conversation with a fellow passenger. Persuasive and distinguished with the courtly air of the Kentucky gentleman, T. Lyle Dickey was already a respected and wealthy attorney with a practice in Ottawa, the La Salle county seat--familiar territory to Wallace. There was work there for a man with knowledge and determination. Dickey saw such qualities in his pleasant traveling companion, spoke of what opportunities existed in his own firm, and soon Springfield and Lincoln were forgotten.[14]

Wallace's law career under Dickey's sponsorship had scarcely begun when the Mexican War was ignited by what many called the provocative actions of expansionist-minded President James K. Polk. Whatever his moral reservations about the origins of the conflict, Wallace was lured to the colors by the urge to "see the elephant" and the exotic wonders that beckoned in distant Mexico. The sentiments and influence of his mentor, Lyle Dickey, no doubt played a part, since the elder attorney soon plunged into the business of raising a company for the coming expedition south.

Wallace enlisted as a private in Company I, First Illinois Infantry. Promotion followed quickly. By the time the regiment reached San Antonio, Wallace served as adjutant to Colonel James Hardin--a man he respected and loved. But Wallace was no ordinary backwoods lawyer. A keen mind and articulate pen, as well as a streak of common sense, distinguished him from his fellows. Illustrative of that was his candid self-appraisal when the regiment encamped upon the site of General Andrew Jackson's 1814 victory over the British near New Orleans. Writing home, he noted: "Slept upon the ground where Jackson achieved his glory, but felt none of Byron's enthusiasm upon the plains of Marathon, perhaps because I was very tired, probably because I am not Byron."[15]

Such was this man--a patchwork of contradictions, a paradox at once genteel and familiar with Byron's sonnets and Blackstone's commentaries on the law simultaneously infected with an inner fire impelling him toward action: to walk gingerly along the tightrope, to peer over the edge into the chasm below, to dare the odds. His decision to join the Mexican expedition brought only incredulity from fellow student and college debater, S.M. Fellows.

> What! You become a soldier? Why if you wish to do that you should enlist in the royal guards of Prussia, where you could be surrounded by your peers. Perhaps though your disposition should lead you to prefer a situation where your eminence would be conspicuous. But really, Wallace, are you in earnest about military glory? Do you think you could face the cannon's mouth and rush upon that glittering steel of an enemy? Not that I would wish to intimate a want of true courage in your composition, but I should almost hope you were deficient in this kind of brutal courage...[16]

Similarly, young Wallace's benefactor and friend, Professor Pickeny of the Rock River Seminary, reminded his former pupil that "war is a sorry game, which, were people wise, kings would never play at..."[17] Only weeks later the outnumbered American expeditionary force under "Old Rough and Ready" Zachary Taylor found itself in desparate combat against the Mexicans on the plains of Buena Vista. Here the First Illinois and young Lieutenant Wallace met the "elephant" face-to-face. Confusion, searing heat, courage, dust, and savage brutality characterized the engagement. Hardin's First Illinois became separated from the main American force. Many Americans were spitted upon Mexican lances as they fled down a ravine. Only the timely intervention of cannon fire from an American battery prevented total slaughter. "The first shell whistled close to me and burst within fifty yards...," Wallace recalled. "I've heard many sweet sounds--the voices of lovely women, and the melodious breathings of sweet instruments--but the whistling of that shell was the most grateful sound that ever greeted my ear..."[18]

Stumbling through the debris of battle that day, Wallace gazed upon Colonel Hardin. The ravaged body bled from four gaping wounds torn by the Mexican lances; a broken sword lay in the dust. Nearby were the tattered bundles of other dead who, having been wounded earlier in the fray, had limped or dragged themselves to the mouth of the ravine, only to be mercilessly slain by the same Mexican cavalry. The stinking rot of the battlefield presented a stark, ugly panorama leaving Wallace distinctly unsettled and unwilling to describe the unsavory scene in letters home. He was, however, less reticent about attributing the victory to the "bull-dog courage and perserverance of the volunteers" while expressing deep doubts concerning the competency of regular army officers, from Taylor on down.[19]

Peace saw renewed success for the returned soldier. He was now firmly established as a partner with T. Lyle Dickey in Ottawa where, because of the presence of the State Supreme Court, the legal profession flourished. By 1852, Wallace successfully ran for the office of county state's attorney, achieving a fine reputation. His growing eminence and sensitive spirit were in no way an impediment to a deepening relationship between the 29-year-old veteran and the 18-year-old daughter of Judge Dickey. Ann, even as a precocious 12-year-old, had captured Will's eye when he first arrived in Ottawa in the mid-1840's. Upon her 16th birthday they confessed mutual love. A two-year engagement followed, capped by a gala wedding and a Chicago honeymoon.

By the close of the 1850's, Wallace was an influential factor in the newly created Republican party. He stood on the platform with Lincoln during the first debate with Douglas, and later worked feverishly for the "Rail Splitter" when Lincoln sought the Republican presidential nomination in 1860. Wallace's political preference was all the more surprising when compared with the strong Douglas-Democratic leanings exhibited by his father-in-law and associate, Judge Dickey. Such partisan feelings evidently posed little threat to his friendship or to family relations. In fact, Wallace was already building a fashionable stone house only a few hundred yards from Judge Dickey's imposing mansion. Both homes enjoyed a lovely view from their location atop a wooded bluff just north of Ottawa.

The Wallace family had resided in their new home only a year when Lincoln's call for volunteers sounded on April 15, 1861. Surely it came as little surprise to Ann that her husband would respond, considering his political loyalties and personal code. Neither the prospects of further financial success nor even the warmth of their newly adopted daughter, Isabell, could dissuade the thirty-nine-year-old attorney. This rebellion inspired in him only contempt and outrage against what he described as a "prodigious crime against the freedom of the world." The specter of two distinct American nations was anathema to him, and compromise had been rejected by radical elements on both sides. There seemed, he thought, little choice left but to resist the great crime or succumb.[20] This was the man who would command the Eleventh, a sentimental, passionate man deeply in love with his wife, his child, and his country. Bidding good-bye to Ann at the St. Nicholas Hotel in Springfield, May 5, he rode out to camp and prepared his ragged band for the coming ordeal.

Orders had come down instructing the regiment to entrain for a journey 200 miles south to establish a camp near Villa Ridge, Illinois. Only six miles north of the tip of the state, the village stood astride the strategic Illinois Central tracks. Everything was in flux at this moment; even the loyalties of many Illinois residents were doubted. Nowhere was this more evident than in the deep southern tip of the state where the populace was largely indifferent, and often even hostile toward the Lincoln government. Sabotage, even outright rebellion, could be expected. All were excellent reasons for posting the Eleventh at Villa Ridge. A howling windstorm slashed at the treetops as the more than 800 men in Wallace's command set out in columns of four, bound for the Springfield depot. Private Carrington, of Company B, recalled:

> How proud I was as we marched down through the streets of Springfield at 4 p.m. to take the train, with the drums and fifes playing "The Girl I Left Behind Me." We were formed in columns of platoons and kept the step fairly well, with bright muskets, frying pans, camp kettles, and red blankets tied over our shoulder. The flag we so proudly bore, our hearts swelling with soldierly pride and patriotism...cheered all along the way, we shouted until hoarse to the men, women, and children who waved their hats, handkerchiefs, and seemed full of enthusiasm. It is all hurrah Boys, so far.[21]

The exuberance of the moment dissipated almost before the shouting faded in the distance. The troops found themselves packed elbow-to-rib cage in cars sufficient for only two-thirds their number. Ahead lay two full days of travel, with frequent stops, some apparently explainable, others a complete mystery to the irritable passengers. No provision for food had been made, so hunger only added to the increasing misery. Sharp criticism and complaint surfaced quickly and was suppressed only in part by Colonel Wallace's sincere assertion that he himself would not eat before his troops did. The jostling, sooty train ride seemed interminable. Finally, the train pulled off on a country siding, and the order came to disembark. Lieutenant Bird of Company D wrote home of the refreshing scene that greeted the sweaty, sleepless troops. Here was a perfect campsite situated amidst a "magnificent forest" and boasting a deep spring with sparkling, cold drinking water.

Immediate preparations were made to form the camp, and put up the necessary buildings for shelter of the troops. All the companies will go under roof tonight. The buildings are simply rough boards, covering a scant joist frame with wide cracks between the boards, and rough board floors, with roofs of the same material. But in this season of the year, and in this genial climate, they will be abundantly comfortable. The men have put up substantial bunks along one side of the buildings similar to the old fashioned berths that you and I used to see ranged alongside the cabins of steamers quarters. We shall get along very comfortably indeed in them. Indeed the change from Camp Yates is almost luxurious. Quarters will be much more clean and healthy...[22]

Despite the idyllic setting, an enemy soon made its appearance. A deadly, unseen foe lurked about the camp and thrived in the unsanitary environment created by ignorant country boys. Typhoid fever, diarrhea, measles, and other assorted maladies, at which the surgeons could only guess, left dozens of the men bedridden, groaning wrecks. Private A. L. Swap of Ottawa recalled how the surgeon calmly informed him one day that he must leave the dispensary since his impending and inevitable death by typhoid would have a deleterious effect on the morale of the surviving patients.[23] Finding shelter in a nearby private home, the 180-pound soldier dwindled to a 100-pound skeleton until deep sleep broke the fever. Rising from his sick-bed, the boy asked for, and gobbled down a quarter piece of blackberry pie with no ill effect whatsoever. In spite of the ordeal, the soldier returned to the ranks a few weeks later, re-enlisting in the 37th Illinois. Others, though, were less fortunate, as Lieutenant Bird described:

> At the usual hour for battalion drill the regiment was drawn up in line, and the deceased's remains (H. Hamilton of Ottawa) were conducted down the front of the line, preceded by the music and followed by both of the Ottawa companies. The music played a dead march and it was the most solemn music I ever heard. The fifes piped in subdued tones and the drums kept one continual muffled roll, which never ceased until the mournful procession had deposited the corpse on the cars, which took all earthly that remained of the young man to his home that night. I can give you no idea of the solemnity of the music on this sad occasion. It can only be realized by listening to the plaintive notes of the fifes and the low but ceaseless roll of the drums...[24]

Such scenes were miraculously few among the Eleventh. Only ten men from the regiment perished from disease during the first three months of enlistment compared to much higher figures from other units. Much of the credit would go to regimental surgeons A.W. Hise and H.E. Goodwin, who formulated and helped enforce a strict set of sanitary regulations. They insisted the men bathe weekly, air their quarters and clothing each day, thoroughly cook their food, and remove all wastes and slops far from the confines of camp. These precautions, coupled with the fact that the more communicable diseases soon ran their course, left the regiment with other more pleasant concerns such as searching out "Reb" spies said to lurk just beyond the camp's perimeter.[25]

Understandably enough, the men on guard were uneasy, imagining in these early days all sorts of horrors that might be concealed in the darkness. "Every stump was a rebel," recalled one recruit, evoking the image of a terribly frightened boy grimly clutching his musket while peering into the forbidding shadows. The situation was made more uncomfortable since everyone knew that the bolder among the regiment made nightly forays into town for drink and other merriment. The return past the sentinels was a touch-and-go proposition which, for certain men, made the expeditions all the more exciting. "Some of them will get a ball yet, and then they will not think it so much fun to run the guard," Lieutenant Bird wrote home.[26] That tireless correspondent also described what the constant alerts had done to one of the more sensitive among the volunteers:

> Another unusual precautionary measure was taken in camp on Wednesday night in putting on double guards. This opened the men's eyes again considerably: and they were on watch "right smart." They slept with one eye open all night I warrant. These extra precautions, while warranted by the suspected presence of spies, made the men certain that a battle was at hand and one of the officers in the regiment, somewhat noted already for his excitability, assured his men that we would be positively attacked before morning. I hope that when he awoke...and found himself yet alive in his bunk, he felt ashamed of himself as his conduct had been foolish. I notice that he has not had any "attacks" since...[27]

Eventually the terror posed by the night vanished and picket became mere routine. In fact, the regularity of camp soon became wearisome. The supposed galmour of military life wore ever thinner among men who prided themselves on an independent frame of mind. They had elected these officers, hadn't they? Who were these men now to hold such haughty airs? Such were the thoughts expressed by the more rebellious. They had enlisted to fight rebels, not to burnish belt-buckles and tody to a lot of supercilious prigs. "I'll be damned if I'll stand guard," is how Private Terrence Moran of Company B phrased it. The remark, directed to Captain Shaw, won him eight days in confinement and a diet of bread and water. Colonel Wallace was determined that discipline be enforced, and was soon to impress upon the men that this military business was not something to be trifled with. The court-martial was his weapon, and the commander wielded it with a vengeance. The Eleventh was not to rot internally as were so many other volunteer regiments. Wallace was insistent that the men behave regardless of how homesick they might be or how foolish an order might appear. His basic philosophy was rooted in the statement that the men of the Eleventh must not degenerate in conduct since "because they had become soldiers they need not cease to be gentlemen." Drunkenness, insubordination, petty theft, and other failings of human nature would not be tolerated.[28]

Discipline won a key battle in mid-May when recruits Charles Robinson and Martin Henry were brought before the colonel and charged with gross misconduct. During an unauthorized visit to Mound City, Illinois they insulted a number of local ladies, forcing the city marshall to escort them back to camp. A panel of officers convened and found the two guilty of all charges. The defendants were dismissed from the service for the high crime of bringing dishonor to the regiment. Three other recruits received light sentences ranging from a mere reprimand to confinement with light rations. An example was needed, however, and Privates Henry and Robinson were singled out for the purpose. Their eviction from camp was conducted with all the spectacle that military formality deemed important. "Notable and impressive" is how Lieutenant Bird recalled the resulting ceremony:

> As the regiment came on to dress parade at 6 O'Clock last evening, these two men were marched out in front of the line...with the fifes and drums in advance, and a rank of eight men marching in their front, and another eight in their rear. The front rank marched with reversed arms, so that their bayonets were pointed at the breasts of the prisoners, and the rear rank with their bayonets following close behind. In this order the prisoners were marched along the whole front of the regiment, to the lines of the camp, the music playing the rogue's march... The scene was a very impressive one, and very generally affected the men in the regiment. I think there was hardly one in the line but felt that he would never go through such a humiliating and disgraceful punishment...

Convinced that constant activity served the dual purpose of dissipating the pangs of homesickness and instilling a sense of purpose in the men, Colonel Wallace launched an intensive training program. He appointed Captain James H. Coates as the official regimental drill master. A dapper, slender man with a decidedly English appearance, Coates evidently possessed no special background for the position. Nonetheless, he did a creditable job. "We like to have him show us how to handle a musket," commented Private Carrington. "He is so plain, and tries to teach us the principles of Scott's Manual, the shoulder or carry arms...." The drillmaster's unassuming ways were a decided contrast to Adjutant Charles Hotchkiss, described by young Carrington as a "fleshy little man" always "puffing and perspiring," scurrying up and down the ranks babbling on about the regiment like a worried housewife dusting the settee prior to the pastor's visit.[30]

Slowly the loose collection of individuals melted into a single entity: a trained animal responding without thought to barked commands, swinging along with easy stride that comes from long hours of drill. By early June, Captain Nevius of Company D bragged to his brother in New York state:

> Our regiment is getting along fine. It has the reputation as being the best drilled regiment in the West. You may think that I am boasting some but it is a fact. My company, I am proud to say, still takes the lead in all the exercises. We have received so many compliments that I am sick and tired of them. [31]

Outfitted in new uniforms including a gray coat and pants with light blue trimmings and a blue cap, the men struck a highly military appearance. When General Ben Prentiss reviewed the command on May 17, he came away highly impressed, saying the Eleventh was ten percent better trained than any regiment in his command. Lavish compliments were also provided by General George B. McClellan who inspected the men at the camp. The former railroad magnate was commander of all Union troops in the Midwest; soon he would head for the eastern theater, bound for the Army of the Potomac and controversial fame. Writing his wife of the progress the regiment had made, Colonel Wallace announced that the Eleventh was "better disciplined," and "better drilled" than any in the district:

> Discipline comes hard on volunteers, and I am obliged to be severe sometimes, and expect some dissatisfaction, but I believe I have the confidence of the officers and men of my command, and if we should have an engagement they will find this discipline the very making of their reputation as a regiment. I think I have succeeded in inspiring a proper "esprit de corps" as the French say, and all seem animated with a desire to make this the crack regiment of the service...I am proud of them.[32]

Stern and yet solicitous of his men's welfare, Colonel Wallace by pure force of character and example not only set about making these men soldiers but also earned their loyalty and respect. He made great demands but returned to the regiment a concern that bordered on tenderness. All this was obvious even to the casual visitor. Mary Newcomb of Effingham, whose husband served as a sergeant in Company G, would later recall the commander as "a splendid officer and a good man...noble looking, well poised...of fine appearance and a pure gentleman in every respect. He had a generous heart and sympathized with every man's troubles." Burdened with duty, his days stretched far into the early morning hours, and even then the constant alarms would drag him from fitful sleep. As befitted a responsible commander, Wallace projected confidence and optimism among the men. He was twenty years older than most in his command and represented solid, dependable authority. The fact that he was also a man with all those familiar frailties would have probably shocked the typical enlisted man. Of course, it would hardly surprise Mrs. Wallace who weekly listened to the inner man mirrored in long, tender letters home. Alone in his tent, Will could admit to being "weary with many cares." He could open his heart and yearn for peaceful times:

> How would I like to lay my head on your dear breast for an hour and feel your fingers about my temples and your sweet breath creating an atmosphere of peace and love about me. It is now 2 O'Clock at night. All is quiet about me. The stars are bright in their silent watchfulness and all seems peaceful and promising. How I wish this...night be a true augury of peace to the country. I am so tired. I can say but one word to you tonight and that is I love you...[34]

Fragile sentiments faded into hatred on May 25 with the roar of a shotgun fired half a continent away in Alexandria, Virginia. Captain Elmer Ellsworth, the friend of so many in the Eleventh's Zouave company, lay dead at the hands of a Rebel assassin. Minutes before, the young officer had hauled down a Confederate banner from atop a boarding house within sight of the nation's capitol. Ellsworth had been Lincoln's military attache and his murder was billed in the Northern press as that of a martyr for the Union. Lieutenant Doug Hapeman of Company H in the Eleventh, marked in his diary how "the news...cast a gloom over the camp and the flag was at half-mast during the day."[35] Other men in Company D swore revenge and were described by one officer as at the "highest pitch of desire to meet the enemy." Their company commander, Captain Nevius, was especially distraught. He had learned the rudiments of military drill from the slain Ellsworth:

> The fallen officer was one of my best friends. Many is the hour he has taught me the Zouave drill, and twice last spring he offered me a commission in his regiment as soon as I was through with this campaign, but it is all over with now. Our country has lost a valuable officer, and myself, as well as many others, a true friend.[36]

Within a week of the grim tidings of Ellsworth's death came an opportunity for revenge. Citizens from nearby Caledonia, Illinois claimed the Rebels on the Kentucky shore "had frequently threatened them and their place," according to Lt. Bird. Messengers referred to the Southern village across the Ohio as a "hot secessionist hole." Captain Nevius, in company with a small contingent from the Zouaves, was soon scouring the riverside for transport. Seizing two small skiffs, they pushed across the river and landed in what appeared to be a completely deserted village. Lieutenant Bird related the incident as follows:

> Only one solitary man could be seen, who said, while trembling in his shoes, that all the rest of the men had gone out into the woods hunting stray cattle. At the levee of the village was moored a sort of trading barge, owned by the principal man of the place, who was a very violent secessionist. On this boat was a tall flag staff. The boys took their red and white handkerchiefs, and borrowing a piece of blue calico with large white spots on it of a woman whom they found...with these and a plentiful supply of pins they soon manufactured a very respectable flag of the stars and stripes pattern and hoisted it on the staff of the secession boat with large cheers. On the flag they wrote-"Compliments of the Rockford Zouaves: Our Motto--Remember Ellsworth."[37]

Reportedly, the Rebels on the far shore pledged death for the first man who unfurled the American flag on Southern ground. Further threats implied that a Yankee incursion would fall afoul of the fabled Kentucky rifle even though that weapon had long before become militarily obsolete. The small Union party was armed only with pistols and bayonets jammed into their belts. "So we concluded we would try them," recalled Captain Nevius. "So we raised a Union flag on a high flag staff and then the Star Spangled Banner, give three cheers for it and waited for someone to do something, but they would not gratify...." After an hour's wait, the raiders returned north across the Ohio. They proceeded a bare 20 rods or so before the Rebel hamlet stirred, and timid faces peeped out of assorted hiding places at every hand. In striking contrast was the Union shore marked by cheers from the residents of Caledonia who assured the returning saviors that they had raised the first National flag on the Kentucky side.[38] Union bravado had purchased a bloodless triumph which was trumpeted for days about camp. Melodramatic, perhaps, but such activity was heaven-sent since the ennui of Camp Hardin weighed heavily on recruits still more fearful of boredom than combat. Mary Newcomb recalled:

> At this place the boys had no taste of war. They had a good time--no battle, not much guard duty, and but little picket duty. They concluded that war was a holiday and that they would eat, drink and be merry. They arrived at the hasty conclusion that the Rebels dare not fight, and the war was not going to amount to anything and they would all be at home in a few weeks...war had no terrors, for they had not been in any conflict...[39]

Another foray was made across the Mississippi River into Thebes, Missouri a few days later by Captain Smith D. Atkins and Company A. At such an early date in the conflict many considered this uneventful patrol to be a daring stab into enemy territory. True, there had not been one single casualty, and the enemy had not even been sighted. Yet Smith's reflemen did return with plunder, of sorts. They captured a Rebel flag discovered flying from a Mississippi trading barge moored near Thebes. Upon their return to Camp Hardin, the company presented the trophy to the normally placid Colonel Wallace. He seized the opportunity to harangue the regiment about trials to come and punctuated his comments by throwing the captured banner to the ground. Discipline forgotten, the men broke ranks and jostled one another in frantic efforts to tear, spit on, or stomp the quickly shredded ensign. Emotions were strained; the men desperately needed relief, a safety valve. [40]

To some degree the mounting tension was alleviated with the announcement that two companies from the Eleventh were scheduled for a sham battle. It was with unbounded enthusiasm that the men of Captain Rose's G Company and Captain Nevius's Zouaves greeted the news. The fight was conducted with zeal by men barely beyond childhood and still filled with an adolescent ebullience. It was singular, many officers remarked, how the men could raise such excitement over a staged battle. Many seemed beside themselves and were only kept from serious mischief by an officer's upraised sword. Lieutenant Bird described the affair as a great children's game played with all the feverish intensity common to boyish make-believe. Through the fields and woods of southern Illinois they maneuvered, retreated, changed front, fired imaginary volleys--and then, best of all, fixed bayonets for a mad dash at the enemy:

One of our men told me that he itched all over to stick his bayonet into the men of the retreating company...At the same time the retreating men did not seem entirely at ease with so many bayonets within a foot of their rear and kept casting quick glances behind and hurrying up their steps.[41]

At the conclusion of the fray, Lieutenant Bird sagaciously observed that this "realistic" training provided fine entertainment for all involved. Furthermore, he noted that in the practical sense a sham battle had a distinct advantage for all participants in that "one is alive afterwards to look over his mistakes..."[42]

Diversions were scarce, making these dream battles all the more valuable. Certainly the sweaty exertions entailed in such romps were preferable to the growing monotony. Then too, unsupervised free time often served as a fertile ground for unsettling thoughts, at least for the more introspective. The frenzy of spring had been replaced by the summer torpor of army existence. Time was in abundance--time to think, time to ponder, time to fret, time to brood. Ahead lay an uncertain future; if only a man could pierce the fog that obscured the road ahead. All the while, the prospects of combat ate away at the corners of a man's mind where self-doubt and other frailties incompatible with honor dwelt and thrived. There was probably not a man in the entire regiment who, at least once, didn't question his own fortitude. Would he disgrace the family? Would he fall dead at the first volley? Even worse, would a Rebel bullet, bayonet, or cannon shot tear away at his vitals leaving behind only the crippled caricature of a man better dead than alive? For that matter, what about the regiment, the army itself? General McDowell's vaunted Eastern troops fled the field at Bull Run. True, they were merely Eastern men but even so the imagination chilled at the possibility. Dull, distant cannon thunder from Federal batteries at nearby Cairo would occasionally float north over Camp Hardin and sharpen the apprehension and uncertainty. Days wore by slowly like a Sunday church service attended by fretting and unattentive children.

Evening at Camp Hardin often elicited a melodious serenade performed by the men from the Rockford Zouaves. With sheet music and candle in hand they would wind their way down the regimental street to the colonel's bungalow. There they entertained with popular strains far into the night. Another diversion indulged in by the men was called a "visit." Strictly formal protocol was followed in such cases. Typically, the men of one company would form a human snake and then weave their way in hilarity through the neighboring company areas urging others to latch on.

One night practically the entire regiment snaked its way down toward Wallace's billet with raucous enthusiasm. This huge "visiting party" arrived at the colonel's doorstep and demanded a speech. This request granted by the indulgent Wallace, they responded with a lusty rendition of the "Star Spangled Banner" culminating in three cheers for the commanding officer. These, and similar boyish antics, provided the grist for a thousand campfire stories destined to be told and retold for a half century to come.[43]

Even a deadly serious call-to-arms midway through June degenerated into a farcical parody. Its ludicrous elements smacked of the burlesque and even caused participants great amusement once time healed embarrassed egos. The deadly foray was initiated after certain citizens of Mound City, an Illinois River town, sounded an alarm. Their community was separated from the fearsome Rebels only by the Ohio River and reliable sources indicated that Southern firebrands were, at the very moment, mobilized for a raid on the defenseless community. Armed to the teeth, on one stifling hot summer night at about 11 p.m., a detachment from the Eleventh sallied forth to the town's protection. Mound City was only twelve miles distant from Camp Hardin, and so with luck the rescuers might well arrive on time to show how western men could fight. Lieutenant Bird of Company D remembered it was a moonless, starless night when the column plunged into the deep woods:

> Then the fun commenced, and I never had more of it in the same space of time. It was no use trying to see anything or each other. Now we would come up all standing in a deep mudhole, then tumble over a log or a stump, and next plump against a tree. One of our guides fell over stumps twice, and your correspondent ran full front against a big tree, and has never seen that tree yet...Our guides kept the road by their feet, and We frequently had to keep in their track by feeling of each other's backs. The march was tried to be conducted in perfect silence but a tumble... or a collision against a tree would bring out an exclamation more emphatic than elegant...[44]

Like so many blind mice they wove through the dark forest until the expedition reached a small, isolated sawmill. Their presence was detected immediately by a brace of hounds who bayed out a warning. Suddenly the sound of men clattering down stairs followed as the mysterious occupants of the sawmill dashed off into the blackness. Their rapid departure was interpreted by the Union patrol as sure evidence that a Rebel scouting party had been surprised. With rifles at full-cock, they pursued with breakneck speed through the undergrowth until they were brought to a confused halt, surrounded by ominous grunts and squeals:

> We found we had made a brilliant charge upon a drove of scampering hogs...Secessionists were thick all around us, but somehow or other they all had a peculiar exclamation of alarm whenever we came upon them--very much like a grunt. Every little while we would stir up a nest of them...They would spring up from under our feet and scamper away farther into the dark woods.[45]

Doggedly pushing on, the bedraggled expeditionary force felt its way through the forest, cursing, wheezing, and despairing of ever finding a road again, much less Mound City. The march was only interrupted once again as two privates plunged head first into a watery ditch, soaking themselves and their weapons in the process. Pausing momentarily, the two dried their rifles and wrung out their soggy clothing as much as possible all the while mourning their intemperate decision ever to go a "solgering."[46]

Incredibly, dawn found the drawn, thorn-scratched men finally on the road leading to Mound City. Bird and his associates were amazed to discover the inhabitants securely asleep in their beds without having been aware of the slightest sound or sight of approaching raiders. Indeed, Bird described the town as "dead as smelts" with the streets "grown up with May weed, with nothing but footpaths running through." His puzzlement soon dissipated, however, upon a conversation with one of the more candid citizens. This fellow blandly asserted that the alarm had been sounded only for the purpose of attracting a permanent Union garrison to the economically depressed community anxious to make a little money from the soldier boys. Wearily, Bird and the other would-be saviors turned from town, and trudged in the early morning light back toward camp.[47]

Despite the apparent futility of this and similar expeditions, it all, intended or not, served a purpose. Each day the men became more familiar with the military life. Rapid marches in search of Rebel spies and other imaginary ghosts toughened them and taught simple lessons never found in *Hardee's Tactics* or in any other infantry manual. These pleasant outings were complemented in camp by target practice. Old flintlock rifles, coverted to percussion, had been issued to a disappointed regiment. "Turnip-slingers," the men called the cumbersome, inaccurate .69-caliber monsters. Even Private Carrington, a man comfortable with weapons of all sorts, quickly learned to detest these hybrid rifles:

> When discharged [they] nearly knock a man down. Mine is not so bad as some. If we could hit a barn at 100 yards it would be a happen so. It requires no skill. The original flint locks would be better as we could pull the trigger and dodge before the explosion would take place. Recoil was incredibly severe and caused black eyes, bloody noses, black spots on faces and shoulders. Old muskets kick like a mule, nearly knock a man down. Some of the boys are afraid to shoot.[48]

As the months passed, Colonel Wallace grew confident. He felt certain the Eleventh would acquit themselves well in any circumstances. By and large, his cadre of officers was an impressive lot, particularly 27-year-old Major Thomas Ransom, who had already proved himself indispensable. On a personal level, the two officers shared similar outlooks, prompting Ann Wallace to remark that her husband and the Vermont-born Ransom were "kindred spirits." On brief, hurried visits home to Ottawa, Colonel Wallace invariably brought along his young major whose quiet demeanor, educated background, and striking good looks won him favorable comment. In camp, the two would often ride together far into the night confiding their thoughts, and speculating about the future.

Conversely, Wallace placed less and less trust in his executive officer, Lieutenant Colonel Joseph W. Filler of Effingham, an intemperate newspaperman who, as a lad of eleven, had entered the profession in his native Ohio. As a "tramping journeyman" the boy had published ten papers and worked on establishments in 18 states--all before reaching the age of sixteen. During the Mexican War, in campaigns from Vera Cruz to Mexico City, he had served as both sergeant and lieutenant in Ohio units. At Camp Hardin, his weaknesses soon dominated, fueling the rumor mill with stories that the lieutenant colonel was never far from the bottle even during duty hours. Intemperance horrified the puritanical Wallace, who was appalled to observe his executive officer reeling drunkenly at more than one regimental dress parade. Even more shocking was Filler's entrance into camp, staggering down the regimental street barely supported by an equally soddened private who had playfully equipped himself with the officer's sword and sash.[49]

Blistering rebukes from Colonel Wallace brought repeated promises that such incidents would never be repeated. Thus the issue stood when, on orders from General Prentiss, the regimental commander left Camp Hardin for a brief official sojourn in Washington. His departure ironically coincided with the arrival of orders for the Eleventh's movement by the "cars" to the seat of the war. Wallace's regiment was to entrench at Bird's Point, a strategic jetty of land in Missouri just across the Mississippi River from Cairo. From here the Union troops would assist in guarding the great watery crossroads formed by the confluence of the Ohio and Mississippi Rivers. Cheered on by a sizeable crowd, the regiment, for the last time at Camp Hardin, fell in at 9 a.m., June 20. With Filler at their head, the 700 strong column boarded a troop train at Villa Ridge and set steam for Cairo 12 miles to the south.

After being properly baked by the raw June sun for a number of hours in transit, the troops detrained at Cairo. This rowdy river town was perched at the very tip of the state and resembled, at least in the wet season, a vast morass upon which floated a motley collection of wooden buildings, livestock and half-submerged plank sidewalks. Thousands of Union troops either passed through Cairo every day or were stationed at nearby Fort Defiance. Many soldiers could be seen lounging on store steps, browsing through the stores, or wandering to the train station for a "look see" at the latest arrivals.

Mustering up by the tracks, the Eleventh then made its way through the primitive streets bound for the Cairo levee. There they awaited the ferry which was to transfer them across river to Bird's Point. Lieutenant Commander Filler, who had been indisposed during most of the preliminary preparations at Hardin, disappeared again in search of a bottle while Major Ransom and the regiment sweltered in the summer heat. Finally, Major Ransom took matters into his own hands and moved the regiment by ferry across the river without incident. On the Missouri shore the Eleventh settled in for the first of many evenings on this narrow belt of land with its superb view of the great watery crossroads which flowed below. It was a majestic panorama which prompted sensitive Lieutenant Bird's description:

> Two mighty rivers flowing on either side...mingling their waters in one broad sheet of a lake as it were...which can be viewed for several miles to the southward at the great "father of waters" sweeps on to the Gulf...their banks covered by dense and scarcely unbroken forests, until their waters sweeping by magnificent curves seem to bury

themselves up in the depths of those stupendous forests. To me that vast and graceful...expanse of water and forest seemed so grand and beautiful...[50]

Chapter Two

A Rash, Brave Fellow

Missouri, in that tumultuous year of 1861, was a society fragmented by terror, fear, and hatred. Partisans on both sides transformed the state into a portrait of violence: shotgun blasts in the night, the long rope draped over a stout limb, animal mobs rooting through the St. Louis streets, barn burnings and bushwhackings. The dividing line between personal vendetta and political priciple blurred. So did the delicate balance between war and murder. The entire state was a great cauldron of civil strife whose fires hardened and shaped a brutal breed best represented by "Bloody Bill" Anderson, William Quantrill, the James Boys, and the Youngers. Irrespective of politics, they were all linked by a callous disregard for human life and the common decencies. When the Eleventh occupied Bird's Point there was already an incipient guerrilla movement abetted by the presence of regular Confederate armies operating in other portions of the divided state. Union sympathizers fled north and east by the hundreds. For many, the destination was Camp Lyon at Bird's Point whose commander, Colonel Wallace, promised protection behind Federal bayonets.

This refuge was admirably situated to serve as a base of operations for projected Union excursions into southeastern Missouri. In addition, Camp Lyon's artillery provided supplementary fire support for Fort Defiance at Cairo and other Federal batteries whose iron muzzles sealed off the vital river crossroads. The Eleventh wasted little time in settling down at the Point since they had the good fortune to find prepared intrenchments dug out by Shubner's German Regiment, now transferred elsewhere. In those first days Captain N.L. Rockwood marched out at Wallace's order to seize rolling stock on the Cairo and Fulton Railroad at a point four miles beyond Sikeston. The action was motivated by intelligence reports which intimated that the railroad was administered by a man who was a "noted secessionist residing in Bloomfield." The mission was accomplished without incident although for some unexplained reason Wallace felt it significant enough to inform Secretary of War Simon Cameron upon its completion.[1]

At this early stage in the conflict the Eleventh prided itself on being farther south than any other Federal unit. Consequently, they expected an imminent response from the bellicose Confederates who muttered all kinds of dire threats in the Southern press. On the first Sunday in the new encampment, Wallace received intelligence indicating that large numbers of Rebel guerrillas could be found at a place upriver from the Point. Major Ransom departed that very day with Companies A and B along with two more companies from nearby Cairo. They boarded the steamer *City of Alton* which ferried them a few miles before the expedition jumped ashore for a wide swing inland designed to entrap the Rebels between the river and the Union steel. After a rapid, difficult march the winded troops finally discovered a long-abandoned Confederate base camp. "The birds had flown," one infantryman remarked.[2] Ransom's men returned to Camp Lyon after four days on the march. Their arrival at the Point was witnessed by Private Carrington who described the returning heroes as "such a blistered up set I never saw before." This first foray into the still rugged Missouri hinterland had definitely sobered the more romantic among Ransom's company. "Footsore and weary, many of them could scarcely wear shoes or shirt for a week or more," Carrington asserted. "Very few complained, thinking all this the natural order of military life..."[3]

Their home at Bird's Point could hardly be calculated to raise the spirits. It was a windy, sand-swept spot skirted by corn fields and cotton patches and dominated by Colonel John Bird's mansion. Except for a decrepit, abandoned railroad depot, a small sawmill, and dilapidated slave shanties, the two-story frame home was the only noteworthy structure in sight. In these primitive surroundings the Eleventh established the rudiments of military housekeeping. The men's efforts were conducted under the glare of the outraged property owner, Colonel Bird, who was an alleged Confederate supporter. A few weeks earlier, other Union troops had unearthed a munitions and arms stockpile hidden at Colonel Bird's residence. Despite this fact, he remained at large although his demeanor changed radically after the incident. Lieutenant Bird of the Eleventh remarked that the surly Southern gentleman was soon "as good as pie." It is doubtful that his benevolent mood survived, however, since the new Federal occupiers promptly expropriated his home for a garrison hospital and headquarters. Bird's unwanted guests were making the best of things, although few had anything positive to say about their bivouac. A terrible heat was made more galling since the men had only river muck for drinking water. Furthermore, the hot river winds gusted with regularity and aroused the omnipresent sand. At times, the wind even blew down the Sibley cone tents which served as meager shelter for the Eleventh. Lieutenant Bird moaned:

> The dust is very annoying indeed. Everything is covered or filled with it. It covers our clothes, mixes in our food, fills our mouths, ears and eyes...[4]

Colonel Wallace was beset both by the hostile climate and the constant threat posed by nearby Confederate forces whose strength and position remained a worrisome mystery. Uncertainty was increased by the limited intelligence reports that were alike only in their contradictory nature with widely varied assertions about the enemy's location, plans, and morale. These burdens were aggravated by a serious deficiency in transport which limited Wallace's range of operations, or at least this was thought to be case in those early days before troops demonstrated a talent for living off the land. Wallace was sorely tried with numerous responsibilities as post commander at Camp Lyon, which was now occupied by the 18th Illinois Infantry and a company of Chicago Artillery as well as his own Eleventh. Unfortunately, the commander was hamstrung in his efforts to establish order by his executive officer's erratic and drunken behavior.[5]

Filler behaved badly those first few days at the Point. His highly intoxicated condition in one instance brought forth a harsh rebuke from Wallace which resulted in only temporary reform. The intolerable situation climaxed on the evening of June 24th when the sharp report of a shot brought the entire garrison to arms. One can imagine Wallace's exasperation when he learned that his drunken executive had fired the shot apparently on a mere whim. There seemed little alternative: Colonel Wallace placed the offender under arrest and immediately initiated court-martial proceedings against the Mexican War veteran. Charged with drunkenness and conduct unbecoming an officer, Filler had few options. Either he could endure a trial with certain conviction as the outcome or resign his commission in disgrace. He chose the latter. A few days later Colonel Wallace received a communique from W.D. Alexander of Effingham noting that the enraged Filler had sworn to lead "the 11th Regiment to the Devil." The information reported that the former officer was "considered a dangerous man" and seemed bent upon returning to the Point to reconnoiter, and then to offer the information to the Rebels along with the services of a company of cavalry composed of other Illinois men sympathetic with rebellion. Taking what precautions he could, Wallace returned to his duties undaunted by the prospect of assassination. Now he could proceed with the business at hand, feeling an implicit trust in Major Ransom who would soon succeed as executive officer.[6]

Surviving correspondence does not indicate that Wallace regarded the prospect of murder at the hands of a malcontent as a real possibility. It was just another rumor added to the growing heap. Every day Union loyalists from Missouri arrived with a few pathetic belongings and tales of Rebel harassment and murder. The military information they provided often clouded rather than clarified the tactical picture. The only certainty was that General Jeff Thompson of the Missouri State Guard was gathering strength in southwest Missouri and would relish the destruction of Camp Lyon. His intentions were a mystery, however, made more puzzling by unsubstantiated and alarmist reporting in the Northern press. One Illinois periodical estimated that during this period Thompson had a force of 8,000 "well armed and well drilled" Rebels within 20 miles of Bird's Point. Eleven thousand more, it was said, could be found at nearby New Madrid, Mo., and three thousand others scattered throughout the state.

This same newspaper described Thompson's troops as almost piratical in nature and appearance. Their motto, so it was said, was: "Beauty and Booty." According to backwoods buckaneer Thompson, Union invaders deserved no quarter. Most thought it was only a matter of time before a major clash would ensue.[7] Wallace took every precaution. He posted a vigilant guard at the Point and threw out aggressive scouting parties into the interior. The men at the Point were transfixed by the almost mythical Thompson; indeed the entire rebellion seemed inextricably bound up with their formidable image of this Confederate general. One day, he opened artillery fire on Union transports on the Mississippi; on another, his men expropriated thousands in cash from a Charleston, Missouri, bank--a few hours' march from the Point. He called himself the "Swamp Fox of the Confederacy" and was the "man most wanted" by the boys in the Eleventh. Missouri historian John McElroy painted an indelible, although slightly mocking, portrait of the Rebel paladin:

> He was a tall, lank, wiry man, at least six feet high, about 35 years old, with a thin, long, hatchet face, and high, sharp nose, blue eyes, and thick, yellow hair combed behind his ears. He wore a slouch white hat with a feather...A white-

handled Bowie knife stuck perpendicularly in his belt in the middle of his back, completed his armament, and he was never seen without it. His weakness was for writing poetry, and he "threw" a poem on the slightest provocation. Fortunately none of these has been preserved...[8]

Early in July, Lieutenant Bird accompanied a patrol of the Eleventh whose mission was to discover the location of the legendary rebel and his band. Their tramp took them in all directions from the Point. It was a random scout that eventually covered a 20-mile deep arc into the Missouri hinterland. They didn't find the deadly "Swamp Fox", but instead encountered a loyal Union man. He described himself as an Alabama native, newly arrived in the West, and now fleeing his Missouri neighbors. After a lengthy interrogation the man provided the names of more than a score. These former friends, he stated, were all active Rebels. Whatever their real guilt, these unfortunates were soon rousted from home and field by Bird's infantry. All suspects were transported to the Point for temporary incarceration and interrogation conducted without the niceties of English common law. The informer was granted safe conduct across the river into Union country where he might enjoy a more hospitable climate. Bird's patrol continued with their round-up, somewhat startled at the reception they received. Their journey exposed them to a populace that was wary in the extreme. To all intents and purposes they viewed the Eleventh's presence as that of a foreign force operating against the will and wishes of the people. Expedience demanded that the civilians project a guarded politeness but little else.

We visited a number of very fine plantations, but many of them were deserted by their secession owners who had fled in mortal fear of the troops at Bird's Point to a more congenial and safer atmosphere in Secessia. Others still remained at their plantations, but had sent all their negroes south, lest we should steal them all.
They seemed to try to preserve a sort of semi-union, semi-secession, each side of the fence attitude, so as if possible to preserve the good will of both sides. They do not seem to have a very intelligent idea of the merits of the conflict, but were waiting to see how their state was going...Right or wrong they went with Missouri, and that was about all the idea they seemed to have about it. All these were chary of giving us any information...[9]

Fortunately, the Eleventh and its sister Union regiments were occupying a position of relative strength based on a triangular system of breastworks with the base resting on the Mississippi River. Seven pieces of artillery had been installed before June was out, and were situated so that they provided mutual fire support. Colonel Wallace found it doubly reassuring that in case of Rebel attack, the post could easily be reinforced from the Cairo side. Even so, the prospect of a night strike by the secessionists bothered him. The three-month enlistments were nearly up, and by early August his command would be severely depleted. Many men would head home, either on leave before enlisting for three years, or to join other regiments for a variety of reasons. Then too, there were those who found the military all too dreary, and would return permanently to civilian life.[10]

Many men at the Point retained much of the original enthusiasm, enhanced by the proximity of an enemy some felt was more inclined to verbal aggressiveness than actual combat. One of the most eager was Captain Garrett Nevius, commanding Company D. He had been extremely close to the slain Elmer Ellsworth, now deified by the Northern press as the first victim of the Southern conspiracy. Like many others in his company, Nevius remembered fondly how the late Ellsworth had drilled him in Zouave tactics. Nevius, a former Rockford photographer, was sincere in his commitment to the Union.

Every day adds to our strength, and in a few days we shall be in a situation to defy any force that can be sent against us, and a visit from them would be gladly received for we are spoiling for a fight. It is not probably that we shall advance any further south before the first of August or some (time) later. Extensive preparations are being made for the descent of the Mississippi, as soon as the heat of the summer is over. We are at present further south than any other body of Volunteers in the Country. It is only about one hundred miles to Memphis the place which we all long to see so much, but before we can get there we have got to capture some very strong holds...And, of course, a great deal of hard fighting will have to be done. But we are ready for it, let it cost what it will. We all feel that we cannot sacrifice too much for our country. As for me, I am ready to give anything, even to the last drop of my blood if required. We cannot give too much to restore its former purity and greatness, and if I can be the means of assisting in doing it, I shall feel proud.[11]

Picket duty at the Point was a decidedly more nerve-racking occupation than it had been at Camp Hardin. The Missouri night held more than just the apparitions of imaginative minds. There, in the shadows, were real men, lurking near the lines seeking knowledge of the Union disposition and, at least in one instance, simple revenge. Such was the case at 9 p.m., Saturday, June 29, when the drummers sounded the long roll bringing from all over the post half-dressed men clutching muskets and cartridges. Private Carrington recalled how such a summons created a veritable beehive of "bustle and excitement" as men stumbled about the ill-lit tents in search of shoes and trousers. "Where's my cap?" Carrington wrote. "Got cartridge box on upside down, everything mixed up, but these tangles gradually came out all right, grab a musket and get in ranks, we marched out in double quick time..."[12]

This time, the men found a shaken picket from another regiment. He told of hailing a man in the darkness who, in reply, fired a pistol but missed his target despite being within arm's distance. Knocking the weapon aside, the sentry drew back firing his musket and also missed the mark. At that point, the intruder slashed at the picket's arm with a knife and vanished into the darkness. Rumor had it that the assailant had been a Southern spy drummed out from camp the day before by the 18th Illinois. "The same old coon," Carrington recorded, "had evidently returned to exact his vengeance on the nearest sentry." Picket duty, which had been such a yawning routine, now bristled with all-too real danger, especially among the boys from the 18th and 22nd Illinois who had joined the Eleventh at the Point. Lieutenant Bird, a veteran of nearly three months, observed their nervous behavior with a certain amused, philosophical detachment. He was present during a typical phantom battle wich brought forth a frantic midnight alarm. Frightened sentries charged a ragged volley and scampered quickly back toward camp:

> ...the firing mostly occurred on their wing of the pickets and when the proper officers went out to ascertain what they had fired at, they insisted that they had not fired at all, and some of them that they had not heard a gun. It was evident, however, that they were somewhat scared at something, for...they were all found to have retreated some 50 rods from their posts in towards camp, all closely hugged down in the thick underbrush, and only after repeated calls answering to officers in search of them...The boys do tell some laughable stories about the behavior of their men when the long roll

beat to call out the regiment...They do say that a number of them had pressing occasion to wash their nether garments the next morning both for personal cleanliness and to obviate a rather unpleasant odor which seemed to attach to their persons...Others made unseemly haste to wrap themselves up completely out of sight in their blankets, and were not seen at all until they emerged from their hiding places after daylight...The 11th had got used to these night alarms, and takes them cooly.[13]

Convinced crisis was imminent, Colonel Wallace slept fully clothed throughout the close of July. He never failed to inspect the picket lines whenever nervous sentries reported activity. By July 31st, the three-month volunteers were mustered out and paid $58.65 in gold and silver. Only about 250 out of more than 700 recruits would re-enlist for a three-year period. Company I from Ottawa was going home en masse. At a time when Rebel attack appeared momentary, the Point lay practically deserted. Wallace wrote home to complain how "the responsibility of a battle was upon me; without adequate means to meet the emergency...it gave me great anxiety."[14] By rights even the three-year men could leave for a brief furlough which further exacerbated the situation. In the interim, the Eleventh shrank to one half its authorized strength while a worried Colonel Wallace brooded about coping with a sudden Confederate onslaught. One member of the Eleventh jotted down a brief letter home on August 2nd. He shared the post commander's fears, asserting with conviction that:

...This place is expected to be attacked every moment. Last night an attack was considered certain, and three additional companies arrived here from Cairo, but returned this morning. Yesterday afternoon details were sent out to cut down trees so as to make approaches to the Point difficult. The boys here are in a high state of excitement, and are ready and eager for a fight. If this Point should be attacked and taken, which I doubt very much, you may be sure the mortality list will be large...I can assure you the boys do not relish the idea of being taken prisoners of war, after the treatment our prisoners received at Manassas. They will die fighting to the last man rather than surrender...[15]

Despite the great danger, the author of the letter, identified only as John from Company B, declined to criticize the men who had failed to extend their three months enlistment. His viewpoint was that most of them were patriotic, but they felt it necessary to return home for business and family reasons. Others, John felt, were motivated by dissatisfaction with certain officers. Almost all, in his opinion, would probably later rejoin the colors and enlist in some other regiment rather than the Eleventh. Even Colonel Wallace felt sympathy for many of those going home. He felt they should be "treated kindly." Many had expressed reticence upon enlisting since they felt the government might expect them to bear the financial burden. There was no immediate answer to such questions. Even Wallace was unsure about the extent of support forthcoming from the central government. Long months of hard service, the climate, disease, lack of purpose, and a shortage of supplies had created the present situation. Wallace reasoned it was understandable that many would abandon the course they had set with such fervor at Camp Yates. "They forget now that the country needs their service more than it ever did," Wallace wrote, "that they are now better prepared to render efficient service than ever before and better than others who must fill their places..."[16]

Doubts, fears, recrimination and uneasiness infected both officers and men in the tiny Union encampment which at the crucial hour lay stripped of manpower. Drawn and tired beyond words, Wallace prepared as well as the circumstances allowed. Then, he waited. Almost anticlimatically, with the first shriek of a steam whistle round the bend, all the nightmarish fears evaporated. The throaty screech heralded the arrival of seven army transports making their soot-smoky way toward the Point. On board *The City of Alton* was the commander of all Union forces in the West, Major General John C. Fremont. Major General Fremont, a one-time Republican candidate for the United States presidency, combined high political connections with equally impressive credentials as an explorer in the Far West. On his arrival, he was appalled at the situation in Missouri. He had placed St. Louis under martial law and considered much of the state to be in "active rebellion against the national authority."[17] He, too, had been deeply concerned about the situation at the Point and brought substantial reinforcement--good men from the 2nd Iowa, 2nd Missouri, the 17th and 19th Illinois, and two companies of Chicago Zouaves. Their landing was a festive occasion described enthusiastically by an anonymous soldier of Company B, Eleventh Illinois:

>   As the boats drew near the landing the big guns on this Point and Cairo spoke their welcome...in tones of thunder, and it was returned by the guns of the *City of Alton*--the boat

on which Fremont and his staff came on. It was indeed a sight worth seeing, to have a view of the fleet coming down the river amid the cheers of the men...and the firing of cannon, with every inch of their decks covered with the living multitude on board, answering the cheers of those on shore...[18]

Wallace greeted the "Great Pathfinder" at the landing with genuine relief accompanied by the roared approval of the men. He then guided the prominent Western explorer on a brief tour of the defenses while the raw soldiery gawked and commented on the specter presented by this near-mythical figure. Fear was now replaced by a desire for a great strike against the enemy. In the Eleventh, the anonymous John was enthralled by the new commander. His very presence alone, he wrote, instilled in the men the "utmost confidence." The reinforcements and the spirit incited by General Fremont left the boys eager for a "chance to give them (the Rebs) a sound thrashing for their impudence." John was confident that any encounter, despite the odds, would result in Union victory. He proudly acclaimed that the men at the point were "composed of the best fighting stuff Illinois can boast of."[19]

A brief calm followed during which Colonel Wallace finally allowed himself the pleasure of a brief visit to the North. Before departure, however, he was named commander of all the troops at Camp Lyon. His normally modest air faded just a bit when he transmitted the news home and called Bird's Point "the most important point in the West."[20] His fortunes were on the rise thanks to the patronage provided by a stump of a man named U.S. Grant. That grizzled cigar chewer urged the promotion because he believed Colonel Wallace possessed military attributes of the highest order. He wrote that duty forced him to draw the attention of the nation's leaders to this promising officer who was "every inch a soldier, a gentleman by nature and a man of great modesty and great talent."[21] Colonel Wallace rode north in high spirits, and most probably felt little anxiety about the Point in his absence since his trusted young lieutenant, Colonel Ransom, remained behind. Wallace referred to Ransom as "my particular friend."[22] But upon his return to the Point on August 23rd, Wallace was astonished to find his executive pale, bloody, and abed with a serious pistol wound in the shoulder, the result of a recent encounter with the "Swamp Seceshers" at Charleston, Mo. He listened to the particulars and could only shake his head in wonder at the exploits of this "rash, brave fellow."[23]

The affair occurred August 19th when 250 men from the 22nd Illinois set forth from camp bound for Charleston, Mo. Informants indicated a large force of rebels under a Colonel Hunter had made their appearance there, a scant twelve miles from the Union garrison. Colonel Henry Dougherty led the Federal counter-stroke. His small force boarded a train immediately to chug west in the waning evening light. Aboard as a volunteer was Colonel Ransom, eager to finally come to grips with an extremely elusive enemy. A burned trestle halted the train a few miles outside of Charleston. The command disembarked and continued afoot for the remaining three miles to town.

At the outskirts Colonel Dougherty split his command in two, sending out two companies in a flanking movement while he, in company with Ransom, "moved straight up the track." They soon overran a thin screen of Rebel cavalry pickets, and then 100 yards from the courthouse, came face-to-face with some 200 Rebel horsemen "drawn up in front of us." One volley from the attacking Federals drove them off to the right where they collided with the flanking companies which set off another violent firefight in a nearby cornfield. Dougherty and the main Union detachment then stormed out into the courthouse square and engaged a strong force of Rebel cavalry and infantry. "From the corners of the streets and houses the enemy poured a shower of balls, the city illuminated by the blaze of firearms," was Dougherty's recollection of the midnight melee.[24]

"Our boys stood the fire as well as could be expected but few showing any signs of being scared; the bullets flew thick around us," wrote Lieutenant Lemuel Adams of the 22nd.[25] Another participant recalled how Dougherty screamed out to Ransom that they must "take the Courthouse or bust."[26] The patter of Rebel fire churned up the dust at their feet or whistled high over their heads. Rushing ahead, some Union troopers burst through the Courthouse doors and windows while others engaged Rebel horsemen who swarmed about in the square. "There were some fearful contests--some hand-to-hand fighting," one Union soldier remembered. "The enemy were impaled upon the bayonet, pulled from their horses, knocked over with the butt of the gun, or of the pistol..."[27]

Ransom was accosted in the darkness by an unidentified horseman who screamed out that he was "killing his own men." Unfazed, Ransom responded that he knew what he was doing and demanded the man identify himself. "I am for Jeff Davis," screamed back the shadowy rider. At that Ransom barked back: "Then you are the man I'm after." Both drew pistols but the wheeling horseman opened fire first. A bullet ripped into Ransom's shoulder, but only staggered the Union officer. His response was to shoot the Rebel dead in the saddle.[28] Nearby, Colonel Dougherty engaged another rebel, shooting his attacker after the Rebel struck him down with a blow of a clubbed rifle. About the Courthouse square lay the bodies of at least thirteen Rebels, with probably another fifty dead in other parts of town. Forty horses and thirty prisoners were rounded up. Lieutenant Adams recalled that they were a "hard-looking set." Captured Southern weaponry ranged from rifles and shotguns "of all shapes and dimensions" including an 18-inch Bowie knife. Prisoners and trophies in tow, the Federals returned to Camp Lyon where they received a tremendous welcome.[29]

Wallace and the Eleventh were particularly proud of the role played by Ransom, a man already singled out as an officer with an uncommon ration of ability and battlefield courage. None knew then that the future was to dictate an ever closer relationship and identification between Ransom and the regiment. He, and not the benevolent Wallace, was destined to spur the Eleventh into its most memorable combats--winning both for himself and the unit an unimpeachable reputation for Western grit. As revealed by his wartime exploits, and in the pages of surviving correspondence, he was an ambitious perfectionist driven by a nameless, powerful inner fire. Through the years of civil war Ransom hurtled along a dangerous, perhaps an even suicidal course, that bore an eerie resemblance to the path chosen a generation before by an equally stoic father.

Death entered the life of Thomas Edwin Greenfield Ransom at the age of fourteen when he comforted his mother at grave's edge on a cold, snowy February 22, 1848. They watched his father, the late Truman B. Ransom, interred with full military honors. Aside from loving memories and a dress sword, the family's worldly inheritance was paltry. Their legacy was of the sword and a tradition of service to the young nation traceable to Colonial times. Ransom was a beacon-word for perseverance and pluck in New England where the family banner was planted at Lynn, Connecticut, in the early 1700's by Joseph Ransom. Truman Ransom's great grandfather Matthew, and his son George, campaigned in the Revolutionary War, suffering with General Benedict Arnold during an heroic but futile winter campaign north to Quebec in 1775. Other Ransom relatives were among the slaughtered at Wyoming, Pennsylvania, victims of British-inspired savages. These were the family honors bequeathed to Truman upon the death of his father, Amasa, in 1819 at Woodstock, Vermont, a death which left the family "in nearly a penniless condition."[30]

At thirteen, Truman was apprenticed as a chairmaker and painter to Artemas Lawrence, who proved a gentle master and allowed the youth an opportunity to read and study in spare moments. An obvious ambition incited in Truman a longing for education which might provide a foundation for some other existence rather than that of a craftsman. Upon reaching a compromise arrangement with Mr. Lawrence, the young lad enrolled in the newly founded military school at Norwich, alternating school with labor. Truman promised his benefactor to double his normal output during working sessions. Once the ordeal of work and study was complete, Truman's career rapidly blossomed. He became a pivotal force in the Vermont militia which in time adopted many of his innovations suggested in an 1835 report to the governor. In 1840, he ran on the Democratic ticket for Congress but lost by a few votes. Similarly he was unsuccessful in an 1846 bid for the lieutenant governor's chair. Ransom was a mathematics instructor at West Point for a short period, but eventually returned to Norwich. There he served as vice-president and then as president of Norwich University before resigning the office upon the outbreak of war with Mexico in 1846. Despite the fact he was the father of three boys and a girl, the 45-year-old university president cast aside his post and accepted a commission with the 9th Vermont Infantry Regiment. Ransom was the regiment's executive officer while Franklin Pierce, a future United States president, served as commanding officer. But it was Ransom who led the regiment in a desperate attack at Chapultepec Castle outside the Mexican capitol on September 13, 1847. The charge encountered savage resistance from a contingent of boy cadets who fought with elan and fanatic devotion. They were overwhelmed, but not before Colonel Ransom crumpled in death with a bullet lodged in his skull. An American eyewitness, Adjutant Drum, described Ransom as "the most brilliant man under fire I had ever seen."[31]

Months later Truman Ransom returned to Vermont encased in a lead coffin. His death forced upon Thomas, his second eldest, harsh realities. Necessity soon led his widow to take in student borders as a simple economic expedient. Her eldest son, Dunbar Ransom, was a West Point cadet who could provide little assistance. It was Thomas who took his father's place and combined work of all kinds with study at the scientific department of Norwich University. At some point, through the influence of an unknown cousin employed by the pioneer Burlington and Rutland

Railroad, he managed to acquire a working knowledge of railroads. These were demanding years to be certain, but evidently happy ones. A smiling Thomas is forever preserved in an early daguerreotype. He is flanked on either side by fellow classmates who pose in an affectionate, carefree manner with arms around the shoulder. Friendship came readily to Thomas who quickly struck up an intimate bond with one of his mother's borders, Grenville Dodge. The two Vermonters shared the same limitless ambition, an engaging intelligence and a youthful infatuation with military glory. Dodge, who would achieve singular honors in the political and civilian spheres, remained a life-long friend and admirer.

It is hardly surprising that the Great West beckoned such young men, eager for achievement and anxious to secure the financial means to guarantee a minimum of comfort for their families. Upon graduation from Norwich in 1851, Thomas Ransom, still a teenager, set course for the prairies of Illinois where his Uncle George Gilson was located at the Illinois river town of Peru. His companion, Grenville Dodge, joined Ransom soon after. Both brought with them credentials as military and civil engineers. These were valuable talents, and the two young men were quickly employed surveying town lots in this boisterous, infant community. Young Dodge recalled how the frontier greeted his arrival at nearby LaSalle with a pistol murder committed before his eyes just after the canal boat docked. After a short journey on the "horse cars", he arrived at Peru in time to witness the body of a soldier recovered from the river. Breathless, he walked into George Gilson's office, then mayor of Peru, to report these ghastly events. Dodge was incredulous at how a preoccupied Gilson barely looked up from his ledgers at the news. He and young Ransom were indeed a long way from staid New England. There were also enticements here in the West, to be sure. Dodge later would reminisce of barn dances and "girls in flaming calico dresses" or prairie fires when entire tracts burst into flames and the town's populace trampled out the blaze as best they could. In 1852, labor troubles at a local mine in Vermillionville brought excitement of a different kind. During a bitter coal strike, Thomas Ransom, Dodge, and Dunbar Ransom were all present as members of a local militia company. Dunbar supposedly presented the "radical" strikers with an ultimatum backed by cannon, an approach that quickly resolved the matter.[32]

That same year, Dodge moved further west into the Indian dominated Nebraska frontier for a brief period and then later settled in Iowa to work as a surveyor for the coming railroad. Thomas Ransom remained in Peru to become town and later county surveyor. He and his uncle George soon became partners in real estate and moved the firm in 1855 to the more attractive boom town of Chicago. There George Gilson, died leaving the responsibility of his family with the distraught, twenty-one-year-old Ransom who accepted the burden without the protest one might ecpect from an ambitious youth. Instead of resentment, Thomas provided affection and financial support. He doted on his cousins, Ella and Frances, with the warmth and solicitude of an older brother. In economic terms, success was elusive in those years before the war. Ransom continued in the real estate business until 1861 when he took on employment with the Illinois Central Railroad as an agent in Farina, Illinois. There he heard Sumter's cannon and raised a volunteer company eventually incorporated into the Eleventh Illinois as Company E.

Possessed of a slender elegance accentuated by refined manner, T.E.G. Ransom epitomized a man destined for command. An erect carriage reflected an inner, rigid moral sense characterized by deep-rooted conviction, and a zeal for order. The mental make-up was in turn built upon devotion to responsibility, integrity, and awesome determination. His younger brother, Frederick Eugene, remarked that for Thomas the word "can't" simply did not exist.[33] This solid moral framework was set off well by his physical presence described by contemporaries as extremely attractive. A steady blue-eyed gaze, firm mouth, and finely etched features created a countenance easy to look upon. His blondish hair was moderately long, and his features were framed by long, thick sideburns running to the chin. An unabashed admirer and friend, one-armed Union General Oliver Otis Howard, pictured young Ransom as "the handsomest man" he had ever met.[34] Gallant good looks, however, could not camouflage an indomitable will which transcended the boyish features. Biographer Dumas Malone draws a stark, iron portrait. His verdict was that Thomas was, "a man of irreproachable character and Cromwellian religious faith [who displayed] courage, power of physical endurance, and coolness in action."[35]

Granite virtues, readily identifiable in the Ransom make-up, document this stern reincarnation of the great Puritan. But beyond the monumental facade dwelt a different, more subtly constructed personality characterized by an affable charm both genuine and attractive. His many friends were encouraged to call him "Green", a nickname derived from his mother's maiden name, Greenfield. Margaret Ransom, a cultured and literate woman, never forgot her son's cheerful willingness to assume responsibilities for others. On numerous occasions, he had demonstrated dependability, maturity and sound judgment. She related how these positive qualities could be discerned early in Thomas's life. His father, she remembered, expressed amazement at the child's precocious concern for others and a willingness to sacrifice, "to promote the happiness of those about him." While perceptions of parents may be clouded by love, these must have been based, at least in some measure, on reality. Margaret Ransom asserted that her son was never motivated by selfishness and never spared "pains or expense" in making the family financially independent and "our daily life pleasant."[36] These insights cannot be arbitrarily dismissed since others, less biased, observed identical tendencies in Thomas Ransom. One contemporary, the Reverend W.H. Ryder of Chicago, concurred in the popular estimate. He perceived the rising 27-year-old Union hero as essentially

> ...retiring and unostentatious. There was no strut about him. He was simple in his manners--quiet, unobtrusive. In a company of gentlemen he would not have been selected as a military man, according to the popular estimate. His power was always in reserve for occasions--and the greater the occasion, the deeper the peril, the more capable did he show himself to be...Ransom was a kind, pleasant, sympathetic man. He had a sunny face, a clear, cheerful eye. He attached people to him...[37]

T.E.G. Ransom was a study in 19th century ethics. Cloaked by a sympathetic exterior was an unyielding, almost fanatical will combining to create a presence and style which catapulted him to prominence. Ransom's character and background were to fuse with the Eleventh Illinois Infantry which he unhesitatingly led toward the sound of distant guns.

Despite the temporary excitement engendered by Ransom's performance at Charleston, the Eleventh, and the other units stationed at Bird's Point, soon were battling the old enemies of monotony and homesickness. Hours of training continued unabated, even more emphatically since the ranks were filling with numerous three-year volunteers completely unitiated in the rigors of army drill. Rumors, of course, provided a constant entertainment, many of which were carried by the constant flow of Union men from the interior. At least two or three families a day were appearing at the picket line requesting refuge from hostile, secessionist neighbors. Outraged by their treatment, John, a soldier from Company B of the Eleventh, wrote home of how the refugees flocked to camp,

...making their escape from the desperadoes and robbers of southern Missouri, who act towards all Union people more like fiends that civilized men. They first rob them of whatever they have, and then they give them so long a time to leave the State, and if they do not leave at a specified time, they will find themselves either tarred and feathered or elevated ten or fifteen feet from the ground with a rope around their necks.[38]

The author of those sentiments was a daily correspondent for a hometown newspaper, the *Lacon Gazette*. The reporter/soldier provided home readers with all the details of camp life as experienced by their friends and loved ones. This particular correspondent was an ardent supporter of General Fremont, whose opportune arrival had been greeted with such excitement by a sadly depleted garrison. The young writer saw the war as something more than just a struggle for union but as something far greater--an assertion that all men should have the same rights, that slavery was an abomination which must be eliminated from the nation regardless of the cost. John saw the war as more than just a struggle for abstract principles; he described the conflict in raw, human scenes witnessed every day at the Point as the floods of runaway slaves appeared daily at the camp gates.

A fair specimen of a "contraband" came into camp last week. He had scarcely clothes enough to cover his nakedness, and those he had on were all tattered and torn. He had made his escape from the splendid home furnished him by some brave and magnanimous Southernor. His body bore the marks of the lash and from all appearances it was no stranger to him from childhood. He was taken outside the guard lines, and told to go wherever he pleased, as they do not keep any "contrabands" here.[39]

Not surprisingly, John greeted President Lincoln's recent rebuke of Fremont's statement of emancipation with great hostility. He felt, as did many, that the "Pathfinder" had been correct in announcing his own Emancipation Proclamation and applauded his intent to confiscate the property of all slave-owners in Missouri. These actions, John asserted, were "hailed with delight by every man at this place" and were worth 5,000 more Federal troops:

We have got the right man in the right place now. And you may rest assured he will give a good account of himself and the men under his command, if meddling politicians and disappointed office seekers will mind their own business and leave him to attend his. But I am afraid they will not...When the news of the restrictions the President had placed upon it reached here, everybody was surprised, and all were fierce in their denunciation of the action of the President. All agreed the restrictions were uncalled for and were altogether out of place, and that the President had no business to interfere. It is feared that Fremont will yet be a victim of red tape; and the West will lose the services of one of the ablest generals in the field. If he should be called away from this field of action by the intrigues of broken-down politicians, and barroom Generals, the consequences would be almost fatal to the great cause in which we are engaged, and would be more disastrous than another Bull Run defeat.[40]

President Lincoln had his own timetable for freedom, however, and he remained steadfast. When the time was ripe, such declarations would be issued from the White House and not from a general in the field, even from one so popular and influential as John C. Fremont. John's strident assertions that Fremont's removal would result in disaster were soon contradicted, however, for on November 2, 1861 the "Pathfinder" was removed from command and replaced by General David Hunter. Lincoln established his authority; his word would be obeyed even it it were to take years before the Fremonts, McClellans, and Butlers recognized the fact. This was to be a war to preserve the Union. If emancipation would hasten the nation toward that goal, it would be declared. If it would prove a barrier to that goal, Lincoln would not concede to its implementation despite the cry of Fremont or the thousands of Johns who thought him right.

The Eleventh was not an "Abolitionist" regiment. For every John there probably stood a dozen who held Negroes in utter contempt. Wallace himself, despite being a staunch Lincolnite, shared the prejudice of most white Americans. The Midwesterner was quick to damn radicals eager to elevate the Negro socially and politically. As were most of their contemporaries wearing Union blue, the rank and file from the Eleventh could abhor slavery, but rarely did it mean they would voluntarily embrace its black victims. Racism was the rule, not the exception. These men fought for the Union and not for abolitionist utopia. The fact that these sentiments were popularly held in the Eleventh was driven home sentiments were popularly held in the Eleventh was driven home by an episode involving Captain Frederick Shaw of Company B, one of the more capable young officers in the regiment.

Shaw, a young attorney, had volunteered his services the very day Lincoln's call for 75,000 troops sounded.[41] Since then, his conduct as a company commander had been exemplary. Solemn, his youthful features camouflaged by a dark, chest-long beard, Shaw was considered by acquaintances in his home town at Lacon, Illinois as a "man of many virtues." One close associate, familiar with the officer since 1854, recalled:

> He possessed a large share of the principles of politeness, very genteel while in conversation, standing erect without emotion of the body, looking you straight in the face. He possessed a good share of intellect. I have no hesitation in saying he was formed by nature and nature's God to command. He had a lofty voice, clear and distinct...It was to the purpose and full of determination.[42]

These virtues did Captain Shaw little good when the same Lacon residents, who had bidden him to war with such great enthusiasm, damned him as an agitator the following winter when his "nigger boy" came sauntering into the all-white, Illinois river community. One small Negro, sent home by Shaw to care for his wife both as a household servant and stable boy, served to arouse the community's fear and hatred. Indignant citizens gathered to protest this incursion by a Negro into a free Northern state. Most regarded this contraband as a slave who represented unfair competition for free white labor. The crowd which milled about the courthouse obviously dreaded other consequences. The specter of further black migration into the North hardly presented a cheerful picture for most. Some of the more apprehensive regarded this single Negro servant as the tip of an impending black invasion. Only the admonitions of one of the county judges served to placate the mob when he questioned how "two thousand intelligent citizens could be frightened at the presence of a nigger boy." It was an issue that finally faded, but not before it was made clear to the young officer from the Eleventh that further increases in Lacon's Negro population would not be welcome.[43]

Racial politics were extraneous in the daily life of the Eleventh at Camp Lyon. Each week in small patrols or in combination with other regiments, the men set out on long, brutal marches in what appeared to be an increasingly futile attempt to close with an enemy whose main concern seemed to be to avoid brassy good-bye, almost always confident that this time they would lay hands on Jeff Thompson's bushwhackers. Invariably the high spirits faded in the choking dust and stifling heat. The Missouri countryside looked devoid of any life except for Negro slaves, children, women, and the rare glimpse of a Rebel horseman as he disappeared around the next bend in the road. Private Carrington of Company B narrated a typical expedition of this type, when the company, along with two other regiments, a company of cavalry, artillery, and a long, cumbersome wagon train, set out on October 4th:

> We got up early, packed up, and with two days grub in our haversacks started for the cars. It was dark and looked like rain. Aboard the cars and rode about four miles, then we got out in the woods to take it afoot. By this time the rain was pouring down. The roads were very muddy, daylight began to appear. We started on, resting once in awhile, until we came to Charleston where we expected to find a large force of the rebels. But the "bird had flown." We then camped on a level place, cooked our dinner, got what little rest we could. Then started on a south course and marched about two miles till we came into a lane with corn fields on both sides. Here we halted, the supposition being the enemy were close at hand. One 12-pounder gun was placed at the head of the lane. We got over in the corn and waited about four hours without seeing anything of them. Then we marched back to Charleston... We took some prisoners, good many of the boys gave out, that is about all it amounted to...all wet and mud coming out of Charleston...Took the cars and landed at the Point about 9 p.m. Broke ranks and got into quarters as best we could all wet and mud...[44]

Except that the men were able to observe with a great deal of pride the bullet-scarred square where their new Lieutenant Colonel Ransom had acquitted himself, the journey was fruitless. Indeed, the only casualty was a Private Thomas Conley of Company K who "while partially intoxicated attempted to force his way through the guard, and was fired on by the sentinel and severely wounded in the shoulder."[45] Colonel Wallace, while disturbed by the breach in discipline, was relieved the wound was not fatal. His own recollections of the Charleston expedition were distinctly more pleasant than Private Conley's. Wallace spent a pleasant day taking tea with a certain Mrs. Rouse,

...who lives in a neat house on the outskirt...overshadowed by a giant willow. The house was prettily furnished with carpets and a piano and a pretty daughter to play...Quite a number of the ladies of the place and neighborhood came out to witness the drills and parades of the troops. The officers and men deported themselves admirably and I think our visit there has had a very good effect...[46]

Through the fall, the story was repeated with equally rugged, and equally disappointing, marches to small Missouri towns such as Norfolk, New Madrid, Commerce, Sikeston, Benton and dozens of hamlets and crossroads. It was a gruelling, frustrating exercise conducted in an enemy country populated for the most part by a wary and, in many cases, hostile people who despised Federal troops. Early November saw the beginnings of the most elaborate and powerful expedition yet planned. A large Union force under Colonel Wallace, including a battalion of the Eleventh, would strike almost due west from Bird's Point, cross Nigger Wool Swamp, and then drive towards Bloomfield for a long-awaited meeting with Jeff Thompson's raiders. Another Federal column under Colonel Richard Oglesby, which included the other battalion of the Eleventh under Ransom, was to proceed by steamer to Commerce, twenty miles upriver from the Point. From there the forces marched southwest toward Bloomfield. A third Union strike force was to leave Cape Girardeau another twenty-five miles upriver, also with Bloomfield as the objective. There, the pincers would surround Jeff Thompson's raiders, crushing them once and for all.[47]

Marching with Oglesby's column, Private Carrington described how the Eleventh moved along with four other infantry regiments, two pieces of artillery, and a detachment of cavalry dragging behind an immense supply train consisting of more than 100 wagons. Despite the impediments provided by such a long, and probably unnecessary, logistical tail, the column made unusually good time, logging twenty-eight miles in one day. Carrington and his companions slipped out of ranks at opportune moments and ranged ahead of the caravan seeking fresh milk and edibles. The expedition seemed to move through a vacuum inhabited only by a few stray Negroes, and an occasional white family looking on with ill-concealed apprehension. Even they disappeared when the Union forces forded the treacherous Nigger Wool Swamp whose muddy pitholes could swallow a man whole. Finally, the weary column spied five Rebel scouts who made an appear-

At another point, Oglesby's column stumbled onto an isolated dwelling whose occupants dashed out the doors in a run for the safety offered by a nearby wood. Such actions were not unusual, considering the secessionists had continually told the inhabitants thereabouts that the oncoming Federal troops were "made up of a set of desperadoes who would not respect either age or sex."[49] The fleeing civilians were run down by the more swift among the company. Ironically, one of the Union men was the son of one of the pursued women. Once recognizing her boy turned Yankee, the mother and son embraced in what was a "really affecting" scene. At least in this instance, the monster had proven less than terrifying. Unfortunately, this was not the case in Bloomfield, where the troops found four Union men abandonded in the city jail. John of Company B told how the prisoners greeted the liberators with grim tales:

> Among them was a Baptist clergyman who had been imprisoned for four months by them and whose life had been threatened several times if he did not turn traitor to his country and flag. They found that threats were useless, so they took him to the woods close by, and hung him till life was nearly extinct, but he would form no alliance with them and their treasonable projects, so they brought him back to prison and kept him in duress until the arrival of our troops. He was greatly rejoiced at his liberation, and says his future home will be in the Northern States. The Union men in Southeast Missouri have had a pretty hard time of it. They have been robbed of all their property, and a great number of them paid for their sentiments with their lives. I have seen a tree in Bloomfield where three men were hung for no other reason...[50]

After the expedition returned to the Point, the men confronted the painful aftermath of battle. The Bird mansion was littered with the wounded from the recent Belmont affray which had ended in a hasty retreat to the boats by Union regiments under U.S. Grant. In fact, the taciturn commander barely escaped death or capture by nimbly riding his mount up onto the deck of the last departing transport while Rebel bullets hissed overhead. Ransom's companion during the Charleston scrap, Colonel Henry Dougherty, was less fortunate--he lay in the hospital with one arm amputated. The Eleventh certainly took notice of these ghastly reminders of what the future held, but the uncertainties soon melted away with the return of garrison routine. Ransom described it as the "dull monotony of camp life" with "all its depressing influences."[51]

On the positive side, permanent wooden barracks were nearly complete even though Ransom ridiculed the results as the grandiose work of an ancient "Egyptian architect."[52] Even so, they would prove warm and roomy in the winter ahead, and surely better shelter than the rotting tents. In his own canvas home, Private Carrington was complaining that the rats had "a regular battalion drill" with "one old fellow acting as Captain." Jokingly, he recorded in his diary that one night "they had their band out; I could hear the fifes squeak quite plain. It all ended in a charge, I covered up head and ears in my blanket, and went to sleep."[53] Any entertainment, even if provided by a rodent drill team, was welcome at Camp Lyon. The men chafed under the often illogical restrictions imposed by military life and longed for excitement. The late fall boredom was broken at one point, however, with the announcement of an impending prisoner exchange.

Colonel Wallace and Major Nevius were both a party to the exchange, although surviving records provide few details. We do know that Wallace and his entourage successfully conducted the exchange near Charleston. The Eleventh's commander informed his wife how one Rebel officer present was most embarrassed when reminded that he still utilized the Federal coin as opposed to the official Confederate currency. Negotiations were climaxed with an elegant dinner attended by the Blue and the Gray. Major Nevius described the incongruity of this pleasant social interlude in a letter:

> This was the first exchange that there has been, either East or West, since the war commenced. The way it was done was this...General Pillow sent a flag of truce to our Camp to know if Col. Wallace would enter into negotiations for the exchange of prisoners. A messenger was sent back to inform him that if suitable arrangements could be made that he would. Consequently a board of Commissioners from both sides was selected...We met...and succeeded in effecting an exchange after which we had a very pleasant visit together. You would not have thought from our actions that we were Enemies. All such thoughts seemed to be thrown aside, and we sat down to a sumptuous dinner which we had got up... more like some old friends who had met after a long absence, than like enemies that we were who would gladly have the opportunity to shoot each other at any other time. The Commissioners from the rebel Camp were from Missis-

The Commissioners from the rebel Camp were from Mississippi and Tennessee. They appeared like perfect gentlemen, too. I never spent a more pleasant time with friends than I did with them ere long on the battlefield; with very different feelings from what we parted company at Charleston, but if it should ever be my lot to fall into their hands I believe that my treatment will be that of a friend...[54]

The Union emissaries returned to Camp Lyon where they confronted a more hostile environment. At this stage, disease was an infinitely more competent enemy than Rebel troops. Bird's Point was a breeding ground for the microbes which returned again and again to torture the men with typhoid, cholera and other agonies.[55] Black measles swept through the Eleventh during this period with a ferocity difficult to associate with what the twentieth-century regards as a childhood disease. Fortunately, Mary Newcomb, the wife of a sergeant in the Eleventh, had grown "lonely for the boys" since first visiting Camp Hardin in the spring. She became a permanent resident at the Point, serving as a volunteer nurse.

I had never seen black measles before...and when I saw them [the victims] turn as black as night, after death, I confess I felt a little nervous about the disease; but I kept well...It taxed us all to the utmost to provide something that the boys would relish as their appetites failed--a little tea, a little toast, a poached egg, a baked potato, a delicate custard, some rice nicely cooked, a baked apple, or a little broiled mackerel--a thousand and one things to be seen every day; no time to visit nor entertain...[56]

Before long, Nurse Newcomb was joined by an assistant, Wade Matthews, a "delicate boy, pale and small, but determined to be a soldier." The slight, sixteen-year-old son of a physician had come to the Eleventh hoping that his enthusiasm would counter his poor physique, but he soon found the grueling marches unendurable. After one particularly futile expedition, Matthews had returned to the Point, "covered with mud, so wet and cold he could hardly undress, and so tired he could hardly speak."[57] With the approval of Colonel Wallace he was assigned as an aide to Mrs. Newcomb who welcomed the assistance. She tended the sick, striving in some way to alleviate the pain and discovering in the process that these soldiers, from colonel to corporal, were after all but men who grew depressed and fretful, who longed for home and those they loved. "...it was Mother here, and Mother there, all the time. It seems to me I can almost hear them yet, calling for a little of this or that," she recalled years later in her memoirs. One member of the Eleventh recollected how the presence of women in the camp had a "great influence over the morale of the regiment," commenting that "a glance at their cheerful and handsome faces will banish the 'blues' sooner than a doctor's prescription."[58]

At pole's end socially from the kindly "Mother" Newcomb was the refined, polished Mrs. Stella Coatsworth, wife to the surgeon of the 22nd Illinois. She was a close companion to Wallace, Ransom and the other gentlemen of the post. Her husband had been seriously wounded at Belmont, and she had endured a long period in which all medical hope for his recovery seemed gone. At one point, Mrs. Coatsworth commandeered a rowboat, crossing the ice-clogged Mississippi in a desperate and successful attempt to bring a medical officer to camp. Although the grim effects of typhoid as well as battle wounds seemed to guarantee only death for her husband, the fever broke and he survived. Mrs. Coatsworth's nine-day vigil had been accompanied by the piteous cries of the other Belmont wounded. War in all its gory futility could not vanquish her romantic ideals; she still managed to see a vision of beauty and grace there in the river encampment.

> The plantation, so late the home of the slave and his master, was filled with soldiers of the free North, and the air resounded with the rattle of musketry and the fiery tramp of the war-horse. The pickets were just returning from their wet midnight watch; footmen, cavalry, and artillery were in full motion; officers were calling out their men for morning drill; and the long lines in order being complete, the whole plain seemed like a vast moving panorama dancing in gay uniform, and flashing with steel. The orchard, the cotton-fields in snowy bloom, the white tents beyond the blue coats stepping toe the morning music, and the golden sky above all, helped to complete the picture, behind which lay the grand tragedy of war.[59]

Chapter Three

Lost All But Honor

Bright skies and a warm friendly sun mocked the calendar on the day before Christmas, 1861. At Bird's Point, thousands of Union troops stood to arms on the parade ground and down at the river landing. Tanned and tawny from recent marches, the Eleventh was mustered in its place for the grand review. No less than five freshly commissioned general officers were expected to preside and add luster to the gala affair. A contingent of garrison ladies, armed with parasols and fans in the unseasonably sultry weather, softened the martial scene. Among the petticoat brigade was Mrs. Coatsworth, who eagerly awaited the coming spectacle. She could blot out in a romantic haze the specter of her husband so recently maimed at the battle of Belmont. A peculiarly 19th-century tunnel vision allowed her to ignore the squalid, disease-infested reality of Camp Lyon and focus enthralled upon "unbroken lines of regiments, brigades and divisions."[1]

It was a grand drama in which yesterday's farm boys were transformed into knights errant led by monumental men who, only months before, had been nothing more exciting than village attorneys or country editors. How she must have thrilled when the mounted Union generals disembarked from the ferry down at the landing. They cantered through the mobilized encampment, doffing plumed hats in salute to an appreciative audience. Conspicuous among the riders was General U.S. Grant, whose equestrian skills offset a rather commonplace appearance. An accomplished horseman from West Point days, he sat comfortably astride a feisty, white stallion named Jack who responded with a will to each command of the reins. The great ritual of inspection took place--shouted commands echoed by unit after unit, the snap of salutes, the blare of the massed bands. Mrs. Coatsworth retired convinced beyond question: not even General George B. McClellan, himself, and the whole white-collar Army of the Potomac, could have presented a more magnificent display than had these rangy Western men.

In many respects, the waning days of 1861 were a tranquil, even romantic time, at least for the officers and ladies at the Point. Mansion headquarters often became host for evening concerts, sentimental toasts in the regimental mess, and elegant meals tastefully taken at leisure. There were evening steamboat cruises on the Ohio River during which the Eleventh's band charmed the celebrants while they glided past the lights of Cairo.[2] Their musical passage was noted with appreciative applause which drifted across the water from the crowded city levee. These pleasant interludes culminated in a buoyantly festive New Year's Eve celebration at Wallace's headquarters. Mrs. Coatsworth and her husband were in the company when the band struck up a lovely tune just as the clock chimed midnight. How pleasant to dream away the early morning hours while the Eleventh's well-beloved bandsmen spun familiar melodies which left the "encampment...aroused and spellbound."[3] Seven regimental bands followed, each in its turn, serenading the garrison. Most everyone gleefully ignored sleep on this the first day of 1862.

This was a strange gaiety tinged with melancholy. At least for the more sensitive and perceptive, it was laced with foreboding. Reading of these early days, one cannot help being reminded of the Waterloo Ball. Visions of terribly young faces materialize, made even more vulnerable by the prospect of what lurked in the shadows of the future. Colonel Wallace dismissed whatever concerns he felt in a fatalistic and chilling New Year's toast. The Eleventh's commander turned to Surgeon Coatsworth of the 22nd Illinois, raised his glass, and urged all present to enjoy these happy hours since they might well enter "enternity" before the year was out.[4] Whatever unsettling thoughts this remark engendered, they surely didn't survive the New Year's Day antics which followed. Camp Lyon capered in celebration. Freed from the daily military routine, the enlisted men romped in a youthful explosion of energy and emotion. In his diary, Lieutenant Nathaniel C. Kenyon of Company K rather smugly recorded the rambunctious frolics of the revellers. Kenyon, the son of a Chicago preacher, described how some of the soldiers reversed their coats, christened themselves Thompson's Rebel raiders, and then galloped on horseback madly through camp. More than a few of the rather unsteady riders, Kenyon noted, concluded the day with sore heads and broken bones.[5] Mrs. Coatsworth, on the other hand, viewed the soldiers' festive jubilation with a detached, almost maternalistic benevolence:

The camp-grounds before daylight were up and ready, and with dawn as wild a season of merriment and arch mimicry commenced as ever graced an Italian carnival. Negroes became major generals, mules were tricked out in ribbons and trails, horses hooded and spectacled, sanitary representatives were led from hospital to hospital in the heaven appointed duty of inspection, and nothing could exceed the hilarity of the occasion...[6]

Winter, 1862, quickly banished the unnaturally balmy weather. The radical weather change was accompanied by an equally dramatic turn of events whose savage reality replaced the gentle holiday atmosphere. There was a rainy, pre-dawn ambush on January 9, 1862 near Charleston, Missouri. The preceeding hundreds of miles of marching culminated in a sordid, confused exchange of fire in the darkness. The brief encounter left the winded soldiers of the Eleventh staring in embarrassed fascination at the Union victims--Iowa men who had been marching just ahead before the night exploded. Luckily, the Eleventh had scant time to dwell on the incident. In January, they joined the entire army in what many believed was the long awaited drive south. If anything, the hostile weather conditions had worsened. Colonel Wallace wrote to Ann:

It is cold, very cold. It has snowed some today and the river is covered with floating ice. The cold weather cannot last long, however, and the men are in fine spirits at the prospect of a forward movement. I have taken every precaution in my power to make them comfortable, and I hope we may make the movement without much suffering.[7]

Wallace's solicitous concern evidently was not shared by fellow officers. Newspaper correspondent Charles Carleton Coffin accompanied the expedition and estimated that not one in ten Union infantrymen even possessed mittens when they landed at old Fort Jefferson, Kentucky, some six miles below Cairo. He described how the miserable riflemen constructed huge bonfires at night and still were forced to stomp about all night since sleep promised only a frozen death. Wallace had expropriated a cabin for his own headquarters when the column neared Mayfield Creek, Kentucky. Outside the men chattered in attempted conversation and beat their arms against their sides to alleviate the numbing cold. Wallace, their commander, enjoyed the limited comforts of the ramshackle cabin, and there scanned again and again precious letters from his far-away Ann. "And, as I read them by the flickering light of a poor candle, blown about by the gusts which enter my present quarters in an ancient and deserted cabin...in the wilds...I felt anew what a treasure of a wife I have at home."[8]

The great drive amounted to nothing more than a reconnaissance in force, a ponderous feint directed toward the Confederate fort at Columbus, Kentucky. This abbreviated campaign witnessed only inconclusive marches highlighted by widespread vandalism as documented by the newspaper correspondent, Charles Coffin. He witnessed the Union invaders wreak "sad havoc among the stock, shooting pigs and sheep for fun."[9] This was the only compensation for the agony endured in this Kentucky adventure. General Grant seemed pleased with the troops' cheerful endurance but punished the looting regiments with fines both for the officers and enlisted. The Eleventh escaped reprimand either through guile or, as Colonel Wallace asserted, because they exhibited a distinctive discipline and bearing. These proud thoughts consoled him when the expedition ended the Kentucky foray and headed toward the Point. Likewise, he was cheered by the demonstrated fact that these men could campaign over the roughest terrain in any sort of weather.

Uniforms had barely dried when the Eleventh was rousted out for another winter slog. The men had not been back for more than a day when rumors of another Thompson raid drove them from the cozy barracks back out into the muck. This time it was for a rugged 30 mile trek west toward Sikeston, Missouri. Major Garrett Nevius dismissed the hardships with the nonchalance of a veteran campaigner:

> On this last expedition we went without tents, sleeping out with nothing but a blanket for protection from the cold winds and storms which prevail here at this season of the year. We got along very well, for we are so accustomed to hardship that we do not mind such things as you might suppose we would.[10]

Most of the men, including Colonel Wallace, bemoaned the never-ending marches into the interior which became ever more tedious and accomplished little. The latest "three days wild goose chase among the swamps," Wallace recorded, left the Eleventh "tired, sore and sour."[11] Frustration at the elusive Rebels and the hostile climate was aggravated by another presumed enemy: the Northern press. Colonel Wallace was incredulous at what passed for the truth in various Illinois and Missouri periodicals. Their vaunted reports from the "seat of the war" appeared to him to be merely gross distortion and exaggeration better categorized as rumor than as news. In utter disbelief, he informed his wife during this period of how one newspaper had already reported Jeff Thompson's glorious defeat and capture.

He ridiculed this journal's supposedly accurate account which noted, moreover, his own heroic demise in a mythical encounter with a Confederate artillery battery.[12] Several other officers and men from the Eleventh were listed among the slain in what was described as a desperate charge. Another journalistic account, equally false but at least more optimistic in tone, related the capture of the Eleventh's old nemesis, General Jeff Thompson. The report confidently stated that the vanquished Rebel officer was, even now, at the side of his captor, Colonel Wallace of the Eleventh Illinois. "I have never known so many falsehoods and exaggerations grow out of nothing as in this case," Wallace sighed.[13] Equally exasperated were the Eleventh's rank and file. Many echoed the sentiments expressed by one member of Company B: "A fight cannot be long delayed, and nothing would be more pleasing to the boys than a chance to show these brave Seceshers how Western men can fight."[14]

Waiting ended in early February when Wallace received orders to ready his Second Brigade for a great winter campaign. His eager command included the Eleventh, the 20th Illinois, the 45th Illinois, the 48th Illinois and the 4th Illinois Cavalry commanded by his father-in-law, Colonel T. Lyle Dickey--all attached to General John McClernand's First Division. With the irony so characteristic in war, the Eleventh turned its back on Jeff Thompson's desperadoes, with whom everyone assumed they would eventually meet in their first major combat. Instead, the proposed campaign was aimed southwest into Tennessee where Grant hoped to thrust an armed host deep into the Confederate center and overwhelm the garrisons on the Tennessee and Cumberland Rivers. Volunteer nurse Mary Newcomb remembered the scene vividly when the Point woke one morning to the news.

As we arose one morning in February the long roll beat to arms. It was the first time the boys had ever heard the long roll; and they knew as little as I did about its real meaning; but we all soon found out. The river had been filling with boats for two days, and we had surmised that we would soon be moved...Everything was in confusion.[15]

Colonel Ransom supervised the provisioning and embarkation of the Eleventh which began at 2 a.m., February 3rd, 1862. Mary Newcomb, who was then 44, was among them as the soldiers gingerly made their way across the loading ramp and aboard the steamer *D.A. January*. She was determined to accompany the expedition as was her boyish, delicate aide-de-camp, Wade Matthews. Rejoining his company as a rifleman, he was thrilled at the prospect of combat. Both searched about in the darkened steamer hold for a refuge from the sleet and cold, but, at best, the *D.A. January* was "a dark, cold, damp place that night."[16] Outside, the sleet storm continued unabated as Colonel Wallace penned another last-minute letter to Ann. This painful communique detailed a tragic event which gave scant encouragement to a man already bowed with worry. Hours earlier his younger brother Mathew, of the Fourth Illinois Cavalry, slipped from the icy deck of the steamer *Chancellor*. Weighted down by heavy wool overcoat, saber, pistol and carbine, the young soldier quickly sank beneath the ice-dotted river, drowning at the very outset of the grand adventure. "Poor Mat!" Wallace lamented. "Had he fallen in action I should not have felt so keenly, as that is the fate a soldier contemplates, but to be thus cut-off in the flush of his youth, with a bright career just opening before him, is indeed most sad."[17]

For the men huddled below, it was a time for fitful sleep or drowsy talk bathed in shadows cast by dozens of flickering candles fastened along the hull. There was little secrecy about the destination: the Confederate bastion Fort Henry whose maze of brown earthenworks dominated the strategic Tennessee River. Only a dozen miles east, across an isthmus between the two great rivers, was the even more powerful fortification of Fort Donelson. There awesome batteries stared out over the Cumberland River. All around were thousands of supporting Gray infantry bivouacked in miles of surrounding intrenchments. Henry and Donelson were the linchpins in the Confederate defense, holding firm the security of Nashville and western Tennessee. Their capture would imperil the communication lines and flank of the Confederate force located as far north as Bowling Green, Kentucky. Similarly, the collapse of the Confederate center practically guaranteed the evacuation of the great Rebel guns from Columbus, Kentucky. Grant's plan was to steam south, disembark his force above Fort Henry and drive an armed wedge of more than 17,000 Union troops right down into the strategic land between the rivers. He felt confident that his ironclad gunboats and stern infantry could rapidly hammer the defenders into submission and set the stage for an invasion of northern Mississippi.

On February 4, 1862, the *D.A. January* anchored in the broad Tennessee River some four miles above Fort Henry. Fourteen other Union transports belched black coal smoke nearby and prepared to land troops. Each vessel was crammed with men, weapons, horses, fodder, wagons and guns. Soon it was the *January*'s turn to disgorge its human cargo on the wooded shore; the transfer was accomplished quickly enough except that one unidentified enlisted man tripped and splashed into the river. The non-swimmer was rescued by one of the officers, and the landing continued without further incident. The men bivouacked about a half-mile further upriver, swathed in heavy blue overcoats. Two gray blankets had also been issued to each man. Nurse Mary Newcomb remembered the somber spectacle of the first encampment on Tennessee soil. In the fading daylight the Eleventh and dozens of other Union regiments settled in as best they could, without tents but still able to curl up in their blankets near the campfire--thousands of which flickered gold against the night sky. The men were "half frozen and shivering," Nurse Newcomb recalled.[18] It was a very special moment made infinitely more poignant as first one man, and then entire regiments, joined in a ragged but powerful chorus. Across the broad Tennessee came the lyrics of an old American hymn, "Rock of Ages." Night brought another heavy, cold rain which drenched the command. Many slept near great burning bonfires, turning now and again to dry out the side of their bodies exposed to the pelting rain, then reversing the process again and again. "And thus we steamed, soaked and shivered all this dreadful night," wrote Private Carrington. "Coming right out of warm, cozy quarters, this night of weather horrors gave many a stout young man his death warrant, but we kept our ammunition dry. The dismal hours of night wore away and morning dawned at last."[19]

Bone-tired men rose in the gray to stumble about in the frigid wet. Some awkwardly attempted to wring dry the sodden wool blankets and coats. Others crumbled bits of hardtack for breakfast or softened the fragments in hastily brewed coffee. With the first real light, Wallace ordered the Second Brigade in line, and the men prepared to set out for Fort Henry. Just before the column departed, the men in the Eleventh glimpsed their old friend, Nurse Newcomb, who had come ashore for a final good-bye. She first spoke with Colonel Wallace who encouraged her to visit down the line, saying: "You may not ever see them all again." Mrs. Newcomb embraced her boys including her husband, who was a sergeant in Company G, and the pale Private Matthews. Ritually she made her way down through the ranks pausing now and again as a soldier pressed into her hand some treasured memento, perhaps a watch or ambrotype, asking she return it to distant parents or a loved one. "Tell them I am in for it, and never expect to get home again," many whispered. In turn, a deeply touched Mrs. Newcomb stopped again and again to murmur, "God bless you and save you."[20]

That first day's march carried the Eleventh only two miles upriver for an early camp followed by another rainy night. On February 6th, the men rose early, only to stand in ranks, idle and confused, until the forward movement recommenced at noon over what one trooper said were "the muddiest roads I ever saw."[21] Rebel detachments had strewn a tangled mass of fallen trees across the rut-speckled "trace", further impeding the march. Artillery had to be dragged and lifted by sheer strength through the morass. A stream, bloated with the winter rains, forced innumerable stops while the men quickly improvised bridges. In other places the "trace" vanished requiring the same dog-tired infantry to double as road builders. General McClernand reported that the seven mile march toward Fort Henry was made "over the worst possible roads." One private in the Eleventh recalled "mud, and water sometimes four feet deep."[22] The men could hear the distant thunder as the Union ironclad fleet engaged the fort's heavy batteries in an ear-shattering duel. The seventeen Rebel cannon challened the fleet's formidable ironclads who soon closed the range to an incredible 500 yards. Meantime, the Union infantry slipped and stumbled its muddy way to the sound of the guns, determined to swing around the left and bottle up the Confederate defenders in their earthworks. Private Carrington of the Eleventh described how all the while the boys heard "those awful guns," even at times glimpsing the Rebel fort through the smoke with the Secessionist flag still flying. Then the firing suddenly subsided. Word filtered back through the slogging ranks that the Rebels had surrendered to the fleet although their approximately 3,500 infantry had already fled the intrenchments and were bound east for Fort Donelson. By late afternoon, the works at Fort Henry were occupied. The Union infantry milled about, in sheer awe at the havoc inflicted by the fleet's guns, and simultaneously scavenged for edibles or souvenirs for the folks back on the farm. "Guns dismantled, earthworks torn up and the evidence of carnage meet the eye on every hand," Colonel Wallace wrote, adding that the Rebel garrison under General Lloyd Tilghman had fled in "panic" leaving behind only a handful of artillerymen.[23] Private Carrington wrote to his father:

The ditches around Ft. Henry are full of water and very deep. At the entrance is a drawbridge. Many a poor fellow would have lost his life in trying to take it by storm. In the Fort, five men (Rebs) were killed, four by the bursting of the big rifle; they got a shell fast someway and the gun burst. The face of one man laid up on the gun, some eight or ten feet of the muzzle rested on the embrasure, while the breech was blown into fragments; some of the pieces weighing 500 pounds or more were scattered about. One of the men had his head and both arms blown off, a red sight...The fire from the gunboats was terrific; I don't see how men could work those guns under such a terrible destructive fire; the parapets and embrasures were torn in great rents where the shells had gone through--scattering death and destruction all around. The log cabins are back of the Fort; shells had plowed their way through the logs from one cabin another. No wonder the enemy left...[24]

Fort Henry capitulated on February 6th. The Federals spent the next five days within the perimeter of the captured strongpoint until the columns struck out once again around noon on February 11th. The weather was warm and springlike, and the men's knapsacks were crammed with two days' rations. One day's march east along Telegraph Road brought the command within sight of the imposing Confederate position at Fort Donelson--great brown earthworks stretching in a vast semi-circle. At the center were the heavy shore batteries protected by 12,000 to 15,000 Rebel infantry glaring down from the hills on the approaching blue columns. On the night of the 12th, McClernand's division, with Wallace's brigade second in line, approached within a mile or so of the works, then proceeded in roughly an easterly direction bound for the Confederate left flank. Captain Smith D. Atkins of A Company, Eleventh Illinois related how the command skirted the Rebel lines so closely that "we could see tents plainly and hear them talk around their camp fires."[25] Oglesby's brigade at one point during the night encountered fire from the Rebel outworks, causing a detachment of Union cavalry great fright. "Wheeling their horses about, they dashed madly to the rear and compelling our boys to clear the road for them," Captain Atkins described.[26] Quickly re-establishing ranks, the Eleventh and the remainder of the brigade braced for attack, but soon the night quiet returned and the march recommenced. At 9 p.m., Wallace ordered a halt. Skirmishers were sent out in the darkness and huddled in the brush only yards away from the Confederate intrenchments outlined against the horizon. As the Eleventh crouched in weariness that next morning, Captain Atkins watched with great interest as Confederate artillery opened with vengeance on Union cavalry bivouacked in a nearby hollow. The brief but harmless fusillade was the opening act in a day of artillery duels. "Fifteen batteries, I think, opened fire and kept it up all day on the rebel intrenchments and round shot, shells and grape flew plenty and fast, cutting off tree tops, and places literally mowing down the young timbers," Captain Atkins observed. "...Taylor's Battery did splendid execution, dismounting rebel guns with their round shot, and sending the Rebs fleeing from their intrenchment when we could get the range, with their shells. Berge's regiment of sharpshooters, each man fighting on his own hook, behind tree, stump or log did very fine work in picking off the rebel artillerymen..."[27] In the late afternoon the Eleventh continued the gradual move to the Rebel left. Dashing across one extremely exposed stretch of ground, Atkins noted the "stzip, stzip, stzip" screech of Minie balls ripping the air over the men's heads or plowing into the soft ground about their running feet. With the onset of night on the 13th, the regiment snuggled in behind the brow of a small hill only a few hundred yards from the Rebel front. The Second Brigade was strung along the front of Wynn's Ferry Road with the Eleventh at the extreme right flank. Beyond stretched the men of Oglesby's brigade and McArthur's brigade, whose regiments extended further right but whose flank still failed to connect with the Cumberland River--a fact which was soon to have disastrous consequences.

Behind the men of McClernand's division lay the key roads leading south, a vital avenue of excape should the Confederate garrison attempt a break-out. But this evening little thought was given to that possibility. The men sought what pathetic shelter was available there amidst the darkening woods with a hard winter rain soaking them to the bone. Despite the frigid downpour, Captain Atkins recalled that complete and utter exhaustion allowed him to sleep as soundly as if he were at home in bed, oblivious to the icy patter which soon transformed itself into a full-blown blizzard. Two hours later the staccato ripple of musketry broke out to the front of the regiment followed instantly by Ransom's bellow, "Fall in, Eleventh!"

...bang, bang, bang went the guns of our pickets, and in less time than it takes me to tell it, our boys were in line. I was surprised, on waking, to find about an inch of snow already fallen, and a wild, fierce snow storm raging; and for two to three hours we stood there, or rather kneeled in the snow and storm, while the bullets went whistling over heads. The Rebels seemed to be determined to worry us out, for their balls did no damage, passing from one to five feet above our heads. Then the fire slackened, but every little while, all night long, the orders often came "Fall in," and we stood by our guns. No sleep... and in such a pitiless storm--the bullets whizzing, our limbs benumbed or aching, feet slopping wet with the slush and mud, and not knowing but that at any moment a wild, charge might come, where cold steel must be met by cold steel...when daylight came our clothing was frozen on our backs and our blankets, stiff with ice and snow, might be stood up against the trees like boards.[28]

Captain Atkins of Company A was a prolific writer, a twenty-six-year-old Freeport, Illinois attorney, a graduate of the Mount Morris Seminary, and a man with unabashed political ambitions.[29] His connections with the *Freeport Journal* were intimate--he would one day own the paper outright, in fact--but for now the aspiring volunteer officer was content to utilize the paper as a forum to display his military achievements. Wallace and Ransom felt that Atkins was absent from duty far too often and there are indications that they resented the *Journal*'s repeated letters to Springfield regarding regimental business. These messages usually dealt with the "pitiful plight" of the Eleventh at the Point.[30] But whatever the animosity, the bickering was quite rightly obscured by the necessities of the moment while the regiment shivered in mutual suffering outside Fort Donelson. Valentine's Day was equally dreary. No fires were allowed anywhere near the front, forcing the men to chatter their way through the endless waiting, many with muskets jammed bayonet down into the slush to allow themselves the luxury of warming frozen hands inside their coats. Later, hot coffee was brought up from the rear by detail to provide the soggy, ice-encrusted men with a small bit of warmth. Snow and colder temperatures came with the passing of the day, punctuated throughout by the incessant call to arms sounded every time the picket fire intensified. Then, too, there was the desultory but deadly sniping that now and again claimed a victim. Much to his own amazement, Captain Atkins observed how the horror soon lost its impact on the men beset by misery and cannon fire:

Our boys were fast getting used to the sight of wounded and dead, growing familiar with the whizzing bullets. They no longer dodged them, but the closer they came, the merrier the laugh, and the livelier jest...Round shot, shell and grape were all tried plentifully on us, but we were too close to the brow of the hill for them to do us much damage. They passed right over our heads, and exploded, or spent their force, in the woods beyond...One (shot) passed close to me in front and one close behind me as I sat reading a letter..."[31]

Union spirits rose dramatically at around 4 p.m. when the crescendo mounted, supported by the dull distant roar from the Cumberland River where Yankee ironclads answered Rebel shore batteries. Many in the Eleventh's ranks joked about this bloody exchange of Valentines. Most were optimistic; these same waddling iron monstrosities had worked wonders at Fort Henry. While the men listened intently, the gunboat fleet probed ever closer to the Confederate gun flashes. The fight was rapidly turning into a slug fest. The ponderous Union ironclads were slashed, gutted and pounded by an effective and powerful barrage. Ignoring the return fire, the Rebel gun crews squinted through the murky powder smoke which, at times, almost completely obscured the oncoming ironclads. Finally Union Admiral Andrew H. Foote closed the range to 400 yards, a fatal mistake which provided the Confederates with easy targets while Federal shells howled off to tear the air far high of the mark. Spent naval shells burst in a roar in the woods beyond. On the river, the ironclads buckled under the point-blank cannon blows. Within minutes, the *St. Louis*'s pilot house was battered, leaving her a helpless wreck. *Louisville*'s steering mechanism was dismembered by Rebel shot. She also drifted aimlessly down river. Both the *Pittsburgh* and the *Carondelet* were bruised, riddled and bleeding. Admiral Foote was seriously wounded but still retained command despite the bite of Rebel shrapnel in one ankle.

All this transpired beyond the sight of the Eleventh. The regiment nested securely in the wooded, snowy hills more than three miles distant. But they quickly guessed the outcome when the cannon faded, replaced by the distinctive Rebel yell. Private Carrington recalled how the victorious Rebel gunners had "sounded like small boys, school boys yelling." An inveterate diarist, Carrington would dejectedly scrawl in his journal how "we were rather gloomy at their being repulsed. The gunboats had been so successful at Fort Henry. The rebel guns (at Donelson) are planted in pens dug out on the side hill close down to the river's edge for cannon shot to take effect. And it is almost impossible to get a shot or shell to take effect."[32] Another soldier from the Eleventh, Private John W. Reading of Morris, was duly impressed with the Confederate defensive works which loomed just over the rise.

No labor had been spared to make the fortification a strong one; nature itself had made it almost impregnable, being a succession of hills averaging 100 to 200 feet high with deep ravines running between them, where the redoubts were built and batteries planted...Just imagine a succession of hills six miles in length, crowned with batteries...and surrounded by trenches, trestle-work and rifle pits, the front covered by a chevaux-de-frise of fallen timber, almost impassable, and you can form some idea of the obstacles...[33]

Formidable or not, the men in the Eleventh and other Union regiments were not in the slightest doubt that soon, perhaps in a matter of hours, they would be ordered forward to carry those works and silence the great water batteries that had beaten the gunboat armada. It was a sobering thought although, as Private Carrington suggested, "in sleep we forget the dangers of the hour..." Another night came, and again the snow, the wet, the fitful slumbers in hollows scraped by hand in the hillside--then once more the pickets falling back, Ransom's voice ringing out, and standing to in the cold. So the night went in endless repetition, the winter air bringing the sounds of sharpshooters searching out in the black for victims.

A pale, winter sun crept into the morning sky on Saturday, February 15, 1862. Grant's army crouched in misery at the outer edges of the great Confederate strongpoint. Suffering men winced against the cold, relentless wind. And, soon, even before first light, the near-constant rifle chatter swelled in intensity on the Federal right wing. Like a forest fire, the noise skipped along the First Division front until the crackling fire sputtered out directly to the Eleventh's front. At about 7 a.m., the regiment's pickets dashed back through the woods and reported breathlessly of a large Rebel force advancing with flags flying. Private John Reading in Co. F saw the Gray mass loom over the hill minutes later, greeted by a concerted roar of musketry. "The Rebels fought well," he conceded, "but not fairly--like Indians they sought shelter of stumps and trees. We suffered them to advance within 100 yards, when we opened upon them with terrible effect..."[34] Twice more, within forty minutes, the attacking Rebels renewed the assault, moving through the wood and keeping up a continuous fire. They fell back each time, although groups made their way at points to within 40 yards of the Union line. Captain Atkins claimed they even came within 25 paces of Company A in one rush:

We stood ready for them, cautioning our men to keep cool, and waste no ammunition, and not fire a gun unless sure to lay a rebel on the ground...Bullets were flying plentifully enough, and, getting them in splendid range, we opened upon them a murderous fire that literally mowed them down, and stopped their advance...The attack was admirably planned, the advancing line of battle being followed by another forty rods to the rear, and the rebels had their intention evidently being to turn our right wing and escape; they fought with the most reckless courage and dauntless heroism, so determined to break through our lines...but the 11th never wavered and for about forty minutes the battle raged as if all the furies had broken loose, the roar of musketry almost deafening, the bullets flying literally like hail, our dead and wounded falling on all sides, when their firing slakened, and then they broke and ran! And such a shout of victory as went up along our lines...[35]

Ransom promptly threw out the line of skirmishers once more. Other men were detailed to proceed toward the rear where they might safely light fires for the purpose of brewing coffee. This steaming brew was then brought up to the men shivering in line of battle who breakfasted as best they could with their muskets within easy reach. File closers, in company with the members of the Eleventh Band, were searching about the hillside for the wounded, carrying and dragging the men back for what treatment was available in the rear areas. Not many minutes had passed when once again the pickets came scrambling back with news of a larger Confederate attack force weaving through the woods right behind. On line with the Eleventh was a special correspondent for the *Louisville Journal*, who described the assualting Rebel columns as an immense force:

As soon as a head appeared above the brow of the hill, bang went a well-aimed bullet at it...Though they (the Rebs) did not fight with the reckless courage of the first attack, they fought longer and more cooly...During the whole time, Col. Ransom was moving along the regiment, and all the company officers were cautioning the men to keep cool, and never fire a gun except it be well aimed at a rebel as, if we did not, our ammunition would soon be gone. The regiment fired at will, every man firing his piece only when he was sure he could hit a rebel, and the 11th wasted no ammunition. When anyone was killed or wounded and that was frequent enough, his cartridge box was taken off and distributed to those yet in line...[36]

After more than two hours the assualt faded. The Rebels fell back through the wood, chased and harried by the rousing cheers from the exhausted Eleventh. A few minutes later, the Rebels poked their heads over the hill once again, but this effort was half-hearted in comparison with previous assaults. Again they "skedaddled," as Captain Atkins noted with great satisfaction. Less encouraging, however, was the fact that for some time the rear area had been filling with hundreds of soldiers fleeing the advancing Rebels who rolled up one Union regiment after another on the right flank. In the chaos, the Union's 25th Kentucky, while moving up in support, fired a volley into the 8th Illinois by mistake, and added to the mounting terror and confusion. By early afternoon, the Federal right wing consisted of Wallace's brigade with the Eleventh at the extreme right flank fighting alongside Colonel John A. Logan's hard-pressed 31st Illinois--all that effectively remained of Oglesby's brigade. McClernand's division was dangling out on the right flank, an inviting target for the continually pressing Confederates eager to turn around on the right. Once this was accomplished it would bring Wallace's brigade and the 31st Illinois under a scalding, raking fire. It was nearly 1 p.m. when, in Captain Atkins's words,

...a most terrible fire opened in front of our regiment, and in front of the 31st Illinois, Col. John A. Logan, which joined us immediately on our right....It seemed as if the rebels had gathered demoniac courage by their partial success in driving back our line, and followed up every inch of vantage ground, and yelling like devils, they poured in their fire like hail--The gallant Logan rode about among his men, utterly fearless of his own life, and succeded in rallying his regiment. The right flank was thrown back to the rear, changing the line of battle making an elbow where the left of his regiment joined ours, and for a time they met and checked the enemy. This left our regiment exposed to a raking right flank fire...Col. Ransom kept moving up and down the lines, as did also Major Nevius, cautioning our men to keep cool...but make every bullet bore a hole through a rebel...[37]

Especially deadly in that bloody wood were Rebel rifles crammed with "buck and ball"--a lethal mix of bullet and buckshot. It was a frontier fight with the Gray riflemen crouching behind stumps and trees and in the brush. They would load and quickly leap into the open, unleashing a deadly blast into the ranks of the Eleventh. Slim, impressive Col. Ransom presented an inviting target as he pranced along the regimental lines atop his favorite mount. Before morning ended, his coat had been ripped six times by Confederate bullets, his hat pierced once, and his horse shot dead beneath him. One Rebel round finally found the mark, smashing into Ransom's right shoulder, forcing him to the rear, streaming blood.[38] Taking command, Major Nevius was faced with an increasingly chaotic situation as the nearby 31st wavered before incessant assaults, breaking at three different times only to rally before the screaming Logan who galloped in a frenzy up and down the battle line. Mud-splattered and bloody, Logan inspired his men to make one more stand while he rode up to the adjoining right flank of the Eleventh, there notifying Nevius that his regiment was nearly out of ammunition and must be withdrawn. Colonel Ransom, his wound temporarily bandaged and treated, now returned, instructing the Eleventh to march to the right into the 31st's line of battle. Private Carrington wrote how this movement toward the right was the most difficult order to obey. "About the hardest thing I know of in battle is to take a fallen man's place, to step up and fill a gap in the ranks that was made by the fatal bullet."[39] The movement was methodical; the men paused at intervals to fire and load, and kept up a continuous fire. Once secure in the positions formerly held by the 31st, the Eleventh braced for further assault. The Rebels' response was immediate. Atkins recorded how the enemy came on pent-up with a "hell bound fury." There in the cold wood they fought. The Eleventh crumbled about its edges under strong pressure from their front actively abetted by other enemy forces on the far right. From that exposed point, a deadly rifle fire tore away at the Eleventh's naked flank. Private Carrington remembered:

> Then the enemy's undivided attention was turned upon us. We in the meantime had kept up our share of the racket, the boys falling continually. "Close up" was the word...Alex Hesse, on one knee in the rear rank in front of me was hit in the shoulder, the bullet went clear through and lodged in the skin of the blade. He looked up at me, put his hand to his shoulder, turned and walked out of the ranks without a word..I never saw him afterwards...I did not hear a

man groan or cry with pain that day. The wounded walked or crawled away down the hill...The dead lay where they fell. The constant "spang, spang" of the muskets on the damp frosty air blended with the roar of Taylor's guns...We closed up, keeping the colors for our center...[40]

The situation's severity was apparent to Colonel Wallace who pressed the First Division for reinforcement. His immediate superior, General McClernand, pleaded this was impossible at the moment, instructing Wallace to act on his own discretion. Wallace, therefore, determined upon a withdrawal from this precarious position by pulling the brigade back roughly southwest along the Wynn Ferry Road, and there re-consolidated his sorely tried command.

The crisis mandated that the Eleventh be withdrawn from their hellish predicament on the extreme right flank. There could be no delay or Wallace's old regiment would be routed. Orders were passed to each regiment detailing the impending movement. Incredibly, the brigade withdrew in relatively good order despite heavy Confederate pressure, but something was definitely amiss on the distant right. It became apparent that the Eleventh was holding its old position, made more dangerous as the retiring brigade exposed the left flank as well as the right. Unknown to Ransom, the messenger detailed to bring the withdrawal order to the embattled Eleventh lay dead in the muddy slush. Totally isolated from support, the men robbing dead comrades for bullets, Ransom's Eleventh waited for the Rebel reaction.[41]

Lieutenant Colonel Nathan Bedford Forrest, sitting in six-foot two inch magnificence upon his mount, was not a man to ignore opportunity. A rough-hewn cavalry genius, he spied the opening within minutes of Wallace's withdrawal. He capitalized on the error by ordering his Rebel horsemen to sweep in on the left while Hanson's Kentucky infantry assaulted dead ahead. Other Confederate units continued the crippling fire from the far right. The entire attacking force concentrated on the beleaguered Eleventh, crushing in from three sides on the weary Union regiment which had so doggedly resisted throughout the day. It was around 2 p.m. when the Rebels came through the woods once again, howling for the kill.[42]

Confederate fire seared in from every side. The Eleventh Illinois disintegrated into a clot of dead and wounded men. Lieutenant James Churchill of Company A suffered a grim shock of awareness that the Rebels were in the rear. "Our men were being shot in the back."[43] German-speaking Henry Uptmor, a private in

Company K, noted the savagery of the fire which now came from the front but even more deadly still from the left rear where Forrest's cavalry clattered through the wood. "The blue bullets were thick, and one wounded me in the right arm between the elbow and the shoulder," Uptmor wrote. "They flew thick as birds in flight."[44] Now the Rebels came on with a roar. Hanson's Kentucky infantry charged the Union front, recoiling from one massed volley from the Eleventh, then recovering and pushing to within forty yards when Colonel Ransom bellowed out the order: "Face to the Rear and charge cavalry." The Eleventh wheeled about in a ragged order and attempted to claw their way back to the main Federal line. Kentucky infantry fired into their backs while they stumbled through the underbrush. Private Carrington realized instantly that the only excape route led through the Rebel cavalry. He joined the retreat that was now degenerating into confused, fearful flight.

> The Rebel Infantry at the same time charged, sweeping up the other slope of the ridge, and being so earnest in the matter we gave way. There was no order given that I heard. The whole line just seemed to melt away and scatter. There was a blind rush to get away on our part, and forward rush on their part to get us. As I saw the right wing trying to get down in the ravine and the left breaking off that way, I turned my musket "at a trail." As it happened the bayonet ran in under a small jack oak tree that had been cut down and left hanging to the stump. Some of the boys crowded in behind me and I was forced to let loose of my musket, for I could not back out, so I had to go on without it. I ran down the ravine and started up the opposite slope, my shoes slipping in the snow for by this time the sun was breaking out and thawing a little...[45]

During the crazed retreat, the Eleventh fragmented into isolated clots of men. Some fought their way through the cavalry, others threw up their hands in surrender, and many were shot down in their tracks. Ransom gathered a small band about the colors and scrambled through the woods against tremendous odds. Confederate fire screamed in at the color guard. Bullets struck Color Sergeant McCaleb three times without apparent effect. Then, a fourth round smashed into his face and the six-footer went down. Sergeant William Armstrong quickly grabbed the banner and tore through the woods in company with Ransom and a few other survivors.[46] It was worse on the right flank.

Company A was in desperate straits when the line broke. In their precipitate withdrawal, they encountered a jagged line of wooden abatis. They were forced to either weave their way delicately through or squirm underneath the obstacle, all the time exposed to a ferocious fire. Company A never recovered; all discipline disintegrated. Later, men from the company recalled how the most savage fire came when they neared the top of a small rise. For others, the most terrible images concerned Forrest's cavalry when that rugged force wheeled in among the regiment firing carbines and pistols.[47]

One victim was bearded Lieutenant James Churchill of Company A. Early in the sprint toward safety he was struck in the left thigh by a .69-caliber rifle ball which hurled him to the ground. The dazed officer regained his feet despite the profuse bleeding and hobbled off to rejoin the desperate race south. He could see Forrest's mounted troops strung out in a ragged line ahead, unleashing deadly aimed fire into the Union fugitives. Rebels blazed away with an odd but effective collection of horse pistols, shotguns, rifles, and revolving Colt rifles. Plunging toward what appeared to be a gap in the Gray line, Churchill darted toward it only to find himself within six feet of a Rebel cavalry man. The Union officer raised his pistol but was struck before he could fire a shot. This time, Churchill was down permanently. He fell heavily into a pile of dead and wounded men. His pistol and sword lay just out of reach. Initially the pain was excruciating in its intensity. The bullet had smashed into a hip-socket, angled down along the thigh bone and lodged above the knee. Churchill quickly faded into unconsciousness.

All along the line it was the same story. Blue-coated infantry darted through the wood with horsemen in close pursuit. A few infantrymen paused to stab with the bayonet at the cavalry, and a few even leaped up in desperate efforts to unhorse their antagonists. It was bloody chaos. When the order to retire sounded and the rush toward Wynn Ferry Road commenced, Private A.W. Gore of Company B was already wounded in the thigh. He paused for a final shot. No sooner had he pulled the trigger when a Rebel bullet passed through one hand and tore away great splinters from the rifle's stock. In shock and terror, Gore dropped his mangled weapon and joined the foot race to safety, "but with much difficulty as I had to go on one leg and one hand. I went about 20 yards and fell behind a log. Sergeant Sweeny fell a few feet from me with a wound in his leg...." Private Gore lay helpless while the regiment was shattered before his eyes. He saw Private H.S. Ellsbury stiffen in mid-flight only a few feet away. The ball tore through the soldier's head but the momentum carried the mortally wounded man onward until he fell across the horrified Gore. Minutes later, another soldier from the Eleventh crashed to the ground nearby, clutching a shattered jaw.[49] Everywhere the men in Blue were dying, throwing up their hands in surrender or groaning in wounded agony. All around, the regiment was being butchered by a scathing fire from Rebel infantry and cavalry.

Wounded twice in the back and once in the side, Lieutenant B.F. Blackstone of Company B somehow managed to stagger away from the hellish melee until suddenly confronted by a mounted Rebel who, "instantly drew his pistol." Blackstone recalled how he was "a second too soon for him." The Yankee's first shot lifted the cavalryman "three feet" out of the saddle to crash headfirst into the ground. Scrambling atop his still living adversary, Blackstone pulled out the Rebel's saber and plunged it through the man's body. Bloody sword in hand, the Yankee officer resumed his flight toward the main Union line now some three-quarters of a mile distant.[50] Similar and equally gory hand-to-hand encounters were repeated all through the snow-painted woods. Private Charles Crane from Company B found himself in a one-sided struggle with three pursuing Rebel horsemen. They galloped just behind him until the fleeing infantryman turned and killed the trio's leader with a cooly aimed rifle shot. Crane immediately dove into the brushy shelter of a large fallen tree evidently sliced down by cannon fire earlier in the battle.

Enraged, the two surviving horse soldiers circled about his nest, ineffectually slashing about with heavy cavalry sabers. Crane scurried through the fallen limbs like a rabbit with a pack of hounds at full bay. All the while the two Rebels hacked away in a frenzied effort to cut down the elusive Yankee. Bleeding from a painful buckshot wound in the back, and with one hand half shot away, Crane squirmed out of sight and crawled through the underbrush behind the horsemen. Rising out of concealment in their rear, the union private struck home with his bayoneted rifle. His opponents' movements were constricted in the heavy growth, and he quickly stabbed both to the ground. An exhausted, trembling Crane didn't even pause to see if he had killed the Rebel. Instead he whirled around and loped off through the hilly Tennessee countryside.[51]

The survivors located the remnants of the regiment in Buford's Hollow about a third of a mile south of Wynn's Ferry Road. A bleeding Ransom was attempting to re-establish order in the hollow. Only about 115 men were counted, many of whom wounded or without weapons. Those woods by the Wynn's Ferry

Road represented a melancholy sight for young Private Carrington who had finally found refuge from the "hissing bullets." One rifle shot had sizzled right along his right hip bone "stinging like a bee" but leaving only a "beautiful round red spot about the size of a ten cent piece." Wandering toward the rear, the nineteen-year-old took note of the orderly Union regiments which were moving up now in belated reaction to the Rebel threat. Such reassuring sights unfortunately were balanced by the spectacle of defeated men dejectedly stumbling about or stopping to exchange horror stories of what had transpired during the morning's fight: "The woods seemed full of men all drifting to the rear, wounded men assisted by comrades moving slowly and sullenly," Carrington wrote in his diary.

We felt we were whipped, the shame of it ground us. We couldn't bear it. I soon overtook Whitfield, with three bullets through one leg, limping along. He threw one arm over my shoulder; I grabbed his hand. "Ouch," he said. I looked and the middle finger hanging by a shred of skin on each side where a musket ball had gone through...We came down to a farm house, already full of wounded men. While the Doctors or Surgeons were quite busy, Billy Green of our Company was bare headed holding one hand with a bleeding thumb, going around swearing at the Rebels, the Doctors, the Government and everything else...[52]

At about this time, a tear-choked Wallace rode up complimenting the men on their magnificent five-hour fight. In turn, Ransom saluted the old commander promising that the regiment was ready to follow any command at any time. "Brave men that could face the devil cried like children," Captain Atkins noted.[53] Then, with the grimy tears rubbed away, the regiment marched to the rear as the Union center composed of General Lew Wallace's division marched up in support. Although it would be impossible at the time to perceive, a turning-point was reached. General Grant was finally on the field after a long conference aboard the *St. Louis*. He ordered General C.F. Smith to assault the denuded Confederate left flank and ordered General Lew Wallace to recover the ground lost on the far right where the Eleventh had bled so freely. Smith's charge on the left caught the Rebel defenders at a most vulnerable moment just as they were rearranging their battle lines. Soon the Union infantry occupied a considerable portion of the entrenchments of vaunted Fort Donelson and drove back a counterattack. Both sides then waited for the morrow when daylight would witness another drive toward the Rebel river batteries.

On the far right, Lew Wallace's men encountered remarkably light resistance. Unknown to them, bickering, indecisiveness and animosity among the Rebel high command frittered away the Confederate advantages. As a result, the Confederates pulled back and gave up the break-out plan despite the success enjoyed earlier in the day. Wallace's counterstroke was only partially successful. When the dark and bitter night cold returned, his troops occupied only a portion of the contested field. Out between the lines, the agonized cries and pleas of the wounded were heard up and down the line. Morale in the crippled Eleventh was nearly depleted. Captain Atkins of Company A admitted the night of February 15 was one of sadness and uncertainty:

> We lost everything on the field: blankets, knapsacks, clothing, bringing with us only our arms and what was on our backs. Our wounded were left on the field to suffer all night, the ground being in possession of the enemy...It was cold, the ground covered with snow. We were without blankets or tents, and almost worn out with fatigue. Crouching over our campfires and shivering, discussing the sad history of the day, a long, sad evening was passed. Utterly exhausted, we slept and shivered and suffered...[54]

Out in the night, the wounded sprawled in bloody helplessness on the battlefield. They had escaped only to confront a different, and in many ways more painful, death. Freezing temperatures, perhaps even as low as 20 degrees below zero, conspired with the wind to torture the survivors. Abandoned by both armies, they groaned in mumbled prayer or screamed out in their anguish. A few feebly crawled through the snow seeking out the shelter of a hollow stump, or blindly searching for a Union picket. One sufferer was Lieutenant James Churchill, twice wounded in the savage encounter with Forrest's men. The officer slowly regained consciousness probably in the late afternoon or early evening, but he was almost totally paralyzed and barely able to move his head to inspect the nearby surroundings. What he finally saw was a disturbing panorama in which more than fifteen dead men could be counted within a radius of ten feet:

> I attempted to get up, but could only raise my head--my hips and lower limbs were as of lead. In a moment the enemy's infantry were passing over me, and in less than five, only their stragglers could be seen...robbing and tearing the clothing from the dead and wounded. I remonstrated, and

told them that it was not in accordance with civilized warfare...The stragglers of an army are usually the worst men in it, and purposely fall to the rear to rob the dead and wounded. Its general character should not be judged by them. The air was filled with the cries of the wounded, to which it was pitiful to listen, some with boyish voices were calling "Mother", others shrieking as though in great agony, many groaning and occasionally one swearing like a Spanish trooper...[55]

Confederate surgeons hastily inspected Lieutenant Churchill's injuries and some minutes later informed him quite bluntly that he would die before morning anyway, making it fruitless to transport him to the rear. Only the walking Union wounded were rounded up for the journey back into the Donelson fortifications. The rest would have to face the night alone on the battlefield. It was a grisly prospect for Churchill. He lay cushioned against three other fallen Union soldiers--one with a bullet hole gaping in his chest. Begging assistance from passing Rebel soldiers, Churchill asked one group to lift him away from this quivering body pile. The men did, although Churchill's screams from the resulting pain caused them to drop him before the move was completed. The pain subsided, however, and soon Churchill found himself chatting, quite amicably, with a nearby Confederate horse soldier. They discussed the merits of the Rebel's .56-caliber Colt revolving rifle. Not much later the advancing Union troops from Lew Wallace's division appeared, initiating a fierce rifle duel. Churchill and the other wounded were stranded between the battle lines wondering whether foe or friend would be their murderer:

> ...the bullets "sist" all around me, but as I was not in condition to dodge, I had to take what came. Several struck the log near me, and the splinters flew in my face...It seemed as though the battle lasted an hour, when both parties stopped firing, and the enemy retired towards Dover. I could hear no noise now, except the cries and groans of the wounded...Night had come, and I was evidently between respective picket lines. All hope of being taken from the field vanished...[56]

Within a few hours, Churchill was again in intense pain from his wounds. He shifted his head position only to find that his hair was frozen fast to the ground. Gingerly the suffering officer reached back with one good hand, slowly working the hair loose, and once successful, remembered to shift position fairly frequently through the night. Despite all his suffering, he remained conscious, his mind turning upon a number of subjects including vivid recollections of Napoleon's fate in icy Russia. The thought strangely enough aided him in his fight against depression. He became convinced that since some of the Emperor's troops had miraculously survived the snowy 1812 disaster, then why could he not prove a survivor in the present one. In fact, the mounting cold served a singular purpose, clotting and freezing Churchill's untreated wounds which otherwise would have resulted in a quick death. Thus the night passed, with the well-educated officer pondering his fate in a philosophical manner amid the dead, often partially naked, bodies of his comrades. For nourishment he would suck on chunks of frozen coffee which he had found in a nearby canteen thrown aside in the chaotic flight. "...what a feast I had," Churchill would later write. Finally, the weary sun glimmered atop the woodline to the east, and with it came the roar of heavy naval fire out toward the river. Dawn also brought individual searchers such as Private Jim Maddon of Company B who crawled up to Churchill asking for the whereabouts of the fallen Captain Shaw. After he obtained the information, he slipped away promising to return soon. The haggard, crippled Churchill lay immobilized with his board-like clothes frozen like iron to the ground. It was to be another four hours before Union troops finally carried him off the field.[57]

At about 9 a.m. the wretched remnants of the Eleventh Illinois, under Ransom's direction, formed up in a small hollow. One man asked whether the Rebels had surrendered. With accustomed grit Ransom replied that he didn't know the answer although either way the Eleventh would be going into action before sundown. With these words in mind the ragged contingent of just over a hundred men began their march. As they neared the Rebel entrenchments, they noticed an incredible sight--white flags were hung everywhere over the earthen parapets or were waved by individual Rebel soldiers. Fort Donelson had fallen, and the great Rebel bastion was at once transformed into a vast Federal prison camp containing more than 12,000 troops, 20,000 rifles, 48 pieces of field artillery, and 13 heavy cannons. Rousing cheers exploded along the Union lines, and Colonel Wallace formed the brigade for a triumphant march into the Confederate fortress in direct opposition to orders from General C.F. Smith's division. "General Smith is not my commander," was the icy reply. "I am going to the Fort; I commenced this battle and it is my right."[58] Minutes later the First Brigade marched down the muddy lane with the shattered Eleventh at the column's head, shell-tattered colors prominently in view. Bands struck up a spirited salute and the Union army strode into the captured citadel. Captain Atkins of Company A emotionally recalled how the bands "were playing national airs" while the decimated Eleventh wove its way down toward the Rebels' water batteries:

> Thousands of Rebel soldiers who grounded their arms, and (we) planted our shattered and torn regimental colors, the second stand so planted on the Rebel fortifications of the main Fort. Down on the river Cumberland lay our gunboats and fleet of transports, that came steaming up, forming a grand scene, and Taylor's Battery fired a national salute...The victory is a grand one--the greatest of the war.[59]

Soon afterward, a completely exhausted Colonel Wallace penned out another letter home. His comments were still laced with pride but balanced by a sober acceptance of the terrible cost. The Eleventh had been brutally handled in its first major battle. Wallace needed only to glance at the shredded battle flag and splintered staff for an eloquent reminder of that fact. Truly, Wallace wrote, "they have lost all but honor and flag."[60]

Chapter Four

Hideous Night

Church bells peeled in jubilant, clangorous celebration on February 16, 1862, and the loyal citizens of Chicago rejoiced in what a *Chicago Tribune* reporter described as a "rampage" of joy. Schools emptied, businesses were abandoned and American flags sprouted from nearly every public building. "The people heard nothing, saw nothing, knew nothing, except that our boys had taken Fort Donelson...," the writer recorded.[1] Grown men romped in delightful pandemonium and reveled in General Grant's surrender utlimatum. It was a bracing tonic for those who still remembered the previous summer's fiasco at Bull Run.

On the battlefield itself, the Union survivors were in a far different mood. Somber men from the Old Eleventh drifted through the scene of Saturday's tragedy in melancholy search for comrades who lay dead, dying, or in pain there in that frigid, lonely wood. Frozen bodies lay in grotesque parody, surrounded by an unbelievable litter: abandoned weaponry, a solitary boot, a dead mule, soggy newspapers, letters fluttering in the breeze, caps, coats, India-rubber ponchos, a great mass of miscellaneous clutter.

One man out of every five in the Eleventh who carried a rifle at Donelson was now or would soon be dead. No Union regiment suffered as did Ransom's stubborn riflemen.[2] Seventy were buried on the field, 32 more were to die in the hospital or at home, while 181 nursed wounds and 88 were missing--most of these now Rebel captives. Three hundred and twenty-nine casualties from 500 engaged--an awesome 66 percent loss--was the final tally. True, the Union army as a whole came through with remarkably light casualties at least when compared with the far bloodier butcher bills they soon would pay further south. Their losses at Donelson, however, were concentrated mainly among those regiments included in General McClernand's First

Division--the chief victims of the powerful February 15 retreat. Colonel Logan's 31st Illinois listed 31 killed, 117 wounded, and 28 missing; the 8th Illinois suffered 54 dead and 188 wounded; the 18th Illinois lost 53 dead, 157 wounded, and 18 missing. General McClernand, in company with the *Chicago Times* correspondent, toured the ground the day following the surrender. His journalist companion recounted:

> A scene never to be forgotten--never to be described...the slaughter was immense. The whole space of two miles was strewn with dead, who lay in every imaginable shape and form. Unionists and rebels were promiscuously mingled, sometimes grappled in the fierce death-throe, sometimes facing each other as they gave and received the fatal shot or thrust, and again heaped in piles which lay six or seven deep. I could imagine nothing more terrible than the silent indications of agony that worked the features of the pale corpses which lay at every step. Though dead and rigid in every muscle, they still writhed and seemed to turn to catch the passing breeze.[3]

Another searcher was Private Henry Uptmor of Company K. The German-speaking trooper who had barely escaped from the Rebel cavalry the previous day by taking refuge in deep, thick underbrush. Now he wandered through the forest calling out the names of his close companions, George Weis and Karl Zerrusen. The three boys had grown up in the tiny German-American farming community of Teutopolis before joining with the Eleventh in the summer of 1861. Henry hoped that he would find his two friends still among the living as he picked his way through the human debris. He was shocked at the sight of the stripped bodies, or when clothed, the pulled-out pockets indicating that scavengers had already swept through in ghoulish pursuit of valuables:

> Soon I came to that part of the field where our regiment had fought. The very first corpse I came upon was that of my sleeping companion, George Gerard Weis, the stouthearted, Godfearing youth. He was lying with his face turned upward, looking toward Heaven with his arms outstretched as if he wished to say, "Dear Father in Heaven take me up to you in your Kingdom, for I am tired of this life on Earth..." The bullet had pierced his lower lip, and came out through the nape of the neck to carry on and on its speed. Soon I found another comrade, another good fellow named

Karl Zerrusen. He was well covered and I found his body still warm, a sign that he had died only a short time before I came upon him. He had been wounded in the abdomen and must have suffered much pain before he passed away...Then I walked around the battlefield to meditate upon it...[4]

At Dover that Sunday, the Union army had almost dissolved as the men set out singly or in groups to view the captured earthworks, or walked around the small village where, in a modest two-story white home very near the river, the surrender terms had been dictated early that morning. It was a gala affair. Men seemingly forgot the necessity of military order and discipline. They intermingled with thousands of supposedly hostile Secessionists, although most of these seemed more angry at the flight of Rebel Generals Floyd and Pillow than at the gawking Yankee conquerors. Wandering down the muddy road through Dover, Private Carrington of the Eleventh noted the good humor of one Rebel officer who joked about spending a holiday in the North this coming summer. Carrington described how the streets were dotted with

...piles of muskets, squirrel rifles, and a lot of fine shotguns, some silver mounted, a good many of these were sent home by the Boys. Our Government had no use for such an assorted supply of arms. A soldier would come along and pick up a rifle or musket, look at it, throw it down on the pile: Whang. It would go off sending a bullet singing off in most any direction. It seems they are all loaded, left so by the Secesh. No guard to look after them, piled up like cordwood. Managed to get a few tents and here we go...so cross and grouchy can't keep from quarreling about everything. The rattle of a leaf startles us, and rasping sound set the shivers going--sounds like the whistle of a bullet. I reckon we're nervous.[5]

Union wounded were transported into Dover every hour. They filled every home and barn and many were simply laid alongside the snowy road in the open air to await the hospital ships. The wounded were being shipped to Cairo and Mound City, and even to hospitals in Indiana and Ohio. On board one such vessel, Mary Newcomb frantically attempted to care for the hundreds of wounded tucked into every nook and cranny of the steamer, one of which was her own husband. "Many were taken down to the coal pit in the hold to keep them warm, as those on deck were terribly exposed," she wrote. "It snowed and froze every night and they were without covering. Many were badly frozen, and all suffered severely, for they were so badly wounded that they could not move much."[6] All about the steamer she scuttled, bringing a kind word, a touch, or a bit of cracker or soup to the suffering. She assisted a certain Dr. Collier who in turn could not do much more than offer the men some lemons or jelly along with heartfelt sympathy. It was as if the battle hadn't ended, for the agony went on, and the death list grew longer. Mother Newcomb was deeply touched by these lads who seemed so grateful at the gift of a bit of ham or a soothing voice. There was Private Allen of Co. G, Eleventh Illinois, terribly wounded by a rifle ball in the lung, yet calmly setting about arranging the details of his impending funeral, assuring Mother Newcomb that his father would pay all costs:

One Sunday morning he saw the sun rising, and called me...We raised him up and he rested his head on his hand; then, looked toward the end of the boat, he saw the flag, and said, as a heavenly smile lit up his face: "We fought to the very last, and the flag still waves..." He sank back and was dead. On the way to Cairo we lost one hundred and fifty men. They were laid together, side by side, and covered with blankets.[7]

She discovered that "her pet", young Wade Matthews, was aboard, wounded and suffering from exposure. "The poor boy had both hands and both feet frozen, and one foot had been shot," she noted with horror. "How I pitied the little pale-faced boy! I washed him, combed his hair and gave him to eat such as we had--for by some means the supplies sent from Chicago had been transferred to other boats, and we had but little to do with; about a barrel of crackers and a barrel of meal to be made into gruel or mush was about all we had, and nearly a thousand, starved, thirsty, dying men."[8] The boy survived, but Mary Newsomb's suffering turned intensely personal when, nine days after the battle, Sergeant Charles Newcomb passed away after a jolting ride on the Illinois Central aboard a train packed with "limbless, armless, sightless men going home." He died a day after reaching home at Effingham, urging at the last that Mary return "to take care of the boys." The funeral was attended by few for this southern Illinois town was, in Mary's words, a "rebel community."[9] Despite the threats, a service was held, and the body interred: one more casualty from the Eleventh.

Back at Donelson around noon on Monday, February 17th, the Eleventh's survivors clustered about a gaping, mass grave.

Within were sixty-eight dirty blue bundles laid side by side at the bottom of the pit. Lieutenant Doug Hapeman recounted in his diary deep anquish and the accompanying rage that so many of the dead men's possessions had been looted. A former printer's devil, he had fought well that Saturday commanding Company H, since Captain James Coates was absent due to sickness. Whatever pride he felt at his own personal accomplishments was overwhelmed when the men shoveled in the first spadefulls of hardened earth. To him it seemed everyone, Ransom and Wallace included, were in tears.[10] Perhaps he recalled how Colonel Wallace had been similarly moved when the shattered regiment had formed up on Wynn's Ferry Road immediately after the February 15th rout. "You were the pride of my heart," Wallace told them. "Now you are the pride of my life." His voice falling, he promised, that "good will bless you, and history will find a place for the gallant Eleventh Illinois Infantry."[11]

"Dreary desolation" is the phrase employed by *Ottawa Free Trader* editor William Osman in describing the west Tennessee country near captured Donelson. A close personal acquaintance of General Wallace, and Lieutenant Hapeman's former employer, Osman was a Mexican War veteran and War Democrat. He had taken the first steamer available for the war zone, determined to see for himself those "terrible water batteries" and speak with the men from the Eleventh who were now in camp near Dover, recuperating as well as circumstances allowed. Osman's hurried visit to the battle site provided ample material for a number of articles. The editor was exuberant in his praise:

> We found the General, W.H.L. Wallace, to our great joy, in excellent health, having been informed in Cairo that he was sick. In his quarters we also found Col. Ransom nearly well of his wound, and on duty, as he had been for several days...And we saw--well, everybody, and that night, and next day and the next, we keep on seeing and shaking hands and talking with the heroes of the bloodiest battle ever fought on the continent, and the more we saw and found out about them and the work they done, the more we felt like doing homage...[12]

Hardly coincidental was the appearance in the *Free Trader* of a highly critical editorial, noting that "praise should not be indiscriminate" regarding the recent victory. Osman posed some interesting questions demanding why on the bloody Saturday the Union right was unsupported from dawn until early afternoon when the massed Confederates finally smashed through. The failure to respond immediately to the Rebel threat, Osman wrote, left the great mass of McClernand's division open to a "galding fire" of nearly double their number. Why, the editor demanded, was support not forthcoming considering the fact that nearly 20,000 Union troops were within easy marching distance of the threatened sector? Such failure was "unexplained and unaccountable." The editorial speculated that "A Heavy Responsibility" lay somewhere in the army leadership.[13] There could be little doubt that the criticism was leveled at U.S. Grant, the little man from Galena now basking in the warm approval of a nation famished for a victory. There is every reason to believe that Osman's opinions reflected those of Wallace and Ransom although conclusive documentation to that effect has not survived. Whatever their feelings, the Donelson victory obscured real questions about Grant's leadership. These were, some six weeks later, brought to national light after the nearly ruinous engagement fought at Pittsburg Landing.

For the present the mood was optimistic. In Ottawa, Ann Wallace beamed with pride at the accomplishments of her husband and of the regiment whose heroic behavior was further tribute to the competence of its first commander. "I think it is more honor to be one of the Eleventh after the battle of Donelson that to be General McClellan himself," Ann wrote.[14] It was a joyous time made more so by the appearance of her older brother, Cyrus Dickey, adjutant of the Eleventh Illinois, home now for a few days' brief leave. The returning officer brought with him the regimental flag, leaving it in his sister's care as it "was in a decidedly dilapidated condition, evidently unfit for reentering the field." Scores of visitors streamed up the bluff to the Wallace mansion, there to view the relic whose staff was pitted by rifle shot, the tip of the metal spear sheared, and the faded banner pockmarked with bullet holes "promiscuously distributed all over its surface."[15] When Lieutenant Dickey announced his impending return to the regiment, the community presented a replacement banner, prompting him to write a flowery note of thanks published that very week in the local newspaper. He requested the town folk respect the old flag now resting at his sister's home. Saccharine and overly sentimental by jaded 20th-century standards, his message reflects in full the sincerity and idealism of an age long dead:

> Under this toil-worn banner the 11th Illinois has chased the rebel marauder Jeff Thompson through every cypress swamp within fifty miles of the Mississippi from Cape Gira-

deau to New Madrid, and in looking upon it our brave boys were cheered on by the reflection that they were not fighting for the miserable section of country through which they were wading knee deep...but for the suppression of rebellion and the re-establishment of that flag upon every foot of American soil.

This same old flag shared with us the fatiques of that memorable march into the heart of Tennessee and from the hills that frowned upon Fort Donelson, waved defiance to rebellion and its votaries. It waved proudly over us through the storm of lead and iron which rained upon us in that hard fought battle. Finally, though riddled by the enemy's bullets and disabled from further service, was the first American flag planted upon the walls of the inner Fort.[16]

Similar sentiments were articulated in the tiny Illinois River community of Lacon, located some 40 miles down stream from Ottawa. There, dozens of wounded survivors from the Marshall County Guards, or more correctly Company B of the Eleventh, were recounting their adventures and joining in the chorus of homage raised to the late Captain Fred Shaw. All thoughts of what had transpired only months ago when the officer had brought back his free Negro were forgotten, and Shaw was enshrined as a martyr. Stories related Shaw's gallantry at Donelson, where he was wounded twice in the early stages of the engagement, surviving his wounds only to fall shot through the head during the stampeding retreat. The entire town of Lacon was literally swathed in black crepe those early March weeks, while the local paper published endless tributes for the area's Donelson survivors.[17]

Surely the easiest to identify was Lieutenant Samuel B. Deane, a rather prim, bookish looking man whose scholarly appearance had been drastically altered by a Rebel rifle ball. Residents marvelled at the purplish, deep indentation on his forehead where a ricocheting slug had impacted. The force hurled Deane unconscious to the ground. He rose minutes later, dazed and bleeding but not seriously injured. Witnesses recounted how the musket ball had been flattened to about the size of "two shilling pieces."[18]

Sergeant James Vernay had an even more absorbing tale to reveal. He was one of those taken prisoner and only recently abandoned by the retreating Rebels at Nashville. There, about forty of the seriously wounded captives from the Eleventh were visited by General Will Wallace himself in an emotional meeting. "It would have done you good to see the poor fellows' faces brighten when they saw me," he wrote Ann. "Scarce one of them but shed tears when I shook hands with them."[19] Among those rescued was the normally dapper and self-possessed Sergeant Vernay, now somewhat undone by his horrendous experiences. The soldier was the son of David Vernay, a former Maryland resident who had fled that slave state some years before, ever "steadfast in his denunciation of its baneful effects."[20] We might then assume with some certainty that the Civil War represented for James Vernay an issue that went far beyond Union versus Secession. Whatever his motives for fighting, he was severely wounded on Saturday, February 15th just as the Eleventh turned about for the mad dash through the closing Rebel lines. A Minie ball passed through Vernay's right arm, grazing the bone, and tearing open a main artery which then spouted blood all about despite his efforts to tie off the wound with a large handkerchief. "My God, if I faint I shall never see my home," he thought, and renewed his efforts, this time utilizing a stick to jam through the improvised bandage, twisting it tighter about the arm. Weaving unsteadily through the woods, Vernay plunged into a turbid, freezing stream immersing his aching arm until finally the bleeding seemed to cease, allowing him to continue until brought to a standstill by a volley of rifle fire delivered by a set of prancing Confederate cavalry.[21] One horse soldier menaced Vernay with a pistol muttering a death threat at the "Lincoln Mudsill." The mud-smeared Vernay cooly replied: "If you are so cowardly as that, you can shoot." The encounter concluded with the approach of a Confederate infantry officer who ordered an end to the threats and sent Vernay back to Dover under armed guard. Vernay and the other prisoners were whisked out of the beleaguered fortress early that morning on a Rebel steamer bound for Nashville. The *Lacon Gazette* published his account of his sojourn there as a prisoner of the Secessionists:

> He says he was generally treated well while a prisoner; but was however, not a few times insulted, when he would give them as good as they sent. He told such that none but mean man would insult the flag of his country, or those who were battling for its defense; to which they replied that further south he would not talk in that manner; that two-thirds of the Federal army would be cut to pieces if they made their appearance in the mountains of Georgia and Alabama.[22]

These brief sojourns home were especially pleasant for the men whose wounds were neither particularly debilitating nor disfiguring. For them the days home were highlighted with the attentions of the ladies and the respect of friends and family. There was certainly a decided tendency on the part of many in the Eleventh to lengthen their visits at the expense of comrades still in service. Colonel Ransom predictably was not among those who sought leave when his nagging shoulder wound forced him to ride in an ambulance as the Eleventh marched from Donelson back to Fort Henry. From there, the unit embarked on the steamer *Memphis* bound south to Savannah, Tennessee, where Grant's army prepared for a drive into Mississippi. Ransom's Eleventh counted barely two hundred muskets at that point. Nearly eight hundred had mustered for the three-year service in August, 1861.

Another major clash was expected, probably at the strategic railroad junction at Corinth, Mississippi; the regiment desperately needed the Donelson wounded back in ranks. Colonel Ransom eventually became so vexed with the reluctant returnees that he drafted an emphatic telegram addressed to each convalescent. In essence, he defined for those individuals the fact that a hospital discharge could in no way be construed as a discharge from service. Prolonged, unauthorized leave would be equated with desertion unless the men returned immediately. Simultaneously, Ransom assured that rail transportation was made available for the men who, for the most part, could not afford transport south. The Eleventh's commander was convinced "an important crisis" was imminent.[23]

Pride in the regiment and faith in its capabilities motivated Colonel Ransom to risk his reputation and career to challenge a direct military order. The incident occurred in the aftermath of Donelson and concerned a headquarters directive Ransom deemed an insult to the men he commanded. Lieutenant Henry H. Dean of Company D related how orders had come down that the regiment was to be transported north for the purpose of guarding Confederate prisoners at Chicago's Camp Douglas. "Ransom and Nevius [both] tendered their resignations and said if we were to be put on such duty as that after the service we had done, they would not have anything more to do with this war. They came down on it, so the order was countermanded, and we were ordered to move with the fleet numbering, according to one participant, more than 75 transports, now anchored off Savannah, Tennessee."[24] Here the Eleventh went ashore and went into bivouac awaiting further movements. Private Carrington described the surrounding areas as a "pleasant and beautiful country" boasting a large loyalist population who had been subjected to the depredations of roving Rebel bands "plundering and hanging every Union man in the country."[25] The atrocities motivated many, who otherwise might have remained aloof during the Federal advance, to join the colors. Major Nevius made note of the phenomenon in a letter to his brother:

> A great many true Union people...heartily welcomed us. They have been greatly persecuted by the rebels, so much so that a great many had fled to the swamps and woods for protection, but have since our arrival returned to their homes. Quite a large number have enlisted in our army, some out of desire to serve their Country and some to save themselves from being forced into the rebel ranks. The rebels are doing all they can to raise their army to numbers equal to our own. They are forcing everybody (who will not volunteer) into their ranks, that they can get hands on. There has always been in this part of the State and Northern Alabama, a good many Union people and true ones they have been too, to hold out against all the persecution that they have been subjected to...[26]

On March 24th, 1862, the Eleventh reached Pittsburg Landing and pitched camp four miles west of the river. Here, by the great Tennessee River, Grant concentrated nearly 40,000 men. Only 18 miles away lay the next Federal target: the Corinth rail junction. Pittsburgh Landing proved a warm, pleasant, wooded encampment for the tired Eleventh although the springtime lethargy was disrupted time and again by drill as well as a divisional review held on April 3rd. The entire army squatted by the river awaiting the approach of Major General Don Carlos Buell who was marching with 35,000 Federals from Nashville. Once united, the plan was to move directly on Corinth where Rebel General Albert Sidney Johnston awaited with what rumor said was an army 80,000 strong. Latrine gossip was, at least in this case, woefully inaccurate. Johnston's force did not exceed 40,000. Moreover, at that very moment, his troops were streaming toward Corinth from all points of the compass.

Grant's Donelson victory had placed the Union army in an extremely advantageous position whereby a bold, quick thrust southwest toward Corinth promised piecemeal destruction for the separated Confederate force. What did transpire was that the Rebel commander, General Albert Sidney Johnston, who was billed by the Southern press as a rising military star, proceeded to justify that faith with action. Johnston marched while Grant paused and Buell dawdled. Determined to annihilate Grant's army at Pittsburgh's Landing before Buell arrived, the Rebel army marched northeast on April 3, 1862. Two days later, the noisy Rebel array was crouched in readiness only a few miles from the Union army. The troops camped on the evening of April 5th, undiscovered, within cannon shot of the Federals whose commander slept at his headquarters in Savannah seven miles down river. "I have ordered a battle for daylight tomorrow, and I intend to hammer them," Johnston told an aide. A few miles away, on board a Federal hospital steamer, Mary Newcomb walked the deck and enjoyed the cool, spring breeze. The boat was anchored off the Landing where thousands of Union troops bedded down for the night. Years later the matronly, saddened woman would recall the scene:

> Saturday is always a welcome day to the soldier when in camp. No tiresome drill...nor everlasting roll-call--on the morrow he can write to the loved ones at home. They felt secure as they lay down on this Saturday night...Everything about them was calm and lovely. The scenery was beautiful, the orchards were already in full bloom, the grass was green, birds were singing in the dense woods, the odor of wild flowers was in the air...[27]

In the early morning hours soon after, the steamer *Minnehana* anchored along the Landing. Among its passengers were Captain James Coates of Company H, Eleventh Illinois in company with General Wallace's wife, Ann. Her husband had only recently been promoted to the command of General C.F. Smith's Second Division since the latter lay mortally injured at the Cherry Mansion in Savannah. Wallace's old Second Brigade was now led by Colonel C.C. Marsh, a sterling officer who fought with the 20th Illinois alongside the Eleventh at Donelson. Mrs. Wallace hoped for a brief visit with her beloved Will as an antidote to vague, unsettling fears she could scarcely explain. To that end, she had worked her will on the military authorities at Cairo who allowed the lady transit to the army at Pittsburgh Landing. With the advent of daylight on Sunday, she intended to go ashore, with Captain Coates as an escort, and surprise Will.[28]

The distant bark of rifles could be heard, but it was dismissed as merely incoming Union pickets discharging their weapons rather than laboriously extracting the charges. It was a slovenly habit engaged in frequently by citizen soldiers on both sides, and so Mrs. Wallace donned hat and gloves for the expected stroll ashore. At the last minute, Captain Coates insisted she stay aboard allowing him to locate the general, whose camp might be some distance away. The slender, dapper officer soon strode away through the waking camps while the picket fire continued ominously out on the edges of the army. It was Sunday, April 6th, 1862.

Wallace's old Eleventh stirred in the half-light. Ths men anticipated an inspection before the day was out and had begun initial preparations while others set about the business of breakfast in the field. Twenty-six-year-old Private Frank Whipple of Company H observed it was going to be a beautiful day and fastened a string between two bushes to air his blankets. So far the war, the real war, had not touched young Whipple, who considered himself a lucky soldier. A case of food poisoning prevented his participation at Donelson where so many had died. Darkly handsome with a neatly trimmed and distinguished mustache and luminous dark eyes, he cut a striking figure that contradicted his farmboy origins in Waltham, Illinois.[29] His luck was in force in the early days at Bird's Point, where as a raw recruit he quickly established a reputation for sharpshooting after a miracle hit on a darting squirrel. Frank Whipple enjoyed the attention and kept the secret a private one.

On his return to the regiment from the hospital, Whipple's good fortune continued even when his steamboat struck a hidden snag at night. The blow was fatal to the steamboat and incited "near panic" among the startled passengers who scrambled off the sinking boat onto a nearby sand bar. Seconds later the craft slid beneath the black water. The whole incident could be dismissed in a letter home as an exciting shipwreck adventure. Perhaps he was indeed a lucky one. But whatever the case, Whipple's placid early morning routine was shattered that Sunday when a Confederate artillery shell shrieked over the regiment's tents to burst with a great roar somewhere in the rear. Rifle fire crackled in the air nearby; the sound seemed centered on the encampment of Sherman's division that encircled a small, wooden chapel known as Shiloh Church.

Those first shots ignited a flurry of movement: men pawed about for rifles and ammunition pouches or hastily buttoned shirts and slipped on boots. Most were incredulous that so many of the enemy could be so near. In Company B's bivouac, Private Carrington had finished breakfast and was hanging his haversack on the cross arms of his tent when the battle opened.

> The the drummers again beat the long roll, that awful, dismal sound, beginning out towards the front and taken up by different Regiments from one camp to another way down the line clear back to the river landing...the quick forming of

regiments of infantry, horses hitched to guns. These great horses galloping with the cannon to the front. Mules and wagons hurrying to the rear. Those blood curdling sounds of the alarm drums increased the excitement--volleys of musketry, the roar of rebel artillery, our own guns, chiming in. Then and there was hurrying "to and fro." Shell and solid shot plowed up the ground, tore through our tents, splintered trees falling far to the rear as several cannon shots passed over our camp, one cutting the hind hoof off a horse. The Regiment fell in and marched toward the firing...[30]

Two hundred men answered the drum call in the Eleventh's bivouac. Thirty-five others had been detached for various details depriving the unit of needed firepower. Ransom's predicted crisis was here, but the Eleventh still lacked the manpower due to the Donelson losses. The only reinforcement was the unarmed Captain Coates who arrived on the scene with his young son, his appearance lustily cheered by Lieutenant Hapeman of Company H., who stepped aside and let his senior take command.[31] The regiment and the remainder of the Second Brigade had marched a half-mile toward the firing. They halted at the Corinth Road and stood facing the Purdy Road. Shattered elements of Sherman's three brigades attempted to reorganize nearby after having been driven from their encampments near Shiloh Church by a powerful, determined assault. In fact, the Rebels were rolling back the Union troops all along the line. Colonel Marsh had the Second Brigade in line with Colonel Abraham M. Hare's First Brigade. McAllister's battery took up a position between the two infantry brigades. On the near right flank, Burrow's battery rode up to the rear of the regiment but the Confederate columns suddenly loomed into view before they could unlimber the guns. Private Carrington described in head-shaking amazement the chilling, awesome sight of Rebel infantry only three hundred yards away. "It was a glorious but a terrible sight," was the concurring opinion of Captain Lloyd Waddell of E Company. "The order was, 'The whites of their eyes, boys, and then give it to them,' and the Eleventh was again engaged. Never, never in my life have I seen...such a death struggle."[32]

Clouds of rifle bullets, mixed with the brutal black blurr of solid shot, erupted from the opposing lines. Marsh's brigade came under a devastating fire from Bankhead's Tennessee Artillery battery as well as infantry fire from S.A.M. Wood's brigade. The Rebels closed to within thirty or forty paces of the brigade's left flank where the 45th and 48th Illinois unbelievably held their fire.

"Some of their [the Rebels'] Regiments wore blue uniforms and carried a blue flag with a single star in the center," Private Carrington explained. "Some of the boys held their fire thinking they were our own men."[33]

That hesitation was fatal. The Rebels opened up a fire that carved the brigade's left flank into bloody chunks. Hundreds were killed or wounded in the first few minutes. Many stunned survivors stumbled to the rear. The 16th Alabama and the 27th Tennessee were at the same time heading for the guns in Burrow's battery directly behind the brigade. Ten minutes had passed since the first fusillade, and the Federal line was already buckling. In those brief minutes the Eleventh had endured a terrific fire. Ransom later described how his already weakened regiment was torn apart by the Rebel volleys which "told with fearful effect upon my line."[34] Conspicuous as always atop his charger "Old Bob," Ransom was one of the first hit. A Minie ball opened an ugly head wound that bled profusely. Major Nevius was hit in the hand and young Lieutenant Silas Field of Company A crumpled to the ground; his leg was almost severed by a solid cannon shot.

In Company H, Captain Coates's unarmed bravado terminated almost immediately. Minutes after joining the battle line, the officer was wounded in the chest and hand. He was forced to turn over the command once again to young Lieutenant Doug Hapeman and make his way toward the Landing and medical treatment. Another well-respected line officer, Captain Henry H. Carter of Company K, was less fortunate. This courageous officer was Ransom's personal choice for major and enjoyed in equal measure Wallace's support. Both remembered his superb fight against Rebel cavalry at Donelson when Company K led the retreat. Carter had received an inconsequential head wound during that daring exploit. At Shiloh, the consequences were eternal. Carter fell dead, shot through the brain, just as the battle commenced.

"Everyone was loading and firing as fast as possible," Private Carrington wrote of those moments, "bullets hissing over our heads and cutting the limbs, twigs and that peculiar chug when a bullet strikes a man."[36] Marsh's left flank was bent backward by the ferocious assault. First the 48th Illinois and then other regiments, in turn, broke before the oncoming Confederates. Faced with a fearful pressure on its front, and now with the possibility of another flank attack like the one at Donelson, the Eleventh wavered, and then fled despite Ransom's screams and shouted orders. The entire brigade front collapsed. McAllister's batteries and Burrow's guns stood exposed to infantry attack. Nearby Colonel

Abraham M. Hare's First Brigade fell back before a fantastic Confederate bayonet charge pressed across the naked plain of what had been a Union parade ground. Complete disaster was prevented, or at least postponed, when Colonel C. Veatch's Second Brigade of Hurlbut's division counterattacked.[36]

In the melee, Company B of the Eleventh remained relatively intact and rallied behind a pile of oat sacks. Here the men snuggled behind the makeshift barricade and leveled an effective fire on the Rebels, killing several artillery horses when they attempted to haul the cannon into closer action. Private Carrington stood his ground here but observed how the Rebels drifted toward the left flank once again where they poured a hot fire on the exposed Yankees. "This movement on their part kept our men falling back taking new positions farther back and nearer the river landing," he wrote.[37] Outflanked again, Company B's riflemen abandoned the gunny-sack fort to join the mass exodus toward the river.

> Our Company was just gone as an organized unit. By this time it was fearful. Wounded men with comrades to help them were limping to the rear...toward the River. Artillery horses cut loose from the guns; cavalry horses with saddle under instead of over...Men with arms, and men without arms; wagons hitched with six mules, the drivers cussing and whipping; all rushing for the rear...Still the muskets volleyed and the cannon thundered, while the smoke, rolling up among the trees, hid the lines at times, then to drift away...As we drifted to the rear I overtook Captain Coates...A bullet struck the breast of his coat tearing out the cotton while another hit his wrist. There was a boy with him, his son. I passed a man lying in a field, a piece of shell had torn a large chunk out between hip and knee. No one payed any attention to the poor fellow...No one ran, just walked on, sullen, panic stricken, the terrors hidden under that cloud of smoke...As we neared the river we saw officers trying to get men into ranks, but they payed no attention to them, but drifted on...Off to the south I saw a whole Regiment come rushing down the hill with the Colonel at the head. Thinking the whole line was broken we turned north and kept on down the river...[38]

Ransom's Eleventh reformed, or at least remnants of the same did so, in Jones's Field some 500 yards to the rear of their original battle line. They resumed their composure during a brief interlude bought with blood by Veatch's brigade, which was now inflicting great suffering on the Rebels and suffering greatly in turn. Ransom was calm and seemed confident, mounted on Old Bob. He soon commandeered seventy men from the shattered 70th Ohio and placed them on the Eleventh's left flank. Together they moved under his command some minutes later when Marsh ordered a counterattack against the Confederates now in possession of the Second Brigade camps. Ransom was gratified that the Eleventh seemed revitalized. "We drove them [the Rebels] slowly back under a heavy fire, and while a rebel battery was laying upon us we still moved gallantly forward."[39] Every foot was contested by a spirited enemy, but Marsh's brigade, by now a hodge-podge of various units, doggedly pushed on at least a half-mile until they neared McClernand's captured headquarters where hundreds of dead were strewn about. It was here that Cobb's Rebel Artillery Battery stood fast and the Union attack hesitated. Ransom was particularly apprehensive about one group of Ohio soldiers that he had recently rallied but now seemed undecided once again. "They were awfully disposed to run, but I made them move up to the work," he reported.[40] Finally, around noon, the Eleventh and the 20th Illinois closed to within two hundred yards of Cobb's guns. From that range they lashed the gunners with small arms fire. Minie balls gouged into the wooden cassions, slew dozens of the cannon crew and killed all the horses.

Within a short time the guns lay deserted, ready for the taking, but the counterattack lost impetus and Rebel infantry stiffened their resistance. Elements from four Confederate brigades were soon arrayed against the Eleventh and the rest of Marsh's brigade. These infantry were then supported by Hodgson's Washington Artillery Battery who sprayed a deadly stream of canister shot into the advancing Blue riflemen. The Federal right was the first to go, including Ransom's hostage Ohio infantry who, he said, "ran like the devil."[41]

General McClernand was incredulous at Ransom's performance in the action. Later he retold that the Eleventh's commander had "although reeling in the saddle, and streaming with blood from a previous wound, performed prodigies of valor."[42] The enraged Ransom fell on the retreating Ohio troops with a vengeance cutting "one of their heads open with my sabre."[43] Another account described his actions as swift and terrible telling how the embattled Ransom confronted one fleeing Union infantryman who, in total panic, plunged his bayonet into the colonel's horse in a mad effort to escape. "Rising in his saddle, Ransom sabred the recreant on the spot."[44] One Union officer who served with the young Vermont-born soldier would later recall that he never saw a man who was so transformed into "something supernatural--so completely changed from his usual self" as when Ransom appeared on the battlefield:

> Ordinarily, he is of a quiet, modest, disposition; but when in battle he becomes tigerlike, fearing nothing and becoming terrible in action, yet maintaining a cool self-possession and presence of mind, and displaying a degree of discretion and military ingenuity that are wonderful...[45]

Even human tigers couldn't prevail against that awful, unrelenting Confederate attack. In the early afternoon, probably around 2 p.m., Ransom's horse had been shot out from beneath him. His head wound still seeped blood, and the weakened commander left the field "totally unfit to command or even walk."[46] Major Nevius assumed command of the Eleventh briefly, but he too suffered from a serious wound. A rifle ball had pierced his hand early in the day and now, he too left the battle. Captain Lloyd Waddell of Company E was the senior line officer left in commission. He now led the regiment which numbered about eighty men. These survivors were tired beyond feeling; the battle had been in progress at least ten hours without letting up. Captain Waddell later wrote home:

> It was an awful sight to look at that little band, besmeared with blood and dirt, with their trusty guns in their hands, looking along the line to see how many of their beloved companions were left to them...It was a sight I never wish to see again. But there was little time to lose, and no time to complain. General McClernand came up, and asked if that was all that was left of the 11th. "Yes," was the reply. "Well, my men," he said, "we must win this day or all will be lost. Will you try it again?" We will! was the response. The boys called on me to lead them. I formed the regiment (or company as it was) on the left of the 70th Ohio regiment, and was again ordered to take our position in front. Ten minutes' time and we were again engaged...[47]

Lieutenant Henry Dean of Company D was with the regiment the "last time we went in."[48] The well-liked, jovial officer was aghast at the slaughter, and at the same time in near awe at the incredible heroism displayed by the rank and file. He would swear that there "was not a coward" among the Eleventh's ranks that

Sunday. Always afterward, Dean could vividly picture the sight of Private Ira Beddo whose right hand was "terribly" mangled but who refused to go to the rear, instead hoisting the regimental colors, allowing the unwounded bearer a chance at firing upon the ever-present Rebels. "He took our colors and told the man to fight, as he had two hands to work with while he (Ira) had only one," Dean recalled.[49] Later Beddo would transfer the flag to another, and grab a musket which he laboriously loaded between his knees and fired across his shattered arm, ignoring the pain. "He is one of the bravest in the Regiment."[50] Grant's army was surely in need of courage that Sunday as it engaged in a head-on punching match with an ever pressing opponent. McAllister's battery alone would fire 2,000 rounds this day, and as Dean noted, inflicted "some awful execution."[51]

About 4:30, the weary Confederate columns massed for one final dash against McClernand's ragged battle line, formed up in the sixth position of the day. "Advancing in heavy column, led by the Louisiana Zouaves, to break our center, the gray Regiments came," McClernand would report. "We awaited his approach within sure range, and opened a terrific fire upon him. The head of the column was instantly mowed down; the remainder of it swayed to and fro for a few minutes, and turned and fled..."[52] Pond's brigade and Wharton's cavalry had been opposite the meager remainder of the Eleventh in that final attack; they too reeled before the rippling Union fire, falling back before the iron storm. It had been a day of utter horror for the Eleventh. Its tattered remnants joined the remainder of McClernand's division along the final battle line strung along the Hamburg-Savannah Road.

In the late afternoon, the Eleventh's old commander, General W.H.L. Wallace, was immersed in the precarious business of withdrawing his bleeding Second Division while under continuous pressure from an aggressive, persistent enemy. All day long the Union center, commanded by General Ben Prentiss, had frustrated repeated assaults. The men fought along a shady, rural lane that ran atop a barely perceptible rise in the ground and fronted with a briar and underbrush tangle barricade. The position, dubbed the Hornet's Nest, was held with granite tenacity by the Blue-coated riflemen until approximately 4:40 p.m. when they were exposed to mass artillery fire. Confederate cannon, lined wheel-to-wheel, fired at practically point-blank range. Prentiss was isolated in the Hornet's Nest. Confederate columns had, at this point, practically encircled the Union strongpoint. Prentiss and nearly 2,000 Federals were to surrender before another hour expired. On the other hand, General W.H.L. Wallace sought to initiate a fighting withdrawal and salvage the remnants of his Second Division which held the right flank at the Hornet's Nest. He was determined to extricate his command and join the Union main line of resistance down near the River Landing.[53]

Lieutenant Cyrus Dickey, brother-in-law of General Wallace, was at his side when the Gray onslaught swept around the beleagured Union position. The handsome officer had fought the entire morning with the Eleventh and then traversed the battlefield to join General Wallace. He found the Second Division slowly being smothered by relentless attackers. The collapse of Hurlbut's division, located on the far left, marked the beginning of a Union disaster. General Wallace and Lieutenant Dickey soon embarked on a personal reconnaisance to affect a withdrawal. Rebel infantry were rapidly filling the woodland between Pittsburg Landing and the hard-pressed Second Division. In this confusion General Wallace rode out into a savage place which was later christened "Hell's Hollow" by Union survivors. A soldier from the 28th Illinois saw the Eleventh's old commander ride out into the very center of the fire storm. Wallace was only a few hundred feet from him. "There I witnessed some of the most obstinate, deliberate, stand out in the open, old style fighting that I ever hear of," Sergeant Branson of the 28th recalled, "the opposing lines being about 150 yards apart..."[54]

The general conducted the reconnaisance mounted atop Prince. He was a perfect target for the Rebel infantry who closed to within seventy paces. Rising in his saddle to obtain a better view, Wallace shuddered, then tumbled to the ground. A Rebel musket ball had carved its way through the general's skull from just behind the ear to exit through the bridge of the nose.[55] Young Lieutenant Dickey was horrified.

> I, with three of his orderlies, picked him up and carried him a quarter of a mile or more, when the firing became so hot on all sides that the men who were helping me let go. And, I was compelled to leave him on the field--as we all supposed him dead--and in five minutes more the lines were between us and him...[56]

Down at the landing, General Wallace's brother, Major Martin R.M. Wallace of the 4th Illinois Cavalry, was shaken when Prince cantered in with an empty saddle. The major soon after encountered one of his brother's orderlies who swore that Will had been killed instantly by Rebel rifle fire. This shocking news was transmitted with deep regret to the supposed widow who was still off shore aboard the *Minnehaha*. Her own intense personal grief was accompanied by fear that the entire Union army might soon be driven herdlike down to the Landing for mass slaughter. Ann was appalled at the scene on the bank where thousands of panicked and beaten men cringed along the landing.

> The...raw troops seemed perfectly insane. The steamer had to keep a slight distance from shore or it would have been swamped by the rush of soldiers. At one time an officer got aboard and ordered the pilot to touch shore and take his men aboard. He threatened the pilot with his pistol. I sat nearby, the only person on deck except the pilot and this officer. The pilot pretended to obey him, but really did not, thus giving the frenzied man time enough to come to his senses...[57]

Pain and confusion were integral parts of this nightmarish scene which took place in a pit of noise: exploding shells, the great din of the battlefield proper, the shouts and screams of men near hysteria, and the hellish sound made by dying horses and mules. Only with the coming of night did the noise abate somewhat, but never completely end. It was then that the wounded men could be heard in a pitiful chorus. Union gunboats on the Tennessee kept up a barrage while, now and again, dazed, weary infantry on both sides blazed at shadows in the darkness. On the opposite shore, General Don Carlos Buell's Army of the Cumberland tramped to the waiting steamers and were soon taking up positions beside Grant's sorely tried troops. Thunder and a heavy, cold, spring rain also came with the darkness as a fitting climax to that crimson Sunday. Private Henry Uptmor, the German-American veteran of Donelson, was huddled on the river bank that night with the few surviving men from the Eleventh. Stricken with "bileous fever", Uptmor had dragged and stumbled his way toward the rear just as the battle opened that morning. He felt too weak to carry a musket and left the regiment when "the advancing infantry were so close to our camp that...they could have shot right through our tents." Uptmor had witnessed an unforgettable kaleidoscope of disaster:

> The wounded were being brought in in great numbers. They were brought in, by all methods, some were carried here, others in ambulance wagons...By four o'clock the enemy had driven our forces back so far that they were only

a half mile from our Landing. Our boats had to draw away from the shore in order not to be sunk by the enemy cannonading. Ths cannon balls tore through the woods in all directions. Musket firing went on continuously all day. We could think of nothing except being captured or killed. The outlook was very dreary and sad...As soon as it became dark, our boats began to transport the troops over the river. It rained during the whole night, and it was unendurable for the sick and wounded people to sleep under the open sky, but there was just nothing that could be done about it.[58]

Not far away, Private Carrington crept into an abandoned tent with five other uniformed refugees. They had found the regiment settled in near General Grant's headquarters with the ragged colors leaning up against a log and "dead and wounded everywhere." They heard that General Wallace was dead while other rumors told of the wounded Ransom being carried off to a hospital boat ranting and, "calling for his sword and 'Old Bob.'" It was a bleak encampment made more so by the knowledge that at this very moment the Rebels occupied the regiment's morning bivouac, pilfering whatever belongings they might find there. At night the rain began to fall. Carrington described the scene:

Soon after dark the two Gun Boats opened fire, sending nine-inch shells up the ravine cutting off great limbs from the trees, and utterly demoralizing the enemy. Every fifteen minutes these guns roared all night: the pouring rain, the flash-like lightning of the cannon, the scream of the shell in its flight through the wood, the bursting report far over the rebel lines and bivouac...night hideous in all our surroundings. We get some sleep.[59]

Morning revealed Grant's army reinforced by 20,000 fresh troops of Buell's command as well as General Lew Wallace's division, which had reached the battleground late the first day after a confused march. The great gamble had failed, and the gambler, the vaunted Confederate General Albert Sidney Johnston, was dead--one of the many victims of the fire which had poured from the "Hornet's Nest" the day before. Now the revitalized Union army pushed west, where they encountered a stubborn, but soon retreating, enemy. The exhausted Confederates were shoved back through Grant's Sunday bivouac and toward the Corinth Road until around noon when Rebel General P.G.T. Beauregard ordered a full-scale withdrawal. The tattered Eleventh Illinois did not participate in the Monday battle, serving instead in the reserves where they listened to the ongoing struggle until the command came to move up into the abandoned Rebel positions. At 5 p.m., the surviving members of the Eleventh wandered through the wreckage of their Sunday encampment. "Our camp was nearly all destroyed, losing most of our blankets and many of the trees were cut off with shells," Lieutenant Doug Hapeman of Company H jotted in his diary. "Dead bodies were strewn all over our camp. We retook nearly all the artillery taken from us yesterday and took some of the enemy's."[60] An anonymous Illinois soldier gave a more graphic description of the battle's aftermath which soon appeared in a Rockford newspaper:

> I went to a gory pile of dead human forms in every kind of stiff contortion. I saw one arm raised, beckoning me. I found there a rebel, covered with clotted blood, pillowing his head on the dead body of a comrade. Both were red from head to foot. The dead man's brains had gushed out in a reddish and grayish mass over his face. The live one had lain across him all that horrible long night in the storm. The first thing he asked me was, "Give me some water. Send me a surgeon won't you? Oh, God, what made you come down here to us? We would never have come up there."[61]

Surrounded by rotting men, horses and mules, the men of the Eleventh walked about in dejected bewilderment. A few recovered their equilibrium and soon were busy mining the dead for valuables. Lieutenant Henry Dean recalled in disgust how one vulture joked that he had joined a new unit called a "rifle company" since they rifled the dead. The man in question, Private Dewitt, then proudly produced two cap-and-ball pistols procured earlier that day. Most in the Eleventh, however, were soon engaged in salvaging their own personal gear. In one tent, they found a nest of Confederate wounded and these were soon transported to the hospital. With night approaching, the more usable shelters were resurrected from the rubble; Private Carrington counted thirty-one shell and bullet holes in his squad's Fremont tent and estimated that there were at least ninety dead horses along the Second Brigade front. There was little room for jubilation on this hard-won field. Lieutenant Dean admitted frankly, in a letter scrawled the next day, how Buell's arrival prevented a massive Union defeat. His own morale, however, was resilient, and the soldier was ready for another campaign against an enemy that he had come to respect:

I am anxious to see whether the enemy will make another stand or not. I saw the Palmetto flag of Carolina, the Pelican flag of Louisiana and the old regular Secesh flag, and they all came down in a hurry. The enemy fought bravely and well, and any man that says they are cowards, or anything of the kind, has never stood up before them to see what they are made of. Our loss, as is the Secesh's, is terrible. The field for miles is literally strewn with the dead--friend and foe lying side by side, and no end to horses. If you could have seen this battle and compared it with Donelson you would think <u>that</u> only a skirmish...Our tent is completely riddled with bullet holes, of all sizes, from a buckshot to a six pounder...[63]

In the awful aftermath, Union soldiers found General Wallace. He was encrusted with blood, and soaked to the bone by the night's rain, but amazingly alive. His broken body was immediately carried to the landing, and there put aboard a steamer. Ann Wallace rushed to his side where she was to remain until his death on April 10th. Wallace faded away at the Cherry Mansion in Savannah feebly clutching his wife's hand in the final moments. His last whispered words were: "We meet in Heaven." Four days later the body arrived in Ottawa draped in black. To the tolling of bells and drum taps they bore the general up the bluff.[64]

Wallace's final march was made up the hill to his beloved "Oaks". Behind the coffin a groom led Prince with boots reversed in the stirrups. The general was buried behind his home in a pleasant wooded area beside children who never survived infancy. Earlier at the Ottawa Baptist Church, the Reverend A. Colman articulated the passionate outrage that followed the Shiloh debacle. The minister swore vengeance in the house of God and denounced the Southern Confederacy which, he advocated, should be "destroyed root and branch." Reverend Colman closed by announcing his intention, "to wage war against that great wrong, that has shed the blood of our friend, and now seeks the destruction of our country."[65] In distant Washington, a more compassionate man, President Abraham Lincoln, was distraught at the sad news from Shiloh Church. He was with relatives and friends of General Lew Wallace of Indiana when confirmation came that the slain General was in fact the Illinois Wallace. This was greeted with unrestrained elation but only earned a sharp reprimand from the president who snapped: "He was somebody's Wallace, wasn't he?"[66]

Chapter Five

A Thousand Ties of Affection

Amputated human limbs festered in a mound nearly five feet deep outside the Union surgical tent. Aswarm with flies, the macabre battle memorial presented vivid testimony to the character and cost of the combat which had erupted on April 6, 1862. Following Sunday's slaughter the reinforced Union army drove the stubborn Rebel forces from the field, but the men in blue gave only perfunctory pursuit. At various times in the future, for various reasons, both sides would claim a victory of sorts, despite the incontestable fact that armies cannot be truly said to win battles of the savage intensity of Shiloh; at best, they can only survive them. Grant's army suffered more than 13,047 casualties in the two-day struggle: 1,754 killed, 8,408 wounded and 2,885 missing. The Confederates lost slightly less. These were great wounds, but the contending armies survived to inflict and endure more pain. For all its horror, the Fort Donelson fight had proven to be a mere rehearsal for the blood-letting at Pittsburg Landing. Few on either side realized that both constituted only a beginning.[1]

In the Shiloh aftermath, even the impetuous Ransom was somewhat subdued. Writing to his close friend, Brigadier General Grenville Dodge, he declared himself ready to participate in another engagement with the Rebels, but then candidly admitted that the Eleventh and its commander were not, "as the boys would say, hankering after a fight." This was understandable. The Eleventh suffered a near 50 per cent casualty rate, and only seven weeks after the Donelson agony. Lieutenant Douglas Hapeman of Company H reported home how the regiment was "all cut to pieces." Fourteen men were buried in a pit at Shiloh. Ten more would die in the hospital or at home, like Silas Field of Company A. After being struck in the leg by a cannon shot, he lingered for weeks, and never recovered from the subsequent amputation. Lieutenant Field died at Freeport, Illinois surrounded by helpless, grieving relatives. In total, the Eleventh's adjutant estimated 96 dead and wounded out of 200 engaged at Shiloh.[2]

Ransom, for one, was convinced that the slaughter was linked to incompetence in the Union high command. After his discharge from a hospital steamer, he was frank in his appraisal in a confidential letter to General Dodge dated April 13. He was not alone in his criticism, and Grant was soon relegated to a command limbo while Major General Henry W. Halleck assumed leadership of the Army of Ohio, Tennessee, and Mississippi. The press slashed away at the much maligned Grant who found himself, probably unfairly, charged with gross negligence, drunkenness, and similar crimes. Critics pointed out that Grant was headquartered at Savannah seven miles down river from the action, and was not even present when the Confederates struck. The issue of surprise was debated endlessly although few believed the canard, alleged by the more sensational journalists, that entire regiments were bayoneted while asleep in their tents. Ransom, though couching his own criticism in vague terms, was adamant:

> We had a devilish rough time here, "Ocean". Buel and night only saved us on Sunday, but we gave them more than they bargained for on the day following. I am not able to give you an account of the fight; will only say bad generalship came near costing this Government the total rout of Grant's column. That is confidential; but I feel, Dodge, as though my life and that of my brave men had been risked often enough with incompetent leaders. If you had been placed as I have, Dodge, and seen the tide of battle turn against you simply from want of foresight and judgment of Generals, your blood would boil as mine does. But I am treading on forbidden ground. Buel is not in advance, and Halleck here. I feel that now we are all right...You have learned doubtless of the death of our brave General W.H.L. Wallace. He was my nearest friend...[3]

Legitimate questions surfaced both in the field and at Washington concerning Union unpreparedness on April 6. Many were puzzled by certain inconsistencies that were observable to all who had even a rudimentary military knowledge. That prolific chronicler of the Eleventh Illinois, Private Carrington, never resolved the dilemma. Years later, the incisive and intelligent veteran confessed his deep admiration for Grant, but was unable to explain away the latter's failures at Pittsburgh Landing. The slaughter at that place left a great scar upon the minds of most survivors. Carrington believed the memories of the awful carnage would remain carved into his mind never to be erased "until death." The questions he posed in a letter to the *Toledo Blade* were penetrating and comprised an acerbic, eloquent postscript to the Shiloh story:

> Why was it that educated commanders, who had seen service should not know that an Army of 50,000 were concentrating only 18 miles away, barely four hours' march, and no preparation? Why were we clearing off parade grounds and drilling instead of throwing up a line of works? There were thousands of willing hands: there was brush and timber in abundance. Spades and axes could have been obtained, cannon planted, rifle pits dug, so we could have held the enemy until noon...We all heard the roar of artillery and musketry on Friday evening, and were in line until late; but on Saturday night we undressed and went to bed, thinking of no danger...[4]

While Grant's reputation was under heavy attack, Ransom's prestige as a regimental commander of exceptional ability spread through the ranks and among influential officers in the Army of the Tennessee. Second Brigade Commander Colonel C.C. Marsh, made special reference to Ransom's gallantry and refusal to leave the field despite his wound. General McClernand shared the same opinion, as did General Grant himself. Both McClernand and Grant recommended the youthful officer for promotion to brigadier general. Bright, conscientious and intense, Ransom was naturally flattered by these, and other equally complimentary, testimonials. He was eagerly ambitious, but still professed to despise the political machinations that so often accompanied promotion. Still, Ransom was human enough to write General Dodge on April 17 and seek his intervention in the U.S. Senate where the Iowa soldier possessed several intimate acquaintances:

> I am well aware that more depends upon the pressure brought to bear in the Senate than anything else, and having but little might in that locality myself, should depend entirely on my friends there, among whom I shall count on you...I make these suggestions frankly, knowing I am talking to a friend confidentially and one whom I trust is ready to do me any favor in his power--at least such is my conviction. If I am asking too much of you, Dodge, why pay no attention to it, and write me candidly what you think.[5]

In that same communication, Ransom vented his hostility regarding the many men who had allegedly won rapid promotion simply due to influence. His disgust was chiefly directed against Brigadier General John A. Logan whose 31st Illinois fought beside the Eleventh at Donelson:

> I have come to the conclusion, when such men as John A. Logan (<u>Illinois Democratic leader, Congressman, and commander of the 31st Illinois</u>), who cannot put a squad through the manual of arms, and who left me on the field of Donelson alone when my regiment gallantly covered his change of front to the rear, with the expectation of being supported by him, when he left me, falling back in great disorder...his regiment never again appearing on the field that day, or in fact, getting all together for two days afterwards. When he gets promoted to a Brigadier for such acts of Generalship, it strikes me that I may not be deemed conceited for allowing my name to be put forward for promotion when recommended by Generals Grant and McClernand, who have been eye witnesses of the conduct of my command in two of the greatest engagements of the war...[6]

Ransom was disturbed by political generals and by those who allegedly failed at Shiloh. Furthermore, his audacious nature could not relate at all to the new commander, General Henry Halleck. Washington, and not the field, was this officer's proper element. His main concern in the West seemed to be aimed at avoiding defeat and not seeking victories. Perhaps his own highly developed and sensitive political antenna detected that the public, and certainly those in Congress, wanted no more bloody victories as at Shiloh. Most expected another great struggle at Corinth, and Halleck's army, 120,000 strong, mounted a drive toward that place on April 24, 1862. Halleck seemed determined that the army tunnel the last three miles to the Rebel city where 55,000 Confederates awaited. Except for an occasional picket skirmish, the advancing Union troops occupied their time in brute labor. Miles of corduroy roads were laid for massive, ponderous supply trains. Forward elements crept ahead, ready at the first shot to hunker down and scrape out firing pits. The Union army's timid advance resembled, in spirit, all the audacity exhibited by a covey of elderly matrons shuffling home from prayer meeting. Ransom's Eleventh was ignominiously, but realistically, consigned to a reserve role within McClernand's First Division. Private Carrington admitted to his diary: "Our regiment is too badly played out to ever stand another hard fight."[7]

Rumors abounded that the unit would be disbanded and the survivors assigned to other commands. Company H, for instance, was literally down to one man following the April 6th catastrophe. A trickle of returning Donelson wounded did bolster the slender muster rolls, but only slightly. The Eleventh began the Corinth campaign with only 165 men under arms who shambled along in the First Division's muddy trail. On May 7th, just outside Corinth, the Eleventh suffered another casualty of sorts. Colonel Ransom finally succumbed to General McClernand's insistent offers to join division staff as Inspector General. Ransom's reluctance was rooted in a deep attachment to the regiment to which he felt "bound by a thousand ties of affection."[8] Finally, he agreed and announced the decision before the Eleventh's tired remnants in an emotional scene recorded by an observant newspaper correspondent:

> We have been together many months, we have passed through two terrible battles, and the thinned rank, the absence of many familiar faces, our large list of casualties, speak louder than words can express the noble part borne by the Eleventh. You now have an enviable reputation. By your gallant deeds the name of the Eleventh will always be remembered--honored. The proudest moments of my life have been while I commanded you, and I have long since learned to love the regiment...[9]

The Eleventh's new commanding officer, Garrett Nevius, dwelt in a world of absolutes. His was a rigid universe where any dilemma of conscience or duty could quickly be resolved by reference to Holy Scripture or the well-worn copy of *Hardee's Tactics*. That astute observer, Private Carrington, noted that "tactics and the testament" were never far from his hand.[10] Colonel Nevius presented an austere facade that spoke more of the pulpit than the sword. Photography had been his trade before Sumter. Somber, deep-set eyes accentuated the natural gravity of his face; a substantial beard and premature balding contradicted his youthful 25 years. Reserved and dignified in manner, Colonel Nevius was somewhat aloof, although intimate letters to his brother Will back in New York state revealed a warmer nature, as well as an appreciative eye for the ladies. It may be supposed that the real man could only be penetrated upon extended acquaintances. Nevius was hard on himself, demanding the best at all times, and deeply committed to the Union. He was equally unforgiving with others, evidently unable to understand, much less sympathize with the average soldier's cravings for ease, sexual gratification or liquor. The new commander was no hypocrite either for he never, as had some commanders, failed to practice what he preached. "He was a man of deep and earnest convictions and of unquestionable bravery," wrote one contemporary, "never deviating under any circumstances from what he considered the path of duty."[11]

No less a judge of character than Colonel Ransom agreed. He mentioned Nevius in dispatches both at Shiloh and at Donelson where the executive officer, at least for brief periods, had assumed regimental command in what was euphemistically described as "trying circumstances." The two men were similar in their devotion to the Union cause although there is evidence that Nevius didn't quite share his superior's zest for combat. Characteristically, Nevius pictured the war as a "hard job" in a May 6th letter to his brother Will. He did not dwell on his own promotion but rather expressed a longing that the present struggle soon conclude: "I want to get through with (it) as soon as possible."[12] Like so many good and gentle men, Nevius was evidently a reluctant warrior impelled in his actions by duty. This is not to say that the new commanding officer doubted the cause. Indeed, he fatalistically swore in that very same letter that the restoration of the Union was worth death in battle. "I may fall at any moment on the field of battle," he wrote, "I think I am ready to meet my fate; if such it should be."[13] Nevius then proceeded to update Will on the military situation the regiment faced as they lay in intrenchments at Monterrey, Tennessee:

> We gradually approach the enemy's works at Corinth fighting with the rebels, who are trying by every means in their power to prevent our advance but so far they have signally failed. One week of good weather and we will be at work on Corinth, unless they evacuate which I do not think they will do...We are about three miles from the Mississippi state line. A few more steps and we shall be in the last state between us and the Gulf. What a change! One year ago we were in Camp Hardin in Illinois. What an eventful year it has been to us all. Who would have thought that it would have taken a year to get fairly engaged in the war. I hardly believed it would last one year, but it has, and fair prospects for it lasting another...Our wounded are doing very well, some of those who were hurt at Donelson have returned to the regiment so that we now have two hundred men present.

With these I expect to whip five hundred rebels, before the war is over with. My hand is not extremely well yet. It troubles me a good deal to write and do anything that requires a steady hand...[14]

Nevius's assumptions proved incorrect. The Rebels abandoned the Corinth railhead on May 30th and headed south. They disguised the retreat with an elaborate charade, giving the impression that outgoing troops were incoming reinforcements. Each train chugged away from the station to a chorus of cheers as if another reinforcement had just arrived. Wooden cannon bristled impotently in the Confederate entrenchments and other trickeries were artfully employed in the grand deception. Union troops entered a ghost town on May 31st with everything of value burned. The Old Eleventh bivouacked outside the captured town until June 4 when orders came down for a move north to Jackson, Tennessee, a community sitting astride the important north/south railroad. Union infantry were needed for track security and for the suppression of enemy cavalry who operated with impunity in this bitterly pro-Confederate district.

At 7:30 a.m., July 6, 1862 the Eleventh was in column headed north with other elements detached from General John A. Logan's division. "The day was quite pleasant and the roads in good condition and no dust," jotted down Lieutenant Hapeman. "The first four miles was rather 'low' but after that the country was the finest I have seen since I left Illinois. The country is rather thickly settled but few of the male inhabitants seem to be at home."[15]

Despite his twenty-two years, Hapeman was now a veteran, having commanded Company H with distiction at Donelson and Shiloh. His abilities won the warm approval of Colonel Ransom in the process and guaranteed that officer's continued loyalty in the days ahead. Ransom liked this boyish soldier, formerly an apprentice printer who began his trade at age 13 on the *Ottawa Free Trader*. Like so many others in the Eleventh, Hapeman was disappointed at the intended destination since camp rumor had been that they were bound for Chicago to recruit and recuperate. Reality, however, saw the Eleventh tramping along in the summer heat through a handful of Tennessee hamlets and small towns inhabited, for the most part, by a distinctly unfriendly populace. It was 5 p.m. on July 8th when the column streamed into Jackson. Hapeman recalled how they,

...marched into town with colors flying and all the bands playing. We had rather a cool reception from the citizens of the place, most of the houses being closed and the people being in the houses. But the niggers did look gay, it being their holiday, and they were dressed in their gayest clothes. Jackson is a very pretty place, containing about 4,000 inhabitants in good times. It had a number of fine residences, and a courthouse, and a fine ladies seminary...[16]

The Eleventh went into camp right outside town where they soon learned that Rebel cavalry were in the area supposedly bent on making a night attack upon the Union picket line. It was a rumor that couldn't be ignored. Unfortunately, on the second night in town, nervous pickets from Company E opened fire on a group of horsemen who had ignored the call to halt. The marauders turned out to be Union cavalry coming in from nearby Bethal. One Yankee horse soldier was dead and another wounded during the unfortunate affray. The tragic incident only aggravated the tense atmosphere in Jackson where residents openly flouted rebel sympathies. Their political beliefs, however, did not prevent the merchants from doing a land office business with the troops charging the Yankees $1 for a tobacco plug, 25 cents for a quart of milk, and $20 for a barrel of flour. "This is the hottest Secesh place we have been in yet," noted Private Carrington of the Eleventh. "The citizens won't hardly look at us, especially the women."[17] Lieutenant Henry Dean of Company D concurred, reporting home in a letter that Jackson prided itself as the first town in Tennessee to raise the Rebel flag. This deep commitment to Secession, Dean felt, was most prevalent in places like Jackson because of the presence of so many rich, influential land owners who had a financial stake in slavery. They tried to convince their "niggers" that Union troops were set on deporting them all back to Africa, painting a monstrous picture of the terrible Yankees. Dean noted how one old black "Uncle" told him that the slave holders portrayed the Northern soldiers "as perfect cannibals and who would just eat them up..."[18]

The Eleventh's commander was quite taken back by the bitter, frigid reception but insisted his own officers behave in the most friendly manner and refrain from committing acts that would confirm the local prejudice about Northern ruffians. "Even the little children have been taught to hate and fear us," Colonel Nevius observed.[19] Despite the fact that white residents plugged their ears when the Eleventh's band struck up "Yankee Doodle" during the march in, Nevius pointed out that by the second evening a delegation of ladies from the Seminary witnessed the regiment's dress parade. "I think that they will get into better humor when they find out what fine fellows we are," Nevius wrote his brother Henry.[20] These pleasant diversions couldn't conceal the fact that the regiment was here for more than just a rest. Rebel raiders infested the area, posing a threat to rail communications in the process of being rebuilt by Federal work crews. In Jackson itself, a detachment of engineers was repairing a number of locomotives which would soon be hauling Union troops and supplies. Colonel Nevius explained the situation in a letter home dated June 9th:

> There is a large force of the rebels together in Tennessee, north of the Memphis and Charleston railroads. Guerrilla bands are roaming around the country harassing the Union people, and burning cotton, destroying bridges, and in many places laying the Country in waste. They think to annoy us by such proceedings, but poor creatures, they are only biting their own noses to spite their own faces. I hope they will enjoy it...Since the evacuation of Corinth, the rebels have been driven in all directions...General Halleck has more prisoners than he knows what to do with. All their railroads in Tennessee west of Nashville are in possession of the Federal forces. Our Gun Boats are at Memphis, and in a few days the Mississippi will be open from Cairo to New Orleans. The glorious work is progressing finally and I look forward to a speedy termination of this unhappy and uncalled for war...[21]

Events contradicted Nevius's optimism which was a bit premature, certainly in regard to the Mississippi River which remained closed. Confederate batteries at Vicksburg and other important places dominated this key water highway. But these were strategic matters, and Nevius was more directly concerned with his own immediate responsibilities in maintaining the military efficiency of the Eleventh Illinois. He was not pleased with what seemed to be, to this most proper officer, a tendency on the part of the enlisted toward raucous, ungentlemanly behavior. The men were increasingly intoxicated, and gambled until all hours of the night in direct violation of orders. In the commander's opinion, discipline as a whole "had fallen on hard times." Nevius felt the situation had gotten so far out of hand that he issued a special order on June 21.

It is necessary...For when men lose four months wages in less than 48 hours it is natural to suppose that they would shirk from duty to take any opportunity to earn back what they had lost--some are led to resort to other means to get possession of their money.[22]

The colonel found it shocking when groups of the men began to sneak off for nocturnal visits to the nearby Negro shanties. There, they "conducted themselves in a most shameful manner which was disgraceful both to them and the Regiment."[23] Nevius was even more upset concerning the leadership qualities, or more properly, the lack of them, in his own executive officer, Captain James Coates. That fall, the colonel felt strongly enough to bring the matter up before the Illinois adjutant general in Springfield. Coates had just won election as major in the Eleventh whereas Nevius was convinced that Captain Rose of Company G was better qualified:

Captain Coates is a fine gentleman, a good officer, and as far as qualifications as drillmaster goes, and I believe a brave man. But he has a serious failing. He is very much dissipated, so much so at times, as to entirely disqualify him for any duty. Were it not for this failing I should prefer him to any officer in the Regiment for a Major....I want someone to assist me whom I can trust at all times, someone whom I will not have to watch half of the time in order to have him fit for duty...Justice to the men of the Regt. and to myself demands that someone whom we can trust should be appointed Major. I can say without fear of contradiction that whiskey elected him last night...In conclusion, say give me anybody but Capt. Coates...[24]

Nevius's distrust extended to his next senior captain, Lloyd Waddell of Company E. This was the same officer who had taken command at Shiloh when Nevius left the field, leading not more than 80 survivors into the final battle late Sunday afternoon. Ransom singled out this gaunt, wild-eyed soldier for his "conspicuous and honorable" role in that terrible conflict when he led the remnants of the Eleventh into the "thickest of the fight."[25] In his personal correspondence, Ransom spoke of Waddell in affectionate terms, referring to him as "Wad." Colonel Nevius did not share these opinions, and remained convinced that Captain Waddell deserved neither respect as a man nor as an officer. By the spring of 1863, he felt strongly enough about the matter to dash out another letter addressed to the Illinois adjutant general demanding Waddell's removal. The letter was a scathing indictment overflowing with abusive and mostly unsubstantiated charges:

> He (Waddell) was one of the first Captains of the regiment yet he has been in only one battle in which the regiment has been engaged. He has always managed so as to be absent from the regiment more than any other officer, and without any very good reasons. He is very negligent in all his duties as an officer so much so that his Company has frequently been made to suffer for it. He is, in fact, one of the most careless Company Commanders we have in the regiment--a fact well known by all acquainted with it. He has no qualifications as a drillmaster whatever. I have endeavored for a long time, whenever he has been with the regiment, to prevail upon him to apply himself to the study of tactics but without avail...Our Army has been cursed too much already with incompetent officers. Unless good, reliable ones can be appointed it is better to have none at all.[26]

These concerns were exacerbated by the continuing manpower shortage. At this point, the Eleventh's strength rarely ever exceeded 250 compared with the nearly 800 who packed the muster rolls at Bird's Point six months before. All these considerations probably were foremost in the commander's mind when he was ordered on July 24th to prepare for a possible confrontation with the Confederates.[27] They were to march on Lexington, Kentucky, where Grayback cavalry were terrorizing loyal Unionists. It was indicative of the growing discipline problem that General John Logan felt it imperative to impress upon Nevius that the men must not straggle or abuse the property of civilians in the area. "I desire you to use your endeavors to cultivate a conservative, friendly feeling with the people where you may," Logan wrote.[28] This would be Nevius's first independent combat mission as a regimental commander. His unit departed Jackson at 11 a.m. that very day and made the 28 miles to Lexington before noon the next day.

Whatever Rebel force had been at Lexington, however, was not present when the Eleventh arrived amid cheers and smiles. The town's sizable Union population extended a thankful welcome. Colonel Nevius was soon informed that the appearance of the Eleventh has precipitated the rapid departure of the town's most vociferous Rebel, an alleged "braggart" who had boasted how he had more than 100 barrels of corn ready for provisioning the Rebel cavalry in the area. These stores were seized with relish by the commander. Nevius was pleased to learn the Union expedition had apparently arrived in time to prevent the persecution or even the executions of loyal citizens in the area.[29] "The secessioners about here have been led to believe that there was a large force of rebels to cross the river at Perryville on Tuesday night last, and that they were to aid them in every way they could," Nevius reported. "Some prominent Union citizens were to be their victims." The Eleventh stayed only three days at Lexington, but equipped and organized a troop of loyalists for the future protection of Union men. After taking this precaution, the regiment departed at 1 a.m., July 28th. A hard day's march brought them back to Jackson, trooping into that town at sundown, where the men collapsed into sleep.

Nevius must have been flattered when he learned that Colonel C.C. Marsh had praised the Eleventh for its deportment on the recent march. He was well known to the regiment, having commanded the 20th Illinois at Donelson, and their own brigade at Shiloh. "Your soldierly appearance on coming into camp today after a march of nearly thirty miles in a burning sun convinces your commander that, for endurance and soldierly qualities, the Eleventh is still the same who so cheerfully submitted to the terrible hardships of Donelson and increases his confidence always strong in your integrity and fidelity."[30] Five days later the Eleventh was on the move again but this time it was "by the cars," and heading north to Cairo for rest and recruiting. Once again, the move was accompanied by even more flattering praise of the "Old Eleventh". The regiment's departure was reported by a *Chicago Times* correspondent on the scene at the Jackson depot:

> The havoc of war finds in this regiment an illustration at once powerful and sublime. A thousand men, by the bullets of the enemy and the casualties of the service, in one short year had been whittled down to two hundred. Gen. McClernand appeared before them with such thoughts as their changed condition must have inspired to bid them good-bye. He paid them in glowing terms the highest tribute that could come from their commander. In every fight they acquitted themselves like heroes. They had killed more of the enemy and received heavier losses than any other regiment in the service...The General was frequently interrupted by hearty cheers and expressions of anxiety to be again led to face the enemy, and as he retired cheer after cheer followed him. Their splendid [the 11th's] instrument band played all the

popular airs as the soldiers were arranging themselves in the cars. Just before the train started, Gen. Logan appeared on the platform. He addressed the men for a few moments, complimenting them on their bravery and services, wishing them success in filling up their ranks with such heroes as themselves in which case no enemy of equal force could stand against them. The train started off amid the uproar of contending shouts.[31]

Cairo, with its mud and mosquitoes, was a drab anticlimax. The men of the Eleventh found themselves assigned to the 63rd Illinois' former barracks which were incredibly filthy and required a massive clean-up operation. Disheartening as well was the fact that the regiment was on constant guard duty made more onerous because of depleted ranks. Reduced numbers prevented a proper rotation of the duty which most veterans, in particular, detested. A few even expressed preference for active campaigning. As the humid, oppressive southern Illinois days dragged on, the disappointment mounted even higher when it became obvious that there would be no flood of recruits for the "scarecrow" Eleventh. Recruiting officers, detailed to promote enlistments in Illinois, met meager success. Politics and money were at work. Potential infantry recruits flocked to the new regiments which offered lucrative bonuses for enlistments. At the same time, Springfield authorized the creation of more and more regiments opening up more command slots for the ambitious. Most often the older units were usually in desperate need of additional manpower. Captain Cyrus Dickey of the Eleventh mentioned the problem in an August 11th letter to his sister, Ann:

> The 11th Regiment is resting here and getting fat and saucy, but with little prospect of recruiting its numbers. We have recruiting officers out but volunteer enlistments are slow and no other means have been furnished to fill our ranks. I think that the government is almost criminally negligent of this duty. There is no General, that would not prefer old regiments...to twice the number of men under untried officers with no experience in field service.[32]

There was one redeeming feature about the Eleventh's three week sojourn at Cairo. Their old commanding officer, T.E.G. Ransom, was serving as military commander of the strategic river town. His heartrending farewell to the Eleventh was proving a bit premature and it appeared Ransom's intent to keep the regiment by his side in upcoming expeditions.[33] Unfortunately Colonel Ransom's morale was not much better that that of his old regiment. His efforts at seeking promotion to brigadier met with frustration despite the efforts of his boyhood chum, General Dodge, and his latest commanding officer, Brigadier General William K. Strong. Ransom even attempted to secure a personal interview with President Lincoln on a quick trip East. "I saw everybody," Ransom wrote Dodge, "was cordially received by the Illinois delegation and others and by your friend Kasson...who promised to do anything he could for me. I made no effort in my own behalf, as I saw it was no use. The president was engaged in more important matters, and the number of Brigadiers for the State too many..."[34] Ransom's dream was his own brigade, containing in it the "Old Eleventh." Yet, in spite of the promises from so many influential military leaders, the dream seemed destined never to materialize. Increasingly frustrated, and convinced that he was "laid up on the shelf" in the backwaters, Ransom brooded on the situation he would describe in a letter to General Dodge:

> Perhaps if I have a chance in the field I may win a commission, but I have not such an expectation of getting one unless something else turns up, when I may have an opportunity to show myself...When I go into the field again, if possible, I want to get with you; can it not be so arranged?...Please to go to work with this point in view, as I am exceedingly anxious to get with you <u>and not go into the command where I have been so long</u>; of course, I do not say this to anyone else, and I have reason to know that a certain General will try to get me back. You understand--I am out, and want to stay out...[35]

The Eleventh was briefly stationed at Paducah, Kentucky. Rebel activity in the Fort Donelson area soon demanded their attention, and the regiment boarded a steamer on August 27. It landed at Fort Henry and took the familiar route to the old battleground whose Union garrison was threatened. A few days before, Forrest's Rebel raiders clashed with Blue troopers in Dover itself and burned the town after a spirited fire fight. On Saturday, August 30th, the Eleventh reinforced the post and was hard at work on new breastworks early the next day while keeping an "eye out for guerrillas." The men of the Eleventh worked beside men of the 71st Ohio and the 13th Wisconsin and were supported by Flood's Artillery Battery. By Monday, the situation seemed secure enough so that many from the Eleventh toured the old Donelson battlefield. There they constructed a rude fence around the mass grave which contained so many old comrades. Carrington revisited a farm house that had served as an impromptu field hospital during the fight. "The Lady told us the smell of gunpowder and blood was yet in the rooms where our wounded had lain, and several died. It was a sight when we were there the evening of the battle."[36]

The old battlefield brought back melancholy reminders at every turn. Captain Henry Dean, now commanding Company D, pointed out in a letter home how the snowy roads of February were now filled with "dust ankle deep" and the temperature was well over 100 degrees. It was his viewpoint that the newly raised regiments should be sent out in the field allowing units like the Eleventh the luxury of garrison duty up North. Dean's only explanation was that the regiment had earned a "reputation for fighting, and it looks as though we are to do our share, at least as long as there are any men to fight."[37] Dean wrote how his own company barely mustered 28 men, compared to 76 who answered roll call before Donelson. It just didn't seem fair that the survivors must go back again and again while fresh troops were at hand. Yet, despite these reflections, Dean remained confident that the "Old Eleventh" still could handle itself in any meeting with the Rebels. "The guerrilla has sent word that he is going to take this place," Dean wrote, "but we have 'heavy doubts' to the contrary. Our boys are ready..."[38] Still the bravado could not conceal the apprehension about another fight which might result in terrible casualties as had Donelson and Shiloh. Unpleasant thoughts were reinforced by the dreary surroundings.

> The ground where we fought is all overgrown with weeds and bushes, and can scarcely be recognized as the same place. The fort is washing away fast--the guns have all been removed--the barracks have most all been used for the wood. In fact, there is nothing left here scarcely to mark the place except the old ruins and the number of graves of both Union and Secesh that can be seen on every side...[39]

An old graveyard is an unnerving sight for men huddled behind new earthworks and awaiting new battles. They must have greeted Ransom's arrival on September 4 with relief. His presence certainly promised an end to this tedious waiting. On the very next day the Yankee garrison sallied forth after Confederate forces believed operating near Clarkesville, 35 miles up river. Colonel W.W. Lowe commanded the expedition which included the Eleventh, the two other infantry regiments and 600 cavalry. A vigorous pursuit was launched and Rebel pickets were encountered September 6th by advanced cavalry scouts. Inexplicably, Colonel Lowe practically stepped aside to give Ransom total command at that point. The very next morning the Eleventh moved from its evening encampment at his orders. By 8 a.m., the Eleventh closed with a line of Rebel skirmishers about five miles outside Clarkesville. Ransom ordered Nevius out on point with three companies from the Eleventh, deploying them in a skirmish line on either side of the main Clarkesville road. They encountered Rebel skirmishers not two miles out of camp, and shoved the enemy back in a running, hide-and-seek fight among the forests and cornfields.

Thick dense woods with underbrush was on each side of the road except occasionally a cornfield. The rebels were hid in these and had many fine shots at us but as many men were deployed...they failed to do us any serious harm, for our skirmishers took advantage of the trees...About noon we came in sight of their main road to town runs, in front of them on both sides of the road was open fields. They were fortified behind a rail and stone fence, also a couple houses and barns...[40]

Nevius halted his skirmish line about 500 yards from the Confederate position and awaited Ransom and the main body. Two field pieces were quickly planted near the main road and shortly after they opened a brisk fire which continued for about ninety minutes. The Rebel line extended across a crossroad near Riggin's Farm, situated atop a substantial rise which gave them a fine view of the Yankees below. While the preparatory artillery fire continued, Ransom ordered his cavalry to the rear while placing his infantry on both sides of the road. There the infantry crouched in relative safety to enjoy the artillery demonstration; six-pound rifled shot smashed into the fence line near the crossroads with savage effect. "Rails flew left and right...," Private Carrington observed with satisfaction, although the barrage almost claimed the lives of five or six Union skirmishers who had collected around a tree far in advance.[41] The artillery spotted this clot of men, supposed them rebels, and directed a volley of cannon shot which exploded ten feet up in the tree unleashing a "shower of dust, bark and dead limbs." Carrington watched the men scurry in every direction accompanied by howls of laughter from the regiment. "It was real funny to see them get away from the falling limbs, pieces of bark and the cloud of dust that enveloped the tree," he wrote.[42]

It was a vicious, accurate bombardment against men armed only with shoulder weapons. The Confederates could only burrow ineffectually in the earth while round after round plowed into the strongpoint. Carrington was stunned when, after about 50 cannon shots, the Confederate line evaporated. The Rebels fled toward Clarkesville. Ransom ordered the advance, and the Union men emerged from cover with "bayonets at the charge." The Eleventh's decimated band struck up a rousing chorus of "Yankee Doodle". Elated at the scene, Ransom would later recall how the remainder of the Confederates gave way. "It was too much for the Butternuts. They broke without giving us a volley."[43]

The men were greeted at the rail fence by a Rebel waving a white flag. About him lay the crumpled bodies of those who had been killed or wounded during the cannonade. The Bluecoats paused, catching their breath and gawking at the fallen enemy. "Two men were lying nearby," Carrington wrote, "one with his head shot off, the other with both arms and part of his breast torn out by one shell."[44] In all, 17 Rebels lay dead along with 40 wounded and 50 or 60 captives. It was a fine bag and Union losses were negligible. The Eleventh counted one wounded, Lieutenant Blackstone of Company I, who shot himself in the leg with his revolver during the excitement. All that was left was for Ransom's command to march into Clarkesville and accept the town's surrender. Unfortunately the troops were a bit overexuberant. One group broke into a dry goods store, distributing the contents as their rightful booty. Colonel Ransom soon learned of it and rode right up on the sidewalk and into the store itself. He slashed about right and left with his saber at the startled thieves. "They skedaddled in a hurry," remembered one man from the Eleventh.[45]

Clarkesville had been defended by Rebel cavalry under Colonel Thomas G. Woodward, a protege of the famed Brigadier General John Hunt Morgan. Their defeat at Riggin's Hill had been a humiliation for the proud horse soldiers, but they brought off the retirement in a professional and orderly fashion despite a hard pursuit. Ransom felt that if Colonel Lowe had "taken my advice a little earlier though, we could have bagged three or four hundred of the rascals."[46] The Riggins Hill victory was incomplete, in Ransom's eyes, although such a bloodless triumph must have been a pleasant change of pace after Donelson and Shiloh. Then too, the march back to Fort Henry was not without amusement. The Eleventh and the other Union regiments lived off the land.

> While in Clarkesville we took and destroyed quite a large amount of public property, and during the whole time we

were gone we lived entirely off the country through which we marched. We reached Donelson day before yesterday and yesterday marched to this place [Fort Henry], and now are waiting for a boat up from Paducah to go to that place...The weather has been warm, and the roads so dusty that at times we could not see a hundred yards back of us. A dirtier lot of men you never saw, but we lived freely as we had all the peaches and apples we could eat, and <u>chickens</u> and <u>turkeys</u> are now very scarce on the road...[47]

More than a year and a half had passsd since those early Missouri expeditions when the Eleventh was shackled with a retinue of wagons carrying what most supposed were the bare necessities for campaign. In the intervening months, they learned differently. Now it was rifle, ammunition, and a few days' rations of coffee and hardtack. Restrictions on foraging were erased when the men swept through the enemy countryside. Officers like Nevius fretted over the men's morals, their penchant for foul language, and vulgar sport, but few doubted their fitness as soldiers. When it came to it, these Western men could march as well as or better than their Rebel counterparts and fight with equal tenacity. In camp, the men of the Eleventh and other Western regiments were as adept at improvising as any soldiers who ever cursed an officer or dodged the provost marshall. *Chicago Journal* correspondent Benjamin Taylor described this special breed of Western soldier in an article that appeared in late 1863:

If there are men in the world gifted with the most thorough self-reliance, Western soldiers are the men...No matter where or when you halt, there they are at once at home. They know precisely what to do first and they do it. I have seen them march into a strange region at dark, and almost as soon as fires would show well they were twinkling all over the field, the Sibley cones rising like the work of enchantment everywhere and the little dogtents lying snug to the ground, as if, like the mushrooms, they had grown there, and the aroma of coffee and tortured bacon suggesting creature comforts, and the whole economy of life in canvas cities...[48]

Soldierly virtues would be useful in the coming months, especially with the advent of a new campaign in the fall of 1862. Grant was in command once again, and planned a massive drive south. The objective was Jackson, and then the Vicksburg river fortress. The "Old Eleventh" was assigned to the great expedition after a mundane month in the Paducah area. In late November, the men packed aboard box cars for the ride to LaGrange, Tennessee, the jump-off point for the new drive. The regiment was now part of the First Brigade, Sixth Division. Even more appealing was the announcement that the newly promoted Brigadier General T.E.G. Ransom would command the brigade. An old Scotsman, and prominent Chicago steel manufacturer, Brigadier General John McArthur commanded the division. Spirits rose with the prospect of decisive action, and at Ransom's good fortune. "The men like Ransom lots," Carrington remarked in his bulging diary.[49] Most were equally enthusiastic about the new march which was to be made by 100,000 well-armed, well-fed, and by now veteran Union infantry. The plan was simple. Grant's army was to plunge south from LaGrange along the Mississippi Central Railroad, encounter the Rebel army under General Joe Johnston probably at the Tallahatchie River, defeat it in detail, march on into Jackson and then move east toward Vicksburg. Simultaneously, an army under General William T. Sherman was to move down the Mississippi by boat and assault the Vicksburg fortress to complete a vast pincer movement. On November 28th, the main column left LaGrange in damp, chilly weather. At the spearpoint marched the understrength Eleventh Illinois who slipped in the yellow mud of northern Mississippi.

By November 29th, the Eleventh penetrated to a point near Waterford, five miles south of Holly Springs. The next day witnessed an ongoing skirmish. The Eleventh's riflemen cautiously moved out, exchanging shots with a thin screen of retiring Gray infantry, and losing one man in the bargain. Private Uptmor of Company K recalled how this skirmishing continued until the riflemen had proceeded to within about a mile of the Tallachatchie River where the Rebels held a main line of resistance hinged around two forts, or earthwork complexes, on each side of the river. "They opened battery fire upon us," Uptmor wrote, "and the bullets (shells) flew thick and heavy over our heads. We lay still here for awhile, then our artillery came up in front and began to shell the enemy, and they did the same to us. The enemy had good gunners and several times their bullets went right through our ranks."[50] At this point, Colonel Ransom ordered the regiment to move out in columns of four, seeking a more advantageous position, but taking an enormous risk when the long Blue column traversed a large open field within easy artillery range. Private Carrington wrote:

We ducked every time one passed. They (the Rebs) worked the guns pretty fast thinking to annihilate us before we could reach shelter. When it comes to firing on a whole Regiment marching by the right flank...across a field in full view...and not hit a man, it must be considered poor artillery practice.[51]

The regiment cringed under the raking cannon fire but most of the rounds screamed high overhead, exploding into the woods far behind. It was nervous work, made more so by the feeling of utter helplessness so often remarked upon by infantry who have endured a heavy bombardment. Terror feeds on each passing minute, and the mind begins to ponder what might happen if one of those black iron balls should plow through the crowded ranks. Carrington later wrote:

It's tiresome lying flat on the ground. Finally Private Bragg stood up, adjusted his cartridge box and equipments, and with an oath said: "Maybe you fellers over there would like to kill some of us?" We laughed. Heretofore all had been silent in the ranks for we did not know what instant a shell would tear some comrade's life out, and to be buried in such a lonesome spot. We dreaded this, to see a man killed and buried alongside the road, then pass on and leave him seemed so hard.[52]

The cannonading continued for three more hours; shells gouged out the earth and sprayed the black dirt over the regiment, or burst nder a rail fence. "The pieces hummed towards us but no one was hit," Carrington described.[53] Wooden slivers the size of a man's arm could be deadlier than cold iron. Lack of water, and the obvious futility of laying under a constant bombardment, convinced the officers that a withdrawal was necessary.

In camp, seven miles north, the men busied themselves for the next day's expected assault on the Tallahatchie River forts. But the fight didn't materialize as the Rebels inexplicably withdrew leaving behind their abandoned works and a burning bridge as souvenirs. Captain Henry Dean of the Eleventh wrote:

During the night the enemy had executed one of their "masterpieces of strategy" and "skedaddled", leaving as strong a position as I have seen since the war commenced. Our Regiment was in advance of the whole army, and, of course, was the first to enter the enemy's works. Their main fort was on the south side of the Tallahatchie River, and they had burned the bridge; and we being in the advance were obliged to rebuild it for the main Army to cross, which was an all night's job. As soon as it was daybreak we started after the Butternut crew double-quick, and arrived at Abbieville about 9 o'clock, where we captured about a dozen stragglers but the main force had gone on "Dixie-ward."[54]

The Eleventh marched into the Mississippi hamlet which was left relatively intact by the retreating Rebels although the railroad depot, another railroad bridge, and piles of commissary stores had been put to the torch. The regiment stayed but one night and then encamped a mile south of town, where they would remain until December 18th. The remainder of the Union army continued toward Jackson. At 10 a.m., that date, the march led the Eleventh to Oxford where the men witnessed with satisfaction the arrival of four trains packed with Rebel prisoners. "All quiet, the boys in good spirits," Carrington noted in his diary.[55] The march was going well with little resistance since most white inhabitants had fled before the Union advance. But the march was far from uneventful. Colonel Nevius described how the regiment plunged on through a nearly deserted land populated only by droves of slaves who greeted the Yankees at every plantation house:

Most of the people desert their homes before we arrive in sight. Some of the Negroes are having fine times living in their master's houses. They are now boss and hands, and seem to like it too. The other day some rebel sharpshooters took a position in a large mansion on a hill, and with the aid of a cannon annoyed us very much. The only way to get them out was to shell them out. One of our rifled cannon was brought up, and fired a shell which went through the house from one end to another. Such getting out of a house I never saw before, Rebels and negroes all mixed together...[56]

Ahead was Jackson, Mississippi. Prospects seemed bright for Union victory, perhaps even the beginning of the end for the Confederates in the West. Surely the Rebels had suffered at Donelson, Shiloh, and most recently during a bloody unsuccessful assault at Corinth. Major Coates and Captain Dean, both of the Eleventh, had been detailed as members of the provost marshall at Oxford and observed, based on prisoner interrogation, what they thought were sure signs of Rebel collapse. "They all agree in saying that their army is very much demoralized, and that if we leave them alone for a month they will fight among themselves and go home," Dean wrote from the Abbieville camp. "Deserters are coming in continually, and all unite in saying: 'The Southern Confederacy is played out.' To me it looks more like winding up this rebellion now than ever before."[57] Dean was almost buoyantly optimistic in his analysis. He wrote his home town newspaper in Rockford, Illinois and predicted the boys might be home in the spring, assuming that the Eastern armies did their share. "We keep a stiff upper lip, and wade through the mud, knowing that every step we take brings us nearer the Gulf..."[58]

Heady optimism and dreams of going home by spring were shattered on December 20, 1862. Rebel raiders under General Earl Van Dorn galloped into Holly Springs "yelling like so many devils." He and his men had ridden right around the advancing Union army to strike hard at this key supply center.[59] Elements of the 29th, 62nd, 101st and 105th Illinois Infantry Regiments offered sporadic resistance while the 2nd Illinois Cavalry gave a better account of itself at the fairgrounds outside town. It was all to little avail. The Rebels quickly assumed command, paroled their prisoners and began methodical destruction. Rails were torn up and three Union locomotives wrecked. Millions of dollars in Federal stores and ammunition went up in flames. Grant's plans for the winter campaign vanished in smoke. His supply line was cut, leaving the army isolated in a land thought incapable of feeding such a vast host. The decision came almost immediately, and on December 21st, the Eleventh Illinois pulled up stakes for the disappointing march back north, retracing their steps through an enemy land stripped now of every foodstuff and repeatedly looted by many of the passing Union regiments. One Illinois soldier remembered:

> The destruction and devastation along the line of the Federal Army's retreat, is beyond all description. No one could form any idea of it unless they actually witness it. There is not a house left on the road from Oxford to within a couple miles of this place [LaGrange, Tennessee]. The town of Oxford is almost totally destroyed...the spirit of destruction characterizes the soldiery. Frequently the residences of three or four large plantations, with their rows of Negro quarters, could be seen in flames from one standpoint, and at night the whole heavens were lurid with the blaze of burning dwellings, barns, cotton-gins, and anything combustible...[60]

The only mention of the retirement comes in Private Carrington's diary. He made mention of the "colored people of all shades and sizes" draped along the roadside fences gazing in awe at the retreating thousands. These were the same Yankees who had been marching south with such confidence just a few days prior. Inquisitive slaves called out to the marching soldiers, asking: "Whar yourn's gwine with yo' sharp stickers on yo guns." Others simply exclaimed: "Never did see so many Yankees," accompanied by another remarking: "Look way up yonder, mo coming." The blacks would stare and chat with the Union troopers, and then fall in the rear of a regiment.[61] Most of the blacks carried a pathetic, small bundle of personal property. They were going North to freedom. Carrington drew a vivid portrait of the scene: "Women carrying babies, besides huge bundles on their head. Men, boys and girls--poor things they suffered more than if they had stayed on the plantations. Many, however, remained and took care of Master's property as best they could."[62]

Smoldering Holly Springs gave mute testimony to failure when the Eleventh marched back into the city on December 22nd. The men made camp in front of the courthouse and awaited further orders. Christmas was spent amidst the debris of defeat, a cold and cheerless holiday. Perhaps they discussed the fate of the 109th Illinois Infantry whose members now were under mass arrest for suspected Confederate sympathies. Many said the southern Illinois unit was ready for immediate surrender when Van Dorn struck Holly Springs. And, there was no doubt that the regiment failed to respond even though their camp was only five miles outside the great Union supply center. The men in the 109th were quick to admit they detested Lincoln's recent Emancipation Proclamation which, in their view, turned this struggle into war for "Nigger Rights." Strangely enough, the Holly Springs incident was to have great impact on the Eleventh within the near future, even altering the very personality of the regiment. These events, however, were still in the future when the Eleventh marched out for Moscow, Tennessee, on December 30th. There they braced for another predicted raid and pondered the future. On January 6th, 1863, Colonel Nevius provided his brother Will with an update:

Our Division marched from Holly Springs to this place (Moscow, Tenn.) one week ago yesterday, but all of it, our Brigade, except us goes on towards Memphis, and will be stationed on the Railroad to guard it from the guerrillas who are very plentiful in these parts. They keep us continually on the alert. Day before yesterday Gen. Grant sent us word to look out for Van Dorn, who is said to be moving for this place. Let him come. He will find this place not another Holly Springs. We will welcome him, as his rank calls for, if he should come, but I hardly think he will. Grant's army is at the present at a standstill, but I do not think it will remain so long...[63]

Chapter Six

Blaze of Musketry

This man Grant was always coming at you, never allowing a moment's respite, stubbornly refusing to accept that the Vicksburg puzzle was insoluble. After the Holly Springs fiasco, he was like a tenacious wrestler who had been momentarily frustrated, but was far from beaten. Grant groped and fumbled for a better grip on the Confederate jugular. He knew that the great Mississippi River was the key and that the Rebel grip on that watery artery must be broken. So it was in the spring of 1863 that Grant's army shifted across the river to the western bank in search of a different angle of attack among the fetid swamps and bayous of northern Louisiana. On January 26th, the "Old Eleventh" was already encamped at Young's Point, Louisiana, located five miles upriver from Vicksburg. For these weary Midwesterners, the almost tropical environment stood in stark contrast to the familiar Illinois prairie. Private Carrington placed tongue firmly in cheek when he wrote:

> We are camped on the west side of the river. Can even now hear the boom of the heavy guns as our mortars and gunboats throw a shell now and then to stir them up. Our camp is behind the levee on a large plantation. The owner and Negroes are gone; the fields are grown up with cockle burrs, nearly as high as a man's head. The country is very low and leveed all the way below Helena. Where there are no plantations, heavy cyprus and canebreaks line the river. Oh! This is a beautiful swamp-the sunny south...I expect we'll have a gay time here yet. Rain and mud since we landed.[1]

In the wearisome cold and wet of early spring, the regiment had settled in for only a day or two before the bloated Mississippi began to seep its way through and over the protective levee. Work details were immediately assigned the arduous, exhaustive task of dumping huge quantities of dirt and brush into the ever widening crevasses that appeared on the threatened levee. "The river is the most dangerous foe we have at present," one soldier remarked. Yet all the brutal work was fruitless as the regiment suddenly received new orders. The Eleventh, along with five other regiments, moved further south by steamboat. The next morning, the regiment disembarked at Lake Providence about 30 miles further from Vicksburg. Almost immediately a party of foragers from the division promptly collided with a force of Rebels estimated to be 300 strong. They traded volleys of musketry before both sides pulled back. The encounter put everyone on the alert that night although nothing more in the way of the enemy materialized. The Eleventh set up shop about four miles west of the Mississippi River on the shores of Lake Providence, which provided a pleasant vista despite the dismal weather. Lieutenant Colonel Nevius was extremely pleased:

> Our camp is on the banks of one of the most beautiful little lakes that I have ever seen. It is ten miles long in the shape of a crescent and about a quarter of a mile wide. My tent is pitched in the door yard of the finest house that I have seen in the southern Confederacy. Most of the white inhabitants belonging to this section of the country have fled to other parts. The few that remain have too many interests here to attend to, to go way, or they would go too for they are bitter Secesh. But they are beginning to feel the horror of war in all shapes...The man who owns the plantation...is a very wealthy man, worth several hundred thousand dollars...but most of it is in this section of the country. Yet, notwithstanding all his wealth, he cannot get the necessaries of life to put on his table. There is not a soldier in our Army, but what has better meals every day than he does. Most of his slaves have left him. Others he expects will go, and he lives in continual fear of what he has left, and the soldiers. Nearly all his stock is gone, taken by either the Rebels or the Federals, so that he is left, almost entirely without means of going from one place to another unless he goes on foot. He told me a few days since that he should be compelled to ask for help, or starve.[2]

Life at Lake Providence was relatively simple for the rank-and-file of the Eleventh. They were spared the heavy labor of building a canal designed to bypass Vicksburg. Instead, Ransom's brigade provided camp security. The men spent a great deal of time on watch, but still were left with bountiful free hours in which they chatted, played cards, wrote home, or dozed away in their tents while the almost continual rain pattered on the canvas. It was a marvel, Private Carrington wrote, how imaginative the soldiers were in these idle moments. They carved finger rings from coal, made elaborate pipes from sugar cane, and constructed all types of bracelets and jewelry out of shells.[3]

Variety was interjected into this routine by an occasional forage expedition into the interior where the steadfast Rebels secreted vast stores of corn as well as livestock--much of the latter branded "Property CSA." Colonel Nevius wrote of one such expedition:

> We embarked on board of a fast steamer about two o'clock one afternoon, and just daylight the next morning landed about fifteen miles above here and came round in the rear of this section and secured 235 beef cattle, 50 sheep, 40 fat hogs and 75 splendid mules, 18 good work horses, besides a chicken and a goose for each man, and was back on board with all our plunder by dark...Most of the inhabitants in this section of the Country were very wealthy before the war, but the matter is rather mixed now for nigger property is very uncertain these times. Especially where our Army goes. I was talking with a man a few days ago who said that the week before he was the owner of one hundred Negroes. Now...his wife would have to get their own meals. So it goes. None but those who experience it know what the horrors of war are. I hope that none of my friends may ever experience it.[4]

Private Frank Whipple, an ever lucky soldier, was a party to similar forays upon the civilian population in what was fast developing into a very modern breed of total war. Fifty years after Appomattox he would tell his young son, Warner, of the times when the Eleventh descended on those hapless plantations to strip them of nearly everything. He related seeing southern women in a home seemingly unconcerned, sitting sewing, while soldiers destroyed, or removed bales of cotton, caught poultry, used the rail fences for fires, and roamed over the yards and gardens.[5]

Such depredations became increasingly common. These were either actively encouraged by certain Union officers or, in most cases, tolerated by commanders in no mood to weep over the misfortunes of a few rich Rebels. Private Carrington spoke of the steamer *Empress* docking at Providence with a load of forty-three wagons, all to be used for the transport of Rebel cotton stashed everywhere among the swamps. Daily, the Union detachments would return either with bales of CSA cotton or beef cattle or other valuable property that might well sustain the beleaguered Confederacy. On March 22nd, a foraging party from the regiment invaded the premises of a plantation said to be the property of the late Senator Stephen A. Douglas, the same man who had ridden through the cheers of the Eleventh and other Union regiments at Camp Yates in 1861. The troops made themselves right at home listening with great interest when the "Darkeys" mentioned how it had been a long time since they had seen their illustrious owner. A small party of the Eleventh would made one plantation temporary foraging headquarters. The Yankees were comfortably ensconced under an open cotton shed, the heavy, wet bales stacked around in a square providing them with an excellent fort in case Rebel troops should make an unexpected visit.[6]

For many of the Union boys these expropriations were a delight, a kind of officially sanctioned Halloween spree. One man, who never was one to ignore the rules, saw it all very differently. That was the Eleventh's old commander, now Brigadier General T.E.G. Ransom. In command of the Second Brigade at Lake Providence, Ransom was appalled at the conduct of Federal troops. On February 12th, he issued a severe reprimand to the regiments under his authority, including his own Eleventh:

> The outrageous conduct of a few lawless members and followers of this Command has brought an imputation of disgrace upon us all. Houses have been entered and pillaged. Old men and defenseless women have been abused and insulted. Old paintings, family relics, libraries...have been wantonly destroyed, robberies of money and jewels have been committed...destitute old Negroes have been robbed of the scanty subsistence left them by their fleeing masters. These things have been done under the pretext of subsisting on the enemy, and have been too lightly regarded by many of the officers...[7]

If there was bitterness and cruelty among the ranks in the Eleventh it cannot be condoned, but these feelings should be understood in the context of the times. At about the same time as foraging expeditions were ravaging the countryside, the Donelson prisoners were trickling back to the Eleventh. Those who survived Rebel prisons were not conducive to magnanimous feelings toward their former jailors. These were the men who had been rounded up by Forrest's cavalry when the regiment beat its hasty retreat through the Tennsssee woods more than a year previously. All had been quickly loaded aboard the same Rebel steamer which bore the Confederate General Floyd away from the doomed fortress. They were not lucky enough to have been left behind at Nashville, as were Lieutenant James Vernay and a handful of others. For these men, it was only the beginning--the first steps on a journey into a great darkness. Lieutenant Nathaniel C. Kenyon, Company K, Eleventh Illinois, was one of these travelers. His bleak odyssey began when he threw up his arms in surrender just after the line collapsed on Saturday, February 15, 1862. Those early days in captivity left him kindly disposed toward the majority of his jailors whom he described as, "Mostly gentlemen, treating us with uniform kindness."[8] As the months wore by, however, Kenyon's brief notations in his battered diary became studded with invective scrawled by a man bewildered by the whimsical cruelties inflicted by the ever-present guards. The captive Union officer was ever more despondent as each new rumor regarding exchange proved to be false.

Kenyon and the other Yankee prisoners were shunted all through the south, locked up in a score of improvised jails at Nashville, Atlanta, Tuscaloosa, Castle Thunder, and eventually Libby Prison in Richmond. "They guard us as closely as though we were wild beasts," Kenyon noted on March 9, 1862, while rumbling along in a freight car headed deeper and deeper into the hostile South.[9] The journey was concluded aboard a steamer which brought them to Tuscaloosa and a meeting with a certain Captain Henry Wirz, Swiss-born, and speaking with a guttural German accent. "As big a tyrant as ever ran," was Lieutenant Kenyon's verdict regarding this callous jailor.[10] (This was not, however, the Colonel Wirz who disgusted the nation a few years later after his tenure as camp commandant over a little piece of hell called Andersonville.) While at Tuscaloosa the men from the Eleventh suffered often at Wirz's hands who seemed ready, if not eager, to throw a man in chains upon the slightest pretext. Kenyon pondered the illogic in that offenders were often "pardoned" after promising they would never again violate the rules, but no one ever seemed to know just what "the rules" actually were. The lieutenant seethed in anger when the guards increased their brutalities. On April 17, a soldier was shot through the head for merely looking out the prison window. This abhorrence for his captors was reinforced by the often beastly, vulgar habits in which they indulged. Kenyon was from Chicago, a preacher's son, whose prison reading often touched on Dickens's *Tale of Two Cities* or Goldsmith's *Vicar of Wakefield*.[11] He was not impressed by one boorish Rebel guard who pointed out a passing Southern belle as his mate from the previous evening, saying: "You know that gal up thar, don't you? Well, I sat her the other night, you know. I sat her until plumb daylight, you know, and a danged smart gal she is too."[12] Increasingly Kenyon, as did many of his companions, turned inward, living in a fantasy universe. This was a mental refuge secure from daily monotony and the stench of unwashed, emaciated bodies. Kenyon wrote:

> There is one privilege that cannot be taken away from us, that is the freedom of thought. There is some little consolation in these dreary walls if it be nothing more than the roaming of our minds to the friends and scenes left at home. We can imagine where they are in what direction their thoughts are diverted and at night when visiting dreamland...how vivid are the impressions there received of scenes visited and friends communicated with...[13]

Except for daydreams, the only other event which the men relished was the evening meal, although the quality and quantity dwindled with each week. Kenyon recalled an endless, nauseating menu featuring rotten meat, or corn with the cob ground up. The result was a coarse revolting human feed, sometimes supplemented with dry lumps of blackeyed peas, a diet hardly adequate for a man in robust health, much less one convalescing from typhoid or nursing an infected battle wound.[14] There was no medical care, Kenyon asserted. Each day another Union prisoner died, principally as a result of hard prison fare and primitive living conditions typified by the fact that most made their evening beds on stone or wooden floors without blanket or coat for warmth. On June 25th, 1862, Kenyon confided to his diary how he assisted with the burial of two more victims:

> I helped put two men in their coffins last evening. They had lain so long, they were fly blown and the stench was almost unbearable. They use our men as though they were no account whatever, not according to them the common decencies of life.[15]

One week later he witnessed an even more grisly scene. The guards shot down a French-speaking Union soldier "without cause or provocation." Shot in the bowels, he died in agony--in Kenyon's viewpoint, "another victim to the inhumanity of the C.S.A." By the Fourth of July, Kenyon was still mentally healthy, and even contemplative:

> I little thought that this, the anniversary of our independence would find me a prisoner of war, not permitted to celebrate it as accustomed to and among those whose forefathers fought side-by-side with ours to gain this independence. Ah, little good did their suffering and privations come to if this work of desolation and disunion were permitted to go on unpunished and looked into futurity and seen the Union thrown to the four winds and their cherished principles trampled upon would they so freely have shed their blood through a long seven year war to gain a temporary peace? Many of them engaged in that struggle are scarcely in their graves when here their children are engaged in a war such as was never known...one portion to sustain the government in whole, the other trying to overthrow it an establish another which has in its very elements the seeds of discord...[16]

Kenyon's diary is a litany of crushed hopes and fading spirits. As the summer of 1862 burned down upon the sweltering prisoners, their condition worsened, particularly with the humiliating, painful onset of rampant diarrhea. Conditions did not improve after Union General Prentiss led a futile escape attempt September 14th while at Atlanta. The result was more stringent restrictions on the prisoners' freedom while the would-be escapees won a term in close-confinement:

> Before they took them away, they searched the building, bunks and baggage, and took away all files, canes and other instruments that I suppose they thought might be used as weapons...They appear to be as afraid of unarmed Yanks as though they were monsters that possessed supernatural strength.[17]

So it went, the tedious, unnerving limbo inflicting deep mental scars along with the physical ones. Kenyon philosophized regarding the natural ebb and flow of spirits. He observed that morale was highest at the beginning of each week, reinforced by the latest parole rumors. This optimism, he noted, seeped away, reaching a nadir on Sunday, "which is a very blue day, everyone with a face drawn down hardly venturing to crack a smile." The cycle was repeated, week after week, month after month, never ending, unless by a trip to the "Dead House."[18]

Kenyon's sojourn in the South finally did end with a trip to Aiken's Landing, Virginia, on October 13, 1862 where an exchange took place after more than eight months' captivity. Understandably, many were bitter, as reflected by Adjutant Hull from the 9th Michigan who labeled the Southland as "Dixie--The land of Snakes, Scorpions and Traitors."[19] Four hundred men in all, evenly divided between enlisted men and officers, were involved in the body trade at Aiken's Landing. "It really seemed as though we could hardly realize our change from the confines of Hell almost into the hands of our own government...,"[20] Kenyon noted in his diary. Incredibly, the young officer would return to the Eleventh within less than 30 days, joining the unit at Abbieville during the Holly Springs campaign. He was soon commander of Company K, taking the place of his old comrade, Captain Henry H. Carter, fallen at Shiloh. This little bantam-cock was soon back in the ring with little evident effect from the gruelling prison experience.

Adjustment came harder for others. In one case, it would prove an insurmountable barrier for a delicately handsome soldier with deep vulnerable brown eyes. Sergeant Frederick Eugene Ransom, younger brother to General Ransom himself, became a walking scar following his eight-month trial.

The 20-year-old sergeant had fought with Company E of the Eleventh at Donelson where he witnessed the tragic death of a boon companion, Sergeant Joe Leith. Ransom was wounded in the arm and captured by a tall, bearded horseman from Forrest's command. Eugene, as his family called him, was the youngest child who early on faced the challenge of living up to the accomplishments of his martyred father who fell at Chapultepec. Older brothers, Thomas and Dunbar, had gone West in his early years, the latter a regular army officer in the far northwest while Thomas surveyed the raw pioneer earth in Illinois.[21] In 1856, Eugene joined Thomas in Peru and for two years attended an academy for boys before moving on to Fayette in southern Illinois. There Thomas recruited what became Company E of the Eleventh. The younger brother served in the ranks, apparently quite contented, while Thomas rose up the promotional ladder, winning plaudits on every side. Dunbar, now an artillery captain in a New York company, distinguished himself at Bull Run for his professional capability and coolness under fire. For Eugene, the war was a brief one that ended in ignominious surrender on February 15, 1862. This marked the beginning of a much more intense battle: the struggle to regain his health. Eugene was among the paroled at

Aiken's Landing in October, and immediately enrolled as a patient at the General Hospital in Annapolis, Maryland. Some of his experiences are revealed by a poignant letter written December 12, 1862, by his mother, Mrs. Margaret Ransom, then of New York City. She was determined her son be transferred from Annapolis to Belleville Hospital where she might visit the depressed and ill boy. She requested the transfer through Dr. Simpson, medical director at Belleville, writing:

> Such being the case, will plead my excuse for taking the liberty of soliciting your kind attention. My son was wounded and taken prisoner...and confined some eight months...He has suffered so severely from ill health and cruel treatment while at Macon, Ga., that life was undesirable. For three months he lay unable to help himself, covered with vermin, and without a change of clothes throughout the imprisonment. His head is disfigured and become callous in consequence of lying so long on boards or stone. At one period, while in a weak and starving condition, he sat by the fire to warm himself. The rebel guard came towards him and kicked him into the fire, and both of his limbs were badly burned. My brother-in-law who saw my son soon after his arrival at Annapolis stated that the parts burned were still untreated, and also that the scars were quite deep and permanent. Will you pardon this detailed account of the hundredth part--of what is said--to have been the sufferings of my poor son? I regret to annoy you with them, and would not do so, did I not deem it necessary to show you how much he requires our care and sympathy...[22]

In May, 1863, Eugene Ransom rejoined the Eleventh after the unit had embarked with Grant's army on the great Vicksburg march. He, Kenyon, and so many others, carried into the campaign a personal burden etched in their souls by the prison ordeal. Their experiences would be related among their comrades, planting in many the angry seeds of hatred and vengeance that would result in the mass vandalism of the type that repelled General Ransom. He clung desperately to romantic notions that war could be waged by gentlemen in honorable combat. It was a fading dream, ever more apparent as the fighting grew increasingly bitter. Casualty lists soared beyond the human imagination, and the prisons in Richmond, Virginia and Rock Island, Illinois spat out their skeletal survivors. A grim awareness dawned that this was total war, a struggle to the hilt in which the concepts of chivalry became ever more absurd. The exhilaration of 1861 had been replaced by an implacable, relentless hostility, an Old Testament thirst for a final accounting.

Despite the enormous losses, the personal suffering, and the general weariness that comes following a long and bitter struggle, Colonel Nevius had few doubts regarding the fighting efficiency of the Eleventh Illinois Infantry in the opening months of 1863. Early in February, he wrote a close friend, Fred A. Horsman of Rockford, how "the health of the regiment" was excellent, adding that the Eleventh would "give a good account of itself as heretofore" during the expected summer campaigns.[23] Even more importantly, the continual recruiting problem was resolved in late April when the 109th Illinois Infantry Regiment was amalgamated into the Eleventh.[24] This was the "traitor regiment" which had spent the winter under armed guard. The 109th provided 389 presumably loyal recruits for the old Eleventh. For the first time since Bird's Point, the regiment would be at nearly full strength with 839 soldiers answering muster in late April. "...the men are good soldiers and do their duty as well as the older members of the regiment and a majority are well pleased at the transfer," reported Captain Henry Dean on May 1. His opinion was shared by Private Carrington who observed in his diary that the "new boys" were good fellows, easily fitting into the life of the regiment, evidently without serious questions raised concerning their loyalty or dependability.[25]

Colonel Nevius's optimism about the fighting efficiency of his re-vitalized regiment did not extend to the home front during that weary springtime. As were so many other combat officers, Nevius was aghast at the rising peace sentiment in the North. Especially prominent was the growing phenomenon called "Copperheadism." The movement was led by Senator Clement Vanlandingham of Ohio who was soon escorted to Rebel lines for his seditious activities. Nothing seemed more sure of incurring the wrath of the Northern rifleman than learning that dissension and defeatism were making deep inroads into civilian public opinion. It was doubly ironic that the men most involved, those who were paying the terrible price every day in wounds, sickness and death, were by and large the most loyal, the least disheartened. The Eleventh's commander addressed this issue in a scathing letter north which appeared March 7th in a Rockford, Illinois newspaper:

> I hear that you people, up North, are getting tired of the war. All I have to say, at present to all such is come and help us end it, by whipping the rebels. It is the only way it

can be ended with any credit to ourselves and justice to the generation that will follow us. I wish you to say to all such as think that the army is anxious to return home, that it is a fact, but not until they have whipped the rebels into the Union again, unless it is to punish the rebels at home. If some of those at home, who are crying peace, would hear the threats that are made by the brave boys who enlisted nearly two years ago to fight for the Union--and are not yet tired of fighting for it--they would be very careful what kind of peace measure they imposed on the country. If the voice of the whole army could be heard on this matter in our Legislatures, they would think about looking for some other country to live in when the soldiers returned home, for I will assure you their vengeance though slow, will be terrible...[26]

When the weather grew more conducive to campaigning, the re-born Eleventh girded for the coming ordeal. The beginning was marked by the sound of thunderous cannonading on the night of April 16th, 1863. A Union gunboat flotilla ran past the Vicksburg batteries, losing but one man in the process. "Altogether it was a decided success," Colonel Nevius wrote home, "for our side. It gives us complete control of the river between Vicksburg to Port Hudson...Tonight (April 22) it is the intention to run six more transports below Vicksburg."[27] It was part of Grant's grand strategy, for these would ferry his army across the Mississippi from Hard Times Landing to Bruinsburg where they would then strike out on hard, open ground for the Confederate armies at Jackson and Vicksburg. But the first requisite was that the vulnerable transports successfully negotiate a formidable gauntlet of heavy artillery supplemented by a number of primitive calcium searchlights and bonfires designed to illuminate any passing steamer. Steamboat crews were not eager at the prospect, and Grant sent out a call for volunteers, preferably men with river experience. Even Colonel Nevius was tempted by the opportunity:

As soon as it was known that volunteers were wanted more than enough made application to go...So great is the desire to get a chance to be one of the selected ones, that officers are volunteering to go and act as coal heavers. More than half of my officers made application to go but I could not let them all go so I selected out those whom I wanted to try it. If I was not the only field officer with my regiment, I should be tempted to go myself, but as it is, I will not think of it...[28]

That night, the frustrated men left behind at the Eleventh's Lake Providence camp once again heard the cacophony of cannonading when the steamers dashed past Vicksburg. Last in line was the *Horizon* commanded by Captain George Kinnard with Lieutenant James D. Vernay of the Eleventh Illinois acting as executive officer. Rebel batteries were well warmed to their task by the time the *Horizon* churned past. They riddled the steamer with 15 heavy shot. Cannon balls smashed into a smoke stack, plowed into the cabin admidships, and crashed into the hurricane deck. Miraculously, not one shell struck her in the vitals.[29] Captain W.S. Oliver aboard the *Tigress* would later recall: "Only those who faced this terrible concentrated fire, or who witnessed it from Vicksburg...can have the faintest idea of its beauty...The gunners at work could be distinctly seen and a newspaper could be read with ease from the hurricane deck..."[30] Oliver's own boat was smashed into a drifting shambles, and finally sank two miles below the batteries. The other five boats were "riddled from stem to stern" but would still serve their purpose.[31] The first part of the plan had been completed. Now the army could march.

Grant's army crossed at Hard Times, streaming over the river into the exposed Confederate underbelly--finally free from the turbid swamplands and tired military dogmas that insisted on formal, well-defined supply lines. This new army traveled light and moved with amazing speed along the dusty Mississippi roads. The men supplemented their diet, or supplied it in whole, from the surrounding countryside. The Eleventh Illinois was not among the first units over the river because, along with the remainder of Ransom's Second Brigade, they were assigned the important, but hardly exciting, rear guard role. They moved out on April 26, 1863 at 2 a.m., each man with 100 rounds of ammunition and ten days' rations. Their departure was accompanied by a strong admonition from General Ransom:

> All unnecessary firing, straggling, entering houses, pillaging or abuse of citizens, will be punished with the extreme vigor of military discipline. The commanding Genl. is determined that the Brigade shall maintain its fair reputation for soldierly conduct everywhere...[32]

With this warning stinging in their ears the men were off. They helped build a roadway from Richmond to Perkin's Plantation, and safeguarded the communication lines connecting the rear elements with the advance guard. It was vital, if tedious, work as the brigade was engaged, in Ransom's words, in the exhaustive task of "cleaning up the whole debris of the Army in advance..."[33] May 10th arrived, and word came that a new communications line had been opened from Young's Point. The Second Brigade could abandon its former duties and set out in pursuit of the advancing Union army crossing the Mississippi. On May 12 the brigade marched and were ferried over at Grand Gulf, Mississippi. Only a few weeks previously, Colonel Nevius had written with great optimism about the new campaign.

> We are now in splendid condition for a fight. We were never so well prepared before. How long it will be before we shall have done, none of us can tell, but if you don't hear of some warm work near Vicksburg before another thirty days go by, I shall be disappointed...The troops are ready and anxiously waiting for the order to cross the river, Then look out...[34]

Grant opted for a daring strike eastward. He dispatched his army toward Jackson with the objective of splitting the Confederate forces in two, leaving the Vicksburg garrison isolated from further reinforcement. This was the course the Eleventh followed when it marched from Grand Gulf. The men choked and gasped in the billowy dust stirred by thousands strung out ahead. Perceptive and observant as always, Private Carrington wrote of the expressions on the faces of these marching soldiers:

> Strong hearty fellows, hardened by miles of marching. We notice their faces, some look tired, some gay and careless, others sober as they realize what all this means. Then the jolly joker, keeping a whole regiment in good cheer. So they go. Many of these stalwart forms will meet a soldier's fate in the coming days...[35]

It was a hard march through an exotic countryside. The Midwesterners gawked in wonder when the column skipped over a decaying eight-foot alligator carcass sprawled in the dusty road. The command departed from Grand Gulf in blistering heat on May 13th, marching 18 hard miles until the halt sounded. Carrington remembered:

> I scrambled over the fence, took off my cap, loosened up my equipment, while the boys brought a canteen of water. Resting in the shade of the magnolias that were in bloom, I soon rested. When the bugle again sounded the forward,

took my place in ranks all right. (The nearest I ever came to giving out on the march.) The yellow dust was nearly four inches deep as the other divisions had marched ahead of our Brigade with artillery and cavalry, besides wagons and all that goes to make up an Army on the march. The dust would hang on the eye brows, hair moustache, settle all over our uniforms and equipments. Faces streaked with perspiration until we were a hard looking outfit...[36]

The march was a horrible ordeal. The men were grateful for an early 2 p.m. encampment near a crystal clear creek. Private Henry Uptmor would always remember the lovely grove nearby with its merciful shade and the cold, clear brook water. "We can thank the dear good Lord for having provided such a beautiful place for us, where we may peacefully rest," he would write. "No one knows what this means to a soldier, how precious it is to him who so often must be under the open heavens."[37] The respite was only temporary, for this would be a week for hard marches. The regiment ground out 13 miles one day and 20 the next. At every opportunity men of the Second Brigade ignored General Ransom's specific injunction against firing civilian dwellings. Revenge was to have its way and the army rapidly become an armed host of incendiaries. Ransom was angered at the senseless destruction and, at one point, halted the brigade to threaten harsh punishment for any soldier engaging in arson. It was a futile gesture. Even as Ransom spoke, Lieutenant Colonel Joseph Stockton of the 72nd Illinois Infantry saw a half-dozen homes just down the road begin to curl into smoke and flame.

On May 16th, the Eleventh passed through a dead man's land outside Raymond, where the advanced elements had fought a bitter fight a few days before. It was an awful wasteland strewn with broken weapons, hastily dug graves, and trees disfigured by bullet and solid cannon shot. Later in the evening, the men heard the muffled cannon and distant battle sounds of another battle in full progress which incited Ransom who, in Carrington's words, was "wild to get in with his Brigade."[39] It was not to be, and with sunset the Eleventh ventured out into an even more recent battlefield on which the dead had been gathered in preparation of burial. This brutal meeting place would later be called Champion Hill, and the battle here marked a turning point. Even at that moment other Union troops were leaving the strategic rail junction and supply depot at Jackson in smouldering ruins. Grant's army had accomplished the grand design. He had splintered General John C. Pemberton's army from General Joe Johnston's force and then smashed the former at Champion Hill. Northern-born General Pemberton was left with no choice but to retire toward Vicksburg with the Federals in close pursuit. It was a significant accomplishment although the great mass of those participating had only a vague concept of what was transpiring. Certainly Private Carrington of the Eleventh was too appalled at the grisly aftermath for lengthy reflections on military strategy or historical consequences:

> In a ravine lay a great number of the rebel dead, mostly Georgia troops. They had worn large white hats--many of these were lying on the ground with bullet holes in them showing the deadly fire of our men...nearly all were shot in the head. I noticed when the brain is pierced by a bullet, the body stiffens in the position the soldier occupied when struck. If at a charge, the hands and arms remain so. He may drop the musket, or if in the act of loading, the right arm will be extended or raised...Near a Spring the Boys found quite a pile of pictures and trinkets taken from the pockets of the Confederate dead. One...brought me a picture of some "Mother in Israel" who will wait and mourn for the son who will never return.[40]

There was little time for philosophy. The very next morning the column was on the march, pushing to the Big Black River where a half-hearted Confederate stand withered before an attack spearheaded by Brigadier General M.K. Lawler's brigade. More prisoners and more captured cannon, came into Union hands while the men busily prepared to bridge the mud-brown river--the only barrier between them and Pemberton's reeling army. Four bridges were built, with one assigned to Ransom's brigade. The Eleventh's old commander supervised every move. His immediate order was that an old cotton gin and a few other nearby buildings be torn down for usable timber. Huge trees bordering the river were quickly toppled into ths stream "still fast to the stump." These would serve as the underpinning for the makeshift structure. By 9 a.m. the next morning, the troops were marching once again, bound for Vicksburg only 17 miles distant. Young Ransom was catching the eye of high command for his efficient deportment as brigade commander. U.S. Grant would remark that the 28-year-old was competent, at the very least, for corps command. He described Ransom as "a most gallant and intelligent volunteer officer."[41]

In the days ahead there would be a need for intelligence and gallantry, for Pemberton's fleeing thousands were already recovering from the week's heavy punishment. Behind an interconnecting maze of trenches at Vicksburg, the thirty-five thousand Confederate troops braced for an assault which had to be conducted across open ground, providing a natural field of fire for the defenders. The important question was: Had the dazed Rebels recovered their morale following Champion Hill, Raymond, the Big Black, and the other recent Union victories? If they hadn't, all the fortifications in the world couldn't save them. Grant's army smelled blood, and was pawing at the door to Vicksburg. Grant made his first assault May 19th at about 1 p.m. on a hot and dry morning. Ransom advanced a "strong line of skirmishers," fanning out in front of the brigade, feeling out the Confederate defenses.[42] It was cautious work for the Eleventh while the men scrambled up and down the steep ravines. "Occasionally a musket bullet passed over our heads singing its unfriendly song," Carrington recalled.[43] By 2 p.m., the regiment pressed to within 500 yards of the prominent Rebel works known as the Third Louisiana Redan in plain view. It was then that the order to advance was given. Rebel artillery raked the charging Union lines.

> I could see in an angle of the rebel Fort, the cannoneers working a small gun while we were in full view and not more than three or four hundred yards distant. They fired shot after shot while we kept up a lively dodging and soon reached cover.[44]

Ransom's troops were stalled in a tangle of underbrush and abatis stewn in front of the Rebel positions. The assaulting infantrymen were helpless while the enemy poured into them a "terrific fire of musketry," according to Ransom's official report.[45] Private Uptmor of Company K would write how the terrain, along with the primitive obstacles placed by the defenders, doomed the assault. "It was not possible," he wrote, "for the mountains were too steep and too much wood had been piled up and hammered together...the enemy had organized within and had the opportunity to kill us all, and our losses were so heavy that we soon saw we had to retreat."[46] All across the board it was the same mournful story: heavy resistance from Rebels grown confident behind a formidable defense position dug into the hilly, ravine-spotted countryside. Grant's army made miniscule progress during the assault, and suffered heavy casualties. Miraculously, Nevius's Eleventh lost only a few wounded, as did Ransom's brigade which now included the 95th Illinois, the 72nd Illinois, the 14th Wisconsin, and the 17th Wisconsin. Total Union casualties on the 19th were 900 killed and wounded. Ransom's men dug intrenchments, and were soon blazing away at the enemy. For the next two days it was a constant sniper's battle, and occasionally the fighting drew battery fire from both sides. At night, the Union mortars belched out their great sputtering, red projectiles in high lazy arcs that ended with roars in the Rebel fortress.

During the early hours of the morning on May 22nd, General Ransom reconnoitered the Confederate defenses. He and several other Union officers found a vantage point that provided cover from the Rebel snipers. It was there that Ransom betrayed the morbid humor of the fatalist. Everyone had been using a fine set of field glasses belonging to a certain Colonel Wright of Chicago. Ransom turned toward that man, it was told, and "jocosely" remarked: "Colonel, if you are killed I want you to leave that glass to me." Lieutenant Colonel Stockton of the 72nd Illinois interrupted the exchange to remind Wright that he had promised the glasses to his son. In fact, he had stated so in his will. Later in the day, Colonel Wright was wounded on the field, and died weeks later in Chicago.[47]

May 22nd, 1863, was a fine spring day with the Deep South sun burning down its warmth. It marked the beginning of a massive Union assault against the Vicksburg intrenchments. Grant ordered an attack by all three army corps from one end of the defenses to the other. Ransom's brigade was up at dawn's light, forming in column, and then preceding toward the forward area where the men would then creep ahead as close upon the Rebel works as possible. Order and counterorder came while the morning hours wore away. The men lay there fidgeting in the hot sun, wondering what the next few minutes would bring. It would hardly be a surprise assault because the Rebels were already splattering the Union advanced positions with a continuous spray of rifle fire. Ransom's brigade was lucky enough, in that the terrain allowed the forward elements to approach within 60 yards of the Confederate lines. It would only entail a brief dash to reach the enemy heavily massed behind the earthen fortification. The Rebels would undoubtedly open up with fury when the first Bluecoat appeared out on the naked ground below. Private Carrington wrote:

> We formed in columns of companies right in front, closed en masse. As it happened, our company was at the foot of the hill. The intention was to forward and deploy advance. Lying here waiting for other Regt's to get in position, and for the word to forward...chewing [sugar] canes that

were growing at our feet to keep our minds from what we knew was coming. A woodpecker lit on an old dead snag sounding a tattoo with his bill [and]then flew away with a 'churp'--Happy woodpecker. Saw a man in our uniform, unharmed...walk up the hill to the right of the column lying there. He reached nearly the top when a musket bullet struck him in the shoulder and sent him whirling. He came down the hill and landed on a brush pile--'kerslap' there he sat looking so foolish. I had to laugh in spite of the deadly surroundings...[48]

Ransom initiated the battle by calmly walking out into the fire zone and calling on his brigade to assault. His men emerged in the open with a unanimous shout which dwarfed the cannon roar now rising from the front.[49] Instantly, the column front disintegrated before what Ransom described as "one continuous blaze of musketry." All the while "the artillery on my left threw enfilading shot and shell...with deadly effect."[50] Nevius was at the head of the "Old Eleventh". He had barely yelled out, "Now men, charge with a will," when struck in the forehead by a Rebel musket ball. Carrington saw the limp body dragged back moments later, "the blood and brain" flowing from the gaping hole in Nevius' skull.[51] As at Shiloh, the first few minutes were the most deadly. Ransom's brigade suffered a twenty-five percent casualty figure during an unbelievably brief time span. One anonymous infantryman from the Eleventh recalled how the forward elements were "mown down as grass." He described the charge as "most terrible, for no matter where we might appear, the rebels, from their works, would have a cross fire upon us from four different directions."[52] This participant claimed that nine out of ten attackers would have fallen had the assault been pressed. Instead, after the first traumatic shock, the majority of the brigade "crawfished" back a few rods, seeking cover from the never-ending Rebel fire.[53]

"The bullets and the shells flew over our heads...One is not safe from them a single second," was how Private Uptmor of Company K remembered that awful day.[54] After the first onslaught, the survivors were being picked off as they squirmed into shallow depressions in the ground or sought refuge behind the bodies of the fallen. Private Frederick Hardten and Sergeant Frank Whipple from the Eleventh "hooked the ground near a stump" only to have a sputtering 24-pound cannon shell roll between them. "We gave it a roll down the hill, and it went off below in the deep Ravine," Hardten would later write. "I can't help but remember Company K, the 72nd Regiment. Colonel Starling said: 'Come on

Company K! Come on Company K! I'll bet on Company K!' And Company K did not go but remained."[55] There in the very center of the fire storm, General Ransom demonstrated a supernatural courage. He continually exposed his person while mustering the remnants of the brigade for a final push into the Rebel works. He seized the colors of the 95th Illinois, waving the standard back and forth as a rallying point, crying out: "Forward men! We must and will go into that fort!" The 14th Wisconsin spearheaded the impulsive rush right to the very brow of the enemy's intrenchments, where the men huddled temporarily safe, yet unable to go over the top which was raked by Rebel fire. Ransom was very near the enemy works where elements from his brigade planted four stands of colors.[56] Ransom's men clung beneath the Rebel earthworks. They were like the child who has clambered high up a sheer cliff face to reach a point where courage can no longer drive him higher nor can he retrace the precarious path that brought him there.

Twenty minutes, or at most a half-hour, passed with the brigade huddled under the enemy guns. It was time enough for Ransom to realize further progress was impossible while a retreat could leave the retiring column dangerously vulnerable. General Ransom opted for an orderly retirement, setting an example by striding back out in perfect view of the Rebel lines and climbing atop a large stump crying out: "Men of the Second Brigade! We cannot maintain this position. You must retire to the cover of that ravine, one regiment at a time, and in order. Move slowly. The first man who runs or goes beyond the ravine shall be shot on the spot. I will stand here and see how you do it."[57] The 17th Wisconsin provided a covering fire while the remaining regiments withdrew under Ransom's watchful eye. During the movement, a captain from the 72nd Illinois, a Ransom intimate, crawled out on hands and knees begging the general to step down from his dangerous perch. The only reply was a snarling: "Silence!"[58]

Ransom's charge and subsequent withdrawal were witnessed by members of the 124tb Illinois who were then taking up positions further in the Union rear. They enjoyed a panoramic view of the futile struggle. "We could see the wreaths of blue smoke curling over the rebel earthworks as their rifles cracked, right and left, directly under our exploding shells, as though they were not harming them in the least," recalled Chaplain R.L. Howard.[59] "Our men advanced, under Blair and Ransom, on the double-quick, in full view of our position. Some reeled and fell, others pressing on, gained the works and planted their flags upon them, but they could not enter, and after a fierce struggle for a few moments they sank down on the outside under the friendly cover.

It was of no use, they were too few, and the enemys fire was too galling...The wounded crawled under the shelter of logs where they could. The dead lay there in sight..."[60]

Ransom's withdrawal left behind a number of troops from the 17th Wisconsin who were so far forward that they had to await the cover of darkness before crawling back toward Union lines. The attack had been a bloody repulse although the Eleventh was fortunate in incurring only 53 casualties, as compared to the battered 95th Illinois, whose losses were 161 killed and wounded. Ransom's brigade alone suffered 476 casualties that terrible May 22nd. In total, Grant's army expended 3,199 in dead and wounded for negligible gain. Private Carrington of the Eleventh wrote in his diary how the regiment was greatly "disheartened" following this bloody repulse. Another survivor from the "Old Eleventh" would bitterly write how the attack resulted in "nothing gained." One soldier mourned the loss of Colonel Nevius, writing that "a more noble, brave and patriotic man never fell. Every man seemed to feel that all was gone and lost in him. I fear that the 11th will never be again what it has been...."[62]

Chapter Seven

Lighting in the Evening Sky

Three days passed before they buried the May 22nd dead. The ghoulish duty was performed during a brief cease-fire which barely allowed time enough for a hasty interment on the spot. Details from the Eleventh Illinois participated in this ghastly chore. Men shuddered at the sight of those festering corpses, ballooning up under the callous sun. Henry Uptmor of Company K would remember, even 60 years later, how the fallen "were nearly consumed with worms."[1] Equally horrified was Private Carrington of Company B. He graphically described how the dead lay with "their faces turned black and fingers like bird's claws."[2] Thankfully, there would be no more wild charges across this killing ground. Grant was reconciled to a patient siege following the bloody failures on May 19th and May 22nd, 1863.

The spade, rather than the bayonet, would lead the way into Vicksburg. The Union army took to the ground all around the perimeter of the Rebel fortress. At night men from the Eleventh Illinois and the other Union regiments scratched out the rudimentary beginning of a vast trench network, nibbling ever closer upon the Confederate works. Lieutenant James H. Coates now commanded the Eleventh Illinois. Evidently, he had conquered, or at least controlled, his heavy drinking. Nevius always considered his executive officer a man of many virtues marred only by this one crucial failing. Certainly, he was one of the most experienced regimental officers, enlisting at Camp Yates for the ninety-day service and then rejoining at Bird's Point for a three-year term. The Eleventh's new commander was a native of Norristown, Pennsylvania, born there in 1831. At the age of 14, the lad journeyed to Philadelphia and enrolled in a military school for boys, learning the complex army drill which would later prove eminently useful. Lieutenant Colonel Coates journeyed west in the early 1850's, taking up residence at Peru, Illinois, at about the time that young Ransom was surveyor in the same Illinois river town. No evidence exists, however, to indicate that during this period the two were acquainted. Coates was engaged in the grain business at Peru, and in neighboring LaSalle, but just before the war's outbreak he moved the concern into Chicago.[3]

The call to arms brought him back to LaSalle to raise a company among his friends there. Traveling with those volunteers to Camp Yates, he discovered that the Illinois quota for three-month volunteers was already filled. Coates was undaunted, offering Colonel Wallace his services as a drillmaster without either commission or pay. His brief military biography states that Coates subsisted, during those first few months, on donations provided by fellow officers. Now in the summer of 1863, this slender, mustached, thirty-one-year-old officer found himself commanding the veteran Eleventh, succeeding the highly respected Wallace, Ransom and Nevius, two of whom already had been shot down in battle. It was a heady responsibility, particularly since the regiment was in the midst of the siege on Vicksburg. Nevius's memory was still fresh in the minds of the regiment. The newly promoted Colonel Coates expressed that loss with characteristic 19th-century sentimentality, in a letter written to the fallen officer's mother residing in Lodi, New York:

> My Dear Madame: It is with feelings of the most exquisite pleasure, that I am enabled through the directions of the officers and men of the old 11th, to forward to you as token of regard, for the mother of the late Colonel, The Flag of the Regiment, carried by it through many charges and trying scenes. ...Please accept it my Dear Madame as an offering of friendship to you, from rough but grateful soldiers, and, as you at times look upon the faded and tattered Stars and Stripes, may your heart be gladdened by the positive reflection that your lamented son held a firm and undying hold upon the affections of the officers and men of his command. The officers and men unite with me, in many and kind wishes for your long life and happiness: and with many personal assurances of regard, I remain, Madame, your obedient Servant.[4]

General Ransom, as commander of the Second Brigade and immediate superior to Coates, still imprinted his personality on the Eleventh Illinois and the other four regiments within the command. Ransom was constantly in the firing lines, superintending the tedious digging, instructing the men where advanced batteries should be placed, and displaying a talent for organization. Typically, Ransom's total contempt for his health needs during the siege worried his subordinates.[5] The surgeons were also deeply concerned about the general's eroding physical condition. When the Rebels were rumored to be contemplating a sortie, or when intelligence reported the possibility that a Confederate relief column under General Joseph Johnston was approaching from the east, Ransom would re-double his already strenuous efforts. He allowed himself only four hours sleep a day when these crises threatened and restricted that brief rest period to mid-day. By these means Ransom was awake all through the evening and early morning hours--times thought most likely for Rebel attack. "He superintended his own section of the works with unceasing vigilance," wrote a contemporary magazine author, "always acting under a sense of personal responsibility for the lives committed to his care."[6] Captain Cyrus Dickey documented in his letters home how General Ransom won everyone's admiration for his May 22nd exploits. As assistant adjutant, Dickey had been at Ransom's side during the costly assault. The young officer was awed by his commander's audacious valor: "Ransom shone, as usual, above all the others," he wrote his sister, Ann Wallace in Illinois. "There are none like him in this battle...always where the danger was greatest, always cool and confident."[7]

As the siege matured, the Union forces slowly tightened the coil. There was a routine in this systematic strangulation. It was almost as if events followed a master script in a stately ballet of death. During the hours of daylight, movement in the killing zone between the lines was non-existent. Both sides maintained a patter of rifle fire that, on occasion, soared in its intensity until it resembled the full-blown roar of open battle. More often the muggy, summer air was silent, split apart only by the sniper rifle's isolated crack. Like so many venomous reptiles, these cold marksmen would wait for hours on end for any enemy soldier to grow careless or too curious; then, they would strike like a rattler. Sniping had become a profession and, within a few weeks, few Union or Confederate soldiers dared even to expose a hand above the parapet. Private Carrington described how he would hold up a shovel over the trench, fascinated when the shining metal was struck by four and five bullets in as many seconds.[8] Nighttime was better; the digging would resume as the infantrymen clawed out first a shallow indentation for protection, then deepened and widened the slit. By the next morning the Rebels gazed upon another ominous new extension in the Union rifle pits. The greatest amount of the digging proceeded under cover of darkness, although in certain areas which provided sufficient protection troops continued excavation by daylight. The Rebels were increasingly nervous, often keeping up their harrassing rifle fire all through the night in a vain attempt at frustrating the construction efforts. On May 25th, Carrington described his first experience in the firing line:

> Early this morning finds us in the rifle pits. My position was at an angle exposed off to the right. Having a spade, I soon fixed the ditch deep enough to protect me...Their line of works is about 200 yards in front. I aimed at the top of their pits and fired. I got a return shot quickly, struck the dirt about two inches below the top...We exchanged a few shots but as I had no protection for my head, concluded to rest awhile. Not a man could be seen on their works. The man next to my left was located behind a stump that happened to be in that part of the line. He also opened fire, got a shot in return that hit the stump making the splinters fly. It was so close, he turned pale and sat down...[9]

With each passing day the siege lines became more extensive and infinitely more elaborate. Ransom constructed a covered way large enough so that an artillery piece could be carried right up to the front lines. This deep trench was completely protected from enemy fire, as the top was covered along its entire length by heavy logs piled high with dirt. Cannon emplacements were designed with protective mantelets which could be swung open from the inside just before firing, and quickly closed before Rebel bullets swarmed in answer. Private Carrington asserted that plowshares were confiscated from nearby farmers and converted into bullet-proof shields for the Union snipers. A slot was cut through the steel for the rifle before the assembly was placed atop the parapet, and then packed in from with dirt-filled gunny sacks for added safety. Imaginative expedients like this provided a degree of immunity, but even secure rifle posts were extremely dangerous as marksmen on both sides developed uncanny proficiency. They watched for the tell-tale darkening of an enemy loophole, indicating a soldier had taken up his firing position, and then drilled the careless soldier right through the head. Darkness wasn't always a guarantee, either. Later in the siege, Corporal Charles Hindman of Company I unwittingly lit a match before checking his watch for the time. He fell dead instantly from a Rebel bullet which sped right through the loophole, crashing into his skull just below the left eye. It was a superb shot made in the pitch black night.[10]

The Eleventh was burrowed into the hillside by the time Surgeon Oliver G. Hunt from Sandwich rejoined the regiment in early June. The medical officer was incredulous at the grimy living conditions made infinitely worse by the brutal Mississippi sun now burning down with sizzling intensity. Surgeon Hunt wrote home to tell how the regiment nested in the hillside where men lived like so many "ground hogs." He painted a revolting picture of trench life, recording how the Eleventh's encampment "abounds in dirt, ticks, lice, fleas, mosquitoes, lizards, and last, but not least, snakes." Not surprisingly, Hunt describes the campaign as one of the most arduous yet undertaken.[11] At the brigade hospital the tents were crowded with sickened, exhausted soldiers. Every day the number of patients grew, with more than 90 sick and wounded in the hospital by June 7th. It was an unreal, bizarre world. Hunt observed that he went about half-erect for hours "fearing that the top of my head would be blown-off if I dared straighten myself out...Woe to the man who showed himself on either side." A relatively well-educated, keenly perceptive individual, Surgeon Hunt provided a vivid portrait of siege life for the folks back home:

> From sunrise to sunset, and from sunset to sunrise, there is one constant and continuous cannonade going on, and this is also accompanied with constant fire of musketry and rifles. You have some idea of it from your recollections of Shiloh but here it is worse if anything, and the devoted city, with its inhabitants, is fast being destroyed, and still the rebels refuse to surrender. A great many women and children refused to leave the city when Grant offered them the privilege and now they can't get away...Many women and children have been wounded and maimed, and now are living in holes in the ground--the only refuge from shot and shell. The view by night is grand and sublime...We first see the flash of the mortars like lightning in the evening sky, then comes the distant booming of the explosion...rumbling and reverberating up and down the river, like the thunders of a tornado, then we see rising up immediately before what seems to be a small shooting star. This goes up for a distance of at least one mile and a half, and seems to poise itself over the doomed city, when it commences its descent. Sometimes it reaches the ground before its explosion, but often it explodes in air, vivdly lighting up the whole scenery. Although we are accustomed to the noise and not even notice

it in the daytime yet it becomes so loud in the night as to keep us awake...[12]

Rebel batteries threw out a withering counter-barrage. The Union rear area became as dangerous a place to be as the most exposed rifle pit. Captain Cyrus Dickey estimated that sixty 100-pound shells struck the Second Brigade front every day. On June 17th, he related how Ransom's headquarters came under heavy nine-inch mortar fire literally leaving bushel-baskets of shrapnel littering the ground nearby. Dickey was amazed that the unnerving bombardment caused so few casualties, writing: "It is astonishing that these missles do not do more execution."[13] Illustrative of this phenomenon was an incident in which General Ransom and Major Waddell of the Eleventh attended a staff meeting conducted near the Union siege guns. About fifty officers were present including General McArthur, 6th Division Commander, and General James McPherson, commander of the XVII Corps. The conference was shattered into adjournment by a large Rebel mortar shell which buried itself three feet into the earth and exploded right in the center of the incredulous officers. Captain Dickey claimed that the blast completely buried Major Waddell while "scattering dirt over the whole party."[14] Incredibly, not a man was seriously injured. The great killer continued to be aimed rifle fire and not the noisy but usually ineffective cannon bombardment.

One of the more imaginitive members of the Eleventh soon thought he possessed the solution for this deadly sniping game. Private J.D. Lyon of Company B was an ingenious soldier who envisioned a bullet-proof look-out. A soldier could plink away farom this protected vantage point all day at the Confederate lines. In his dreams, Lyon constructed this perfect sniper's perch that was impervious to bullet, shot and shell. His brainstorm was received with little enthusiasm. Undaunted, the determined Lyon proceeded to implement his project singlehanded. Every night for two weeks Lyon labored on his dream. He planted poles in the ground, surrounded by hogsheads packed with clay, and topped it off with a platform shielded by heavy wood. He completed the structure on June 2nd, climbed up into his perch before dawn, and poked his Enfield through the narrow firing slit in eager preparation for the day's shooting. Carrington recorded the results:

> Just back of Fort Hill, [Third Louisiana Redan], he saw two Johnnies, sitting in the smoke of a small fire eating

breakfast. He first sighted at one then the other. Finally, [he] decided to take the right hand man--only about 75 yards. Aiming, pulled the trigger. As he did so someone just west of him over their breastworks must have been watching for the report of his musket. From the noise under and around and on the outside of that "look out"--there must have been a dozen shots fired...Three bullets penetrated and went right through those hard seasoned staves (two thicknesses) and one hitting the opposite side. He wasn't long in getting down...Break of day did not catch any of the Boys in that place. But after dark it was a fine place to watch the mortar shells and the night firing artillery, etc., to gaze at the stars and wonder what they were doing at home.[15]

 The men tolerated, and even joked about, the strange world they inhabitated. Its idle moments could at any time explode into violence whether from a random shell or the sniper's premeditated attack. The rank and file from the Eleventh lounged in the relative safety of the more elaborate rifle pits, reading worn back issues of newspapers from home, or tattered editions of *Harper's Weekly* or perhaps *Frank Leslie's Illustrated Magazine*. A few feet away their on-duty comrades blazed away at the Rebel lines through the narrow, visor-like rifle ports. Back behind the outer line, the men might curl up in hillside caves shaded from the sun's direct glare by crudely constructed bamboo roofs. Often these "shebangs" nearly became instant graves for the inhabitants when a shell landed nearby or when a sudden summer rain caused the hillside to shift, burying the sleeping soldiers in suffocating mud.[16] Interestingly enough, many soldiers avoided digging personal shelters, but would rent a hole when the Rebel shelling worsened. Captain Dickey informed his sister, Ann, how good holes were a fine real estate investment for the more enterprising and energetic among the command. "During a bombardment from the enemy these caves are at a premium," Dickey wrote. "The boys who have not dug caves for themselves try to buy out others who have...Good caves today run-up at $2.00 to $2.50 this afternoon, but are at a discount this evening since the Lines have become quiet..."[17]

 This was a very intimate war in the trenches around Vicksburg. The proximity of the lines allowed, at many points, opportunities for nightly conversation between the rival forces. Captain Dickey wrote home in late May how one advanced trench in the Second Brigade area was so near the Rebel lines that he could easily toss a chunk of dirt over the parapet into the enemy rifle pits. Daily evening dialogues were often conducted in a perfectly normal conversational tone as the troops "poked" jokes at one another. "They are not much disposed to deal in compliments," Dickey noted.[18] Comrade-in-arms Carrington concurred. He recalled one evening's exchange beginning when a nearby Yankee called out, asking how the Rebels liked their new commanding general. "What General?," came the hesitant reply. "Why General Starvation," was the chortled retort. On another occasion, an unseen Rebel demanded that the Yanks tell him when they intended to visit Vicksburg. This brought forth the quip: "Soon as we get hungry for mule beef." And, so, the nightly repartee continued until first light, when the killing resumed.[19] Union confidence was at a high by early June, reinforced now and again by the occasional Rebel deserter crawling in bearing grisly tales of suffering and misery within the river fortress. Surgeon Hunt of the Eleventh wrote home June 7th:

> I have just seen Major Waddell (11th Ill.) who is officer of the day and is just from our front. One of our men yesterday took a peep just for a moment over the hill, and got a ball between his eyes, which killed him instantly...I have on several occasions, suffered my curiosity to take me to the same place, and have as often had a leaden messenger of death flit by my head. Since then I have been entirely satisfied with the range of vision up to the sky and my rear. The rebels are starving in Vicksburg. Maj. Waddell this morning saw a rebel major who had just deserted from the city, and who stated that last night they ate up the last morsel of meat, and now have nothing but corn, which they parch and eat. He says that most of the women and children are collected together under the bluff near a large church...He told Waddell that he saw them just before he left, and they were the most pitiable looking objects his eyes ever rested upon. They would fall upon their knees to every officer that came amongst them, supplicating that they save them from destruction...General Grant said yesterday evening that in three days his boat would land at the wharf in Vicksburg--God grant that it may be so.[20]

Hunt's optimism was premature. Grant would not glimpse the Vicksburg wharf for many weeks, while the Eleventh Illinois and the other besieging regiments continued the deadly sniping as they burrowed their way nearer the enemy entrenchments. The "Old Eleventh" and its former commander General Ransom were not forgotten back in Illinois; news of the May 22nd attack made a great impression. On June 1st, the *Chicago Tribune* mourned that "the Eleventh is always brave; it has a reputation which cannot be called in question, it has been proven on too many battlefields..."[21] Five days later that influential paper saluted General Ransom as a superb soldier with the "record never surpassed, and hardly equalled, in the history of this or any other war."[22] Ransom's fellow officers were equally impressed, taking part in a special awards ceremony held just behind the lines in the latter part of June. Corps Commander General James B. McPherson and division Commander General John McArthur spoke in glowing terms of Ransom's military virtues and honored him with a gold medal commemorating the May 22nd attack. The twenty-eight-year-old General also received a sword, sash, a pair of fine revolvers, a set of field glasses, and other accouterments valued at $600. "The elegance and expense of the gifts, together with the high officers present and participating, rendered the occasion rather an unusual one of the kind," reported the *Chicago Tribune* correspondent. "No Illinoisan will doubt the worthiness of the recipient."[23] Ransom's stock was rising both at home and within the army, most notably with red-bearded General William Tecumseh Sherman, XV Corps commander. Courage was a quality understood and appreciated by this blunt-spoken, no-nonsense officer who expounded the philosophy of total war. "Cump" observed the May 22nd onslaught and was at once captivated by Ransom's daring. Years later he would recall those first impressions:

> His appearance was almost boyish, with blonde hair, blue eyes, a fair complexion, and, though of slender form, he had the bearing of a gallant soldier. War is the supreme test of manhood, and an hour--a minute sometimes--reveals the spirit which is in the man; the grasp of the hand, the flash of the eye, the unspoken word which trembles on the lips...tell more than a volume can record. I saw Ransom during the assault of the 22nd of May 1863--saw his brigade dash against the battlements to be hurled back... I then marked him as of the kind of whom heroes are made.[24]

The men in the Eleventh were helping to create a more lasting tribute, in the form of a massive redoubt jutting out deep into the Rebel lines near the Third Louisiana Redan. It was christened Fort Ransom. From here the Eleventh daily harried a tiring enemy. There was a price for this sport, of course, exacted by rock-steady Rebel riflemen who zeroed in on the narrow firing ports. Lieutenant Robert Jehu, a native-born Englishman from

Welchport, fought with Company C in the Eleventh during this constant skirmishing. Lieutenant Jehu watched when Private James Cain caught a musket ball in the chin; the missile glanced off and "severed the jugular vein." The soldier bled his life away in the dirt within ten minutes despite all his shaken comrades' efforts at first aid. It was an unnerving experience.[25] Lieutenant Jehu noted in melancholy how the slain rifleman had left behind a wife and child "in circumstances which are to be commiserated and pitied." On June 26th, Captain Nathaniel Kenyon of Company K almost suffered a similar fate while sniping away at the Rebels from within Fort Ransom. Peering through a firing slit, the former prisoner-of-war was struck by a Rebel slug which furrowed along his left temple above the ear, leaving behind an ugly, jagged four-inch trail. His apparently lifeless body was dragged back behind the front lines and examined by an army surgeon who pronounced him dead. One trooper from the Eleventh wouldn't accept this dire verdict. He pulled a trusty whiskey flask from his blouse, and poured the contents down Kenyon's throat, reviving a very shaken but alive infantry officer. Less than a month later, Lieutenant Kenyon, his scar still a vicious purple, would marry while on leave in LaSalle County, Illinois.[26]

As the siege wore on the Eleventh Illinois became very familiar with a strange creature who not only endured the suffering but thrived. Known only as John, this individual was one of a number of Chippewa Indians serving with the nearby 14th Wisconsin. Indian John astounded the Union soldiers with his exploits. He would creep out in the near-open in plain daylight, somehow concealing his position until his dark eyes caught a target moving in the Rebel works. "After careful aim he fires," Carrington wrote, "then rolls over and over to get away from the return bullets that are sure to come. The smoke reveals his hiding place."[27] At day's end the swarthy sniper would saunter past the Eleventh's encampment bound for General Ransom's headquarters for his daily reward: a jigger of whiskey. John's deadly proficiency was documented in the July 2nd edition of the *Chicago Tribune*.

> A particular rebel sharpshooter had been popping away at the Indian's port hole for a number of days. Indian tells two or three members of his company to point their rifles at reb's place, and after reb has made one pretty close shot, Indian bounds up with a death yell. Reb, beside himself with delight, raises himself up to look at the supposed dead redskin. Indian's comrades send two or three bullets through the rejoicing reb who has fired this last shot...[28]

June 25th marked an explosive end to routine slaughter with the thunderous detonation of 2,200 pounds of gunpowder buried beneath the Rebel positions at the Third Louisiana Redan. Carrington, recently promoted to the rank of corporal, recalled the sight as a "spout of dust high in the air: a blubber you might call it mixed with timbers, boards and men."[29] The Eleventh was in reserve when the men from Logan's division on their immediate right flank plunged into the smoking debris with fixed bayonets. The assaulting infantry established a narrow foothold inside the Rebel fort, which became the focus for brutal, sometimes hand-to-hand, combat. "The fight was close and desperate," observed Corporal Carrington, "night finds the boys in possession of half the Fort..." Fort Ransom's two 12-pound howitzers played a key role in the battle, blazing away when Rebel reinforcements stumbled up toward the wrecked strongpoint. The next morning saw the bitter conflict continue with Logan's men scrambling after primitive Confederate hand grenades which bounced and sputtered into the improvised trenches. Sometimes a brooding, black six-pound cannon ball came rolling down at them, exploding with deadly effect among the huddled Union troopers.[30] The fighting finally ended at about 4 p.m. with Logan's battered assault force pulling back from the ruined fort in a fighting retreat. Despite their keen disappointment at the repulse, the men in the Eleventh enjoyed a comic footnote in this otherwise tragic operation. Lieutenant Jehu from Company C described in a letter home the details concerning a black man's unexpected arrival in the Union trenches. "Logan fired a mine under the fort in his front," Jehu explained, "which removed vast quantities of earth, and hurled large numbers of the enemy in the debris besides blowing five white men and one colored into our lines, killing the white men whilst Sambo lives. Upon being asked how high he had been, Snow Bird said 300 yards, and that as he was falling down he met his master going up."[31]

Numerous anecdotes such as that helped serve an important purpose, diverting attention from the dire scenes that daily greeted the Eleventh's weary, lice-infested infantrymen. Following Logan's failure, they must have been less than excited upon learning a similar attempt was planned for their immediate front. On July 1st and 2nd, General Ransom personally supervised the construction of another tunnel under the still formidable Third Louisiana Redan. A thousand pounds of gunpowder were placed at the shaft's terminus, awaiting the signal for another assault.[32]

However, the attack schedule was interrupted when a Rebel delegation appeared just before noon on July 3rd out in front of McClernand's corps, followed by a cease-fire all along the lines. The quiet came, bringing an eerie sense of solemnity as the dusty soldiers warily eased out from beneath the protective earth into the sunshine. After initial trepidation, thousands from both sides were lounging above the trenches, unabashedly gazing in curiosity at their enemies incongruously sitting and standing within plain view and easy range. Something grand and of enormously grave consequence was occurring after 46 days of siege. Of this, the men were only vaguely aware, although the rumor mills ground on, fed by the doubt which grew when no official word came that day. Lieutenant E.P. Thomas of Company G in the Eleventh later recounted to his sister Hattie that the men still remained in doubt until the 9 a.m. officers' call on July 4th. Colonel Coates informed his assembled company commanders that Confederate General Pemberton had agreed to an immediate surrender, adding with a grave expression that General Logan's division would be the only Union unit participating in the actual occupation of Vicksburg.

    Col. Coates there hesitated and looking up was the very picture of despair or disappointment for we had all calculated largely upon going into Vicksburg. He then remarked that he had another order to read the substance of which was that until further orders Gen. Ransom's Brigade would be attached to General Logan's command. At that announcement we sent up one of the gayest old shouts on record, and immediately "vamoosed the ranch" to watch for white flags...[33]

    Minutes later the tattered defenders streamed out from their entrenchments and proceeded to stack muskets outside the defense lines. Corporal Carrington noted the absence of any Confederate battle flags among the booty, because they were either hidden by the Rebels, or torn into small shreds by Union soldiers as souvenirs of the proud Rebel garrison. The whole process of laying down arms was conducted in a dead silence by the Confederate infantry which had resisted with such admirable tenacity. Few present doubted that this was an important pivot point in the struggle now that the Federal army had almost split the Confederacy right down the middle. But little did anyone realize that at that very moment Lee's bleeding Army of Northern Virginia was dragging itself southward after a great repulse at a Pennsylvania crossroads called Gettysburg. Both in the east and in the west the

Rebel fortunes waived before an exultant, confident Union army. Later Private John W. Reading would recall:

> At precisely half past twelve, the signal for advance was given; instantly the Bands commenced playing a martial air; colors were unfurled to the breeze, a single command was given, and the column was in motion, with steadily measured tread, and with the exception of the music, in profound silence, that steady column of veterans moved forward each regiment saluting with its colors as it passed the Commanderin-Chief and staff, then moved away to the right until lost to view amid the labyrinths of Logan's Fort. Soon, however, it emerged from a covered way, and crossing the parapet of the Rebel Fort Hill [Third Louisiana Redan], marched up the open road for Vicksburg. Here the rebel army was drawn up on each side of the road, with arms stacked and colors cased, gazing in mute silence on the advancing columns...It was ten minutes past two p.m. when the troops were halted and arms stacked around the Court House Square...for a few moments the most profound silence reigned throughout the conquered city, not a word was spoken, not a drum beat, not a soldier moved, the intense stillness was beginning to become oppressive, when an officer stepped out upon the dome of the Court House and unfurled the American flag. Then the long pent-up feelings of the soldiers found vent in one prolonged deafening shout of triumph. Cheer after cheer, shout after shout...tears coursed down their sunburnt faces.[34]

The "Old Eleventh" had come a long way since those first ludicrous drill sessions at Camp Yates in the springtime of 1861. The men were now veterans striding through the hollow ruin of the once proud riverport whose guns had defied the Union for two years. Most of the Yankees were tired men, weary from the long fighting, and mainly curious about their recent enemies, for whom the majority seemed sympathetic. German-born Henry Uptmor certainly had reason enough for hatred, having endured the slaughter at Donelson, the panic at Shiloh, and the bitter siege at Vicksburg. Instead, when he walked amidst the rubble, Uptmor felt a great sadness. His heart was touched by the suffering among the defeated and dejected citizens and soldiers of the Confederate garrison. "Sympathy surely took possession of me when I met the wounded and sick of the enemy forces who came humbly toward us and begged for a piece of bread," he recalled.

"Each one of us gave them all the bread we had with us. It was deplorable indeed." Uptmor had nothing but admiration for these gaunt men in "Butternut" and Gray as they chatted with great animation regarding the recent conflict.[35] The Union veteran was convinced that only the shortage of food forced the Rebel surrender. Rebel soldiers told him how many of their men had not eaten anything whatsoever in the last few days.

Grant stated that Vicksburg's fall delivered 29,500 prisoners, 172 cannons, and 60,000 stand of small arms. The last were, in many cases, more modern than weapons carried by the victorious Yankees, many of whom promptly equipped themselves with the latest in English arms. In those early days following the surrender, the Eleventh was bivouacked as camp security in the captured Rebel trenches, or assigned as prison guards. Many of the officers were engaged in the laborious paperwork involved in issuing paroles to the Rebel captives while others spent free time exploring the enemy's defensive network. The Yankees marvelled at how any Confederates survived the horrible bombardment. General Ransom conducted a hostile Confederate officer on a tour of the mine planted directly underneath the fortifications at the Third Louisiana Redan. The detonation would have blown Ransom's guest into a thousand particles had events delayed surrender past July 4th. "Yet such was the fascination of Ransom's personal address," wrote a contemporary magazine author, "that even in the deadly mine the intended victim was won to a warm admiration of the Union General as a soldier and as a man."[36]

Lieutenant E.P. Thomas, Company G, Eleventh Illinois, was ecstatic about the victory. He called it the greatest of the entire war. In a letter written to his sister, Hattie, the youthful officer boasted that the triumph was on "the Donelson order" but even grander. Thomas, in almost gloating terms, noted that the surrender netted one Confederate lieutenant general, four major generals, and nine brigadier generals, along with enormous amounts of material. As a whole, he was impressed with the captured Rebel infantry, describing the men as "miserably dressed" but a fine looking set. Three days after the capitulation, he wrote:

> It might have been once a very pretty place, but it is terribly dilapidated now. There is scarcely a house but...our guns have riddled. There might once have been four or five thousand inhabitants here. There are still many citizens here, and are all drawing rations from us to live on. I should think it rather humiliating. God grant that my Mother and sisters may never be reduced to that...Oh, may the Father of

Mercies care for them and bless them. I am using paper captured here; it is full blood Secesh and bad to write on.[37]

In those days immediately following surrender, the "Boys" from the Eleventh scoured through the ruins in a grown-up treasure hunt looking for souvenirs. Corporal Carrington's wandering took him through the Shirley House, a prominent battlefield landmark located near Logan's lines. The white-framed home served as an occasional Union observation post and headquarters for the 45th Illinois Infantry. It had been an attractive dwelling, but in the battle's aftermath Carrington found pure shambles. He described the entire home as "peppered" with bullet holes, the interior nearly demolished. Wallpaper hung in shreds behind shattered pictures dangling from the scarred walls. Shattered plates, furniture, and personal belongings lay strewn all about.[38] It was a portrait of devastation, and it made a tremendous impact upon the Union infantryman. More encouraging, at least from a Union perspective, was the content of a letter found by Private M.A. Smith, Company C of the Eleventh. The missive, dated March 23, 1863, was addressed to Jeff Hicks in Vicksburg and written by a friend nicknamed "Rosie" serving on another Confederate front.[39] "Rosie" was pessimistic, admitting that his unit had been "whipped every time we met the feds," and forced to "run like thunder." He described his fellow Confederate soldiers as "such a mass of naked, hungry, broken down men I never saw before and never wish to see again." The author was depressed and convinced that further resistance was futile:

> Jeff, I wish this foolish struggle was over, and we could all get home agan. Jack is yet at home, enjoying all bliss and peace. This is not fair. He ought to be made to fight for what he helped to bring on us, but let him go--he will reap his reward...Everyone is tired of this war, and the most rabid Fire-eaters are anxious to compromise this matter and stop it...You must keep the contents of this letter to yourself, for it would not do to tell the truth to the officers now...Save yourself now, for when this tom-foolery is over we will have prosperous times.[40]

Unfortunately for both sides, the "Rosies" in the Rebel army were still outnumbered by "loyal" Confederates. For the most part, these enemies were good, strong men firmly convinced their cause was just and righteous. They were men the Eleventh Illinois had come to respect for tenacity and bravado displayed on so many battlefields. Even so, the Eleventh was not hesitant about continuing the campaign. Too much had been sacrificed for a compromised peace; this would be a bitter war without mercy. After the Vicksburg victory, the veteran regiment embarked on a new tour of duty. They were slated to serve as occupation troops in the lovely city of Natchez located 80 miles down river. On July 18th, the troops boarded the steamer *Luminary* for the voyage south to join Ransom, who in company with additional Federal units had entered the city a few days earlier.[41]

Ransom's advance party had made its appearance at the Natchez wharf on the afternoon of July 13th, quickly jumping ashore and within minutes seizing key points. Virginia-born Mrs. Mary Shields, mistress of the palatial "Bird's Nest" mansion in the venerable river town, was shocked at the sudden Yankee occupation. "Several regiments came up the hill from the river screaming and hooping like wild Indians," she remembered. "My father was taken prisoner and brought to his home by a regiment, which had been increased by Negroes. Those black men in their bright blue uniforms were a fearful sight to a Southerner."[42] Mrs. Shields related how faithful house servants interceded, assuring the Yankees that her father had treated them well and quickly negotiated his release. The fiercely pro-Confederate Southern belle was horrified at the invaders' behavior. She claimed soldiers quickly emptied the barn of horses while companions barged into the "Bird's Nest" itself, searching for valuables.[43]

Not so strangely, Union commander Ransom viewed events from a different perspective. He was highly pleased with this bloodless invasion. He reported to XVII Corps headquarters how his forces achieved total surprise and were in firm possession of the city. By 4 a.m. the next day, the always enterprising general mounted 200 infantry for what turned into an extremely profitable foraging expedition netting 5,000 CSA cattle. Another sortie ambushed the trailing elements of a large Confederate wagon train on the Louisiana side. They returned with prisoners in tow as well as with 312 rifles, 203,000 rounds of small arms ammunition, and eleven large crates packed with artillery shells--all bound for Confederate General Kirby Smith and his troops.[44] Ransom was elated and U.S. Grant offered his hearty approval of these developments. Vicksburg's conqueror possessed great confidence in Ransom's ability at holding independent command. "He has always proved himself the best man I have ever had to send on expeditions," Grant wrote. "He is a live man and of good judgment."[45] Ransom would need that quality in the days ahead, during which he would be challenged by strange new civil problems in addition to military considerations. In the next few months, Natchez' government would consist almost solely of General T.E.G. Ransom, who persisted in carrying on a firm but benevolent policy. "My troops have worked hard--frequently forty-eight hours on duty--and have behaved admirably," Ransom reported. "Hardly a case of pillaging, or even of disrespectful treatment of a citizen, has occurred, and the people constantly express their gratitude and happy disappointment in their treatment."[46]

Natchez was a lovely, graceful town which charmed the gawking Yankee visitors. They were awed by the elegant white colonnaded mansions with their beautiful landscaped vistas. "This is the finest place that we have ever been in in the South," Private Whipple wrote his brother. "I don't think there could be a more handsome place."[47] Whipple, a Shiloh and Vicksburg survivor, was enchanted with the melodious church bells ringing out over the hillside city. He expressed his disbelief that the war continued in such an idyllic surrounding. The Union soldier attested that the majority in Natchez were bitter Rebels. He attributed this phenomenon to the fact that "wherever you find wealth, you find hot heads..." Private Theodore Copple of Company C, Eleventh Illinois, was even less sympathetic toward aristocratic Natchez society. "This is the first place ever we got into but what we could tell the slave from the whites," Copple wrote his hometown newspaper in Centralia, Illinois, "but here it is impossible. Girls and boys, whiter than a great many of our Copperhead brethren, are in bondage. Men own their own half-brothers and their own children in bondage. If this is not sin in the first degree I would like to know what is."[48]

The Eleventh's arrival in Natchez was rather uneventful except for one reckless exploit featuring the impetuous George McKee, C Company commander, who had recently been promoted to major to replace Lloyd Waddell. Details are fuzzy, but McKee was serving as provost marshall in those first days of occupation, and, while on the rounds, spied a gray-clad figure disappear into a doorway. Even though he carried no firearm, McKee dismounted and followed. Confronting a coatless gentleman in his room, the Union major informed the suspected Rebel that he was now under military arrest. "Beg pardon," came the reply. "You must be mistaken in the gentleman." McKee was undaunted, briskly warning the Confederate: "No mistake--No nonsense, Sir. Put on your coat."[49] The Rebel uniform was then produced while Major McKee patiently waited as his prisoner collected a few personal belongings. In the interim, a black "contraband" sidled into the room with the whispered message that two other Confederate officers were making their escape in a carriage just outside. McKee took the first prisoner's verbal parole before running out, leaping into the saddle, and clattering off in a dusty two mile pursuit. Sheer bluff was his only weapon when he overtook the carriage and demanded immediate surrender. "The rebels were very much crestfallen when they found their captor had only his sabre," one account notes, "while they had pair of revolvers and sword." McKee's impulsive bravery was a gambler's virtue, but a military handicap, as the Eleventh would learn in the very near future.[50]

Occupation duty in Natchez produced few such daring escapades. Life for the invaders was a pleasant routine, far removed from the gritty trench life they had grown accustomed to during the Vicksburg siege. Mrs. Shields was outraged by the spectacle of supposedly loyal Confederates socializing with these blue-coated intruders. She scoffed at those "Belles" who enjoyed company with Union officers mounted on what the staunchly Confederate lady emphatically described as "borrowed" horses. Then, too, there was the frightening influx of thousands of black slaves from the interior, tramping in every day and filling the temporary campsites established by the Union forces. Ransom was busy carrying out General James B. McPherson's instructions that the "strong, able-bodied" blacks be recruited for the new colored regiments. The existence of these armed Africans appalled white Natchez residents. "A negro regiment was formed at what was called the Fork of the Roads, each company commanded by a white man," recalled Mrs. Shields. "The Negroes were well armed, dressed in uniform and drilled daily. Whenever a citizen was to be arrested and whenever a Confederate soldier was supposed to be around...a squad of Negroes was sent to make the arrest. The arming of the Negroes was a terrible thing and difficult to bear patiently."[51]

Mrs. Shields made little effort to conceal her contempt for the occupiers. This obvious disdain resulted in an ugly incident at Federal headquarters where rations were freely distributed among the town folk. Her mistake was in disdainfully avoiding the front entrance which featured the national flag draped over the doorway. The performance was observed by several Union officers who confronted the die-hard rebel when she began to leave through the flagless entrance. Mrs. Shields bragged that a "double line of soldiers with fixed bayonets" blocked the passage but stood aside when she marched briskly ahead.[52] Ransom's reaction was instantaneous. His order, dated July 22nd, 1863, read:

Mrs. J. Shields, whose public conduct at the headquarters of the General Commander was insulting to the Flag of the Union and the officers and soldiers of this command, is denied the protection of the Flag, and is hereby notified to leave this city and our lines within twenty-four hours, with her family. Mrs. Shields will be allowed sufficient transportation for a reasonable amount of baggage...The Provost Marshall will be charged with the execution of this order and will take inventory of the effects of Mrs. Shields and occupy her premises for the use of the Government...The property retained by the Provost Marshall will be confiscated...

By order of

Brig. Gen. T.E. Ransom
Commdg.[53]

War breeds hatred. Neither Ransom nor the Eleventh Illinois was exempt, particularly as the conflict stretched out into the third year with fair prospects for continued hostilities. It was hard to love their enemy, although the infantrymen in the "Old Eleventh" usually gave the Graycoats grudging respect. The same was not true with the Union soldiers' favorite target for venom and ridicule: the Copperhead or Northerner who sympathized with the Confederate rebellion. Idle days in Natchez provided many of the men with the opportunity to pen their detestation in long, virulent letters home. Company C was most prolific since most came from Centralia in Marion County; there, in deep southern Illinois, the Copperhead movement flourished among a population with roots in Tennessee and Kentucky. Private Samuel C. Copple of Company C had little use for these Southern sympathizers, claiming that a traitor in the North was not entitled to any rights except the "right to hang..."[54] He sent home a threatening letter to the *Centralia Sentinel* promising a dire fate for Copperheads when the Union veterans returned at war's end:

We would like to be home now to make those Copperheads keep still and hunt their holes. We look upon them as being ten-fold worse than a Rebel in the rebel ranks, for they have no excuse. They are the most inexcusable of all men, and have brought disgrace upon themselves that will mark them through life. Their children, will look upon them and stamp them as traitors and enemies to the best government instituted by man. Oh, Copperheads, you had better turn to

Uncle Sam before it is too late; before he confiscates your property and banishes you from the country you have disgraced.[55]

Robert Jehu shared those sentiments, calling the Copperheads "snakes through the underwood creeping." The naturalized American was even more virulent in expressing hatred for these Rebel sympathizers, these backstabbers who proudly flaunted in public "Butternut Badges". The enraged Jehu portrayed them as "men in comparison with whom Arnold was the truest of patriots, and Judas a philanthropist of purest intent..."[56] The Centralia boys were incensed when rumors circulated which indicated that an assistant provost marshall had been shot in ambush by deserters and Copperheads prowling Marion County. Many feared the alleged shooting might be the first act in a threatened Copperhead sabotage campaign popularly described as a "Fire in the Rear." Private Jacob Copple expressed little concern regarding a Copperhead "Fifth Column", commenting in an August 27th letter that any such effort was doomed to failure. He condemned the Southern sympathizers saying, "hard things should be called by hard names." In the letter Copple challenged two Copperhead acquaintances:

You are virtually as much a rebel as you were in the rebel army. Yea, more your position is more degraded and despicable than the Southern soldier,...the rebel soldier is honored and respected as a soldier, by us, but what respect or honor can they expect to have who will stay at home while we fight their battles, and play into the rebel hands behind our backs?[57]

Duties at Natchez allowed little time for Ransom to engage in these evidently satisfying fulminations. His tenure as post commander was extremely trying, as headquarters was constantly crowded with petitioning citizens. Captain Dickey, acting as adjutant, wrote to his sister Ann elaborating on the varied and bizarre responsibilities involved in governing a conquered Rebel community. At one moment a "dashing widow" might walk in demanding her stolen carriage horses be promptly returned. She would be followed rapidly by two Negroes "out of breath" reporting Rebel cavalry on the Louisiana side "shooting all the Negroes who refused to go to Texas." Naturally, the more sophisticated came bearing gifts as a prelude to their requests. Offerings ranged from fruit baskets to a "huge demijohn of old sherry aged in a Natchez garret for 26 years." One of the most constant problems revolved around the Negro encampments bulging with ill-clothed, filthy, and, often, diseased slaves who died by the hundreds.[58] Black camp guards complained they were insulted on numerous occasions by Ellet's ill-disciplined Horse Marines. Ransom's life was made miserable by the Marines and their bandit-like ways. Mr. A.T. Bowie wrote the general on August 4th, reporting one of their more despicable acts which occurred at the John Routh plantation:

> They then burst open a barrel of whisky, made all of the Negroes drunk, and in that way learned where his valuables were, consisting of silver-ware, liquors, meats, clothes, table and house linen, and even scuffled with him for his purse. They took the amount of $25,000 worth of property...Mr. Routh is an old man of nearly seventy years; had his house, gin, barn, stables, and everything burned last spring. These Marines also threatened to take him prisoner; did take his grandson...in jail at Vicksburg...[59]

Existing records fail to reveal Ransom's reactions. He was surely no "mollycoddle" when it came to rebellion, as evidenced by his severe treatment of Mrs. Shields. Yet, his own basic human nature and a deep-seated conviction in fair play would lead one to believe that the youthful brigadier despised the shabby depredations committed by such troops as Ellet's Horse Marines. These concerns, however, were soon left behind with new orders in October. Ransom was bound for the Texas coast, where Major General Nathaniel P. Banks was mounting a Union invasion force.

Chapter Eight

Dying Is No Easy Thing

Darkness brought the Yankees to Mustang Island, an insignificant 20-mile-long sand strip tucked away off the far southwestern coast of the Lone Star state. More than 1,000 armed Federals waded through the surf on the evening of November 16, 1863. In command was Brigadier General T.E.G. Ransom, newly assigned to the Third Brigade, Second Division of the XIII Army Corps. The pint-sized invasion was the first stage in a Union attempt to frustrate Texas blockade runners. At either end of Mustang Island were the crucial Arkansas and Corpus Christi passes which allowed ships access to the port of Corpus Christi. Once Union troops established batteries overlooking these narrow straits, they could entomb Confederate shipping at dockside, or, at the very least, severly impede ocean traffic up and down these narrow watery avenues. Aided by 11-inch naval cannon aboard the U.S.S. *Monongahela*, Ransom's command overwhelmed a Confederate battery at the island's southern tip on November 17. They netted, at little cost, three heavy cannon, 100 prisoners and a Rebel schooner.[1] By November 29th the brigade was actively besieging a larger enemy bastion, Fort Esperanza, located on Matagorda Island a few miles to the northeast. Disappointingly, the thousand-man garrison stole away in the darkness. Their departure was announced at 1 a.m. with the explosion of the fort's magazines. Sporadic explosions continued through the early morning hours.[2]

This less than glorious victory concluded active operations along the coast for Ransom's brigade. On the positive side, the forays had at least interrupted blockade-running traffic. Certainly France was served notice that the Federal government had not abandoned the southwest despite its preoccupation with events further east. In a personal vein, this brief military footnote propelled Ransom one step up the promotion ladder. General Cadwallader C. Washburn of the XIII Corps cited his services as "prompt, gallant and efficient."[3] On January 4, 1864, Ransom was promoted to command the 4th Division. He spent the early spring of that year in desolate isolation on Decrow's Point near Matagordo Bay. "Not a bush or shrub grows on the Point," wrote Colonel James M. Shields of the 77th Illinois on February 2nd. "All is sand...Ransom, formerly of the 11th, commands this division. I must say that he is deservedly popular as a gallant and efficient officer; as is his adjutant, Capt. Dickey."[4]

Ransom's Texas adventure was a brief, inconclusive interlude in appropriate parallel to the campaign as a whole. From the outset, the Union efforts in this remote theatre of war were hamstrung by inadequate forces, vague strategic goals and lukewarm leadership on behalf of the overall commander, Major General Nathaniel Prentiss Banks. Ransom, the Eleventh's premier soldier, arrived in Texas in early November, 1863, at the mouth of the Rio Grande where Federal soldiers already occupied Brazos de Santiago. General Ransom's first assignment was to serve as post commander at Brownsville, further north up the river. In the political sense the Union presence allowed the French in Mexico a clear look at the American flag flying once more on Texas ground. The Brownsville flag itself had special meaning for General Ransom, since loyal citizens of the Rebel community had presented him with the banner not long after his arrival. They informed him that the flag was associated with the defense of that town during the Mexican War and had been hidden during the Confederate reign. Ransom treasured the memento, which flew over his headquarters for the duration of the war. It was probably in prominent display that spring at Decrow's Point.[5]

While the XIII Corps drilled and complained in its barren new home, plans were well underway to consolidate the Union forces for a grand invasion of northwestern Louisiana. Motives for the expedition were complex and varied. One compelling factor was the presence of twenty thousand dangerous Confederates who lurked in and around Shreveport under the astute command of General Richard Taylor--the late President Zachary Taylor's boy gone Rebel. This potential threat must, sooner or later, be eliminated if the Union desired a free hand to turn east and subjugate the important city of Mobile. There were political motives as well, along with a very real economic enticement. Immense quantities of CSA cotton was stored up the Red River, worth millions of dollars in hard Yankee cash in the starved northern markets. This too was undeniably a factor in General Banks's decision. He would strike hard into northwest Louisiana in pursuit of victory and cotton. In distant Washington, President Lincoln brooded with worry. He had listened before to similarly confident men of the same stamp as Banks. Almost always their pompous predictions were only the verbal preface to defeat and disaster. Then again, perhaps Banks would shatter the chain and achieve in the military arena the same success which had been his in civilian life.

In the years before the war, the press had dubbed Banks the "Bobbin Boy" of Massachussetts. His lowly factory-hand beginnings, followed by moneyed success, were badges of honor in this raw society of self-made men. His career was meteoric, marked by great competence in business matters, particularly the growing giant of the railroad. His material wealth was soon complemented by political eminence. He was a U.S. Congresman, and was elected Speaker of the House; then, he served as governor of Massachusetts from 1858 through 1861. Unfortunately for the Union, an acknowledged personal bravery was his only discernible military virtue. Banks's war service was marred by indecision and defeat best illustrated by the memorable whipping he suffered at Stonewall Jackson's hands during the Shenandoah campaign of early 1862. This able rebel soldier tutored Banks in the killer's art, but the lesson hadn't taken. Subsequently, the war took him to New Orleans where he replaced the equally ineffectual General Benjamin Butler.[6]

One great victory would blot out the early failures. This was certainly on Banks's mind when he contemplated the campaign in Louisiana. All the elements and tools of victory were present in the logistical, strategic and psychological sense. He commanded a confident, hardened army. They were a blend of opposites. Veteran western troops, cavalier in military attitude, were uneasily allied with "white collar" easterners whose parade ground splendor gave cause for snickers and, maybe, a secret envy on the part of their rough-hewn comrades. These were mostly good men, led at most times by capable and brave officers. General Banks could take heart in the reassuring fact that his advance body of infantry was led by Brigadier General T.E.G. Ransom, whose growing reputation was a complete antithesis to his own. The XIII Corps was now commanded by the Eleventh's old colonel. His two divisions totaled approximately 4,500 bayonets. In early March of 1864, Ransom led his lean marchers toward the Confederates who waited on the upper reaches of the Red River.[7]

On paper, the plan was good. General Banks's 20,000 troops would march up the Red River bank supported by a powerful gunboat flotilla, mounting 210 cannons, under Admiral David Porter. At Little Rock, Arkansas, General Frederick Steele was to proceed south with 15,000 men and ultimately rendezvous with Banks at Shreveport. By March 20th, the Union column under the latter's direction had already reached Alexandria, Louisiana. General Ransom was pleased with his new outfit, which included the hardy 4th Division led by Colonel W.J. Landram, and the 3rd Division commanded by Brigadier General R.A. Cameron. It was a small corps boasting a fine reputation for "Western Grit" on a par with Ransom's "Old Eleventh."[8] These men had little respect for the military niceties, which explains their great distaste for the eastern soldiers attached to Banks's army. Lieutenant W.H. Bentley of the 77th Illinois, 4th Division recalled how he and his men were little inclined toward civility with the rebel populace. He noted that the ambush of two foragers from the 48th Ohio and 24th Iowa on April 2nd was particular cause for anger among these Western men:

> The flanks and rear of our army were constantly annoyed by these cowardly sneaks--men who had not the courage to enlist and fight like soldiers, but stood at their gates and bowed as the army passed, and then, seeking the cover of the brush, acted their mean, contemptible part in the capture of and killing of our men. On some of the residences were placards bearing the inscription: "NEUTRALITY--FRENCH PROTECTION HERE," and the French flag fluttered in the breeze. But the Western boys had been too long in the service to show much respects...for the boys showed their contempt for all such claims, by acts of wholesale destruction as they passed along.[9]

Western men were an unruly lot, fine in a fight, but about as receptive to traditional military discipline as a young mustang is to a harness. General Ransom knew them well, respected their many virtues and never discounted their vices or soldierly shortcomings. During the march to Alexandria, the first major stop on the road to Shreveport, he quickly established his authority as corps commander. Ransom demanded his units move out each morning promptly at the designated hour. When this was ignored, the guilty regiment soon trailed dust with the rear guard. It was doubly unpleasant since the trailing unit usually arrived in camp around midnight whereas the others shed their packs as early as 4 or 5 p.m. By such experiences they learned that Ransom, despite an affable nature, demanded pure and simple obedience.[10] But even he could scarce control the troops regarding forage habits. Western troops had, by now, determined that wholesale looting was their right, and was even a God-pronounced punishment for the recalcitrant Rebels. They were brash and cocky, not easily intimidated by more morally fastidious officers nor, for the most part, by impending battle. Each night they snuggled in cramped two-man, "dog tents" and protested fate with a yelping satiric chorus that sometimes stretched for an hour or more. "Of course there could be no sleeping while it lasted," wrote Lieutenant Bentley of the 77th. "With such pastimes as these the boys varied the tedious monotony of the march..."[11]

Evenings were far less festive for General Ransom. He was a serious man beset by heavy responsibilities, and was at all times cognizant that his decisions could have disastrous effects on the present campaign. Despite these burdens, the twenty-nine-year-old general took time out on March 26th to correspond with a very young cousin in Illinois. Ransom had been supporting the family of his uncle George Gilson since the uncle's death in 1856. He was deeply attached to the two daughters, Ella and Frances, regarding them as sisters. In the midst of an arduous, complex campaign, General Ransom set aside a few moments in which to write:

> My Darling Cousin: I was delighted today in receiving a kind and affectionate note from my little Ella, and since she shows so much proficiency in letter writing, I insist on placing her upon the list of my regular correspondents, trusting that Frances will occasionally favor me with a specimen of her penmanship and composition too. I cannot express to you the pleasure that I feel in the knowledge of the fact that you are both interested in your studies and are especially improving with such evidences of your appreciation of our efforts to educate you. We shall be amply repaid for any trouble or expense that may attend your education. It is my wish that little cousins should be educated, so that they may fill any position in refined society with honor...[12]

This most charming letter was written without the posturing and patronizing tones evident in most communications between adult and child. Ransom respected his youthful cousins as adults, and treated them as such. His letter also touched on the mundane, complimenting Ella on a role in a school play in which she portrayed an empress. "I can only say I am sorry for the Emperor," Ransom teasingly wrote. "He will have to look well to his sceptor."[13] The closing passages contained a brief description of the surrounding countryside with Ransom pointing out how

Ella's French studies would have great practical application in this Louisiana country. He described the region "as a garden spot" populated "by wealthy people who are surrounded by everything that wealth and refinement could supply." Ransom urged his counsins apply themselves in their studies, and enclosed a $10 note emphasizing the money be spent "judiciously for young ladies' trinkets." In a brief post-script, he returned once more to matters at hand:

> How would you like to ride along my lines of 18 regiments of infantry, four batteries and a brigade of cavalry? My column on the march is three hours passing a given point and is usually about six miles long. I should have liked to have had you see my command today as they came thro' Alexandria with Bands playing and flags displayed. I felt very proud of them of course--You must excuse my vanity. I would not advise you to indulge in it. Soldiers are allowed to possess a reasonable amount; young ladies usually have their share whether admitted to or not.
>
> Again Yours, Green[14]

There was little pause at Alexandria. Ransom's beloved XIII Corps left early the next day, pounding out another hard, eventless march through the hostile Louisiana countryside. General Banks was adamant that the expedition proceed with speed. He was confident, even outspoken, in his conviction that success loomed only days away. Certainly, there were good reasons. The Army of the Gulf contained dependable, seasoned troops supported by an equally veteran fleet. Yet, at the same time, there were certain misgivings concerning the Red River, which seemed reluctant to allow the squat ironclads free passage. Indeed, the expected spring rise was extremely tardy and forced Porter's fleet to squirm over the Alexandria rapids. The Admiral was aware that his fleet would be isolated upriver if the water level sank any lower.[15] It was a gloomy prospect. On April 6th, the army reached Grand Ecore, where Banks ordered a swing west away from the Red River and Porter's fleet, and deep into the pine forested backcountry. Banks's army plodded north along a narrow, red mud rut strung along for miles and surrounded by an immense near-wilderness.[16] Banks gambled that the Rebels would not offer battle before the Union army reached Shreveport, where Union land and water forces would converge and crush the enemy between them. At that very moment Confederate General Dick Taylor was massing his outnumbered troops near Mansfield 35 miles south of Shreveport. He had chosen to ignore the oncoming Union columns from Little Rock, throwing out only a thin screen in that direction to bargain for a little time. Taylor scraped together about 15,000 men who were concentrated at Mansfield in preparation for Banks's advance. Confederate General Taylor assumed that once the main Union pincer from the south was blunted, his forces might then turn and deal with the threat posed by the Union men coming from Little Rock.

As Banks's column pressed ahead it gradually strung itself out nearly twenty miles from head to tail. The rear elements could never come up in time if the enemy struck at the column's head, which was comprised of 3,500 cavalry under Brigadier General A.L. Lee. The situation was made even more precarious since Lee's cumbersome, 100-wagon supply column was directly behind the cavalry, and ahead of the nearest Union infantry support consisting of Ransom's XIII Corps (Detached). Further back, the story was similar with another 700 wagons sandwiched between Ransom's units and General A.J. Smith's XVI Corps bringing up the rear. The thirty-four-year-old cavalry leader, Albert L. Lee, was aware that this order of march was hazardous in the extreme, particularly considering the narrow, single road on which they marched.[17]

Ransom was equally concerned. Military judgment led him to doubt the soundness of a premature advance by forward elements while the main infantry body lagged miles behind. There was the imminent possibility that the Rebels would mass and engage the Union troops at the column head, where they would enjoy tatical superiority.[18] Early on the morning of April 7th, Ransom informed General Banks that they "were in the presence of the enemy in superior force," explaining how he could "feel it in the air."[19] Ransom's suggestion was to pause, allow the immense column an opportunity for consolidation, and then advance in force. The advice was ignored. General A.L. Lee, commanding the cavalry out ahead, asked for infantry reinforcement as well. These repeated requests were ignored by Major General William B. Franklin, second-in-command, until that officer was overruled on April 7th by General Banks himself. It was 10 p.m. that night when General Ransom received the order while in camp at Pleasant Hill.[20] Twenty minutes later the First Brigade of the Fourth Division was ordered to proceed and join Lee's cavalry encamped eight miles up the road. The First Brigade, accompanied by General Landram, moved out at 3 a.m., and rendezvoused with the Union horseman at daybreak. Together they pushed ahead as the Confederates faded before them, only pausing for a few random, long-range duels with few casualties on either side. It was constant skirmishing with the hard-pressed infantry doggedly keeping pace with Lee's horse soldiers. Landram's troops were exhausted after proceeding nearly 16 miles in such fashion, prompting the commander to request that Ransom relieve them with all dispatch. The corps commander had already done just that, but the reinforcements became entangled in the cumbersome cavalry supply train which blocked the narrow road. Ransom urged them onward, and then galloped past the stalled column, heading for the First Brigade which was still skirmishing with an increasingly aggressive enemy:

> I arrived at the front, five and one half miles from Saint Patrick's Bayou, about 1:30 p.m. I found that our forces had just driven the enemy across an open field, and were shelling him from a fine position on a ridge...It was determined to halt here in order to allow the Second Brigade to come up and relieve the First...I went to the front of the line of skirmishers and carefully reconnoitered the position of the enemy. We were able to perceive two batteries and a large force of infantry in line of battle in the edge of the woods...and also considerable bodies of infantry moving down the road leading to our right and rear...[21]

There was constant skirmishing all the while as the Union troops formed up. The mass of infantry was on the right flank under the command of Colonel Landram. The left was held by Colonel Dudley's cavalry brigade supported on their immediate right flank by Nim's battery situated atop a small hill very near the Mansfield Road. Based on personal observation, Ransom was convinced that any potential Rebel threat would come on the left against the skittish cavalrymen. At 3 p.m., General Banks appeared on the scene. He agreed with Ransom's estimations and ordered the 96th and 83rd Ohio Infantry to move from the far left over to the exposed right flank. This disposition was arbitrarily countermanded minutes later by Major Lieber, an officer on Banks's staff.[22] There was little time left for argument. By 4 p.m., General Taylor's rugged infantry swept in on the Federal right wing, coming on in two waves accompanied by the familiar Rebel shriek. Ransom ordered Landram's weary brigade forward to meet the challenge, and the main battle ensued. The first Confederate wave dissolved before disciplined, accurate rifle fire. "We drove back his first line in confusion upon his second," Ransom recalled, "but recovering, he again advanced till, unable to endure our heavy fire, he halted about 200 yards from our front, where many of his men laid down and returned our fire."[23] Despite this temporary success, Ransom's fears from the early morning quickly materialized. Taylor had concentrated on the isolated Union forward elements bringing into action 4,800 Bluecoats. The attack on the right was only the beginning, followed minutes later by a powerful drive on the Federal left flank--where Ransom had predicted in vain they would assault. Dudley's cavalry broke before the oncoming gray infantry, leaving behind Nim's battery which in turn was flanked and captured en masse.

Ransom described how his XIII Corps was grasped in a "nutcracker" formed by the developing Rebel attack coming on in a giant V to swallow the outnumbered Federals. Both far right and left flanks were soon enveloped and exposed to a terrific fire. Ransom attempted to stabilize the situation by ordering the 83rd Ohio to pull out from the fairly secure right, and reinforce the beleagured 23rd Wisconsin on the tip of the opposite flank. It was a futile gesture because the left flank simply didn't exist at all by the time the Ohio boys switched fronts. Ransom immediately ordered them rearward where they might reinforce the Chicago Merchantile Battery which had only recently appeared on the field. Ransom was laying the groundwork for an orderly withdrawal. He instructed adjutant Captain Dickey, and Lieutenant Joseph D. Tredway, aide-de-camp, to ride out on the wavering right with orders for Landram's division to pull back along the same line. The two officers spurred ahead until Captain Dickey suddenly toppled from his horse with a Confederate bullet lodged in his brain. Tredway reined in and ran over to the fallen officer, lifting him from the ground and calling out his name in a reflex, mechanical fashion:

> My only thought then was to save his body. This I endeavored to do alone and by calling on others to assist me. But by this time the rout of the first line was complete and the enemy were pressing us so closely that none would stay to help me. Finding that I could do nothing alone, I was compelled to leave him and the place where he fell was soon in the possession of the rebels...In my grief and bewilderment I neglected to do one thing for which I shall never forgive myself. It did not occur to me to take his sword and other articles on his person till it was too late...But I believe that if it had been my own brother who fell at my side I should have felt and acted the same...[25]

Dickey's death delayed the transmittal of the crucial retreat orders, contributing to the complete disaster on the Union right. Minutes afterward, Landram's battered division collapsed before the ferocious assault. It was a chaotic, terror-filled conflict with the odds stacked high against the outflanked, outgunned Western troops. The organized retreat turned into a rout, with the 48th Ohio and 130th Illinois suffering horrendous casualties; survivors threw up their hands in surrender. "The Regiments fought by detail, and by detail were defeated," noted Lieutenant W.H. Bentley of the 77th Illinois. "As the timber was dense with underbrush, and the line of the enemy constantly advancing, surging around farther and farther on our flank, our troops were in the dilemma of having the enemy in front and rear...Hundreds of the boys were captured, the enemy pressing us from all quarters..."[26] Ransom was in the thick of it. He rallied some of the fleeing infantry and ordered them immediately behind the Chicago Merchantile Battery for a second stand. It was a hellish ordeal with men falling all around. At one point a Rebel cannon ball howled right past General Ransom, tearing off the head of a nearby officer's mount like an invisible cleaver.[27]

The traumatic battle shock would prove psychologically overwhelming for many. This was the case with Lieutenant Colonel Lindsey of the 48th Ohio who cringed behind a fallen tree while his soon to be mortally wounded executive officer, Major Bering, led the regiment.[28] Ransom could neither forgive nor understand this sort of conduct, which he termed "disgraceful." General Ransom was still mounted while rallying the men around the sturdy Chicago Merchantile Battery. Lieutenant Henry Roe vividly remembered the scene:

> Every man stood to his post. Not a word was uttered, save an order which was obeyed with a will. Then volley after volley told us to the awful carnage that was going on in close proximity to us. Soon our suspense was ended for the brave men that had supported us in eight hard fought battles before this and had never fallen back an inch before, came running from the woods... their ranks broken and cut to pieces but still fighting till the last ten times their own numbers hand to hand. On came the enemy in unbroken line their first line eight thousand strong. Our men soon fell in the rear of "Their Old Battery"... that is what was left of them. We opened on the Rebs. Thanks to the practice we had at Vicksburg and other places there was not a shell wasted. Every shell burst in their ranks. Our six ten-

pounders fairly shook the earth. I never knew the boys to load and fire so fast before, even on drill. We cut their line completely in two. Had we men to have charged them the day had been ours. But their right and left came unbroken and they came around in the skirt of the woods and open an infalading fire upon on us. We were then compelled to fall back about five hundred yards to the edge of the wood where we opened on them again with terrible effect. It was in this second position that Gen. Ransom fell from his horse shot through the knee. He was speaking to me at the moment he was shot...[29]

Confederate artillery shrapnel had smashed into Ransom's left knee, knocking him from his horse at this most critical juncture in the battle. Cameron's Third Division had finally arrived at the front. For a moment, the situation brightened, thanks mainly to the splendid performance by the Chicago Merchantile Battery. Ransom would see no more of this battle, however, as a few sturdy infantrymen hoisted the seriously wounded officer on their shoulders and stumbled toward the rear. Cameron's lines would hold for more than an hour more before the Confederate numbers once again overlapped on both flanks. There followed a hysterical rush toward the rear, past the shouting figures of General Banks and General Franklin who were desperately attempting a rally. A few units, like the Chicago Merchantile Battery, retired in relative good order only to find the single, narrow road completely blocked by abandoned supply wagons. Teamsters cut the reins, mounted the mules, and fled. They left behind a three-mile roadblock guaranteeing total disaster. C.H. Dickinson of the Chicago Merchantile Battery saw chaos unfold:

On came the enemy. They were close upon us, and our supports had given way a second time, and many of our boys were wounded before we limbered up and fell back. Here commenced a scene of indescribable confusion. By some strange blunder, the baggage train of the cavalry divisions had been brought up to this point, almost in front of the battle. We were in the dense pine woods, with but a single wagon track and this filled with wagons, all flying to the rear. Out of the track on either side went the artillery and all else, till the woods were a moving sea of wagons, guns, caissons, cavalry, riderless horses, ambulances with their freight of moaning, dying humanity, bouncing over logs, ruts and underbrush...Close upon us, and flanking us, were the enemy, pouring in their leaden hail all the time. On we blundered...till everything was brought up in a heap by a ravine. To save the guns was impossible. Nearly half the horses were shot. We cut loose the rest and fled, all who were too late...[30]

Taylor's advancing forces seized 200 wagons brimming with Yankee supplies, 20 field pieces, and innumberable small arms dropped in panic by fleeing owners. The pursuit ended two miles from Sabine Crossroads, when the disorganized Confederates collided with the First Division of the XVIV Corps commanded by General W.H. Emory. An hour-and-half long fight broke out with a determined enemy recoiling again and again before what General Banks would later describe as "an immovable wall of fire." That night the Union forces stealthily pulled out from their positions, falling back to Pleasant Hill where they were joined by General A.J. Smith's XVI and XVII Corps. They dug in, awaiting the expected Confederate attack most assumed would come with daylight on the 9th. Sabine Crossroads, or the Battle of Mansfield, had been a costly and embarrassing drubbing for General Banks whose men now revelled in calling him Napoleon P. Banks. His forces had been fed piecemeal into Taylor's grinder, giving the outnumbered Confederates the opportunity to achieve numerical superiority at each key moment of contact. There had actually been three separate battles that day: the first when Landram's Fourth Division folded, the second when Cameron's Third Division temporarily stemmed the tide, and the third that evening when Emory's powerful First Division dealt the oncoming Rebels a bloody nose. Approximately 12,000 Union troops saw action that April 8th; more than 2,235 were killed, wounded or captured.[31] Federal casualties were more than double the Confederate losses while Ransom's XIII Corps was shattered physically and psychologically. Private Lemuel Burke of the 119th Illinois described the pathetic plight of the survivors who came streaming in the next morning, dishevelled, disarmed and disoriented, and "all telling desperate stories of defeat and carnage."[32]

General Ransom miraculously escaped the trap. On the evening of the 8th he sprawled on a cot in a large frame home situated along a timber line at the edge of what was called Pleasant Hill, incongrous since the area was a plain nearly a mile wide, distinguished only by a ravine which ran through the clearing from west to southwest. Lieutenant Colonel William H. Heath of the 33rd Missouri Infantry sought out the wounded officer that evening, having heard the camp rumors regarding the XVII Corps' destruction. He found Ransom propped up on an army cot:

> The parlors where General Ransom was lying swarmed with generals, of high and low degree, who all with one voice agree that the expedition against Shreveport was a dismal failure and that nothing remained now but to get back with as little further loss as possible to New Orleans and reorganize. From the western window I could look out, as General Ransom talked, and see General Banks' fine and well equipped army...all rushing helter-skelter from the timber...I had never before witnessed such as apparently needless route, and as no enemy seemed to be pressing them from behind, I wondered much what made each so urgent...I drew General Ransom's attention to the scene...Rising on his elbow to get a better view, he denounced the fleeing army, in the terse language of which he was past master, as cowards and poltroons, sarcastically comparing them to the wicked, who flee when no man pursueth. Smarting under the universal verdict of failure...and the necessity of going back to New Orleans, "way back," he expressed it; he finally burst out with: "Oh, for heaven's sake get out of the way there, you cowards, and let Smith get his corps up. I know he'll fight."[33]

The day had brought nothing but disaster and dejection. Ransom's closest friend, Captain Cyrus Dickey, was dead near that damnable crossroad in the middle of nowhere. "The General can think and speak only of his death," wrote aide-de-camp, Lieutenant J.D. Tredway. Ransom had known the tall, handsome attorney ever since Camp Yates. He'd been a frequent visitor to that Ann Wallace's home on the heights. And now--after Donelson, after Shiloh, after Vicksburg--Cyrus was gone. In addition to an acute mental suffering brought on by his friend's death, and the de facto demise of the corps he loved so fervently, Ransom was wracked with pain from a grievous and dangerous wound. Four army surgeons examined his battered left knee in the early hours; two advised immediate amputation while the remainder seemed reasonably sure that both Ransom and the leg might recover together. The general closed the debate by rising in his cot and announcing: "Well, gentlemen, as the house is equally divided on this subject, I will, as chairman of the meeting, decide the question. I shall retain the wounded leg, lead included."[35] Neither were his spirits revived by the constant, pessimistic bickering engaged in by general officers crowding into the parlor--each bringing his own pet horror story of retreat and impending doom. At one point, Ransom's comments praising General A.J. Smith's excellent qualities as a fighting commander were interrupted by a curt demand from one general officer as to which Smith this might be. It was a reasonable request, considering that there were several Union and Rebel generals on the field bearing the ubiquitous last name. Unfortunately, the questioning officer rudely spun away before Ransom even finished identifying this particular Smith as commander of the XVI Corps. "Shrugging his shoulders in a significant way, [he] blurted out: 'Oh, damn it, there are so many Smiths.'"[36] The encounter provided the only light moment of the entire day, as Heath described:

> But we of the 16th Corps always felt that our Smith was one of the few, the immortal Smith's that were not born to be sneezed at by quartermasters...But new duties now began to claim the attention of the generals and one by one they drew away from Ransom's bedside. As they disappeared I ventured to ask him who the two big men in the brown overcoats were, who seemed to have so much to say...He said the big one was General Franklin and the other General Emory. In some confusion, I confessed to him that their solicitude about the trains had led me to believe them quartermasters. Ransom laughed; it was the only time I saw him laugh that morning...[37]

Ransom's battles in Louisiana ended with the Sabine debacle. His painful wound demanded a long period of recuperation in more comfortable circumstances. As a result, he would not be a party to the aftermath on April 9th when Banks's army beat off a spirited Rebel assault at Pleasant Hill, incurring heavy casualties on both sides. Banks was enthusiastic about resuming the Shreveport drive that evening, but found himself almost a minority of one. His chief commanders, those same muttering pessimists who crowded into Ransom's sick bay the night before, spoke only of retreat. Faced with their united professional opinion, Banks's new-found confidence flagged instantly. At midnight, the Army of the Gulf turned in its tracks, leaving behind the seriously wounded. General A.J. Smith, XVI Corps Commander, was seething at the turn of events, even suggesting at one point that General Franklin depose Banks as commander and lead them on to Shreveport. Private Lemuel Burke of Company K, 119th Illinois, echoed the prevalent feeling among the disgruntled Westerners:

> Oh, the bitter thoughts that forced themselves upon us as we contemplated the thought of leaving our wounded to the tender mercies of the rebels, and many of them yet uncared for, and our...brave dead unburied...I believe that every man in Gen'l Smith's command felt fully confident that we could have held, and not only have held but could have pursued the enemy and driven him before us. This day we began to hear the reports of prisoners who had made their escape after the battle [Pleasant Hill], and they say the rebels were whipped and abandoned the field...fleeing in a disorderly manner, such was their fright.[38]

Northern newspapers quickly zeroed in on this fiasco in the West whereby a fine Union army found itself whipped by a force less than half its strength. Many were calling the defeat "the Bull Run of the West," and demanded investigation. Every segment of this ill-begotten campaign reeked of incompetence. Admiral Porter's fleet had barely managed their escape over the shallows at Alexandria, and then only after a prodigious engineering feat. Banks's coveted Mobile command would never materialize following such blatant ineptitude. General Ransom's reputation survived the blistering criticism from both the national press and the powers in Washington. His performance at Sabine Crossroads was heralded as heroic in the extreme. Few, if any, fellow officers questioned his role in the blunder-filled campaign. The *Chicago Journal* correspondent at the scene filed a remarkably accurate dispatch detailing the general's unsuccessful efforts in convincing his superiors that an unsupported advance would result in disaster. The story appeared on the front page on April 17th concluding in the final paragraph, that:

> It has been a terribly unfortunate affair, but no one here attaches the least blame to General Ransom, who acted under orders, and, until disabled, did all that any officer could do under the circumstances; but with an overwhelming force to contend against, and no reinforcements, what could be expected but just such a rout?[39]

Even more emphatic in his defense of General Ransom's conduct was Lt. Henry Roe, who had seen his Chicago Merchantile Battery lose its guns and blood at Sabine Cross Roads. This embittered young officer directed his fury toward General N.P. Banks:

"I will...only tell you that our once powerful battery, as well as our noble little 4th Division, was sacrificed that day through the ignorance of a political General... Our Brave young Gen. Ransom here advised that we should wait until reinforcements should come up to our assistance before advancing any further. But <u>Gen. Banks</u> was Commander in Chief and ordered an advance, in other words, ordered troops that had never known defeat before, on to be sacrificed. The whole Rebel Army were in the woods beyond, drawn up in splendid Battle line..."[40]

Ransom's convalesence was typical of the man. He seemed constantly on the move despite the fact that his left knee remained stiff and painful. After a brief rest at New Orleans, the General took passage north for Chicago where he resided in the fashionable Tremont House, receiving in his parlor streams of well-wishers. Early May found him a guest in Judge T. Lyle Dickey's hilltop mansion on the bluff above Ottawa, Illinois. It must have come as a shock for both when Ransom learned the Judge's son, Cyrus, had briefly survived the terrible head wound thought mortal by Lieutenant Tredway. It seems a Confederate major named Winston discovered the young Captain Dickey still breathing, and indentified him as the same Union officer who had befriended his mother and sisters in occupied Natchez. Major Winston cared for the wounded stranger for five days until Dickey finally succumbed. The entire incident was reminiscent of General Wallace's fate at Shiloh, where he too was abandoned as dead, discovered alive the next day, and then lingered on for days before death.[41]

During this period in the north General Ransom was on crutches and nursing his Red River wound. He dismissed the concerns of friends by pointing out that a "stiff knee was better than no knee at all." He would have his photograph taken during this visit at the nearby LaSalle studio of Bowman and Rawson, posing in the fashionable Napoleonic mode with the right hand tucked into the unbuttoned tunic. His expression in the photograph is care-worn, the hair thinning a bit already despite his youthful 29 years. But the effect remains impressive. Ransom looked exactly like the archetypical Union hero. Ottawa newspaper editor William Osman echoed popular sentiment in reporting Ransom's visit as a pleasant honor, adding: "Wounds are nothing new to this gallant officer, who bears ugly scars about his person, the tokens of rebel attentions..."[42] After concluding his visit in familiar LaSalle County, the general returned to Chicago, pausing for a sitting at the Darling Studio in the Marine Bank Building.

Here Ransom was sketched by the same artist who had portrayed his father nineteen years before, just prior to the Mexican War which claimed his life.[43] The young general was obviously not intimidated by the ominous parallel, and soon embarked for New York City where his mother, Mrs. Margaret Ransom, then resided. He must have cut a dashing figure on the Eastern boulevards where many might have recognized the Western soldier from having read of his exploits in the May 14, 1864 *Harper's Weekly*. Ransom's finely etched features had been reproduced for the national magazine in a wood-block cut based on a photographic portrait by Mathew Brady himself. His profile was prominently displayed on the page opposite General Phil Sheridan's--another emerging Union hero in the spring of 1864. Chafing at the restrictions inherent in such a long convalescence, General Ransom eagerly awaited a return to active duty. His boyhood chum, General Grenville Dodge, had requested Ransom for his XVI Corps currently fighting under General Sherman in northern Georgia. The transfer was accomplished on August 2, when Ransom assumed command of the Fourth Division. Ahead lay a momentous challenge as Sherman's army approached Atlanta, a proud and strategic Confederate metropolis guarded by General John Bell Hood. It wouldn't be an easy campaign although by this stage Union leadership was, on the whole, as competent and certainly no less audacious than its southern counterpart. Sherman was a case in point, and so was the psalm-singing, one-armed Gettysburg veteran, General Oliver Otis Howard, the Army of the Tennessee's commander. The deeply religious officer was highly pleased with Ransom's arrival, first observing the Western soldier during a church service at headquarters:

> He was about the height of General Hooker, apparently not more than twenty-six or twenty-seven years of age, of handsome build, strong and muscular, with a figure that artists like to look upon; his head covered with a lightish brown hair, in itself a model, well proportioned, with a high forehead and a broad brow. His eyes were of a darkish cast; which gave a quick piercing expression to his face--pleasant when at rest, but severe and decided when under excitement. He was dressed in a full uniform that day, neat and tidy throughout; and it struck me that I had never in my life seen in appearance a nearer approach to perfection; and, indeed he was a handsome young man. His manners were gentlemanly and tempered with kindness; but he gave the idea of great decision of character. He was well informed

upon everything that concerned public affairs and public duty...Such is my first recollection of Ransom...[44]

    By late summer, 1864, the Army of the Tennessee was entrenched outside the besieged city of Atlanta, their lines forming the far right Union flank. Only days before, Sherman had shifted the army from the opposite flank, moving them behind his line, then swinging out around the city. Bullheaded Confederate General John Bell Hood met them at Ezra Church on July 28, 1864 with his typical impetuous brand of assault. The attack netted little more than massive Rebel casualties. When Ransom arrived, Sherman's army was settling down in siege, cheering their approval at the methodical artillery bombardment which daily sent tons of screaming metal into the Georgia city. His long-sought association with fellow Norwich graduate, General Grenville Dodge, was short-lived, terminating August 19th when a ricocheting Rebel bullet smashed into the corps commander's forehead. Dodge survived, but the serious wound required he relinquish command in order to recuperate in the north. The newly arrived Ransom replaced him as commander of the XVI Corps just as the Army of the Tennessee embarked on a daring sweep around the Confederate left flank, heading in a long arc for Jonesboro on the key Macon Railroad. Sherman had tired quickly of the siege, and now swung all three armies out from their entrenchments in this daring operation, leaving only a corps under General Henry W. Slocum in the trenches outside Atlanta. Five days' hard march saw Ransom's XVI Corps only a mile and a half away from the coveted railroad at Jonesboro when General "Black Jack" Logan's XV Corps came under heavy attack at about 3 p.m. Confederate Generals Stephen D. Lee and Patrick Cleburne pressed the attack throughout the afternoon, suffering 1,700 casualties. Ransom's corps was not actively engaged as a whole although their new commander estimated they had inflicted approximately 500 casulties during the fray while suffering two killed and 16 wounded. Total Union casualties at Jonesboro were only one fourth that of the assaulting Rebel forces.[45] Ransom's infantry entered Jonesboro in the early morning on September 2nd just as a Rebel hospital train chugged out, loaded with wounded from the recent battle. Atlanta's great supply artery was severed, leaving Hood dangling in isolation in the crumbling ruins of that dying city.

    Ripping up railroad tracks, skirmishing with small Confederate patrols, all the while in constant movement, Ransom's corps headed south toward Lovejoy's Station which they would scourge in proper "Sherman style." He then headed back north toward

East Point five miles from Atlanta now occupied by Slocum's Bluecoats. On September 13th, Ransom corresponded with the wounded Dodge, providing an obviously insistent friend with as much detail as possible regarding the events following his relief:

> It is said that "Republics are ungrateful" and I have heard it often conceded that Major Generals, particularly when wounded, expect impossibilities of their subordinates. This must be so, or you would not give me a lecture for not writing you on the 1st inst. when you left on the 25th ult. Doubtless ere this you have received my letter...giving a detailed account of the movements of your command up to that time and will, I hope, give me full credit for the immense draft upon my "Midnight Oil" that such lengthy efforts involve...Howard has recommended me for Major General, and I presume the document will be favorably endorsed by Sherman, though I have no information on this point. Howard told me last night that Grant had ordered Sherman to push the enemy and keep him in our front by all means, and that in order to carry out these orders, a new campaign would be commenced by the 1st of October; this of course, is not known in the Army and will be a great disappointment to all, as a respite and general recruiting is anticipated, and officers expect that a reasonable proportion of them will be allowed to go home...Though the General [Howard] expressed his determination to retain a corps in the field for you, yet the Lord only knows what he will do with Logan and Blair bucking at him...I shall watch your interests and that of the Corps constantly and do my best to keep all right, but you well know how much better you could do this yourself.[46]

Georgia was constant war. The contending armies were on the move nearly every day inflicting and suffering enormous casualties. It was an extremely arduous campaign demanding tremendous exertion, both physical and mental, from the participants. Rebel General John Bell Hood, brazen as always, struck north after Atlanta's fall, dragging Sherman in close pursuit with young Ransom commanding the XVII Corps for the absent General Frank Blair. Ransom's fervent conviction was that the commander belonged up front observing events as they occurred, responding with immediacy, and by physical presence encouraging the troops. Sherman was highly pleased with Ransom's exertions, reinforcing those first impressions gained back at Vicksburg during that fatal May 22nd assault. At one juncture in the Georgia campaign,

Sherman turned to an aide just as Ransom galloped off: "Do you know that young man?" Sherman asked. "That is General Ransom, rising man, rising man; one of the best officers in the service; been shot all to pieces, but it doesn't hurt him."[47] Sherman was in need of such men that fall when the impetuous Hood tore away at his own rail communications in a desperate attempt at duplicating Sherman's own recent strike around Atlanta. On October 5th, the Rebels struck hard at General Corse, fortified at the key supply and rail center in Allatoona Pass, and met a sharp rebuff. With Sherman in deadly pursuit, they then swung west and then north again toward Rome, Georgia, determined upon slashing across Sherman's rear areas.

Hood had an eager pursuer in the person of General Ransom, who spurred on his XVII Corps through Rome, then on through Resacca and Dalton, nipping at the Confederate's heels all the way. The Rebel commander turned southwest at this point, moving through Snake Creek Gap on his way toward LaFayette. In his wake was a jumbled, tree-stewn entanglement nearly five miles long. The obstacles were torn away by Ransom's men who hacked their way through the narrow gap that same night. They nearly reached the Confederate encampment, but Hood was once more on the march heading toward Gaylesville, Alabama. During these endless marches, interupted time and again with the crackling sound of skirmishes, Ransom awed subordinates with his energy and unquestioned valor. Magazine writer J.P. Thompson would assert in a brief Ransom biography how the General conducted the campaign with utter disdain for personal safety:

> At Atlanta, heavy firing on the line was so very frequent, that general officers usually contented themselves with sending a staff officer to learn the cause; but General Ransom never failed, by night or day, to visit the line himself immediately on the commencement of a fusilade, for fear that it might be a serious matter. He always persisted in visiting, frequently, his picket or skirmish-line...and would seldom allow any of his staff to accompany him, on the pleas that this would be an "unnecessary exposure"...This brave generosity he carried to excess, often putting his own life in danger when the exposure of one far less valuable would have answered the same purpose. But when anyone charged him with exposing himself unnecessarily, he always indignantly denied it.[48]

Exposure, coupled with long, exhausting hours in the saddle, slowly eroded Ransom's strength. Beginning on September 30th, his condition grew ever more serious, causing great concern among his staff. Lieutenant J.D. Tredway, aide-de-camp, recalled how both army surgeons and his friends urged Ransom to abandon his command as early as October 15th, and return to the North for treatment. "But as we were then skirmishing with the enemy," Tredway wrote, "he resolutely refused to do so saying that he believed a battle was pending which it was his duty to have a part."[49] Two days later, according to Tredway's recollection, the weakened general dismissed any possibility that he might seek medical attention in the North, stating: "I will remain with my command till I leave it in my coffin."[50] By the time the XVII Corps entered Gaylesville, Alabama, Ransom was confined to his cot, suffering the increasingly sharp spasmodic pain associated with diarrhea. Ransom's disability occured at a crucial stage in the campaign. Sherman had detached part of his army northwest toward Nashville, which was the expected target for Hood's forces, and dispatched the remainder on a grand sweep through Georgia. The XVII Corps was slated for the latter mission, but it was apparent Ransom would not be its commander. General Sherman recalled visiting the stricken Ransom at Gaylesville:

> I rode to the camp...and found General Ransom in a negro cabin. He lay on a rude improvised bunk, tried to be cheerful, and insisted that he was "all right," or would be in a day or so, but I noticed that his hand was dry and feverish, his forehead cold and clammy, and the pupils of his eyes distended, just as I had noticed in my own son, Willie, a few days before his death...Outside the cabin I asked the doctor what he thought. He said little, but I read in his face that Ransom's time on earth was short...As Gen. Ransom could not mount his horse, he was carried toward Rome, the nearest point for a railroad, in a litter...This was on the 28th...and I started from Gaylesville for Rome the next day, and overtook the cortege on the road. The men had constructed a sort of canopy to screen his face from the sun, and as my party approached they set the litter down on the road...There was little change since our previous visit. He certainly had a perfect memory and full consciousness of all that was passing. I remember to have joked him at traveling in a style of Oriental luxury....He smiled and made some pleasant reply, and we remounted and rode on.[51]

By 11 a.m., Ransom was fading so quickly that the escort pulled up at the John Berryhill home six miles from Rome. The staff commandeered the house as an impromptu hospital. Dr. Ormsby of the 45th Illinois Infantry was in attendance. He finally informed Ransom at 1:30 p.m. that there was no hope. At Ransom's side was the faithful Lieutenant Tredway as well as a comrade-in-arms from the Eleventh Illinois: Captain George Doanne of Morris, Illinois. The latter officer was a devoted admirer whose honor Ransom had vigorously defended when rumors had been spread regarding Doanne's alleged cowardice at Fort Donelson. It was a poignant scene recalled by Lieutenant Tredway:

> Up to this time the General had expressed the belief that he would live and though I believe the announcement was totally unexpected by him...he listened...without betraying a particle of emotion either of surprise or fear, and replied that he was as well prepared to die then as he should be 40 years hence...Cpt. Doanne of his staff endeavored to revise his hopes of life by saying: "General, you must not speak of death, you will be with us yet for many years." The General turned towards him with a smile and said: "Why, Dory, I am not afraid of death, I have faced it too many times to let it frighten me now. Subsequently," he said, "no, boys, I am not afraid to die, I do not like to die, but I am not afraid of it. I should have prefered to breathe my last on the battlefield but as it is, I am dying in the line of duty...I have often wished to know what there is for us in the hereafter, now I shall learn...I am not alarmed...[52]

Serene in these final moments, Ransom calmly urged his friends to select some personal effect as a memento, and expressed regret at leaving behind unpaid personal debts. He was detached and quietly philosophical regarding his fate, asking Dr. Ormsby at one point whether he would ever wake once asleep. It was not a gentle death. The spasmodic pain convulsed the general at intervals, inciting his comment that: "There is nothing funny about this thing death."[53] As always Ransom was candid, and without pretention, admitting that ambition was no stranger. His last audible comment was: "As a soldier, I have always tried to do my duty...I do not claim that what I have done was owing to patriotism entirely, though I believe I have as much of that as most men. Patriotism and inclination led me the same way."[54] From there his comments trailed off into incoherent mumbling. At 2:45 p.m.,

October 29th, 1864, General Thomas Edwin Greenfield Ransom, died--exactly one month from his thirtieth birthday.[55]

Ransom was buried in Chicago, a city he once described as the "mighty metropolis of the West, where wordly gain seems to absorb and cloud all the finer feelings of our nation."[56] On Sunday, November 8th, Ransom's body lay in state at Bryan Hall. "A steady and unremitting procession of the citizens...came to take a last look at the face of the departed warrior."[57] The coffin was decorated with floral wreaths and evergreen garlands, while the catafalque was draped with the national flag also bearing the names of his most famous battles. In the afternoon, the casket was drawn toward the city cemetery accompanied by the city's peeling bells and the firing of the minute gun in Courthouse Square. Every doorway and window ledge on the funeral path was jammed with spectators gaping at the solemn procession led by the blue-coated 24th Ohio Battery. The reporter for the *Chicago Times* described how the mournful pageant passed through ranks of flags draped at half mast.

> The day was unusually dark and gloomy. Heavy black clouds hung over the city as if the elements even sympathized with the mourning of a people over the departed hero. Only on the far distant horizon the heavens were breaking into light and splendor suggestive of the glorious dawn...[58]

Chapter Nine

Don't Scare a God Damn!

Federal authority in the defiant state of Mississippi rarely extended for more than a few feet beyond the bayonet-tipped rifle of the Union soldier. These Western Rebels endured with ferocious pride despite a parade of defeat from Corinth to Champion Hill. Founded, at least in part, on a tacit acceptance that this bitter resistance would make total occupation of the state extremely expensive in blood, men and equipment, strategy dictated that Union forces limit their presence to key strong points. Heavily garrisoned and entrenched bastions at Natchez, Port Hudson and Vicksburg were an integral part of the plan. From these points the Bluecoats controlled the river. And, from there, Yankee strike forces could embark on forays into the hostile interior, whether to chastize the wily Nathan Bedford Forrest, to wreck or re-wreck vital railroad track, or to lure Confederate attention and reinforcements from more strategic Eastern battlefields.

On this violent stage, and ruled by this strategic script, the Eleventh Illinois Infantry was to enact some of its most hazardous exploits. Until Ransom's departure for Texas, the regiment had been present at the focal points of the war in the West, whose place names were already memorable chapters in American history. Now the unit was relegated to the backwaters while the main stream of conflict flowed eastward. Back there, in Virginia and Georgia, the final great battles would explode. Meanwhile, in savage Mississippi, the Eleventh waged a far less romantic war. No matter how costly, or how bitterly fought, the struggles on this battlefield were consigned to the back pages of the Northern newspapers and ultimately sentenced to the war's bloody footnotes.

Future battles would not be momentous in effect although waged, at times, with unequalled ferocity. Death's finality was no different regardless of the combat's insignificance. This new era dawned for the Eleventh when the unit returned to the captured citadel of Vicksburg aboard the U.S.S. *Fort Wayne* on October 13, 1863. The city's melancholy ruins were a dreary postscript to the Natchez interlude. For the first time, the regiment became acquainted with a new phenomenon as they labored alongside Negro troops in repairing the city's defensive network. Black men in blue uniforms were anathema in the South, and hardly more popular among white Union troops infected, on the whole, with the racism prevalent throughout 19th-century America. Most often, "the Boys" in the Eleventh rarely even mentioned blacks in diaries or letters except perhaps in passing, and then in highly patronizing tones. They enjoyed describing the colorful Negro garb, mocking the simple plantation hand's pathetic attempt at aping white society, and mimicking the tortured speech patterns and shuffling "Uncle Tom" mannerisms. Especially adept at the latter was the regimental adjutant, Captain Henry Dean, whose letters often recorded Negro dialect. His imaginitive phonetic rendering of these conversations doubtless provided great amusement for friends in northern Illinois. Even Lieutenant Eugene Ransom of Company E, the general's younger brother, shared in the fun. Years later he sketched a scene labeled "The Lazy Nigger Contraband." The drawing depicted a shabby, grinning black caricature cowering before a Union soldier armed with a bayonet, about to stab the lottering "Nigger" into action.[1]

Typical too was Sergeant Frank Whipple of Company H, whose father had subscribed to William Lloyd Garrison's radical journal, *The Liberator* before the war. The son may have despised slavery, but it was plain that Federal union and not equal rights for Negroes motivated his war service. Young Whipple was certainly unaffected by Garrison's eloquent propaganda to that effect. As early as March 16, 1862, he penned home a letter from Savannah, Tennessee that summarized his racial viewpoint. "Down here you see plenty of darkies," he wrote. "Our camp is full much to our annoyance. Father wanted I would bring home one. I think, if I should, he would be sick of his bargain. I think they are better off where they are. I am sure satisfied to let them alone."[2] Later, in the spring of 1863, he listened without enthusiasm when Adjutant General Thomas addressed the Sixth Division on the subject of Negro troops. Volunteers were needed to officer these newly created regiments, but even the lure of promotion wasn't enough. Whipple wrote home to say he was emphatically uninterested and preferred to stick with the "Bully Old Eleventh."[3]

Although racism was prevalent, tolerance was not unknown in the regiment, nor was ambition. For whatever reason, a number of Eleventh veterans joined the black outfits. This included Captain Samuel B. Deane of Company B, a Donelson survivor who bore an ugly scar on his forehead from that encounter. He served as a major with the Sixth Mississippi Colored Infantry. Likewise, Captain William D. Parkinson, formerly of Company B, commanded a company in the 8th Louisiana Infantry (African Descent). This Shiloh and Donelson veteran was memorialized as "every inch the man" after his death from disease while with his black soldiers at Milliken's Bend, Louisiana, on July 13, 1863.[4] It is impossible to speak with total accuracy, but the consensus among the Eleventh's rank and file was, at best, skeptical. Sergeant Warren Peck, another former member of Company B, told his comrades how exasperating life was as a company commander in the Sixth Colored Mississippi. Blacks seemed childlike and always wanting something, he observed with great disgust. Less hostile was Sergeant Carrington, who still couldn't suppress a chuckle as Negro recruits fumbled with their newly issued gear and "get their cartridge boxes on upside down." Despite the teething troubles, Carrington admitted that most black recruits seemed "very willing to learn," and speculated that with time: "It will be rather dangerous...when they get hold of a musket and bayonet."[5] Until that time they labored, as did the Eleventh, with the less glamorous spade. In between fatique duties, both races flocked to water-filled shell holes for a bath and frolic.

Boredom was the greatest enemy in the late fall of 1863 and the early spring of 1864, both for black and white soldiers at Vicksburg. Morale wasn't improved after work details kept exhuming badly decomposed bodies hastily buried during the late hostilities. Sergeant Carrington frankly mourned for the far more pleasant attractions of Natchez. His only positive comment about the return to Vicksburg concerned the troops' relief that the Yellow Fever season had faded with the first frost. One amusement, at least at first, was to explore the crumbling earthworks. Carrington wandered in nostalgia amid the trenches which formed Fort Ransom. He was also keenly interested in the Rebel dugouts as well, particularly the civilian bombproofs which served as shelter for the populace through the siege:

> The cuts along the Jackson road have doorways on the sides...then large rooms made and arched...Here the citizens spent the nights safe from bullets and shells. The clay is of such a nature that it stands a long time just as it is cut, a name carved on the side of the road remains there. Our bullets were more dangerous than the big shells. Bullets

singing down that road hit and killed and wounded a great many while the shells could be seen coming so they could hunt their holes...I saw where 13-inch shells had burst in dwelling houses, tearing out partitions, knocking down plaster and fairly wrecking the house. Some burst five or six feet in the ground, many burst in the air; pieces weighing 50 or more pounds...would strike the ground hard. Woe be to anyone that was struck by these jagged pieces of iron hot from the Mortar.[6]

On the lighter side, there was a theater doing business in the city, attracting every night a good number from the Eleventh. Others spent idle moments in spirited games of "Seven Up," and "Chuck Luck" even on Sunday, much to the prudish Carrington's outrage. More innocent diversion was provided in impromptu athletic events ranging from foot races to an improvised shot put contest utilizing the 24-pound and 32-pound cannon shot scattered all about. It was a quiet time, in their new winter homes awaiting another Christmas in the South.[7] At Vicksburg, the Eleventh made do with rather primitive winter quarters consisting for the most part of tents set above dugouts three or four feet deep. The subterranean nest was then heated by a fireplace carved from the clay at the very rear of the dugout, and topped with a two or three barrel tall chimney. "A soldier can be homelike in camp if he will work a little," Carrington noted. He spent the days perusing a treasured copy of *Harper's History of the Great Rebellion* and back editions from the *New York Observer*. Christmas came and went with little incident; many, like Private Henry Uptmor from Company K, celebrated by attending Holy Mass. New Year's proved little change, except that real winter set in on the very first day, "...the north wind howling all around our tent," Uptmor recalled.[9] For most in the Eleventh it was a gloomy holiday time with little chance for either furlough or an end to hostilities. They huddled in their nests in between the picket or labor details, alternated at times by inspection, parade or some other military tedium. It was a humdrum existence that would soon end as a result of one man and an idea.

General William T. Sherman despised inactivity with the same ferocity he reserved for the Mississippi rebels. The enemy still, despite the Vicksburg campaign, challenged Federal authority at most points inland from the Mississippi River. The general formulated a plan that January to destroy the remaining rebel units within the state and smash the key railroad junction at Meridian, located due east from Vicksburg very near the Alabama line. It was a plan based on advancing the XVI and XVII Infantry Corps out from Vicksburg in a drive straight for Meridian, while General W. Sooy Smith's Union cavalry in Tennessee would head south into northern Mississippi and engage General Nathan Bedford Forrest's formidable horsemen. Sherman envisioned a series of feints that would hopefully confuse the enemy and draw forces away from the main drive on Meridian. The Eleventh Illinois would be the bait in one such ploy built around a water-borne strike force on the muddy, turbid Yazoo River whose mouth emptied into the Mississippi just above Vicksburg. The Eleventh Illinois, in company with the 8th Louisiana Infantry (African Descent), and elements from the First Mississippi Colored Cavalry, constituted this amphibious assault force.[10] The expedition would be commanded by Colonel James Coates of the Eleventh, who would relinquish regimental command of the 11th to Major George McKee. The mission was multi-faceted, although the primary goal was to draw off Confederate forces from the Meriden area. Simultaneously, Sherman hoped the river-borne troops might collect "cotton, corn and other forage" said to abound on the Yazoo River shores.[11] If at all possible, Coates's expedition would ascend far up the curling river to a point near Greenwood where a mounted force might disembark and search out Sooy Smith's mounted Union column which should, by that time, be within close proximity.

Coates's expedition, approximately 1,000 men, boarded the transports *Platte Valley*, *Des Moines*, *Sioux City* and *J.H. Lacey* on January 31st. The convoy was provided with a "Tin Clad" escort including the gunboats *Marmora*, *Exchange*, *Petrel*, *Prairie Bird* and *Romeo*--under the command of Lieutenant Commander Elias K. Owen, U.S. Navy.[12] Thirty-five more black cavalry came aboard at Haynes Bluff on February 2nd just before the flotilla steamed upriver with the gunboats churning in the lead. This was a semi-wilderness whose main communication line was the meandering Yazoo River. The western bank was almost uninhabited, consisting mainly of swampy lowlands dotted with timber and heavy undergrowth. The east bank was dominated by occasional bluffs topped with timber and other growth well suited for any would-be ambuscade. Accordingly, Colonel Coates ordered the men to construct improvised barricades aboard the transports which might give them protection against the Confederate fire that most assuredly would greet every Union foray upriver. The precautionary measure was well taken. The fleet encountered heavy Rebel sniper fire the first day out near Sartartia. Ignoring the incoming Confederate rounds, Colonel Coates ordered his boats straight into the landing and disgorged a detachment from the Eleventh Illinois and the Third U.S. Colored Cavalry.

Black horsemen clattered in pursuit after the fleeing ambushers, killing at least one out of what appeared to be a force of 60 Confederate cavalry.[13] The next morning Coates resumed the upriver voyage which terminated almost immediately near Liverpool Heights, just above Sartartia. The gunboats passed without incident just before 9 a.m., but the vulnerable transports encountered a devastating fire from both Rebel artillery and dismounted cavalry. The enemy were perfectly camouflaged amidst the undergrowth. The transports reversed engines, paddling furiously back out of range while the shipboard Union infantry replied with a steady fusillade. Not one boat was hit seriously, while the gunboat escort, drawn back by the battle sounds, pitched in with its own cannon aimed at the Rebel earthworks atop the heights.[14]

Colonel Coates ordered his transports in just below the bend where the command jumped ashore, formed up in two columns, and advanced on the Confederate position on the heights. Two hundred and fifty men from the Eleventh, with McKee in the lead, formed the left wing while the 8th Louisiana under Lieutenant Colonel F.E. Peebles moved out on the right. Out in front, the dismounted black troopers from the Third Cavalry formed a skirmish line under the direction of Major Jeremiah B. Cook. Another 300 infantry from the Eleventh were positioned in the immediate rear as a reserve commanded by Captain H.C. Vore. The Union landing party encountered rifle and cannon fire. Colonel Coates witnessed his troops go on the attack:

> The hills in this vicinity are amost mountainous and difficult of assault, yet our skirmishers steadily advanced and drove them from their first position. They rallied, however, but not until I had thrown out to the right of his [McKee's] line one wing of the Eighth Louisiana...I am now finding both detachments closely pressed, ordered the balance of the Eleventh Illinois...under the command of Captain H.C. Vore...to their support, throwing the latter as a reserve and in the rear of about center of the line of skirmishers. The enemy now opened briskly with two pieces of artillery, also infantry fire.[15]

The rebels enjoyed a double advantage in possessing the high ground and firing from the safety of breastworks camouflaged by heavy undergrowth. A depression at the very summit of Liverpool Heights served as a ready-made fortress from which the disciplined Southern cavalry poured a heavy fire on the Yankees scrambling from tree to tree below. When the Union troopers approached the main Rebel lines, their right flank came under severe pressure which was quickly countered by Coates, who dispatched a battalion from the 8th Louisiana to the danger area. At this point, Major McKee, on his own initiative, impulsively ordered his detachment to make a dash at the Rebel strongpoint. It was repulsed by an effective Confederate volley which left two Union infantry dead on the field and three wounded. The usually lucky Sergeant Whipple was knocked senseless when a rechocheting bullet struck him high in the forehead. Strangely enough, his companion, Private Paul Miller, had envisioned Whipple's fate minutes earlier, predicting "that Frank would be shot." Now Miller and the other men in McKee's detachment fell back down the wooded hillside carrying and dragging the wounded. Whipple's forehead was painted in blood dripping from the dark, round hole in his forehead. Another Eleventh infantryman screamed in pain from a rifle bullet through the bowels.

Minutes later, dismounted Rebel cavalry charged down the hillside where they collided with Captain H.C. Vore's troops who stood rock steady. They "were fairly driven beyond the hill," Colonel Coates would report.[16] But satisfaction was brief. Pressure shifted to Coates's far right where Captain Wilson's 8th Louisiana Battalion drove back another Rebel threat only to be repulsed in turn by the newly arrived 27th Texas. It was a hairraising, vicious tussle conducted at incredibly close range where black Union troopers traded pistol shots with the Texas bravos before falling back down the hillside.[17] "As night approached I gave the signal for the detachments to fall back to the boats, the gunboats covering this movement with well-directed shell," Coates wrote. "I am now dropping down the river, where I shall go for about one mile, and will make another attack on the enemy at daylight tomorrow morning."[18]

It was time for decision. Coates confronted three basic alternatives: mount another land attack at Liverpool, retire down river and admit defeat, or run the batteries at the heights, which would leave the Rebels in his rear. He was well aware that the remainder of the Texas Brigade under wily General Lawrence "Sull" Ross lurked in the area and could suddenly appear if the Union forces launched another attack at the heights. Retreat would be humiliating and a direct violation of his instructions from Sherman, yet the river above the heights provided little enticement. The Yazoo narrowed under the Confederate gun positions at Liverpool with passage further complicated by the presence of the sunken steamer *Ivy*. Coates's miniature armada would be forced into taking the bend at a crawl--a perfect floating target gallery for the Rebels.[19]

The verdict was to run the batteries, proceed upriver, and accomplish the mission assigned despite the risks entailed in leaving the enemy to his rear. Coates was licked at Liverpool Heights, but managed to withdraw in good order with relatively few casualties considering the length and character of the combat. The Eleventh lost four killed, twelve wounded, and eight missing while the Eighth Louisiana Infantry and the First Mississippi, together, reported only two killed and eight wounded. Furthermore, not one steamer in the flotilla suffered serious damage, and carried enough fuel for at least ten days of travel. One consideration too, was Coates's growing confidence in his black troops who had shown praiseworthy elan in the Liverpool Heights encounter. He reported to General McArthur in Vicksburg how they "nobly performed their part of the duty assigned them and acquitted themselves most handsomely, displaying the courage, coolness, and discipline of the most experienced troops."[20] It was high praise indeed, coming as it did from a veteran officer commanding what one officer in the Third Colored Cavalry admiringly described as "the crack regiment of the 'Sucker State.'" Lieutenant Colonel F.E. Peebles of the Eighth Louisiana was equally proud emphasizing in a letter home that, "the colored soldiers fought with so much bravery and gallantry as to elicit not a few commendations from the officers and men of the Eleventh Illinois, from Coates, down."[21]

Their usefulness as soldiers was complemented by their effectiveness as scouts, spies and messengers. In fact, Colonel Coates entrusted his plans to run the blockade to black hands as the fleet anchored below Liverpool on the evening of the third. Sergeants Washington Vincent and Isaac Trendall, both from the Third U.S. Colored Cavalry, volunteered. They were described by a white officer as "mulattoes, young, brave and quick witted."[22] These former slaves were intimately familiar with the local terrain, making them ideal candidates for a mission which could easily mean instant execution at the hands of Texas cavalry. They silently stole away in a small boat sometime after 10 p.m., headed toward thick cover on the nearby shore, and then slipped unseen through the Confederate picket line. The troopers were clad in the shabby rags common to plantation hands as an added precaution against discovery. Ten hours later they trotted into McArthur's headquarters mounted atop two Texas cavalry mounts, with two more in tow behind. They borrowed the horses from a quartet of

Texas cavalrymen momentarily preoccupied with the attentions of certain female "inmates" of an isolated house.[23]

Naturally, Colonel Coates was unaware whether they had been successful when he ordered his flotilla upriver at about 4:30 a.m. on February 4. The Eleventh's infantrymen crouched behind a barricade of timber, hardtack crates, and other obstructions that would provide some protection from the expected Rebel fire. It was deathly quiet as the lead gunboat cruised past the heights without eliciting a single rifle shot but then the quiet exploded when the five transports came into full view of the Confederates.[24] Rebel riflemen delivered a steady, accurate fire down at the wallowing transports. Bullets gouged and tore away at the thin-skinned vessels. On board, the Union troops fired back blindly at the bluffs, or aimed at the tell-tale puffs of gunpowder. Men were being wounded, and a few fell dead aboard the beleagured Union steamers. Private Uptmor on *Des Moines* turned just in time to see his companion, James Reed, collapse with a bullet right through the leg. It was a tulmutuous few minutes remembered most vividly by Major Edward Main of the Third U.S. Colored Cavalry:

> The rebels on the bluffs could not be seen; they fired from behind trees, rocks and from wherever they could find cover, but the storm of bullets from the transports found every nook and cranny along the face of the bluffs...It was like pandemonium turned loose. The scene was exciting and awe-inspiring to the highest degree...The crash of small arms, the defiant yells of the combatants, echoed back from the silent depths of the uninhabited swamp on the west side of the river, the shrill whistles and labored breathing of the steamers as their huge paddle-wheels lashed the murky waters of the Yazoo into a foaming torrent, the flaming bluffs, vomiting forth sheets of fire...[25]

Once safely past the heights--partly due to the fact that a shortage of shells limited Confederate artillery fire--Coates counted his casualties, which were again surprisingly light. The Eleventh had one man wounded on the *Des Moines* and three severely wounded aboard the *Sioux City*, while one black soldier aboard the *J.H. Lacey* was mortally wounded. No time was wasted in setting about Coates's secondary mission, to seize valuable cotton and other supplies along the riverside. Before the afternoon ended, his men stripped several plantations of 200 cotton bales valuable on the market, but even more useful as proof against small arms fire. The expedition's commander specifically instructed that some bales be placed around the vulnerable steamer boilers where a well-directed Rebel shell might prove fatal.

The fleet was anchored at Goosey's Mill about four miles below Yazoo City. Captain Owen led two gunboats further upstream on a scout which led to a brief exchange of cannon fire with a Rebel battery at Yazoo City. Two Confederate shells struck the *Exchange* with little effect, although they struck dangerously near the boiler. Owen drew back almost immediately, without a reply while Confederate sharpshooters from only 250 yards away plastered his closed gunports with rifle fire. Besides, his mission to secure information on the defenses was now accomplished. He steamed back down toward Goosey's Mill where Coates's troops had already set up bivouac ashore.[26]

Captain Owen grossly overestimated Confederate strength at Yazoo City, which he thought contained at least five batteries and an eight-inch monster gun. In truth, the gunboats had engaged only two small artillery pieces. Accordingly, a retreat downriver was ordered, taking the flotilla without incident past Liverpool Heights to Sartartia, where Coates observed Confederate cavalry on the prowl. Once again, the Eleventh Illinois and their black allies went ashore to pursue. The chase ended in a duel between the two picket lines when the enemy reached the strategic Liverpool Heights position. The Union commander pulled his amphibious force back aboard at about 5:30 p.m., and then ringed the landing area with a strong picket. The next day Coates postponed his drive upriver, waiting through the morning for the ironclad *Louisville*. His patience was exhausted by noon, and still there was no ironclad in sight; Coates determined to push up river despite the odds.[27] He was unaware that the Confederate cavalry were at that moment destroying their fixed artillery batteries at Yazoo City in preparation for a march on Sherman's main columns headed toward Meridian. The Yankee feint on the Yazoo had been correctly analyzed by Brigadier General William H. Jackson who ordered "Sull" Ross to temporarily abandon his Yazoo River positions.

When the Union steamers hove into sight at the Liverpool Heights bend, the tense Union infantry fully expected a fight as they hunched up behind the cotton bales and peered up at those forested hills. There was not one shot, to the amazement of Colonel Coates, who then anchored at the familiar Goosey's Mill landing. From there he dispatched Captain Owen and two gunboats toward Yazoo while simultaneously Major Jeremiah Cook set out on shore with a small mounted scout patrol from the Third U.S. Colored Cavalry. The black horsemen clashed with a small Confederate cavalry force then in the act of pulling out of Yazoo City, which now lay open to Yankee invasion. Coates ordered his transports ahead, docking at the city in the afternoon on February 9th. His command was reinforced the same day by 250 more troops from the Third U.S. Colored Cavalry who had made their way overland from Haynes Bluff under Colonel Embury D. Osband's command. It was an uneasy occupation aggravated by a recent incident at Snyder's Bluff where black Union troops executed two Texas cavalrymen thought guilty in the fatal beating of a captive black soldier. Supposedly, the white officers of the First Arkansas Colored Infantry stood aside while the enraged Negroes murdered the Confederate prisoners. As a posthumous humiliation, the Rebel bodies were buried underneath the slain black cavalryman. Now, only weeks later, Yazoo City witnessed that ultimate Southern nightmare: armed black men walking the streets unopposed.[28]

Major Edward Main of the Third Cavalry thought Yazoo a pretty place numbering not more than 2,000 inhabitants. He was pleased with the pleasant "highly picturesque surroundings" of this once thriving trade center. In the military sense, he was extremely satisfied with the topography which allowed certain advantages should Ross's Texans return. Natural defenses were reinforced by two earthen redoubts abandoned by the Confederates. One was located on a high promontory above the main Benton Road only about 400 yards due east from downtown Yazoo. The second, similar in design, guarded an access road at a point approximately 1,000 yards southeast of the city. Coates could feel safe here since he was provided with a watery back door if any real Confederate pressure materialized. All about lay the rich, fertile cotton land--classic slave country where the residents were either "poor white" or plantation gentry. Much to the invaders' surprise, the streets were filled with able-bodied, young white men apparently disinterested in the war as a whole, much less this occupation by black and white Union soldiers. Hating slavery, and holding a high respect for his black troopers, Major Main of the First Mississippi was hardly an objective observer. For him the town was a perfect example of what slavery produced--a class society discouraging initiative among the lower orders who "cringed and crawled with all the servility of serfs." He held no sympathy for these Rebels whom he described with venom:

> It was here that slavery was found in its most revolting form. The poor whites lived in the hill country, where they eked out a scanty and most miserable existence...In Yazoo City was found a motley crowd of old "Mossbacks", types of

poor white trash, too old or decrepit for service in the rebel army. These dilapidated specimens of humanity, poor people of a slave-cursed country, were lounging about or sitting on goods boxed in front of tavern or store, frescoing the sidewalk with tobacco juice and discussing "de wah." They were yet even loath to believe that Vicksburg had surrendered, which place many of them had never visited, and they had unbounded confidence in the invincibility of the rebel army...The ignorance, stupidity and superstition of these people was deplorable, and furnished the most convincing proof of the blighting effects of slavery...[9]

The Union task force tarried two days at Yazoo City before setting course upriver. Evidently, Coates seemed confident that his steamers could dare any Confederate attempt at bottling them up on the upper reaches of the river, or perhaps the disappearance of Ross's Rebel cavalry was the deciding factor. Whatever the case, the Yankee transports chugged toward Greenwood, a small town very near where the Yazoo forks out into the Tallahatchie and Yalabolusha Rivers. The voyage was relatively uneventful except for a sharp skirmish with a small band from Colonel Jeoffrey Forrest's Rebel cavalry who were engaged near Honey Island by elements of the Third U.S. Cavalry sent ashore.[30] Three black troopers were wounded in the inconclusive fray.

Awaiting the command at Greenwood was a bizarre figure commonly addressed as Colonel Greenwood Le Flore. He was a chief in the Choctaw Tribe, most of whom now resided in distant Oklahoma. As the Union steamers approached the dock, the old chief constituted a small but enthusiastic reception committee, waving a small National Banner back and forth when the Yankees stepped ashore. The elderly gentleman had fought with Andy Jackson in the Florida wars during which time, Captain Main asserted, the Indian "imbibed a great love for the Union and the flag."[31] He was an adept survivor, witnessed by the fact that he had avoided the mass deportation of the Choctaw ordered by his former commander, "Old Hickory," and amassed a considerable fortune in slaves and land. Somehow through the Civil War years he retained his Federal loyalty and his life here in a bitterly pro-Confederate region. "He told the officers that he had promised General Jackson that he would always remain loyal to the government of the United States," Major Main recalled, and "...he had kept that promise, not withstanding the threats and persecutions of the ultra-secessionists."[32] Colonel LaFlore was insistent that the Union officers dine in his "palatial residence" and urged they recruit as many of his slaves as possible for the Colored regiments, saying: "My negroes, too shall fight for the Union."[33]

Another command decision confronted Colonel Coates at this juncture. Captain Owen grew restive as the water level steadily receded on the Yazoo whose channel was extremely narrow, particularly at a point one mile below Greenwood where the wrecked *Arcadia* presented a formidable obstacle. The Navy officer was adamant that the Yalobusha and Tallhatchie rivers were far too shallow to allow the fleet passage; both streams also were clogged with the wrecks of the sunken *Star of the West* and the *Ed J. Gay*.

Coates agreed that further progress upstream would be unwise, although he opted to remain at least a few days at Greenwood while Colonel Osband and 250 black cavalry searched out Union General Sooy Smith's mounted force which should be somewhere near Grenada. Osband's horsemen departed Greenwood at dawn on the 16th, advancing with great caution toward Grenada some 35 miles northeast. At a place on the main road, about six miles from town, they surprised a large Rebel cavalry command and engaged them in a spirited running fight. About a mile outside Grenada, Osband called a halt since observations indicated General Forrest's main cavalry force, numbering seven thousand, was encamped nearby. The attempt to reach Sooy Smith was abandoned and the black horse soldiers clattered off toward Greenwood with all possible speed. They reached Coates with the news at 2:30 a.m. on the 17th.[34]

Based on the official reports and surviving accounts it is difficult to ascertain whether Coates assumed Forrest's command would strike toward Smith or if he felt his water escape route provided him with a certain flexibility. Anyway, he lingered at Greenwood for another two days, reporting to General McArthur that his troops were engaged "securing as much cotton, etc., as possible during the time." On Sunday, February 28, the flotilla was six miles upriver from Yazoo City at which point Coates ordered the black cavalry ashore with instructions to swing around and come in behind the city while the infantry would land at the wharf. Presumably any wandering Confederates would be scooped up between the two Union columns. Yankee infantry occupied the town without incident, but soon received word that the cavalry had encountered trouble. Major Cook with his detachment from the 1st Mississippi loped off on their captured mules, headed toward Benton on the main road. At about 3 p.m., the men from the Eleventh Illinois saw the scattered "mule soldiers" hurtle back into camp with a strong force of Rebel cavalry on their heels. Behind, strewn along the Benton Road for some miles, lay the bodies of at least nineteen black Yankees shot down in the running fight. Others had been captured, although the Rebel cavalry quickly reined up when they saw the Eleventh Illinois and 8th Louisiana Infantry skirmishers move out. They pursued, if infantry could ever be said to pursue a mounted force, some three miles before turning back toward Yazoo.[35]

    The Eleventh was bivouaced in the main redoubt on the Benton Road with Company A assigned as provost guard in the town proper. The 8th Louisiana settled in at the other redoubt southeast of the town while the black cavalry mounted pickets in a wide screen all around the Federal position, while their main camp was established a few hundred yards northwest of the Lexington Road. Dispositions made, Coates settled down for a wait even as the Confederates massed a powerful strike force against his isolated command. Generals Robert V. Richardson and General "Sull" Ross were back on the scene after a futile effort at stopping Sherman's big drive on Meridian. Together they could mount an attack force probably approaching 5,000 men with artillery support. Both Rebel officers were anxious that the Yankee raiders on the Yazoo be taught a bloody and effective lesson. With luck, they hoped Yazoo City might well be the place for inflicting such an education on Coates and his outnumbered command which totaled 1,500.

    In the days that followed, the Eleventh Illinois hunkered down behind their earthwork walls while Rebel cavalry played coy with the Union picket posts. On March 2nd, some 60 grayclad riders finally struck hard at the outpost line, but quickly fell back before a sally from the Colored cavalry. Another day passed with little of note except when an occasional shot barked out on the threatned picket line. "The enemy...will ride within long range, and fire on our advance doing no harm however," Colonel Coates recorded on March 3rd. "As soon as a body of cavalry moves out, they will run from one hill to another, evidently trying to draw them into ambush."[36] Coates wouldn't buy that amateurish trick, however, and settled down patiently in his position at Yazoo City--still populated with a few civilians who were apparently unconcerned about the impending battle. They were hardly overjoyed at the Yankees' return. Lieutenant Colonel Peebles of the 8th Louisiana described the town as a shambles, conveniently forgetting to mention who had made it so:

    The dwellings were mostly closed, as was every store and public building, except the Court House, which told more plainly than words, how ruthless is war. All the doors were thrown open, the floors strewn with paper, some of them dating as far back as 1839; the county records were thrown here and there about the rooms--everything betokened desolation. A printing office, I passed by, was broken open, and the same chaos reigned there. The sidewalks, made of brick, were torn up. Now and then a solitary female was seen on the street, and the most of them wore the sable badge, doubtless for loved ones, lost in the rebel army.[37]

    There were sound reasons behind Coates's apparent confidence, the main one being he knew that Colonel F.M. Crandell with about 700 men from the 10th Louisiana and the Third Mississippi Colored regiments was on his way toward the key Liverpool Heights position. This back door to Yazoo City would remain open for the Union expedition should events necessitate a rapid withdrawal. Secondly, Coates was happy with his position at Yazoo City because it provided his troops with good protection and cover, and the approaches to the city were difficult. The Union commander wrote McArthur in Vicksburg that he could "hold this place, without a doubt, against five times my numbers." He added in the same communication, dated March 2nd, "...everything looks cheering, with enough fighting to create a healthy circulation of the blood."[38]

    It was blood the Rebels wanted. The Texas Cavalry still smouldered over the alleged atrocity which had occurred at Mechanicsburg. The murder of two men from the 6th Texas was made doubly painful since they had been shot down by blacks, armed by the Federal Government. General "Sull" Ross made known his own concern in a subtly intimidating note delivered to Coates under a truce flag on the morning of March 4th. The Confederate general suggested that murder of prisoners was a Union monopoly as his own men treated captives, "kindly and with the consideration due them as prisoners of war. Indeed, it is the boast of the Texans, that while they have always damaged the enemies of their country...in open, fair fight, they had never yet injured nor in anyway maltreated prisoners." Such a benevolent policy was now undermined by the barbaric incident committed by black Union troops at Mechanicville, Ross noted. "From the threats made by officers and men of your command during their recent raids through this county, I am led to infer that yourself and command indorse the cold-blooded and inhuman proceedings of Colonel Wood."[39] Coates's reply was carefully worded:

I would respectfully reply that your information relative to outrages said to have been committed by Colonel Wood, U.S. Volunteers, is the first intimation that I have received of such transactions, and beg further to assure you that this mode of warfare and treatment of prisoners is as sincerely deprecated by me as by yourself. I desire, however, to call your attention to a fact which in all probability you have not yet been advised, viz, that in a skirmish with a portion of your command on the 28th ultimo 19 of my command (colored) were missing; since then 6 of the number have been found, presenting every appearance of having been brutally used, and compelling me to arrive at the conclusion that they had been murdered after having been taken prisoners. I beg leave to assure you...I will not deviate from those principles dictated by humanity, and it will only be in extreme cases of premeditated provocation that I will tolerate it in any portion of my command:

I am, general, respectfully, etc.,
JAS. H. COATES,
Colonel, Commanding U.S. Forces, Yazoo City.[40]

Whatever may have been the reality, both Confederate and Yankee forces felt little hope for pity in this long deferred contest. Racial overtones, deep-seated hostilities, and the alleged Yankee depredations on the Yazoo all combined to create an ideal environment for vengeful hatred. So it was on March 5th, 1864 when the Texans came howling down the Benton Road at just about 7 a.m. Union pickets held firm against a heavy fire until Rebel artillery barked into action. The Yankees scrambled back toward McKee's earthen redoubt. There, a howitzer from the gunboat *Exchange* was wheeled out in reply. "They had their artillery in front, and raked us...from three different ways," recalled one trooper from the Eleventh. "We had a little 12-pound howitzer, but got a shell fast her before we had fired half-a-dozen rounds...and the rebels poured it into us lively."[41] The Confederate veterans advanced on foot while the cannon fire burst into the redoubt and an adjoining rifle pit filled with about eighty black soldiers from the 8th Louisiana A.D. It was probably at this time, or shortly afterward, that the Eleventh's First Sergeant George B. Shaw was torn apart by three hunks of cannon shrapnel from an exploding shell. The blast also threw Captain H.C. Vore to the ground, leaving him dazed from the concussion and bleeding from shrapnel wounds.[42] Another Rebel shell tossed Lieutenant Eugene Ransom into the air, although the general's brother escaped with little more than a good scare. The battle had barely opened and already the Eleventh was taking a beating with the Rebels now on both flanks. The prospect was good that they would soon be between the regiment and Yazoo City proper. Early in the fight Major Cook withdrew his black troops from the exposed rifle pits into the redoubt where he took overall command since Major McKee was still in the city at Coates's headquarters. The dash from the rifle pits left Lieutenant Eugene Walker of the First Mississippi dead at the fort's sally point and two or three black men dead or dying. Cook was convinced that the enemy was about to assault at any moment, and urged the black and white troops to keep up a heavy fire from the parapet. He'd strengthened the position a few days before by securing heavy boards just above the top of the earthwork walls which left a few inches between wood and dirt.[43] As a result the infantry fired on the Rebels without undue exposure although the wooded guard rail was extremely vulnerable to Rebel cannon fire which exploded with regularity throughout the battle. "There was an old house standing in the fort which made a fine object for them to fire at," wrote one beleagured rifleman from the Eleventh, "and the way they threw shells in was not agreeable."[44]

The *Exchange* was off the wharf with a formidable battery aboard including four 24-pound howitzers and a 10-inch Parrott rifled piece. But Lieutenant J.S. Hurd, U.S.N. held fire for fear of short rounds exploding in the city where Company A of the Eleventh, and Company D of the 8th Louisiana, A.D. were stationed. Instead, Hurd ordered a shore party to transport another 24-pounder into town as close-up fire support for the hard pressed Yankee infantry. Rebel sharpshooters were by now within 100 yards of Redoubt McKee while other Confederate units besieged the 8th A.D. in their stronghold south of the town. Major Ed Main of the 1st Mississippi recalled:

> The enemies' batteries...rained shot and shell into and around the besieged fort, some of the shot bursting in the air over the fort, the pieces falling among the men, killing and wounding men, and others finding lodgment in the earthworks, or ploughing deep furrows in the earth covering the men with dirt and debris, while the Rebel sharpshooters, crouching in gully and ravine, closed in...It was well known that the Texans took no "nigger" prisoners, therefore no quarter could be expected...A flag of truce was seen approaching the fort. Major Cook sprang upon the parapet

where he was hailed by Colonel Mabry of the Third Texas Cavalry...demanding the immediate and unconditional surrender of the forces holding the fort, to which demand Major Cook made this reply: "My compliments to General Ross, and say to him that if he wants this fort to come and take it!"...After the flag of truce incident, the attack was renewed with even more fury than before...[45]

At around 10 a.m., Major McKee dashed toward the Union redoubt despite concentrated fire from the 9th Texas, which was practically astride the key Benton Road only 100 yards from the fort. McKee was now in command. The Eleventh's reckless executive officer took full advantage of a large ravine most of the way, however, and arrived without a scratch. One of his first acts was to dispatch part of Company K, Eleventh Illinois toward town with the idea they might keep open a communications line with Colonel Coates's Headquarters. Private Uptmor was among the chosen. The stolid German was, as always, right in the thick of it. He'd already seen his close friend, Sam McElhainy, shot through the arm and another Company K soldier killed outright earlier that morning. It mattered little, for now Uptmor was busy dodging the Rebel fire as the detachment tried to slip back into Yazoo City. Company K was up against heavy odds which resulted in a number being captured by the aggressive Texans. Private Uptmor would later write:

As I looked around I knew we had to flee or be taken as prisoners. I asked one of my comrades to see whether any path to safety was open to us. He at once darted off in the direction of our fort and I ran behind him with all possible speed. Meanwhile the enemy was not idle. They sent shots at us both, but we remained uninjured; they got a bullet through my haversack...when we got within 75 yards of our people, we had to stop because they were firing on the enemy, and the enemy, all around us, were firing on them. We were really in a bad spot. My companion lay down flat...and I sought protection in a small declivity a little farther back. They then fired over our heads from all sides. Small musket balls bullets and heavy cannon balls rushed over us with lightening speed. We lay there about an hour, stiff with fear and full of gloomy thoughts...[46]

Coates was in little better shape inside Yazoo City, now exposed to savage attack from the north where the 17th and 15th

Tennessee came howling in on the outnumbered provost guard. Captain Orton Ingersoll of Company A of the Eleventh, in company with a black detachment from the 8th A.D., pulled back through the city streets in an on-going, close-up fight. The exultant Rebels were joined by many town residents who miraculously produced weapons and delivered a cruel fire from positions on the rooftops. The Rebels penetrated to within two houses of Coates's headquarters where the advance stalled before a cotton bale fort and the Navy-manned 12-pound howitzer whose canister screamed down the narrow streets with gruesome effect. The intensity of the street combat was overwhelming for the Navy gunners who, with their officer, soon abandoned the weapon and fled down toward the wharf demanding that they be allowed aboard one of the steamboats. Lieutenant McElroy turned a deaf ear to these panicky entreaties, sending out another gun crew for Coates while steadfastly refusing to allow the original crew back aboard.[47] His attitude seemed to be that they could share the common fate; and at that moment the future seemed a long march into the dreaded Rebel prison camps or slaughter at the hands of enraged Texans. It was an unpleasant state of affairs when the confident Rebel commander once again called for a cease fire out on the Benton Road.

Lieutenant Rogers of General Lawrence Ross's staff rode out with the white flag toward Redoubt McKee with another demand for immediate and unconditional surrender. This message contained an implied threat, namely that General Ross "would be unable to restrain his men" if forced to storm the Union position. Major McKee was bellicose in his refusal, or as one man from the Eleventh proudly put it: "He don't scare a God damn!" The Shiloh and Vicksburg veteran shouted back at the Rebel emissary his opinion that General Ross simply intended to murder Yankee prisoners. This brought forth a weak negative from Lieutenant Rogers: "No, not exactly that; but you know how it will be."[48] McKee was not appeased and informed the Rebel messenger that any future communications must be in writing, for the record. "...If he attached me with the present understanding and was repulsed, I would kill every man that fell into my hand," McKee stated.[49]

At least for Private Uptmor this ominous parlay proved a Godsend since the Rebel rifleman held fire while he walked back into the redoubt in company with a few other survivors from Company K. During the negotiations, Uptmor, as well as others within the fort, engaged in shouted conversation with the nearby Confederates. "They called to us that they had built that fort for the express purpose of catching Yankees in it," he wrote. "We were very much afraid that they would do just that for we were surrounded on all sides by five regiments, so that there was no way open for retreat."[50] Twice more in the space of an hour and a half McKee received surrender demands from the Confederates, the first containing little more than a promise of "treatment due prisoners of war." McKee responded, "he had no idea of surrendering" and expressed regret that the earlier threats were not repeated on paper. Once again the Rebels demanded surrender:

> Major McKee:
> Your reply just received. I regret for the sake of humanity that you do not find it consistent with your feelings of duty...to surrender the redoubt, which I can certainly storm and take.
> As to the treatment of your men and yourself, I will try and have them protected if they surrender during the charge; but you may expect much bloodshed. If you have no reply to make, we will resume operations when the white flag is down from both your line and mine.
> Respectfully,
>
> L.S. Ross
> Brigadier General[51]

Ever afterward, Private Uptmor remembered how McKee ordered "fix bayonets" right after the last exchange. The men formed in a great semi-circle, apprehensively waiting for the inevitable Rebel charge.[52] At least four hours had passed since the Rebels surrounded Redoubt McKee. Now, with early afternoon, the script suddenly underwent a dramatic change heralded in Yazoo City by the arrival of two more companies of the 8th Louisiana Infantry A.D. Coates had requested the reinforcements, which fought their way into town from their own encircled redoubt located a half-mile southeast. His force in the town then included six black infantry companies as well as Captain Ingersoll's Company A from the Eleventh. These troops began a methodical drive north through the town while the Navy howitzer was "discharging shell with telling effect into the houses the enemy had taken possession of." In turn, the Confederate batteries opened an ineffectual long-range fire that served only to intensify the growing din. Through the haze, the stubbornly resisting Confederates caught sight of a Federal transport steaming upriver, obviously packed with Yankee reinforcements. It was then they fell back before "a desperate charge" launched by Coates, whose cannon did "fine execution."[53] The Yankees drove the Tennesseeans out beyond the town and threatened the Rebel right flank whose attentions had previously been riveted on the supposedly doomed Redoubt McKee. "Sometimes it requires but a trifle to start a panic which once set in motion is as uncontrollable as a drove of Texas steers when stampeded," observed Major Main of the First Mississippi (Colored) Cavalry. "When the Rebel line in the city broke, the 9th Texas, rebel, occupying a position west of the fort, seeing the stampede of their friends, and fearing that they too would be cut off, also broke in disorder..."[54]

Major McKee glimpsed the perfect opportunity when the 9th Texas fell back within plain view of the Yankee fortress. At this, their most vulnerable moment, McKee with only six men behind him burst out from the redoubt "and with loud cheers actually turned the flank of one entire regiment." Two companies of the black cavalry poured out in support as the shaken Texans pulled away in great disorder. Lieutenant Robert Jehu was at McKee's side in the headlong charge despite having been wounded early in the day be Rebel cannon shrapnel. Jehu was shouting: "Boys, they are running, they are running" when he was fatally shot through the head.[55]

Reinforcements from the 10th Louisiana (African Descent) under Colonel Crandell disembarked immediately after the Rebel retreat, but the issue had been settled. The firing died away until, at 5 p.m., the battle ended with the Yankees still secure at Yazoo City and the blustery McKee bragging that the next time they would go at the Rebels "two blind" with the same result. The "Old Eleventh" lost 14 dead, 40 wounded with sixteen captured or missing on the battlefield. The 8th Louisiana Colored Infantry and the First Mississippi Colored Cavalry suffered together approximately 100 killed, wounded and captured. Coates estimated at least 40 Rebel dead and suspected far more.

Strange that the regiment should endure Donelson, Shiloh and Vicksburg only to tempt total annhilation or surrender in a remote river town. McKee's fortitude had made at least part of the difference between success and failure; yet most would agree the black soldiers had been the trump card. Colonel Peebles of the 8th Louisiana Infantry recorded how captured Rebel officers noted with chagrin that the "Darkeys didn't know when they were whipped."[56] He further related the story of a black infantryman, shackled with ball and chain for some offense against discipline, who broke loose at the height of the street fighting and "fought all day in the thickest of the fight." Peebles couldn't resist a comparison between his own Negro soldiers and their pale allies. "Scarcely a man of them skulked away, as did several of the white soldiers who made their way as fast as possible..."[57] By and large, however, the Eleventh behaved in the best tradition highlighted by McKee's flamboyant performance and impetuous charge. The regiment had been in a most precarious position and was grateful for redemption. Certainly most felt as did one unnamed enlisted man who began a letter home the very next day:

> Yesterday, if I had been told that I should be sitting quietly in my tent today...I could not have believed it, for I felt well satisfied in my own mind that we would be marching towards Richmond as prisoners.[58]

Chapter Ten

Each In His Own Heart Wondering

Pounding, bending, and molding iron until it yielded before his inflexible Scottish will had been Brigadier General John McArthur's vocation before the war. Now the one-time village blacksmith directed his hammer against an enemy even less malleable: the Confederacy and its resolute supporters.

The Old Eleventh knew McArthur well and remembered him as the 12th Illinois' first colonel at Camp Yates. Many recalled his courage at awful Shiloh where McArthur succeeded their own W.H.L. Wallace as commander of the Second Division. His distinctive Scottish plaid cap had been well in evidence during the interminable Vicksburg siege when the Eleventh served within his Sixth Division.

This thirty-eight year old Chicago industrialist was a modern, no-nonsense man, who made his fortune building "steam boilers, engines and iron work of every description" at his Excelsior Foundry. Coates's nearly disastrous Yazoo River expedition had been co-ordinated and supervised by General McArthur, the Vicksburg post commander. He was determined that the Yazoo River area be pacified and that the vital Mississippi Central Railroad just west from Yazoo City be destroyed. It was to this end that supplies and ammunition were stockpiled at Vicksburg in the late spring in preparation for a return visit to the scene of March's ordeal.[1]

When the hardtack boxes started piling up at the Vicksburg Commissary, the veterans in the "Old Eleventh" knew for sure another campaign was in the offing. It had been a quiet time since they pulled out of Yazoo City on March 7th, interrupted only by the predictable picket duty, fatique, drill and inspection--daily fare for garrison troops. Routine ended early on the morning of May 4th when McArthur's 2,000 strong expedition wound its way through the Vicksburg defensive network bound northeast toward

Mechanicsville. It was a strong column supported by eight rifled cannon manned by men from the 2nd Illinois Light Artillery and the 7th Ohio Battery. Eight infantry and cavalry regiments were assigned to two brigades, the first commanded by Colonel B. Dornblazer, and the second by the Eleventh's Colonel James H. Coates. Captain H.C. Vore, a veteran officer, would lead the regiment in Coates's absence.[2] The Union force moved quickly, destroying a Rebel ferry on the Big Black River early on, passing through Mechanicsville the next day, and marching on by Yazoo City, heading almost due west on the Benton Road. Confederate skirmishers constantly harried the column whose destination was obviously the Mississippi Central line just west from Benton. Their attentions were received once again by the black troopers from the Third U.S. Cavalry who met heavy resistance at around 10 a.m. on May 7th as the expedition neared Benton. The Eleventh came up "on the double" but the Rebels shied away once they glimpsed the approach of infantry support for the hard-pressed cavalry.[3]

The Yankee infantry double-timed through the streets of Benton until they reached a wide cultivated field just on the other side of the village. Confederate infantry were positioned in a skirmish line extending for a mile along the outskirts of heavy woods facing the open area. At least four field pieces were in support, their gray iron muzzles pointed directly down the dusty Benton Road. The Union column immediately came under an effective bombardment which exploded along the crowded roadway. The Eleventh's seasoned infantry took what cover could be found while the Union artillery clattered up and assumed firing positions in the adjacent fields. A number of gunners from the 7th Ohio were soon dead or wounded from the raking barrage. Sergeant Carrington estimated the regiment endured the shell fire for about fifteen minutes until the order came to move out into the fields and support their own batteries:

> I noticed while the artillery men were getting one gun in position by hand in among the cornstalks, a shot from the enemy's gun...struck just forward of the muzzle in the ground, throwing up the dirt and corn stalks. If the aim had been a little higher [it] might have hit our gun. As it was our Boys opened fire, and a few rounds of which silenced the Rebel Battery and caused them to retreat. Two companies of the 11th, C and K, were sent out as skirmishers...The [black] Cavalry now followed and kept up a running fight...We marched back of town and camped for the night, very tired.[5]

Yankee cavalry gave chase for about six miles north of Benton before rejoining the main Union body encamped near the skirmish site. Intelligence reports indicated the Rebels were concentrating against McArthur's force, and the wary Scot decided to await developments rather than push on against what might become heavy odds. Sunday, May 8th, passed with little more than a few scattered shots on the picket line. The next few days were much the same, although the troops were quite active in visits to nearby farms, where they requisitioned cattle, sheep and hogs as a delightful supplement to their dreary hardtack and salt pork diet. Carrington described the camp as looking more like a "slaughter house" at the time. "We are getting to be a greasy looking set being without tents or change of clothing," he jotted in his diary. "I would not be surprised if there was not a fair supply of gray backs [body lice] in the Company."[6] The veteran sergeant had watched with great interest the black cavalry's steadfast performance throughout the week admitting, "They did very well." Carrington kept an open mind, unlike some of his compatriots who seemed to have forgotten the Yazoo City battle, and the role played by the black troops. Not so with Carrington, who believed: "They will fight if they have good leaders...Time and they will make good soldiers, as they take great pride in their uniforms and equipments."[7]

Tired of the waiting game, on May 12, McArthur ordered the march to resume heading southeast toward Canton, then switching directions after some eight miles, and going almost due north toward Vaughn's Station. At that place he turned back towards Benton where the force encamped once again late that evening after a twenty-two mile march which hadn't even resulted in a glimpse of the enemy.[8] At five a.m. the next day, McArthur struck out again on the Vaughn's Station route with entirely different results. Confederate skirmishers, encountered at about 8 a.m., put up a brave front until the Union artillery wheeled into position. It was a day of constant skirmishing, marked by the curling flames from a large mansion "riddled" and then ignited by the Yankee troops, one of whom was Sergeant George Carrington. Night brought only an uneasy rest as the men slept on their arms, even twitching wide awake at one point en masse "like a great wave and every man grabbed his musket."[9] Dawn witnessed another march. This time the Eleventh, along with 500 cavalry, moved toward the Big Black River with orders to burn the strategic Mississippi Central trestle. It was a two-mile tramp interrupted by frequent stops which allowed the cavalry time to burn culverts, cut telegraph wires, and "[destroy] the road as much as possible."[10]

Each infantryman trudged along with an extra burden--100 rifle cartridges stuffed in cartridge cases and belts rather than the normal 40. McArthur deemed it wise since he believed the trestle to be guarded by a strong stockade, perhaps manned by as many as 100 or more Rebels. They advanced on the bridge through thick cane, which caused the veteran Carrington great worry as he suspected ambush. At this point the Eleventh was nearly five miles away from McArthur's main body which further upset the old battle veteran, who well knew how the Rebels relished hacking up isolated Union regiments. Carrington wrote:

> We then moved forward until we reached a ditch running parallel with the river. We jumped in this, and then Cpt. Blackstone...issued his famous order: "Forward Eleventh and open on 'em," which we did, Peeping over the edge of the ditch, we saw the Blockhouse...on the opposite side of the river. We began firing at the Blockhouse as fast as we could load and fire, making the splinters fly. Lewis and myself, after a few rounds, stood in the bottom of the ditch and loaded...while Stenger would crawl up and fire, laughing at the racket...occasionally a bullet whistled over our heads and cut the brush and canes. After about an hour's firing, we drew off. Having no artillery with us, or we could have demolished the blockhouse...We could have charged over the bridge and carried the stockade and probably lost a 100 men but the bridge was not worth even what we did loose, according to my way of thinking. We finally fell back, and on out the Rebs fired on us killing a valuable scout belonging to the 46th Illinois. It was the hardest sight to see the mud scooped out at the roots of an old fallen tree and this man buried there.[11]

Another man was lost that day, a private from Company I, 11th Illinois. They buried him in the canebreak before the regiment turned back. They rejoined the expedition about noon, rested briefly, and then the consoldiated Union force turned back westward until a 6 p.m. bivouac about four hours march from Yazoo City. At noon the next day, May 15th, they re-entered the scene of the March 5th fight, tired, hot, and angry. Carrington noted that a commissary sergeant and a squad of helpers had fallen into the enemy's hands while out foraging. Rumor had it they were hung by the Rebels, which raised a "rookus" among the Eleventh. "Boys threaten to burn the town; citizens in terror for fear they will," Carrington recorded.[12]

Those fears materialized at 6 p.m. when the courthouse went up in crackling flames, burning to the ground while here and there throughout the city private dwellings were put to the torch by unknown Union soldiers. Colonel Coates reacted with orders for additional guards at key points in the terrified community. This put a heavy burden on the already weary Eleventh. These precautions were soon followed with news from the picket line that indicated the recently captured commissary sergeant was alive and well. The message had been brought in by Confederates under a truce flag. It had little effect, as Carrington pointed out: "The Boys seem determined to burn the town. Several fires tonight (May 17th). Companies A and G went down to help put fires out; good deal of excitement in camp. Boys can't get over the pounding they got here in March...."[13]

Yazoo City survived, but probably only due to the Eleventh's sudden departure at 3 a.m. on May 18th. McArthur's expedition was off on the road back to Vicksburg taking the old familiar river route through Liverpool Heights, Sartartia and Haynes Bluff. The column paused along the way to expropriate supplies from the surrounding countryside where once again the troops turned incendiary, leaving behind several blackened, gutted plantation houses as stark memorials to their passage. It was a hot march along a dusty, primitive roadway. On the 20th, the expedition camped at Haines Bluff making an early stop at 2 p.m., since the artillery horses were near giving out. The next day brought only a short three-hour march back to Vicksburg, the sight of which produced a great shout from the ranks. Carrington recalled:

> Marched down to our old camping place feeling as happy as if we were just returning home. Soap and water were in great demand. There is a stream of water with quite a fall over the rocks a little ways northwest. In this pool below the falls we take our bath, don clean under clothes and returned to the tents much refreshed and rested. In our tents and camp life once more; all received mail. So ends the march of 18 days. Col. Coates says we marched altogether about 210 miles: a few men were killed and wounded...no cotton but a large amount of property destroyed...Worn out horses and men sums up the whole expedition commanded by General McArthur. Altogether a poor speculation...[14]

McArthur was more optimistic in his official report. He claimed the foray resuled in "a wholesome fear on the part of the enemy, from painful experience, that we have sufficient force at this point to move into the interior when desired."[15] The general felt the Rebels might well withdraw all their forces west of the Mississippi Central fearing a repetition of the Union incursion. Furthermore, McArthur stressed the "vast advantage it has been to the new recruits of the command...increasing their morale and giving them a prestige that cannot be overestimated to troops first brought under fire."[16] The "Old Eleventh's" return to Vicksburg marked the beginning of another dormant period that allowed the men to set back "a spell" without the worry and tension that always accompanied any active campaign. It was dull and monotonous, but so very safe there behind the web of trenches that encircled the familiar old river town. And, of course, there were occasional entertainments, cards, the bottle or a bit of roughhouse to pass the time.

The early summer passed with little event. The regiment had mustered for pay on May 28th. There was money and time for peach brandy, whiskey and beer. It proved a fatal temptation for one young officer, in particular. Lieutenant Eugene Ransom's behavior since returning from his nightmarish prison camp experience was characterized by cavalier disdain for duty. Colonel Coates, with evident regret, finally confronted the issue in a June 2nd communication:

>Captain,
>I send you herewith Lieut. F.E. Ransom, E. Co., 11th Ill. Infantry. Charged with being drunk on Picket yesterday 1st inst.
>I would here say that I have no apology to make for the man or the offense, as it is not the first time that he has committed the same crime.
>I must, however, for the Sake of his Family, ask an indulgence. His Father fell in Battle in Mexico, his Eldest Brother Captain (Dunbar) Ransom, now lies dangerously wounded and his other brother, Brig. Gen. Ransom is so favorably known to all Western Soldiers, as to make it unnecessary for me to speak more than his name.
>I had charges prepared against the Lieut. for a previous misdemeanor, and to save Family from disgrace I had offered him an opportunity of resigning but he has not yet availed himself of it...[17]

The youngest Ransom's humiliation must have been a terrible shock for the prim New England clan. Eugene, himself, seems to have felt there were two codes of behavior at work: one for the colonel commanding and one for lowly lieutenants. Some years later he drew an obvious sketch of Colonel Coates lecturing a young officer on abstinence while displayed prominently in the background is a jug of the Colonel's own corn liquor. "Now promise me, you'll not drink anymore than half I usually drink. Are you satisfied?," reads the caption above Colonel Coates. The accused soldier replies: "Yes, Colonel, but I'm afraid you'll keep me pretty busy at it even if I drink half as much as you."[18] On June 16th, the issue was resolved with Lieutenant Frederick Eugene Ransom's resignation from the Eleventh--the regiment commanded, respected and loved by his older brother Thomas. The reason stated is a vague physical disability, but Colonel Coates attached a damning endorsement which would haunt Ransom for the next half-century. It read: "The Lieutenant has from the reason of almost habitual intoxication and continued Venereal diseases been incompetent for military duty for a long period..."[19] Later in the fall Eugene received a second chance as a rodman on the projected Union Pacific Railroad. His selection was engineered by General Ransom who interceded on his behalf with their old family friend, General Dodge, who co-ordinated the vast enterprise. General Ransom expressed at the time his own disappointment with Eugene's behavior, writing Dodge: "I hope you will find him in New York and send him out at once. I fear he will not meet your expectations as to competency for anything higher, but we can only tell by trying."[20] It was to be only the next chapter in Eugene's lifelong tragedy, whose roots undoubtedly lay in the grimy Confederate prisons where a man's mind often was scarred far deeper than the body.

At about the time Eugene Ransom walked away from the regiment, a new face appeared at Vicksburg whose arrival doubtless meant another campaign. The man was General Henry Warner Slocum, an officer with sterling credentials from the eastern theater of war where he was wounded at Bull Run. This very reserved New York stater was a West Point product: in fact, he had roomed with Phil Sheridan, both graduating in 1852. His laurels included Malvern Hill, South Mountain, Antietam, Fredericksburg and Gettysburg. It was at the latter place that Slocum commanded the right wing during those fateful July days. It was an impressive background, but even so he would need to prove himself once again here among Western soldiers quick to heap ridicule on the "white collar" Eastern infantry. Slocum's physical presence certainly was not overly impressive, but the *Chicago Tribune* appears unnecessarily harsh in a description dated December 17, 1868:

He is probably the handsomest of the Generals. He has a fine face, a Roman nose, large eyes, rather a weak mouth and chin and large forehead. Strength is not depicted in his face, the lines are not strong, but it is a handsome, namby-pambyish face...[21]

Hardly the portrait of a commanding general, but then again the *Tribune* may well have simply reflected a Mid-Western disdain for what most considered an effete, Eastern society. Slocum's presence at Vicksburg was a direct result of a personality clash with General Joe Hooker. High command thought Slocum's transfer to the West might alleviate the problem, and besides, great plans were once again being formulated for the Western armies. Major General E.R.S. Canby in New Orleans saw Mobile as the next target since the city served as a major entry port for blockade runners, and possessed a large industrial base. Nearby Selma contained the great Confederate iron works. Elimination of the two cities could have a tremendous impact on the Confederate armies in the field. Canby's plan was to launch a major assault around July 6 accompanied by a number of diversionary attacks, one of which would emanate from Slocum's Vicksburg fortress. Washington put the plan on the shelf when in late June Halleck demanded 20,000 troops for the Virginia front.

Mobile would wait, but Slocum, who headed the Military Division of Western Mississippi, still felt impelled to move on Jackson if for no better reason than the fact that General Sherman felt it imperative to do so.

"Uncle Billy" Sherman was extremely anxious regarding Forrest's presence in northern Mississippi where his deadly strike force posed an ever-present threat to Sherman's communication lines. The Union general felt that Forrest's freedom of movement might be severely impaired if the Mississippi Central was cut by repeated forays from Vicksburg and Jackson. Thus when Sherman noted in a captured Southern newspaper an account about a new trestle bridge constructed over the Pearl River just outside Jackson, he fired off a bristling note to Slocum. "If you permit the enemy to regain the use of that bridge and the Mississippi Central Railroad," Sherman wrote, "you need not expect military favors from General Grant or myself."[22] In his view, this railroad bridge was of consumate importance to the Confederacy. "Every soldier should be doing something against the enemy this summer to keep him busy and from re-enforcing Lee and Johnston."[23] Slocum needed little encouragement as he drafted orders for a 2,800 strong expedition whose object would be the crucial trestle outside Jackson.

They called it "Chimneyville" in this, the fourth year of the Civil War which had already seen the once graceful Mississippi capitol sacked three times by the Union army. Now with the summer sun at its most vicious, the "Old Eleventh" fell in with Slocum's column bound for their first visit to this most stubborn of Rebel cities. They hiked along a pontoon bridge across the Big Black River on the morning of the Third, and then with the heavy wool uniforms chafing at every step, proceeded through the old battlefield at Champion Hill. With luck they would celebrate July Fourth amidst Jackson's ruins. The familiar old 46th Illinois strode along with the Eleventh on this latest adventure brimming with confidence. One soldier wrote how they set off, "in the hot, scorching sun with a musket strung on our shoulders, and a cartridge box well filled with Uncle Sam's pills, ready to administer to his foes."[24] Major General Slocum was in over-all command, and Brigadier General Elias S. Dennis served as division commander. Colonel Coates headed up the First Brigade, and Colonel Dornblazer led the Second. It was a powerful force that advanced behind an aggressive 600-man cavalry screen. In support were six cannon manned by the 7th Ohio Battery who had performed so ably during McArthur's recent May excursion. Union forces totaled nearly 3,000 men.[25]

Riding at the head of the Eleventh Illinois was an old comrade, Captain H.C. Vore---a Donelson veteran with a good record despite at least one instance in which he displayed a flaring temper. That was back in October, 1862, when Lieutenant Vore engaged in an "affray" with 2nd Lieutenant S.F. Moore in the billiard room at the St. Francis Hotel in Paducah, Kentucky. Details are lacking, but the records show Vore was returned to duty soon after while his opponent, Moore, resigned from the regiment some months later. Except for this one interlude Vore's record revealed a competent, if not brilliant military ability. He was an experienced officer who could be trusted to make no major mistakes.

"The fun began as soon as we moved out towards Jackson," related Sergeant T.N. Lewis of Company B, Eleventh Illinois, "and was kept up...every bush had a Johnny behind it."[27] Four miles west of Clinton, Slocum's column received heavy fire from dismounted Confederate cavalry which initiated a day of constant skirmishing that provided ample fireworks for the July Fourth celebration. Resistance was provided by men from Brigadier General W. Wirt Adams's command, and Brigadier General Samuel Gholson's brigade of Mississippi State Troops. Their troops played the tease with the on-coming Union force by hitting the vanguard with long-range rifle fire only to pull away as soon as Slocum deployed infantry and artillery for a battle proper. The tactics delayed his advance so that the Yankee expedition went into camp late on the fourth, just west of Clinton. The march on July 5th was made with the infantry plodding down the main Jackson Road while the cavalry took a parallel route a little to the north. These two roads joined about five miles outside town, and there Gholson's men manned an improvised road block from which they hit the Yankee cavalry hard when they appeared on the scene ahead of the main Union force. Blue infantry soon arrived, however, and Gholson fell back while the cavalry on both sides traded fire in a running fight which terminated at Lynch Creek. Here the Rebels waited in strength, supported by two six-pounders and a 12-pound howitzer from Company A, 1st Mississippi Light Artillery. These guns had a nice field of fire from their position on the Wright farm and could pour a heavy fire on the Lynch Creek Bridge. Slocum rode up, studied the situation, and ordered Coates's First Brigade to swing northeast in a flanking manuever while the 124th Illinois and the dismounted Yankee cavalry opened a heavy fire on the Rebels just across the creek.[28]

Out in front were the men from the 46th Illinois, followed by the "Old Eleventh" and Battery 1 of the 2nd Illinois Light Artillery. The lead regiment took advantage of cover provided by a ridge line, but soon came into open view upon which the Confederate artillery switched their fire from the bridge onto this threatening Union presence on the right flank. The 46th made it to the cover of a heavy woods, joined soon after by the Eleventh whose old commander, Colonel Coates, now dressed brigade ranks for a final run at the enemy. Minutes later the two Union infantry regiments burst through Town Creek into an open field and there halted while pioneers chopped a lane through the woods behind them so Battery L might come up in support. Coates wanted his cannon in close if the Rebels took a stand; he knew from Shiloh what well-manned artillery could do in a fire fight. And, it wasn't too long until the cannon opened up over Coates's head. For at least twenty minutes, shell after shell roared into the Rebel position ahead until the Confederates wavered and then retired down the Canton Road. Coates's two infantry regiments came on in a foot race, won easily by the 46th Illinois, although the panting troopers captured nothing more than a glimpse of the Rebel rear guard moving out down the Canton road northward.[29] Private Henry Uptmor of Company K of the Eleventh was inured to hard campaigning, yet this constant skirmishing in the dank Mississippi heat left him soaked to the skin and nearly prostrate from exhaustion:

> We had a hard time indeed. The enemy would weaken at times and retreat but now and then they would halt and shell us heavily with their...cannon. The weather was very hot and we suffered inexpressibly from thirst, and it was also terribly dusty to march. At one O'clock in the afternoon, the enemy departed, and we halted and cooled off a bit as well as we could. The Rebels sent a flag of truce to us, stating that they were vacating the city of Jackson...and surrendering it to us. At three we continued our march, and at five o'clock we entered the city...accompanied by the sound of merry music...[30]

Uptmor could see Jackson had been a beautiful city despite the charred rubble and nearly deserted streets. The classic state capitol building still stood relatively unscathed, its pristine white columns a sharp contrast to the remainder of the much-pillaged city. The residents were in fear that the Negro Yankees would add a new dimension in terror. The Rebels were relieved that this would be different from the earlier occupations. Slocum would not tolerate depredations; he was determined that the city escape further scourging. It was enough that the Union appearance in Jackson drove home the fact that Federal power could not be defied, that the very heart of Mississippi could be penetrated with impunity again and again by Union troops. But this was only peripheral to the main purpose, the destruction of the Pearl River Bridge. That was quickly done despite harassing rifle fire from across the river. By 4 p.m. on the 6th, the massed Union bands struck up the march and the column briskly moved down Capitol Street headed west. Their departure was signaled to the Confederates by a civilian atop the Deaf and Dumb Asylum who waved a white handkerchief back and forth until one of the Union Provost Guards knocked him off his conspicuous perch with one well-placed rifle shot.[31]

The Union march home proved a noisy duplication of their advance. The Confederates seemed determined to capture or at least severely punish the impertinent Yankee invaders. A fighting retreat is the most difficult military feat, made infinitely more complicated in this instance since Slocum's column included more than 100 supply wagons that not only slowed progress but made a tempting target for the pursuers who were always short on equipment, provisions, and ammunition. True to form, the Rebel cavalry clashed with their Yankee counterparts as soon as Slocum's column poked its Blue nose out of the Jackson debris. Skirmishing continued until dark when the Union expedition "slept on its arms" about three miles outside the city. Daybreak brought heavy contact at the Canton road junction where General Wert Adams's Rebel gunners opened with a fury. They subjected the Union regiments to severe fire for more than three hours. Coates's brigade with the "Old Eleventh" held the right of the road during this bitter stalemate. Uptmor recalled:

> For as soon as we began to advance, they sent pretty many shells at us as a morning greeting, but it did not take us long to greet them quite heartily in return, and then it did not take very long until we became fully acquainted with each other. Now our guns went into play, and soon they were answering us in just as loud a tone. It was soon evident that a battle was on to decide whether we should go back...or not. Our troops were all fighting desperately by this time and many a brave soldier lay fallen in his blood. There one would be with his foot, there another with his arm, and still another with his chest wounded and could still bet away with their comrades...Bullets were forced through the air by the thousands and the bomb shells torn the air as though they were going to destroy everything...[32]

The way home was finally opened after a spirited charge by the 8th Illinois who chased off the 1st Mississippi Artillery, and ended the long-range pounding. Now the wagon train could be brought up although their progress was still opposed by rifle fire. One soldier from the 124th Illinois in Coates's brigade would ever after recall the comic spectacle. Hardened mule drivers spoke in soothing tones to their creatures until they reached cover. Then it was: "Damn'd You Mule, get up!"[33] Once through, Dornblazer's Second Brigade pulled up the rear where they were heavily pressed by General Gholson's two mounted Rebel regiments. It was a delicate operation that continued for at least a mile; the steady Rebel pressure at one point forced the Union infantry to deploy in full battle line. By 10 a.m., it was the Eleventh's turn at rear guard, reinforced by Battery L of the 2nd Illinois Light Artillery. It was then that Gholson's Mississippi cavalry came on with a vengeance. Lieutenant Colonel John Jones stood with the 46th Illinois only three hundred yards away and marveled at the Rebels' audacity. The horsemen came on "with a boldness and determination worthy of men engaged in the prosecution of a better cause..."[34] The "Old Eleventh" awaited the charge with veteran calm; one soldier described how Captain Vore was apparently unperturbed sitting on his mount in a most casual way with the bullets ripping the air all around. He allowed the Rebel cavalry to close to within fifty or sixty yards. At that point the massed rifle fire from the Eleventh exploded in the very faces of the oncoming riders along with the earsplitting roar from Battery L. Private Uptmor recounted the scene:

> We waited until they were about thirty steps away from us, and then we let them have it. We greeted them right heartily as though this time they did not have the right art to really get further acquainted with us. They maintained their position for a while, and they pushed forward out of our hiding place. When they observed that, they went into flight. They had to retreat over a hill, which gave us every advantage of position over them. We fired upon them with such speed that not many...got over that hill. We took many of them as prisoners. We lost five men and had 16 wounded...[35]

The 46th Illinois joined the Eleventh immediately after the first volley and lent their firepower in the succeeding actions. "By the help of Bolton's battery and the Eleventh Illinois, we enabled to hurl from their saddles scores of rebels," proudly reported Colonel Jones, "and scatter in dismay the whole force who had attached us with such intrepidity and assurance."[36] It had been a shattering blow that left Confederate General Gholson incapacitated with two flesh wounds in the shoulder. Two Rebel captains were dead, and a third dying, along with probably 40 casualties. There must have been a certain satisfaction among the veterans in the "Old Eleventh," remembering as they did how the regiment had suffered when Forrest's cavalry chewed them up at Donelson. They had turned the tables this day, but the satisfaction was marred since Slocum's rapid march dictated that the wounded and dead be left to the enemy. The Yankees suffered more than 230 casualties during the advance on, and retreat from, Jackson.[37] Many, weakened by the heat, fell by the roadside to be captured. Sergeant T.N. Lewis of Company B. of the Eleventh was overcome but had the luck to be paroled only a few weeks later. "There were many acts of individual bravery shown in this expedition which ought to be recorded in history," he told his old comrade George Carrington, "but will never be mentioned among the tens of thousands of brave acts of the war."[38]

Slocum's personal bravery during the campaign won many accolades despite mumbling about the abandoned wounded. The general felt the expedition was a success based on the destruction of the Pearl River bridge, the psychological blows dealt by the reoccupation of Jackson, and the successful withdrawal. Discipline had also triumphed since the expedition had campaigned without the outrages so common among the Western regiments. Only one home was burnt, and that at Slocum's personal order, after observing the owner signal the nearby Confederate forces near Clinton.[39] His benign view was certainly not shared by all, and definitely not by at least two men from Company F of the Eleventh Illinois. These were the regiment's 109th boys, those accused earlier in the war of Rebel sympathies. One anonymous soldier complained in a letter to the *Jonesboro Gazette* in southern Illinois, a paper once suppressed by the government, and receptive to negative correspondence from the front. His letter touched on the Pearl River Bridge destruction but applied a different yardstick: "We destroyed it, but it was at the cost of many a poor fellow's life."[40] This was followed later in the summer by another account from Company F that, in effect, attacking the whole Union war effort as a sham and a fraud:

> I tell you this is a horrible war. What is it for? We kill one another for the negro. If I were out I would not enlist again. I have seen enough to satisfy me. Privates fight hard, while officers are filling their pockets, and when they get them full, they will be ready to make peace...[41]

Late in July, the Eleventh said good-bye to the intrenchments at Vicksburg and greeted an old acquaintance, if not perhaps a friend. That gentleman was Brigadier General Mike Lawler commanding Union forces at Morganzia Bend, Louisiana. The regiment arrived at that point on July 30th after a pleasant 100-mile journey down river aboard the U.S. *Diana*. Lawler's encampment was filled with more than 10,000 troops who that very day received a warning from the local Confederates to vacate Louisiana soil or face the consequences, apparently unaware that old "Irish" Mike Lawler didn't scare so easy. Neither, for that matter, did the Eleventh, as Sergeant Carrington noted: "We are ready for them anytime we would be pleased to meet them."[42] Most of the Eleventh's veterans must have remembered General Lawler from his days as Colonel of the 18th Illinois Infantry--a unit that often was garrisoned at Bird's Point with the Eleventh back in 1861. Surely this great, bearded, beer-barrel of a man would be difficult to forget since he was more than ready to enforce military etiquette with his fists or the point of a boot if necessary.[43] The late General W.H.L. Wallace despised the hard drinking Mexican War veteran, and in those early days in Missouri, served on a court martial board that found Lawler guilty in a brutal murder case. The Eleventh's old commander had been shocked at the evidence before him that indicated Lawler had stood by, even encouraged, the lynching of Private Robert Dickman--a man accused of murdering a fellow soldier while at Mound City, Illinois.

Wallace listened to a prosecution witness relate how the colonel had described the murder as "brutal and cold blooded," adding that to turn the suspect over to civilian authorities would be tantamount to "setting the murderer free."[44] But whatever his guilt, Dickman was driven in a wagon on a "wet, rainy, muddy morning" and lynched by members of the 18th Regiment. Lawler, himself, stated his actions--or more correctly, his failure to act--were motivated by what he "conceived to be a military necessity, involving the good order, the proper discipline and the individual safety of my command."[45] He claimed the men were in a "turbulent and desperate...mood and would have shot down any officer who stood between them and revenge. It was practically an admission on Lawler's part that he dared not impose discipline on his own regiment for fear of physical harm, a strange stance considering that the second charge against him was of "conduct unbecoming an officer."

These specifications appalled the gentle Wallace. Lawler's alleged approach to discipline included beating a private in the presence of the regiment, encouraging a fight between two enlisted men, standing by with his sword drawn to prevent interference in what a witness called a "brutal and demoralizing affair," and injecting noxious drugs into a supply of whiskey smuggled into the guard house.[46] On another occasion Lawler was accused of standing by while his subordinate, Lieutenant Scanlon, threatened a private with a loaded pistol and forced the man "to dance, make time and perform other compulsory movements."[47]

Lawler's guilty verdict was heartily supported by Colonel Wallace of the Eleventh, who by virtue of his own extensive civilian legal background, felt confident that justice had been served. We can only guess at his outrage when the ruling was overturned by General Henry Halleck on the basis of certain improprieties relating to the wording of the specifications and charges. For Wallace it was far simpler. He believed Lawler's old friends, namely General John McClernand and General U.S. Grant, had been behind the action. It was not a secret that Grant thought the blustery Lawler a damn fine fighter as well as a practical man equiped physically and psychologically to ram some good old fashioned army discipline down the throats of recalcitrant Western troops. Even during the time of the court martial itself General Grant praised the accused for "attention to your duties" which resulted "in a well drilled Regiment."[48] Wallace's protests were futile. Much had happened in the three years since Bird's Point: Wallace, of course, was gone, but more interestingly, Lawler was acknowledged as a fine combat officer. His most notable contribution was made at the Big Black River fight on May 1863 when the Irishman led a mad charge netting thousands of Rebel prisoners. The Irishman was busy planning another strike at the Rebels, but it would not materialize for some weeks during which the Eleventh made itself as comfortable as could be considering the insufferable heat, humidity and disease. Morganzia was a place of sickness with dozens dropping off every day from yellow fever, typhoid, malaria and other maladies that quite frankly couldn't even be diagnosed by the army doctors still laboring under the false assumption that the swamp night air caused these deadly maladies. The specter of a long, agonizing death from yellow fever shook even the older veterans in the Eleventh. Private Uptmor admitted his own fears hadn't been helped any when some of the men in the regiment, while frolicing in the river, bumped into a floating body. "It looked horrible," Uptmor wrote. "There was no flesh anymore on his legs, and his teeth were no longer in his mouth. The body looked so maimed as if he had been in a fight on some ship..."[49] This unnerving experience was rapidly followed by another death in camp. Many men were mumbling about an epidemic or even plague being a real possibility at this unhealthy place. The German-speaking private wrote:

> On August 7th, the air was full of black clouds, and it was very hot. In the afternoon, I suddenly heard the sound of mournful music through the camp. Inquiring from one of the men in Company C what it meant, I learned that one of their comrades had died, and they were about to put his remains to rest. They brought the coffin from one of the tents and four of the men crossed two muskets which they used as a bier to carry the coffin. The procession to the grave began, again accompanied by mournful music; which had a very subdued effect on us all. Probably many were thinking: "Will I be the next one?", each in his own heart wondering...[50]

Veterans like Uptmor knew from experience that disease rarely trailed an army on the march, and so must have greeted the news of a new campaign with elation. At least the Confederates were an enemy one could see. There, at least, a man had a chance at fighting back, and death was usually a quick one without the pain and humiliation that disease dealt out. This new expedition set out on August 23rd on board steamers headed for Port Hudson. The Union bastion on the Mississippi River would serve as a jumping off point for an excursion into the Rebel areas on both sides of the great river. The very first day's march from Port Hudson set the tone: it was a fatiguing tramp with the men beset by bugs, boredom and a savage sun. The Eleventh did participate in a small skirmish near Jackson--a small town near Port Hudson--which provided about the only action in those first few days. Two men from Company K were hastily buried, victims in this inconclusive fray. A few days later the column was ferried across the Mississippi River to Clinton where they resumed the monotonous tramp, moving along difficult sandy roadways lined with pine trees. Despite a hard march, the Eleventh missed a fight at Clinton where Union cavalry and Rebel horsemen clashed only a few hours earlier. The only battle in the ranks of the Eleventh was a losing one against the temperature which topped 100 degrees, according to Sergeant Carrington.[52] The wagons at the rear of the column soon were jammed with sickened, exhausted soldiers. All along the line of march the soldiers plundered with a great zeal, their path marked by the black smoke from burning barns and homes. The column returned to Port Hudson on August 29th "without having accomplished anything." Their arrival at Port Hudson was relatively uneventful except for an interracial brawl between black troops and members of the 30th Missouri Infantry, won by the white soldiers who didn't tolerate any "Nigger insolence."[52]

Once more the Eleventh embarked on steamers bound back toward Lawler's camp at Morganzia Bend where they would rest and recuperate for the next few days. It was a brief interlude for on September 3rd new orders came down instructing the regiment to ship upriver for duty at the mouth of the Arkansas River, nearly 160 miles to the north. They rolled the men from slumber at 1 a.m., to board the U.S.S. *Baltic* by 4 a.m., and make steam immediately. Confederate guerrilas were making the Arkansas River area rather unpleasant for Union units stationed there. General Elias Dennis was instructed to remedy the situation with 8,000 men and 17 steamers, one of which carried the "Old Eleventh." The voyage took the regiment past Natchez, where Uptmor described the civilian crowd at the wharf as "looking at us as though they were ready to eat us up."[53] Vicksburg provided the men with an overnight stop, a place to stretch the legs, and then they were back aboard paddling blissfully upriver past Greenwood, Mississippi--"a town that lies in ruins as does so many here and there..."[54] On September 8th, the regiment put ashore and established a permanent winter camp at a pleasant spot on the White River in Arkansas.

It was a fine change for the regiment, according to Sergeant Carrington, who confessed in his diary how the Morganzia camp had been a bit scary with its rampant disease. Here on the White River, the regiment enjoyed a relief both from Louisiana fevers and that terrible humid heat that left so many feeling like limp, wet rags. In addition, the woods nearby provided good hunting with raccoon, bear, deer, rabbits, and squirrels abounding. These soon provided the messes with food, tasty meat supplemented by catfish caught from the two great rivers which flowed only a few minutes walk from camp. It was a time to rest, write home, or chat about Sheridan's recent victories in the Shenandoah Valley out east--an event celebrated with a salute by thirty-seven cannon at the White River encampment.[55] By early October, the regiment set about building permanent winter quarters, often quite elaborate with log walls, a mud chimney, and a canvas tent roof. These cheerful domestic chores were rarely interrupted except for an occasional patrol upriver aboard one of the Navy steamers described melodramatically by one soldier as "forays into rebeldom." In fact, they usually were nothing more than pleasure cruises, though in October one boat was ambushed and two soldiers from the Eleventh slightly wounded. It was a fine time until late October when Memphis let out an urgent cry for Union reinforcements. Forrest was on the march, the same backwoods genius who had so brazenly taken that city a few months before. One of the boys in the Eleventh remembered:

> Nearly all had moved in, and our little town was about completed, when on the morning of the 18th a boat came flying down the Mississippi, with news that Memphis had been attacked by an overwhelming force of rebels, and that the Eleventh was needed to save our forces there from utter annihilation. In less than two hours from the time the Boat appeared in view, we were on board, and soon puffing up the river as fast as steam could take us. Twenty four hours landed us in Memphis, which we found still occupying its old position on the bluff and its good citizens considerably worse

scared than hurt. The militia had been out in line two days and nights, and men who had never before seen a spade, were busy digging rifle pits. The main streets were all barricaded...To the Rebels it was evident "distance lent enchantment to the view" for they "saw as well as they wanted to" at that distance...[56]

Within a week or so it appeared clear the Rebels were not about to suddenly devour this Tennessee city, but the Eleventh remained at Fort Pickering shivering under canvas, doubtless cursing the idiots in command. They yearned for those snug, warm cabins on the White River that were now probably being occupied by some other lucky regiment. Even worse, the Memphis Post Commissary refused to supply the regiment since far too many regiments had passed through, drawn rations without proper authority, and gone on their merry way. The view at Memphis was that red tape must be observed. This enraged Colonel James Coates who politely pointed out that his men and officers desperately required provisions, particularly since they hadn't been paid since April 30. He filed an official protest concluding: "I am led to inquire how these officers are expected to live...? And ask a remedy for the evil."[57] Common sense prevailed and the provisions were distributed although payday waited for another time. The Eleventh was a weary, disgruntled lot inflicted with tiresome picket and the other irritations associated with garrison duty. All the time they were "dead broke" in a city with numerous enticements for the lonely. One soldier in Company F spelled out his discontent in a pessimistic letter home:

> We are now living in dilapidated old tents...We have not seen a paymaster for six months, and you may know we are badly off for our share of the "needful." Cake and notion peddlers shun us, and news boys give us the cold shoulder, well knowing our regiment is as dry as a contribution box...We are praying for a paymaster...There are a great many Negro troops here, who do most of the guard and light duty. They are all being paid off today while we stand back with empty pockets, and wondering if the families we left at home are not needing the necessaries of life, while the scant and pitiable $13 a month we should receive is being paid to fat, lazy, cowardly, over-fed niggers...[58]

Hard words these, and undoubtedly representative of many who wore the Blue. Of course, not everyone in the Eleventh was nearly so bitter. Indicative of that was the November 8th national election campaign which was then in full swing. Like most veteran regiments the Eleventh presented President Lincoln with a majority. The incumbents won handily with 116 votes recorded in a straw poll.[59] This constituted a strong repudiation of the McClellan peace platform, but it could not, in the same fashion, be considered a vote for war itself. Men like the newly promoted Second Lieutenant George D. Carrington were weary of the long bloodletting. They longed for home, family and quiet times. Simultaneously, these same men were convinced that all the previous sacrifice demanded that the survivors press the issue to a close. Only an honorable peace could justify four years of slaughter. With this goal in mind these "tried fighters" of the Eleventh girded themselves for one last push, one last flirtation with death, one final battle. While they awaited the last act, their old commander, General T.E.G. Ransom, lay dying hundreds of miles away in northern Georgia. He too pondered the coming election during his final days. Only weeks before the end General Ransom conveyed his passionate feelings on the subject in a letter to a friend dwelling in the North:

> Have no fears for the Army. The danger is, that you at home will surrender to the traitors in your midst. When in the field, with my brave comrades around me, I never doubt that the rebellion will be completely overthrown, that the nation will live. I was glad to get away from that treason that I heard throughout the North. Annihilate it on the eighth of November.[60]

Ransom's spirit, his indomitable resolve, survived death in the guise of the "Old Eleventh." Despite their grumbles, and the appearance of drafted men in the ranks, this remained the regiment he had forged in his own image at Donelson, Shiloh and Vicksburg. Their own morale was certainly on the rise by October 29, 1864 when they returned to the winter camp at the White River. It was a brief stay that ended on November 10 with orders to proceed up the White River and establish a camp at Duvall's Bluff. A bare twenty days later the military bureaucracy spun out more baffling orders. Once more the Eleventh trooped aboard a river steamer, this time the *Commercial*, and journeyed back toward drab, cold Memphis. Outside familiar Fort Pickering they drilled. Bare hands stung when they gripped the steel rifle barrel, and still no pay was in sight. The Eleventh was now attached to the Second Brigade, Third Division, 19th Army Corps. Lieutenant

Carrington wrote how they were a part of a mobile strike force who would be expected to speed by steamboat to any river town threatened by the Rebels.[61] But by Christmas, 1864, they were far from any river. The Eleventh was laboring on repairs to the railroad tracks near Moscow, Tennessee. Six days later they returned to Memphis for the long-awaited muster for pay accompanied by the happy news that the regiment was going south. "Bully!" noted Lieutenant Carrington. "We are nearly frozen here and glad to leave..." Early on the morning of January 5, 1865, the steamer *John Rains* eased into the landing on the east side of the Mississippi River 18 miles north of New Orleans. Troops of the Third Division, already ashore, or clustered on the decks of the nearby steamer *Autocrat*, welcomed the Eleventh with a volley of catcalls and a barrage of rotten oranges. This initiated a joyous battle. Clouds of oranges filled the air while the men threw, ducked, slipped and laughed. Officers were soon angered when the missles began to splinter the glass windows aboard both steamers. Matters worsened when hardtack and other more deadly projectiles started to land with authority among the combatants. Typically, the mock battle ended as quickly as it began and the strangely invigorated troops filed ashore to set up camp near the town of Kennersville, Louisiana.[62]

Guard mount, regimental inspections and other mundane duties were quickly resumed. From this place, however, the men were eligible for passes into New Orleans. They could reach that exciting, exotic metropolis after a short train ride. The great cosmopolitan seaport was a thrilling experience for most of these callow young men. Indeed, the enticement was so alluring that Colonel Coates was forced to throw a strong guard around their swampy camp to prevent unauthorized jaunts down river. The regiment was inspected a number of times during these days leading many to suspect a movement in the offing. Whatever the nature of this suspected move, all realized that it was probably to be the last campaign.

Every day the newspapers described another major Union victory. The Confederacy was pinioned helplessly by strong armies chewing away at its vitals in North Carolina and in the trenches outside Richmond. "Everything is lovely, and the goose hangs eye," noted Lieutenant Carrington approvingly.[63] In the western theater, events were building toward a savage denoument. Mobile was targeted for the next massive Union drive and the Eleventh was assigned a role to play in this final drama. To that end, they marched through mud under a cold rain toward Lake Pontchartrain. On February 6, 1865, they loaded aboard the steamer

Warrior which finally got underway the next morning. Meanwhile, most of the men dined on stolen crab, an elegant feast for farm boys and store clerks. One day and an evening's cruise took them the length of the great lake and then out into the "dark green waters of the Gulf of Mexico." As the rolling paddlewheel bobbed eastward the men lined the rails to gawk at an escort of dolphins skipping gaily alongside.[64]

Chapter Eleven

The Spirit of Killing

Astride the captured rubble of Fort Gaines at the entrance to Mobile Bay, an American flag rippled in the chilly morning breeze on February 9, 1865. Nearby, the men of the Eleventh Illinois Infantry Regiment disembarked onto the sparkling white sand beaches of Dauphine Island. Out on the great glass-blue expanse of Mobile Bay they could glimpse the squat black silhouettes of Union ironclads. These pragmatic forms were in dramatic contrast to the high-masted, ocean-going steamers gliding by in endless patrol out in the Gulf of Mexico. Fifty miles north up the bay lay the great seaport city of Mobile, one of the last tarnished jewels remaining in the Confederate tiara. Nine thousand Rebels manned her ring of trenches, batteries, and strongpoints. Confederate General Joseph E. Johnston regarded it as the best fortified city in the South. The Eleventh and the other Union regiments who gathered at the bay's rim were expected to pierce those defenses. At least among the Eleventh's veterans, this scenario was deadly familiar. War's irony dictated that the adventure was to conclude much as it had begun three years before in the trenches outside Fort Donelson. Once more the Eleventh was to engage in a seige, one final struggle for yet another Confederate stronghold, guarded--even in these twilight hours--by dedicated and steady-handed enemies.

Union Major General Edward Richard Sprigg Canby gathered 45,000 troops for the assault on Mobile.[1] He was a man of caution and detail, not likely to move until absolutely ready. When his army struck it would be with power and purpose, but for now it waited. Dauphine Island was home to the Eleventh during this interlude. The island was one of two sentinels guarding the entrance to Mobile Bay. Guns at Fort Gaines, located at the eastern terminus of the island, stared across three miles of water at the stout ramparts of Fort Morgan located at the western tip of Mobile

Peninsula. Both former Confederate strongpoints now flew the national banner. But back in August, 1864, they had spat out tons of iron when Union Admiral David Farragut chose to run the Rebel gauntlet with his fleet. He had boldly steamed ahead despite their fire and the hidden peril of "infernal machines", or what we now call mines. In the ensuing naval battle his ships harried the CSA ironclad *Tennessee*, hounding the ungainly crippled creature from every flank. The ravaged ironclad's surrender ended forever Mobile's career as a blockade runner's port, a life-line to Europe. Subsequent Union naval and army operations resulted in the capture of Fort Morgan and Fort Gaines. Now in the spring of 1865, Canby's arrival signaled the final phase--the actual capture of Mobile itself.[2]

Mild weather and gentle Gulf coast winds conspired to make the Dauphine Island encampment extremely pleasant, perhaps in that way even more memorable than Natchez. During the waiting time the men from the Eleventh stretched themselves on the sunny beaches and listened to the surf and the cry of shorebirds. Smiling Negroes abounded, eager to clean a soldier's rifle, blacken his boots, or prepare a hot, tasty meal. These often bewildered, almost invariably hungry, souls would willingly work for the most modest sums, affordable even for the lowly $13 a month earned by Union privates. Memories of the chilly, damp encampments on the White River vanished in this warm hue. Sergeant Frank Whipple would remember all his life the calm days at Dauphine. There the men splashed through the surf in search of oysters which soon became regular features on the regiment's menu. The Midwesterners baked, fried, broiled and ate them raw; for breakfast, lunch, dinner and snack until many grew weary of the storied delicacy.[3]

Somehow Sergeant Whipple found the days almost too long while the regiment awaited the inevitable orders for the assault. It wasn't good to think too much before combat. As a combat veteran, he certainly was aware of that basic soldier's truth; maybe that was the problem. A man who'd been through Shiloh and Vicksburg could see with absolute clarity the real face of battle which, at least for many recruits, was somewhat shrouded in myth and patriotic garble of stay-at-home politicians and giddy girls. Sergeant Whipple was not so blind. He had but to touch the great scar on his upper forehead to remember. When that Rebel slug knocked him into unconsciousness on February 3, 1864, he thought death had come. In the weeks that followed his recovery was uncertain, even after the weakened soldier was discharged from the Marine Hospital at Vicksburg. But, as far as Sergeant

Whipple was concerned, he owed his life to the kindly Southern family at Bovina, Mississippi. Their own humanity overpowered Confederate sympathies and they nursed the Union sergeant back to health.[4] Perhaps this recollection was on his mind during the waiting time at Dauphine. Then again perhaps his own impatience was aggravated by that oddly human fear of being the last man slain in the last battle, as if death at any other time was ever less cruel. On February 26, 1865, the thoughtful veteran wistfully wrote his sister a letter echoing a mournful homesickness:

> I can just imagine what you are all doing at home about this time. Now just see if I don't guess right. I guess that all of the folks are at our house and about this time you are eating dinner... waiting for Father to carve the turkey. He need not give me the drumstick for my share. I will take the next joint, a little smashed potatoes and turnip gravy will do...Take a piece of pumpkin pie? This is...bully! Mother asks her pet if he will have another cup of coffee which offer he accepts and winds up dinner...This island is the only place where I could say that I was lonesome...The sooner we leave the better, but I don't see as we ever will. I wish we were with Sherman. I am tired of this monotonous life.[5]

During those idle weeks Colonel James H. Coates was busily defending the regiment's honor, or at least covering its tracks. Like so many veteran Union outfits, their foraging habits had become cavalier. Even the most sympathetic biographer cannot believe that the regiment remained aloof from temptation. The men themselves reduced it to the level of a joke. They never stole the property of Southern civilians. But on occasion, most would admit to suffering from the "cramps." By this euphemism they meant their fingers or hands often cramped, almost against their will, around a plump chicken's neck or some Confederate's prized watch. Evidently, this attitude took on a new dimension during the Eleventh's stay at Lake End, Louisiana the previous fall. Colored civilians dwelling there had pleaded that this was a regiment of thieves. In a letter to General Steven A. Hurlburt, commanding general of the Department of the Gulf, a representative of these poor blacks claimed that within two days the Eleventh had literally stripped them naked. He told how the regiment had "completely sacked our houses of everything, including our wearing apparel. We are...homeless, have had to a great extent to spend Saturday night in the swamps adjacent to our homes..."[6] When Colonel Coates settled in at Dauphine, he was quickly notified by the division adjutant of these allegations. The supposed victims claimed an amount of $9,634 for damages, a considerable sum in those pre-inflationary times.[7] Whatever the validity of the claims, they were doomed to frustration. Colonel Coates blandly reported to authorities that "some of the fences were destroyed to furnish fuel for cooking...nothing else."[8] So the matter rested.

Civilian complaints were certainly not a priority item. The Eleventh and the remainder of Major General Canby's army girded for the final clash. Union intelligence reports regarding the enemy dispositions were remarkably accurate and optimistic in tone. Of particular value were the detailed descriptions of the outer works by a "turncoat" Confederate engineering officer. Similar reports provided General Canby with a portrait of life within the Rebel city, whose population was probably around 40,000 at this point.[9] Those with hard Federal currency would pay up to $275 for a pair of shoes, $200 for a gallon of whiskey, and $500 for a barrel of flour. Many residents preserved an almost fanatical serenity in the face of what appeared to be overwhelming Union strength. General Richard Taylor, the same Confederate leader who had soundly trounced Ransom at Sabine Crossroads, commanded all enemy forces in southern Alabama. General D.H. Maury supervised the Mobile defenses, per se, with approximately 10,000 troops. The quality of the troops varied tremendously. Turncoat Union soldiers, the so-called "Galvanized" Confederates, were the least reliable. Other regiments had many new recruits who lacked the discipline and experience to cope with tried Union regiments like the Eleventh. Even so, there remained a nucleus of hard-core Confederate riflemen. Many remained steadfast in the final hours and would man the Mobile trenches until Yankee cannon, rifle, and bayonet bloodied them into unwilling submission.[10]

The Union army facing Mobile had undergone a transformation since the war's early days. This was dramatically illustrated in the muster rolls of the "Old Eleventh" Illinois. The men who had made the regiment were mostly dead now in the spring of 1865. Those veterans who still remained in the ranks were a decided minority--around 100 in number, out of 750.[11] Shiloh, Donelson, and Vicksburg had accounted for their share of the corpses and the maimed. Disease and desertion made similar inroads. The regiment's bitter chronicle was reflected in the fate of its first three commanders. They all lay buried by the time their unit braced for the final assault. W.H.L. Wallace, the fatherly man the men had loved, had been slain at the Hornet's Nest near Pittsburg Landing. T.E.G. Ransom, that strangely intense and obsessed young soldier, was gone too. His flame and dash were now preserved only in memory. Garrett Nevius was another now listed among the victims. That dependable, guileless man had been cut down in the mad May 22nd charge at Vicksburg. Only Colonel James H. Coates remained, the fourth commanding officer of a veteran regiment.

Among the ranks there was a small contingent who remembered the early days. Captain George Doanne was one, the same grieving friend who had so recently stood at the dying Ransom's bedside in Georgia. Another was First Sergeant Frank Whipple, that lonely soldier, the man who dreamed of dinner at home surrounded by friends and security. Many more had chosen not to stay the course. Back in August, 1864, the character of the Eleventh had significantly changed when the greater proportion of the three-year men turned toward home. Men like Private Henry Uptmor journeyed home, convinced they had played their role and had taken too many chances on too many battlefields. Now it was the turn of the other men to endure bitter fights like the one at Yazoo City. Other young men could taste the dust and furnace heat the veterans remembered from that pounding July Fourth march on Jackson. When the "Old Boys" left they were replaced by the conscripts, or men paid as substitutes by the affluent. Then too, the 109th Illinois transfers still remained. Months were still left before these men would finish out their three-year term. But, whatever their virtues and vices, the men who served in the Eleventh in 1865 were different men with different motives than those who had gone before.

On March 17, 1865 the new Eleventh abandoned the idyllic bivouac on Dauphine Island to join in the campaign for Mobile.[12] General E.R.S. Canby had decided upon an attack on that city's eastern defenses. To that end, the Eleventh and the remainder of the XIII Army Corps were ferried across Mobile Bay's entrance and disembarked at Navy Cove. The Union army was to march north up the eastern shore of the bay. They would either confront the Confederates in an open fight during that march, or, much more likely, lay seige to Mobile's eastern defenses anchored around two strongpoints christened Fort Blakely and Spanish Fort. The regiment was surely encouraged during the landing at Navy Cove by the formidable presence of four Monitors standing off the shore in plain view despite the growing darkness. The *Kickapoo*, *Chickasaw*, *Milwaukee*, and *Winnebago*, along with other powerful units in the Union fleet, were expected to lend support during the upcoming attack.[13] Confederate intrenchments on the eastern shore were believed vulnerable to naval bombardment. When the Eleventh dozed off to sleep on the 17th, the night pickets could well have pondered upon the dark, silent, steel creatures and taken comfort in their ominous presence just off shore.

Brigadier Elias S. Dennis, commanding the Second Brigade, First Division, XIII Army Corps, ordered his units to commence the march north at 8 a.m. the next day. The command made only four miles before the First Brigade elements joined them and both established an early encampment. Dennis set a harder pace on March 18th, bringing the command to a spot near Shell Point Bayou, fifteen miles closer to the enemy city. The next few days were a monotonous continuation broken only when the regiments stacked arms to assist other units in building corduroy roads. Corduroying meant laying down pine logs side by side over the soft, wet sandy trace. Only then could the supply wagons and artillery trains move up.[14] Intermittent rains drenched the men and further impeded their progress. On March 21, the Eleventh worked nearly all day at this back-breaking task. Many officers plunged waist-deep into the muck to encourage the enlisted men far into the night. After a few hours of fitful sleep, the regiment struck out at 4 a.m. the next morning and made their slippery way over corduroy roads laid by units which had preceded them. It was an awkward, slow march interrupted time and again when the men were called out to push and pull wagons or guns which frequently bogged down in the soft earth. Lieutenant Carrington faithfully recorded his own impressions of the campaign despite the weather and the fatigue of the exhausting marches. His diary entries for the period reflected an exhilaration at the prospect of another encounter with the Confederates:

> There seems to be a fine healthy air in these woods. Chewing gum and the rations taste unusually good. Boys are all eager to meet the "rebs"...All hands in good spirits, not growling...No Army but ours would ever try to march through such a country as this. We have our blankets, grub and "dog tents", is about all the baggage we have along. The boys carry spades and axes, so we are ready to <u>ditch</u> at a moment's notice.[15]

Warmer weather arrived and the Southern roads improved in quality during the next few days' march. On March 26 the advance dueled with Rebel skirmishers. Colonel Coates dispatched six companies of the Eleventh to the brigade's embattled skirmish line and soon a "lively fire" resulted. With the veteran's cautious instinct for survival, Colonel Coates instructed his remaining four companies to throw up intrenchments should the

Rebel pickets suddenly prove to be part of a larger, more aggressive force. He knew that good men provided with good cover could stand off three or four times their number. Even after the firing fell off, he had the regiment digging in until nearly midnight. There were to be no Shiloh surprises at this late date. Daylight witnessed the resumption of the march.[16] Bad weather returned as well to soak the command with an occasional shower throughout the day. At the end of the day the tired men rested just out of range of the Confederate intrenchments at Spanish Fort. Mobile was not more than ten miles to the west. Out on the bay itself were those brutish Monitors whose rifled cannons were expected to punish the Confederates with a hail of iron once the battle commenced. The date was March 27, 1865.

Long dead Spanish settlers had fortified these same approaches to Mobile nearly a century before. They had seen with a keen military appreciation how the natural obstacles of the Texas and Appalachee channels could be reinforced by an armed garrison. Confederate engineers had seen similar advantages which led them to construct the Spanish Fort emplacement. Rebel General Dabney Maury had originally considered meeting the advancing Federals at Olive's Creek with his 4,500-man command. Initial intelligence reports had given him the erroneous belief that his forces would only encounter the Union XIII Corps. During the skirmishing on the 26th, he learned that General A.J. Smith's XVI Corps was very close by and in a position to crush his flank should the attack be pressed.[17] Bearing this in mind, the Confederate commander wisely withdrew his force into Spanish Fort. He instructed Brigadier General Randall Lee Gibson to conduct the defense where approximately 2,000 gray-clad soldiers were shielded by a ring of intrenchments and strongpoints. At the age of 33, the urbane Gibson could be expected to offer an intelligent, energetic resistance. A Yale graduate, and a prewar attache at the embassy in Madrid, Spain, Gibson was representative of the South's ruling elite. He had studied law at the University of Louisiana and practiced that profession in addition to running a sugar plantation in the days before the war. This cosmopolitan soldier fought with great distinction at Shiloh, Stone's River, Perryville, Chicagamauga, Chattanooga, and a dozen other battlefields.[18] He certainly could be relied upon to hold up the advance of the Federals as long as possible. Just as certain was the fact that the Union army was not about to assault such a strong position without careful preparation. Brigadier General C.C. Andrews, commanding the First Division of the Yankee XIII Corps, described the Confederate position in respectful tones:

Old Spanish Fort is a bastioned work, nearly enclosed, and built on a bluff, whose shape projects abruptly to the water. Its parapet on the bay side was partly natural, being made by excavating the earth from the side of the bluff and was thirty feet in thickness. The fort was armed with seven-inch Columbiads and 30-pound Parrotts... Extending around that, in a semicircle was a continuous line of breastworks and redoubts. The right of this line commenced 400 yards down the shore, on the highest and most prominent bluff, upward of 100 feet above the water, with a strong enclosed fort, called McDermett, and armed with ten heavy guns...up the slope of another bluff...was another strong battery...[19]

Approximately two miles of outer works formed a deadly half-circle beginning and ending near the water of the bay. Approaches to the Rebel fortress would have to be made across a killing ground reminiscent in many ways of Vicksburg. Almost all the surrounding woods had been chopped down to form an interlocking barrier. Closer in, a fifteen-foot-thick tangle of abatis formed another obstacle. Primitive land torpedoes had been buried at various points along the approaches. Out on the periphery of the Rebel fortress the men of the Eleventh and the other Union regiments applied pick and shovel throughout the night as they burrowed out the beginnings of siege lines. Vicksburg veterans, like the recently promoted Lieutenant Colonel Nathaniel Kenyon of the Eleventh, ably instructed the newer men in the grimy art where good healthy sweat and hard work could mean a lot less blood and pain later on. They were still digging when the sun rose on March 28.

Acting Rear Admiral H.K. Thatcher's Union ironclads took a severe drubbing during the opening rounds. Their efforts to close with Spanish Fort, and its supporting batteries (Huger and Tracy) on the nearby islands, met with disaster. One of the awesome double-turreted Monitors that had been anchored at Navy Cove, the *Milwaukee*, was sunk by a Confederate mine, as was the *Osage*. Men in the Eleventh could glimpse these disappointing Naval operations from their positions in the siege lines. Beyond the fleet they could also see the outlines of Mobile spread out on the western horizon.[20] Almost all the firing and cannon bombardment ceased with darkness. On the next day the digging and the firing resumed with renewed vigor on both sides. On the Eleventh's front Colonel Coates split the command into two shifts. Companies E through K manned the trenches until noon, until relieved by the men from Companies A through D. Captain George

Doanne of Company C was in command of the second relief which kept up a heavy fire until nightfall. From then on it was only "shot for shot," one participant recalled.[21] The rain arrived with the coming of darkness, quickly drenching the tired men who waded about in water and ooze.

Even less lucky men were selected for special duty by Captain Doanne. He needed soldiers to man listening posts out between the lines and instructed Lieutenant Carrington to post a detail for that purpose. That tired veteran thought it all a lot of nonsense, considering the proximity of the Rebels. Perhaps he was preoccupied with this supposed injustice when returning to the main trench a few minutes later. Rebel rifle fire flamed in the wet darkness and a cluster of Minie balls screeched past the startled Carrington. Almost at the same time one of the boys in the Eleventh sang out: "Lieutenant, get down from there! They can see the outline against the sky and are firing at you!"[22] Carrington abandoned dignity to belly-flop into the muddy trench. We can assume his thoughts about the whims of higher officers had momentarily been dismissed. Later he claimed that, despite the Rebel fire snapping at his heels, the decision to leap into the sloppy ditch had been a rather difficult one.

Midnight was the signal for even more serious fireworks. Approximately 500 Confederate riflemen under the command of Lieutenant Colonel R.H. Lindsay sallied out "in gallant style," according to his superior, General Gibson.[23] It was a battle of shadows fought in a downpour. Some of the new recruits in the Eleventh's trenches were completely bewildered. A few even became separated from the regiment, either through their own confusion or perhaps due to their frightened efforts to avoid the oncoming Rebels. Lieutenant Carrington directed the defense with the majority of the Eleventh who stood steady and replied to the Rebel charge with a constant, if mostly inaccurate, rifle fire. Recalling the action, Carrington wrote:

> They opened quite a heavy fire and drove in most of our advanced pickets. They came tumbling in and crawled over and into the pits. The boys returned the fire and for quite a time it was quite lively. Some of our recruits happened to be short men... Some of these would load, then lay the musket on the banks in front at about an angle of 45 degrees and fire away, the bullet going clear over Spanish Fort and doubtless falling harmlessly in the Bay...Some seemed to think all that was necessary was to keep up the firing, make a noise. Others fired at the flashes of the enemy's muskets. Very few

hits were scored on either side. After the firing died down somewhat, I...placed them on post again when the Rebs came out of their works and charged our left...This was about 1 a.m. For about a half-hour they yelled and charged, with our boys pouring in the bullets. They also returned to us a hot fire of musketry. After losing about 200 men, killed, wounded, and taken prisoner, they fell back into their own intrenchments and remained quiet until daylight.[24]

    Veterans in the ranks were inclined to regard the Rebel sorties as trivial happenings. Despite all the shouting and shooting, the Eleventh suffered but three wounded and not one man hit seriously. For them the only really memorable aspects of the skirmish were the antics engaged in by jumpy draftees. Stories were told how an Irishman came rolling into the trenches just ahead of the on-coming Rebels to announce: "Oh, my Captain Dear! Did you see the sky lights?"[25] He was referring, of course, to the red and yellow splashes of light which marked the presence of Rebel riflemen blazing away with enthusiasm. Similar grist for campfire yarns was provided by a German recruit not far removed from the "Old Country." This raw soldier was one who managed to lose himself during the Confederate probing attack. In the aftermath, the unlucky German appeared out of a nearby ravine where a thicket of brush and fallen timber had given him shelter throughout the night. It was still dark when the soldier tentatively approached Captain Doanne and formally presented his rifle, saying: "I b'eesh a Union man, who b'eesh you?"[26]

    At 7 a.m. on March 30, the Eleventh retired from its forward positions, relieved by other men from the First Brigade. Mud-covered and bleary-eyed, the men shuffled through the already elaborate traverses. These zig-zag approaches to the firing line offered the best protection from snipers or enemy shells. Private Moses Gunn of Company K would remember all his life how a number of men from the regiment suddenly clambered out of the sheltering trench and darted out over open ground. It was a school-boy stunt. They had found the safe but slow march back through the traverses too dull for their tastes. Private Gunn was a drafted man, a religious man, and one who loved life too much for such foolishness. He and the other more cautious men in the regiment watched in disbelief while the Rebels spattered the open area with rifle fire. The fugitives were forced to "turkey" their way for short distances: they would dive behind the protection of a stump or hummock, wait a few seconds, and then bolt out for another 50 yards or so.[27] Bullets skipped by inches away, but all the Yankees made their way safely through to the rear. One may assume the immature heroes of this tale greeted their more conservative comrades with triumphant grins and catcalls. They couldn't know that most veterans never took chances when nothing was at stake. Men like Lieutenant Carrington were too wise to waste their quotient of luck for a thrill or laugh. Men like him no longer saw this as a game. For Carrington, in particular, the important fact was that the regiment would sleep in relative comfort far from the picket line for at least a day and a night.

Not a man realized they had spent their last night in the Spanish Fort lines. At noon, March 30, the Eleventh and other elements of the XII Corps were on the march bound north for the second Confederate stronghold, Fort Blakely. Union General Canby's enormous superiority in manpower allowed him to make this shift with little or no danger to the forces still in the siege lines at Spanish Fort. It was his plan to have the XIII Corps consolidate with a strike force of 13,000 men under General Frederick Steele moving toward Fort Blakely from their base at Pensacola, Florida.[28] By the evening of April 1, the Eleventh was only a few miles from the Rebel fortress. They could hear the mutter of small arms fire that told them Steele had already invested the Confederate garrison. The Pensacola column consisted of the Third Division of the XIII Corps plus Hawkins's division of colored troops. They had been marching on short rations through a barren country and eagerly awaited Canby's promised supply train, which was moving towards them in the same column with the Eleventh. These troops were hurried along, even rising at 1 a.m., April 3, to continue the final few miles towards Blakely. By noon, the regiment was in line opposite the enemy's left center. Another tested Confederate veteran commanded the troops in the opposing rifle pits: Brigadier General St. John R. Liddel's battlefield laurels had been won at Perryville, Stone's River, and Chickamauga.[29] His force at Fort Blakely consisted of approximately 4,000 soldiers fairly secure behind a three-mile semi-circle of intrenchments welded around nine key strongpoints.

As had been the case at Spanish Fort, the Union infantry were quickly at work, day and night. Picks and shovels in the thousands created an intricate network of parallel trenches facing the enemy and linked with each other by numerous traverses. It was brutal work particularly when heavy artillery pieces had to be manhandled into position. These operations were conducted under continuous fire. Both sides pumped out a prodigious hail of lead with relatively little effect. Later, when the nearby siege of Spanish Fort finally ended, Union headquarters estimated their men had fired off one million rounds of rifle ammunition and 10,000 cannon shells in less than two weeks. Firing at Fort Blakely was carried on with the same abandon. Few had a specific target but most thought it advisable to keep up the noise just so Johnny Reb wouldn't develop any ideas about a sudden assault or sortie.

Each night the saproller was pushed ahead at the point of the intended trench. This cylinder was a contraption of basketwork filled with earth which absorbed the Rebel rifle bullets with impunity. Behind this moving shield the men quickly dug out a shallow course deep enough to allow further progress. Behind them more men deepened and widened the pit. Gabions--simple wooden baskets filled with earth--were then placed along the earth walls to serve as revetments. Lieutenant Carrington of the Eleventh claimed the regiment could dig out a 100-yard rifle pit in less than one night's labor. It was a technical task whose challenges must have appealed to the typical Yankee's penchant for problem solving. Every morning saw the black mole-like trails creeping a little closer to the Confederate defenses. This was a mode of warfare that set a precedent for the great trench systems of World War I which still lay more than a half-century in the future. The motive behind the digging was the same in both wars, to provide the troops with a haven from the awesome destructiveness of modern firepower. One Minnesota participant in the Mobile siege, Colonel L.F. Hubbard, recalled how the men disliked this modern trench warfare:

> Many a soldier practically dug his own grave while engaged in this work, as a shell would explode in his vicinity or the keen eye of a sharpshooter would detect an exposure perhaps impossible to prevent. It is difficult to realize, as it is impossible to describe, the intense nature of the strain to which a soldier is continuously subjected while performing duty of this character. While the danger to life is perhaps less than when engaged in battle, the sustaining inspiration of possibly achieving some marked success momentarily hoped for is lacking... There is no inspiration in that kind of service. The soldier's thoughts inevitably dwell upon the possibility that any moment a missile projected by a dead shot from the enemy's line may cripple, or that a shell may explode...and crush him. To labor for hours under such conditions constitutes an experience that is most depressing.[31]

Mobile could hear the daily hate explode around Spanish Fort and Fort Blakely in these April days. Citizens could glimpse from rooftops the mushroom black clouds that marked Union cannon positions on the eastern shore. They could make out the Yankee warships that still nosed their way in toward the Rebel bastions, although in a more cautious manner than they had before. Everyone was in dread of the invisible "infernal machines" reported to infest the waters of the great bay. Within the city the die-hard Rebels prayed that the Union tide might be stemmed, or at least stalled, in time for a European intervention. Among the gullible, or perhaps the more realistic, they sought intervention of a divine order. Prayer services in the city's churches were crowded each evening with solemn petitioners. Many had sons, husbands, and dear friends out there on the opposite shore who even now were under a steady Union pounding. One Mobile newspaper carried on a primitive if enthusiastic propaganda campaign during those final days. Editorials gloated over the shoddy quality of the Yankee munitions and remarked in a positive tone how few shells exploded once they reached Rebel lines. Mobile residents read how the boys at Springhill College had begged General Maury to allow them to join the battle.[32] The staunch Confederate officer must have nodded his head in approval when he read how the game boys threatened to join up even if it meant expulsion. In those same pages the doubting citizen could find courage in letters from the front which were almost always optimistic. Yankee bullets and shells were regarded with proper cavalier disdain. One soldier wrote from Spanish Fort:

> We are having a fine time here sharp-shooting with the Yankees. Ten thousand thanks to the ladies of Mobile for sending us that provision they sent us last night. I think I was the hungriest man on the "map." You ought to have seen with what eagerness I devoured those eggs, meat, and cake...My heart ran out in thankfulness to the fair daughters of the fair city. I was proud that I was such a soldier battling for the rights of such ladies as these.[33]

Spanish Fort was in a precarious position by April 8. General Canby had the place under a concentrated fire delivered by fifty-three siege guns and thirty-seven field pieces.[34] These guns, and others located opposite the Confederate lines at Batteries Tracy and Huger, opened with a vengeance around 5:30 p.m. Union infantry had already dug their way right to the very edge of the Confederate rifle pits and braced for a final rush. During the height of the cannon bombardment, men from the 8th Iowa actually pierced the Confederate left flank. Two hundred or so prisoners were taken and several cannon which were quickly trundled about to fire back into the Rebel fortress. Always cautious, General Canby awaited daylight for the final push. He waited too long. Confederate General Gibson withdrew his entire garrison during the hours of darkness. His men made their way across an extremely narrow treadway or causeway that almost linked Spanish Fort with Battery Huger. More than 2,000 Confederate soldiers splashed their way single file across the 1,200-yard-long, half-submerged land bridge. The track was no more than 18 inches wide and vulnerable at most points to Union heavy batteries. Once across this earthen tightrope, they transferred into small boats for a short passage to Battery Huger. From there they embarked on steamers for the final journey back to Mobile. General Gibson reported how the withdrawal was effected without casualties. "It (the escape route) was concealed by the high grass and covered with moss, and the troops pulled off their shoes, and thus, in a noiseless manner, succeeded in retiring without attracting the attention of the enemy."[35]

Eight miles to the north, the investment of Fort Blakely was proceeding swiftly. The men in the Eleventh were in the pits twenty-four hours at a time, and then rotated toward the rear for a twenty-four-hour respite. At night the men of the Eleventh could hear quite distinctly the roar from the cannon at Spanish Fort. At times they could clearly hear the sounds of cheering.[36] It was a heartening, promising sound which matched the Eleventh's own joy at its surprisingly slim casualty roster: not one man had been killed since the campaign began. Everyone was aware that events were moving at an incredible pace. Rumors indicated that Robert Lee's legendary Army of Northern Virginia was being hammered by U.S. Grant near Appomattox Courthouse. Out in North Carolina, red-bearded General W.T. Sherman was hard on old General Joe Johnston's heels. Everywhere Rebel armies were facing a choice between extinction or capitulation. Outside Mobile, General Canby hurried his own preparation for a final attack on Fort Blakely. He must have been sorely disappointed after letting the Spanish Fort garrison steal away in the night. Now he pushed ahead the attack schedule. Major General A.J. Smith was ordered to shift two divisions from Spanish Fort to strengthen the Union left wing before Blakely. On April 7, that ram-rod old regular rode past the Eleventh's bivouac during an inspection of the front. Lieutenant Carrington dutifully recorded his appearance, noting:

Saw General Smith and staff riding and looking along our lines. Something is up. General A.J. Smith is an old gray man, but a fighter and rides like Jehu.[37]

A great assault against Fort Blakely was building. Union sapping operations had now closed the gap between the lines to within approximately 500 yards. Between them and the Confederate lines stood three separate barriers consisting of wooden abatis. Confederate pickets were located in firing pits at various points in the open zone. Their intrenchments were not contiguous to the main bastion which would mean they must flee over open ground once a major Yankee assault took shape. Consequently, the field of fire would be obstructed for some crucial minutes while the Confederates in the fort paused in fear of killing their own incoming pickets.[38] Charges across open ground, as witnessed by the Eleventh at Vicksburg, were rarely successful against a determined opponent. Cool men behind breastworks could hold off the most spirited attack with near impunity. General Canby's attack decision may well have been predicated upon an assumption that Rebel valor might wither in these final hours. Few men could wish to be among the last needless casualties for a cause long lost. Unknown to everyone on that field, Union and Confederate, was the ironic historical timing. Approximately an hour and a half before the attack signal was given at Blakely, the Confederates' finest army and its most valiant commander had surrendered at Appomattox Courthouse in Virginia. General Robert E. Lee and the Army of Northern Virginia had ceased to exist. Everything that followed was doomed by its very nature to be no more than a violent epilogue to the chronicle of the American Civil War.[39]

Almost at the same minute that Lee was riding Traveller down the road from Appomattox, the Eleventh Illinois filed into the forward trenches around Blakely, taking up positions alongside the 46th Illinois. Strung out in front of these two regiments was a 400-yard skirmish line formed by 700 infantry from the Eighth Illinois. As always, there was the waiting. Up and down the Union siege lines, more than 16,000 blue infantry massed in preparation for attack. Their movements were accompanied by a rising crescendo of artillery fire. One nameless soldier in the Eleventh later recalled how "the Johnies" had taunted them earlier in the siege about their seeming deficiency in this department. One Southern wit even offered to loan them some of their own plentiful stock of cannon.[40] Now, on April 9, the Yankee was vindicated when the surrounding Union lines fairly shook with the thunder of a steady barrage. On the left flank of the Eleventh a quartet of rifled cannon was quickly drawn up right out in the open. Calmly proficient, the gunners immediately led away their satin black horses as they prepared to open fire. Lieutenant Carrington was entranced by the batteries' almost poetic ballet:

> After the gun was sighted by the Sergeant, gave it a jerk and a whang, with a ship-like crack. Keen as a squirrel rifle, only so much louder, was the report, while a cloud of white smoke rolled away from the muzzle. Every man about the place had his eyes upon the Rebel works expecting an answering shot. We could trace the course of the shot as with a soul harrowing swish and screech it struck the top of the works throwing up a cloud of dust and crashing through the timber beyond...White smoke floating so gracefully away. The weave of the men, back and forth, as they sponged the piece, the black water flowing from the muzzle, the red flame as it sprang from the gun...The man running from the limber chest to the gun with the charge. The man at the breech with the friction primer...The quick movements of it all. The Lieutenant with glass watching the effects of each shot. It was a grand sight that war alone can produce.[41]

Confederate General Liddell was astutely aware of his predicament at Fort Blakely. Outnumbered by at least four to one, his forces were at a terrible disadvantage. Logic demanded a withdrawal. His troops might provide better service elsewhere where the situation promised a better chance for survival. After the fall of Spanish Fort, even the military neophyte could sense that Canby's full weight would shift rapidly upon the Rebels at Blakely. Liddell's only sensible course was a night evacuation, as had been carried out with such good fortune at Spanish Fort. His tired men must endure the Union guns for at least a few more hours; then they might effect an escape. But whatever desperate hope they entertained in that regard vanished at 5 p.m. Yankee infantry emerged in the open with a great bellow. Thousands of riflemen were sprinting toward the Confederate fortress, bursting through brush entanglements, leaping over water-filled shell holes, and dodging the tell-tale wires which marked the presence of crude Rebel landmines.

The men in the Eleventh waited while the Eighth Illinois skirmish line advanced in a ragged run. Before them the startled Rebel pickets scampered for the main Confederate intrenchments. Even when the Eighth Illinois approached the final line of abatis about fifty yards from Blakely, the Union artillery continued the heavy barrage. Shells exploded on the Rebel strongpoint, throwing up great brown spouts with every hit. Now it was the turn of the Eleventh and 46th Illinois. Colonel Coates leaped onto the parapet of his trench to bark out the order to assault. Like most of the other officers, he had dispensed with his sword while serving in the narrow, muddy trenches. So instead he waved an intrenching tool back and forth as visual encouragement. One anonymous soldier in the Eleventh related how the "ground literally swarmed with the Blue Coats. With a continuous yell the living rushed on, everyone doing his best to outstrip his neighbor, and reach the enemy's works first..."[42] Rebel resistance "came alive" at this point. Four cannons played their bloody work on the Eighth Illinois for nearly five minutes before the first Yankee infantry reached the Rebel defenses. Lieutenant Colonel Lloyd Wheaton and Sergeant John M. Switzer quickly squirmed through the embrasure of an enemy 30-pounder. The Yankee sergeant smashed the Rebel gunner down with his rifle butt moments before the rest of the Eighth Illinois clambered into the strongpoint.[43] A few hundred yards behind came the Eleventh Illinois who hurdled the numerous ravines and land torpedo trip-wires in their sprint toward Blakely. During their advance the gunfire along the enemy's works twinkled red in the fading daylight. Lieutenant Carrington claimed not one man in the Eleventh fired his rifle in this heart-pounding charge:

> I saw to the left our men on top of the works firing down while the flashes from the inside were aimed up. While these men were yet on top of a redoubt a Rebel fired a cannon almost under where they were standing. This was the last cannon shot fired from their intrenchments. As we jumped down inside they were 'throwing down their "hot Enfields"...One Rebel Captain came swearing he would never surrender to a "damned Yankee." One of the boys raised his musket and fired, the bullet passing through his brain and down he went in a pile. Poor fellow! He might have lived. It was all done so quick no one could interfere.[44]

Hundreds of Confederates abandoned the strongpoint to run for the shelter of nearby timber and down to the Blakely River Landing. Those that remained were either quickly killed or subdued. On the far right flank General Hawkins's division of colored troops smashed their way into the fort. Once over the top, many behaved like foxes loose in a chicken coop. Their cry was: "Remember Fort Pillow." One Yankee from the 46th Illinois reported how many Rebels "ran for the white troops" to make their surrender.[45] Another witness observed that the "spirit of killing" had infected the maddened black infantry. Two white Union officers in the 68th regiment were even wounded by their black comrades when they attempted to intervene. Some of the Confederate defenders drowned in the Blakely River in their panic to avoid the frenzied black soldiers. "A good many were shot down because they would not surrender to a black man," swore one infantryman from the 46th Illinois.[46] Fifteen to twenty minutes elapsed before the killing subsided. Colonel Coates ordered the Eleventh back out of the enemy intrenchments a few minutes later, and led them down to the river searching for more Confederate prisoners. Nearly 3,200 were captured that night. Union casualties for the entire campaign were roughly 1,500 killed, wounded, and captured.[47] For once the Eleventh was lucky. Not one man was killed and only six were wounded. Lieutenant Carrington reflected a few days later on this, the final battle:

> I visited the ground on the right...where the black boys charged and noticed many pools of dark blood. The dead had been taken away...There was a good deal of fallen timber and brush they had to go through. The bullets had cut the branches, chipped the logs. It might have been a pretty hot place...Our Brigade was in the center and not under as heavy a fire... Not a coward was to be found. Every man wanted to gain the works. Not a dodger or a straggler. Every man to the front and over the works they went head long. No firing until they reached the top and not much then as they surrendered...After pelting us for a quarter of a mile, then to throw down their rifle shot and smoky, some at full cock, the hammer thrown back by the last shot. It was hard work to keep from doing some shooting then...[48]

On April 10 and April 11, the Eleventh remained in camp a few miles from the captured Rebel fort. The batteries at Huger and Tracy still flew the Confederate flag, but were already under heavy bombardment and near surrender. The campaign was near an end, as was the war. At 2 a.m. on April 12, the regiment embarked on the steamer *Planter* along with the 46th Illinois. A dozen and more transports left the eastern shore at daylight, bound for landing about five miles south of Mobile on the opposite shore. Close alongside were the grim Monitors and the great ocean-going battleships whose rigging was speckled with Yankee sailors. They landed the First and Third Divisions of the XIII Army

Corps without opposition. These troops, including the "Old Eleventh", entered Mobile with the coming of night to bivouac amidst the outer ring of Rebel trenches.[49] The great seaport town was occupied without a shot fired. Military tradition gave the honor of leading the Union column through the fallen city to the Eighth Illinois, whose men had bled most freely at Blakely. Four years to the day after the cannon roared at Fort Sumter, the American flag had returned to Mobile.

Six weeks passed while the Eleventh marked time in Mobile, surrounded by thousands of demobilized Confederate prisoners. Many were so destitute they possessed only their gray, mostly tattered uniforms. These dejected ragamuffins walked the same streets with the Bluecoats, but few incidents were recorded. Perhaps they had all had enough of hate for awhile. Even Lincoln's assassination failed to ignite Yankee wrath, although Lieutenant Carrington recorded how many swore "vengeance and cry for blood."[50] It was only talk. Members of each army mingled with quiet reserve in the streets and establishments of the community. Whatever the past, they all shared the common desire to resume their civilian lives and be done with drills, details, bugles, and salutes. Not that many a veteran wouldn't carry away a bit of pride--men like Lieutenant Colonel Kenyon of the Eleventh, who had shivered outside Donelson, and rotted for months in Southern jails. This splendid officer was only 26 years of age at the end of the war. In his future lay the great American West, a nearly fatal duel with an Oklahoma outlaw, and more than a half-century of productive life.[51] He must have been pleased when an old discharged soldier from the Eleventh wrote him in late May, a month after the fall of Mobile. Captain William Duncan had marched into Vicksburg with Ransom's column. Now he was a discharged veteran inclined to gloat about his old regiment's combat reputation. He wrote:

> I have a desire to know how the old Eleventh is getting along and to congratulate you on the end of the war. I suppose you expect to soon go home. The times of the men are so mixed up that I don't believe they will muster you out as a regiment. You may have to go with Sheridan and finish the job so well commenced and clean out Kirby Smith and Maximillian...Maximillian would be a few days sport for your old veterans. I should like to see the grand review at Washington...especially the Western Army--the old Army of the Tennessee. It would be worth one year of life to march through with them...[52]

Smug self-congratulations were premature. For scores of Union soldiers, Mobile became a graveyard when the city exploded on the afternoon of May 25, 1865. It was almost as if the war refused to die, as if death and suffering had taken on an existence independent from the decisions and actions of men. At one moment a detail of Union soldiers and some black laborers were unloading a captured Confederate munitions train down near the Marshall Warehouse, located in the northeastern quarter of the town near the river landing. Someone made a mistake; no one ever learned who. The answers and a great portion of the city itself were lost in an immense explosion. Its earthquake dimensions were felt eighty miles away in Selma. Captain James G. Patton of the inspector-general's office reported how "a terrific explosion... shook the foundation of the city, followed immediately by a heavy rumbling explosion of shells and fixed amunition and a shower of shot, shell, grape, and canister, and pieces of stone and brick. A dense column of smoke arose..."[53] The steamers *Kate Dale* and *Colonel Cowles* were shattered by the blast, although passengers aboard escaped serious harm. Dozens of Union soldiers, paroled Confederates, slaves, and common citizens were pinioned in the wreckage of the city immediately surrounding the Marshall Warehouse. An Iowa soldier, Captain Charles H. Thompson, was working in his office at the warehouse when the powder detonated. The first blast threw him to the floor:

> This was followed by a second detonation. The roof of the building was crushed in, and the walls fell outward, killing three soldiers who were standing guard in the streets. As soon as I succeeded in recovering my composure to a certain extent, I rushed to the window, and the sight...almost paralyzed me. Down in the street the buildings were falling outwardly and the walls were lapping over each other in the street. I saw a government mule team, which was approaching my building, crushed beneath two falling walls. Half a dozen soldiers...were killed. After beholding these sights I seemed to lose my mind. I jumped out of the window and ran to a vacant lot, where I fell in a fit. Sometime afterward a detail of soldiers found me. I did not regain my reasoning until late in the evening.[54]

Out on the St. Frances Road, at the western fringe of Mobile, the Eleventh Illinois encampment escaped the devastating convulsion. They were startled by the thunder wave of sound and stood outside their tents and shelters staring back toward the breeze.⁵⁵ It was as if all the four years of war had suddenly been compacted into one window-bursting swirl of smoke. The spell was broken a few moments later when the call to form ranks was bellowed back and forth through camp. In company with many other Union regiments, the Eleventh marched toward the still-crackling inferno to provide men for rescue and fire fighting. Flames sprouted in all directions from the main blast. One entire munitions train was blazing down at the tracks. Intermittently, stores of ammunition would be ignited by the tremendous heat. These sudden land-mine-like explosions severely impeded rescue work. "Shells continued to explode so no one could get near to help those who could not help themselves," Lieutenant Carrington recollected. "It was pretty risky rushing into the fire--falling brick walls, bursting shells...Nearly every window in the city was broken."⁵⁶ By 5:30 p.m., the inferno was subdued, but only after thirty-two square blocks of city had been destroyed. Estimates varied drastically on the casualties. Riding through the smouldering rubble on May 26, Captain Thompson of the First Division, XIII Army Corps, described the streets as filled with dead bodies. That officer estimated more than 1,000 killed and seriously injured. A more conservative U.S. army report placed the figure at 500.⁵⁷

The "Old Eleventh" had smelled gunpowder for the last time. Marching orders came two days later. At 9 a.m., May 27, Colonel James H. Coates led the 750 men of the Eleventh Illinois through the wounded city and down toward the wharf. By 1 p.m. they, along with the members of the Eighth Illinois, were aboard the steamer *White Cloud*. Mobile Bay was blue and serene while the flat-bottomed paddle-wheeler steamed south for a pleasant afternoon's cruise. A few hours' journey brought the boat to Grant's Pass, a narrow stretch of the Gulf waters between familiar Dauphine Island and the coast. In the shadow of a setting sun, *White Cloud* set course west for home.⁵⁸

Photographs

A Mexican War veteran, General W.H.L. Wallace raised the 11th Illinois Infantry when Lincoln made his first call for troops. The general was mortally wounded commanding a division in the Hornet's Nest during the battle of Shiloh. (Photo courtesy of the Illinois State Historical Society, Springfield, Illinois.)

Brigadier General T.E.G. Ransom led the 11th Illinois at the battles of Fort Donelson and Shiloh, and led a brigade during the Vicksburg battle and seige. He died while commanding an army corps in the battle for Atlanta. This portrait was taken by Mathew Brady, probably in the spring or summer of 1864 when Ransom was on recuperative leave in New York City. (Photo courtesy of the Illinois State Historical Library.)

Many of the men who joined the army were country boys still wet behind the ears, as depicted in this sketch by Lieutenant Frederick Eugene Ransom. The volunteers were hardened into soldiers at Bird's Point, Missouri before marching south where many died at Fort Donelson, Shiloh, Vicksburg, and the final seige of Mobile. (Photo courtesy of the Illinois State Historical Society, Springfield, Illinois.)

This drawing, depicting the occupation of Bird's Point, Missouri by Union troops, appeared in *Frank Leslie's Illustrated Magazine.* (Photo courtesy of the Illinois State Historical Library.)

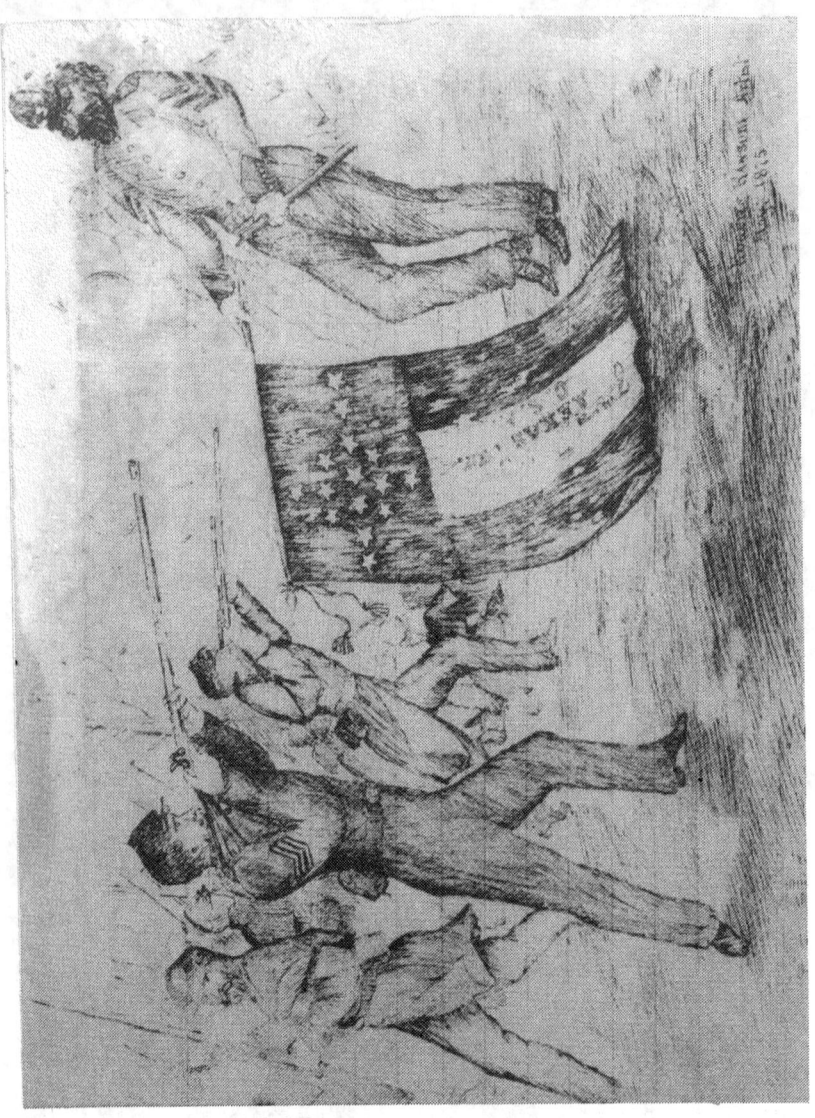

A Rebel flag bearer falls before heavy rifle fire from the 11th Illinois during the battle of Fort Donelson where the regiment suffered sixty percent casualties. The sketch was drawn by Lieutenant Frederick Eugene Ransom, who was captured during the battle. The younger brother of General T.E.G. Ransom spent many months in Rebel prisons. (Photo courtesy of the Illinois State Historical Society, Springfield, Illinois.)

Prisoner-of-war Frederick Eugene Ransom sketched this scen depicting a Rebel guard firing at a Union soldier apparently durii an escape attempt. (Photo courtesy of the Illinois State Historic Library.)

Bloody Shiloh brought grief to Ann Wallace and her adopted child, Isabell, when General W.H.L. Wallace fell mortally wounded with a Rebel rifle ball in his head. He died in his wife's arms a few days after the battle concluded. (Photo courtesy of the Illinois State Historical Society, Springfield, Illinois.)

Years after the Civil War, this photo was taken of General W.H.L. Wallace's war horse, Prince. The general's widow later buried the horse a few feet from the grave of his fallen master. (Photo courtesy of Mrs. Myrna Evans, Oglesby, Illinois.)

Captain Cyrus Dickey was a member of Ransom's staff at Sabine Cross Roads, where he was killed. Dickey, the son of Judge T. Lyle Dickey of Ottawa, Illinois, served with Ransom at Fort Donelson, Shiloh, and Vicksburg. They were close friends, and both were very close to General W.H.L. Wallace, Dickey's brother-in-law. (Photo courtesy of the Chicago Public Library Special Collections.)

Private George D. Carrington served with the 11th Illinois Infantry Regiment from Fort Donelson to the battle of Mobile. He kept a detailed journal of his experiences, which is insightful and crowded with colorful characters. (Photo courtesy of the Chicago Historical Society.)

Captain Smith D. Atkins led the men of Company A, 11th Illinois Infantry during the battle of Fort Donelson, where the unit took sixty percent casualties. Atkins survived to become a brevet brigadier general, commanding cavalry in the Carolina campaign. (Photo courtesy of the Chicago Public Library Special Collections.)

Captain Fred Shaw of Lacon, Illinois brought back a black servant boy to the little town, much to the outrage of his neighbors. Shaw was killed at the battle of Fort Donelson. The fate of his young servant went unrecorded. (Photo courtesy of the Chicago Public Library Special Collections.)

Lieutenant James Churchill was wounded and left for dead on the battlefield at Fort Donelson. He lay there helpless throughout the night, watching as human vultures robbed the dead and the dying. Miraculously, he was found the next morning and taken for treatment. (Photo courtesy of the Illinois State Historical Library.)

Captain Lloyd Waddell commanded the remnant of the 11th Illinois as the first day of Shiloh ended. Colonel Ransom and Major Garrett Nevius had already been wounded and evacuated to the rear. The 11th Illinois suffered fifty percent casualties that day. (Photo courtesy of the Chicago Public Library Special Collections.)

Lieutenant James Vernay of the 11th Illinois Infantry won the medal of honor when he volunteered to man one of the steamboats which ran past Rebel cannons at Vicksburg. (Photo courtesy of the Chicago Public Library Special Collections.)

Lieutenant E.P. Thomas wrote his sister a vivid account of the 11th Illinois Infantry's march into Vicksburg when that key Rebel bastion surrendered. (Photo courtesy of the Chicago Public Library.)

Captain Nathaniel Kenyon was shot by a sniper during the battle of Vicksburg. His comrades thought him dead until they poured a healthy shot of whiskey down his throat, effecting a miraculous cure. Kenyon was promoted to lieutenant colonel before the seige on Mobile. (Photo courtesy of the Chicago Public Library.)

Lieutenant Doug Hapeman fought with the 11th Illinois af Fort Donelson and Shiloh. The young officer later commanded the 104th Illinois Infantry and won a medal of honor during the battle of Peach Tree Creek outside of Atlanta. (Photo courtesy of the Chicago Public Library.)

Notes

Chapter One

A Ceaseless Roll of Drums

[1] Action Report, *The War of the Rebellion: Official Records of the Union and Confederate Armies*, (Washington: U.S. Government Printing Office, 1882-1900), Ser. 1, Vol. VIII, p. 47. (future designation: *Official Records*) Report filed by Colonel Nicholas Perczel, 10th Iowa Infantry.

[2] "Diary of Private George D. Carrington, Company B, 11th Illinois Infantry," (an unpublished manuscript at the Chicago Historical Museum Library); p. 29.

[3] *Ibid.*, p. 29.

[4] *Official Records*, Perczel Report, p. 48.

[5] A letter from Captain Nevius to his brother Henry, January 8, 1862, part of a collection currently in the hands of Winfield D. Nevius of New York State.

[6] John Y. Simon, Editor, *The Papers of U.S. Grant*, Vol. 4 (Carbondale, Ill.: Southern Illinois University Press, 1970), p. 32.

[7] Carrington diary, p. 3.

[8] Carrington, George D., Jr., "Brief Notes on the Life of George Dodd Carrington," (an unpublished monograph in the Chicago Historical Society Library).

[9] Lt. Greenbury L. Fort to the *Lacon Illinois Gazette*, April 29, 1861. Published in the newspaper's May 9, 1861 edition.

[10] *Ibid.*

[11] Charles A. Church, *Historical Encyclopedia of Illinois, and History of Winnebago County* (Chicago: Munsett Publishers, 1916), p. 807.

[12] Captain R. Bird to the Rockford *Rock River Democrat*, May 2, 1861. Published May 7, 1861.

[13] Isabel Wallace, *Life and Letters of General W.H.L. Wallace*, (Chicago: R.R. Donnelley & Sons Publishers, 1909), p.3.

[14] *Ibid.*, p. 9.

[15] *Ibid.*, p. 18.

[16] *Ibid.*, p. 12.

[17] *Ibid.*, p. 22.

[18] *Ibid.*, p. 49.

[19] *Ibid.*, p. 53.

[20] *Ibid.*, p. 107.

[21] Carrington diary, p. 5.

[22] Captain Bird to the *Rock River Democrat*, May 11, 1861. Published on May 21, 1861.

[23] Izora De Wolf, "A.L. Swap in the Civil War," (unpublished manuscript at the Illinois State Historical Library, Springfield.)

[24] Captain Bird to the *Rock River Democrat*, June 1, 1861. Published on June 11, 1861.

[25] Carl Dean Gebhardt, *The Eleventh Illinois Infantry Regiment in the Civil War* (unpublished thesis on file at the Western Illinois University Library, 1968), p. 27.

[26] Cpt. Bird to the *Rock River Democrat*, June 1, 1861. Published June 11, 1861.

[27] *Ibid.*

[28] Gebhardt, p. 36.

[29] Cpt. Bird to the *Rock River Democrat*, May 19, 1861. Published May 28, 1861.

[30] Carrington diary, p. 6.

[31] Captain G. Nevius to his brother, Henry, June 7, 1861. Mailed from Camp Hardin at Villa Ridge.

[32] Wallace, Isabel, p. 112.

[33] Mary A. Newcomb, *Four Years of Personal Reminescences of the War* (Chicago: H.S. Mills and Company, 1893), p. 13. *Lt. Bird concurred in this positive picture of Colonel Wallace. On May 28, 1861, he wrote to the *Rock River Democrat*: "Col. Wallace is daily growing in the regards of his regiment...He is proving himself a skillful soldier and a perfect gentleman. In all his intercourse with the officers and men, he is kind and affable, and in every sense a complete commanding officer..."

[34] Colonel W.H.L. Wallace to his wife, Martha Ann Dickey Wallace, June 4, 1861, from Camp Hardin. (Wallace-Dickey Collection, Illinois State Historical Library, Springfield.)

[35] "Diary of Lt. Douglas Hapeman, Company H, 11th Illinois Infantry", May 25, 1861. *ISHL*, Springfield.

[36] Captain Nevius to his brother Henry, in New York State, June 7, 1861.

[37] Captain R. Bird to the *Rock River Democrat*, June 1, 1861. Published June 11, 1861.

[38] Captain Nevius to Henry, June 7, 1861.

[39] Newcomb, p. 11.

[40] Gebhardt, p. 38.

[41] Captain Bird to *Rock River Democrat*, June 18, 1861. Published June 25, 1861.

[42] *Ibid.*

[43] *Ibid.*

[44] *Ibid.*

[45] *Ibid*

[46] *Ibid.*

[47] *Ibid.*

[48] Carrington diary, p. 10.

[49] Gebhardt, p. 41.

[50] Captain Bird to the *Rock River Democrat*, May 24, 1861. Published May 28, 1861. *A good description of Camp Yates at Springfield is contained in the April 23rd, 1861, edition of the *Chicago Tribune*. **Additional W.H.L. Wallace biographical materials may be found in the following sources: *Sketches of Illinois Officers* by James Grant Wilson (Chicago: James Barnet, 1862); *The Patriotism of Illinois* by Dr. Thomas Mears Eddy (Chicago: Clark & Company, 1866); *History of LaSalle County Illinois* by Michael Cyprian O'Byrne (Chicago & New York: Lewis Publishing Company, 1924); *Old Illinois Houses* by John Drury (Springfield, Illinois: Published by the State of Illinois, 1948).

Chapter Two

A Rash, Brave Fellow

[1] A letter from Colonel W.H.L. Wallace to Secretary of War Simon Cameron, July 1, 1861, on file at the National Archives in Washington--Regimental Letter Book of the 11th Illinois Infantry.

[2] Gebhardt, p. 43.

[3] Carrington diary, p. 11.

[4] A letter from Captain Bird to the *Rock River Democrat*, June 23, 1861. Published July 2, 1861. Also a June 8, 1861 letter published on June 11, 1861.

[5] Gebhardt, p. 44.

[6] A letter from W.D. Alexander to Colonel W.H.L. Wallace at Bird's Point, August 4, 1861. On file at the National Archives, Regimental Papers.

[7] Reported in the August 8, 1861 edition of the *Lacon Illinois Gazette*. Story filed at Cairo, Illinois on August 1, 1861. *Mrs. Margie Bearss, wife of the Civil War historian Edwin C. Bearss is an authority in her own right. She points out that, "the fear of Confederate attack was there but the possibility...was just not there." The Northern press was guilty, she claims, of printing the "wildest exaggerations." Based on her research, Mrs. Bearrs estimates Confederate strength at and around New Madrid, Missouri as being between two and three thousand men during this time period. Union forces at Bird's Point were about the same.

[8] John McElroy, *The Struggle For Missouri* (Washington: The National Tribune Company, 1909), p. 95. *For additional information concerning Jeff Thompson consult: Jay Monaghan, *Swamp Fox of the Confederacy*. (Tuscaloosa: Confederate Publishing Company, 1956); and *Civil War on the Western Border 1854-1865* by the same author. (Boston: Little, Brown and Company, 1955).

[9] A letter from Captain Bird to the *Rock River Democrat*, July 9, 1861. Published July 16, 1861.

[10] Gebhardt, p. 45.

[11] A letter from Captain Nevius to his brother, Henry, June 29, 1861. A part of a collection in the hands of a descendant.

[12] Carrington diary, p. 11.

[13] A letter from Captain Bird to the *Rock River Democrat*, July 16, 1861. Published July 23, 1861. *Also consult the Hapeman diary for the July 29, 1861 entry.

[14] A letter from Colonel W.H.L. Wallace to his wife, Ann, dated August 2, 1861. A part of the Wallace-Dickey Collection at the Illinois State Historical Library in Springfield.

[15] An anonymous letter to the *Lacon Illinois Gazette*, August 2, 1861. Published on August 15, 1861 and signed only as "John" of the 11th Illinois.

[16] Gebhardt. p. 46.

[17] Major General Fremont, "The War In Missouri," in *Battles and Leaders of the Civil War*. 4 Vols. (New York: Thomas Yoseloy, Inc., 1956). Edited by Clarence Buel and Robert Johnson.

[18] An anonymous writer to the *Lacon Illinois Gazette*, August 2, 1861. Published on August 15, 1861.

[19] *Ibid.*

[20] A letter from Colonel Wallace to his wife, August 5, 1861. In the Wallace-Dickey Collection, Illinois State Historical Library, Springfield.

[21] John Simon (Editor), *The Papers of Ulysses S. Grant* (Carbondale, Illinois: Southern Illinois University Press, 1974), Vol. III, p. 205.

[22] A letter from Colonel Wallace to his wife, August 2, 1861, Wallace-Dickey Collection. *T.E.G. Ransom was evidently the perfect executive officer. He and Wallace worked together without rancor. Mrs. Wallace enthusiastically shared Will's positive feelings toward the Vermonter. After Ransom's heroics at Charleston, Mo., she wrote her husband: "Pa (Colonel T. Lyle Dickey of the 4th Illinois Cavalry) got a dispatch this morning from Cyrus assuring us that Col. Ransom's wound is not dangerous. I do hope he will soon be well and ready to stand by you. I don't know how you can spare him. Apart from the sorrow I felt for his own suffering, I am so sorry you will for a time at least, be deprived of the help of so fine an officer and so good a friend..." Letter dated August 23, 1861 at the *Oaks* in Ottawa. On file with the Wallace-Dickey Collection in Springfield.

[23] *Ibid.*, letter dated August 23, 1861.

[24] Colonel Henry Dougherty's report, *Official Records*, Ser. 1, Vol. 3. p. 137.

[25] A letter by Lt. Lemuel Adams of the 22nd Illinois Infantry, 1861. Original on file at the Illinois State Historical Library, Springfield.

[26] Eddy, p. 170.

[27] Ibid., p. 171.

[28] Ibid.

[29] Adams letter, previously cited. *It is difficult to ascertain Confederate casualties at Charleston. Union estimates run from 13 to 50 dead. We do know that Jeff Thompson regarded the incident as a set-back. He placed the officer responsible, a certain Colonel Hunter, under arrest. On August 21, 1861 Thompson wrote the following to Brigadier General W.J. Hardee in Greenville, Missouri: "My officer acted miserably at Charleston yesterday. The enemy attacked them suddenly. My men fell in like veterans, and drove them away, when the colonel took them out of the field and retreated with them, when nearly every man thought he was charging the enemy..." (See *Official Records*, Ser. 1, Vol. III, p. 139.)

[30] Wilson, p. 33. *Also see biography of Truman Ransom and Thomas Ransom in *Norwich University; 1819-1911: Her History...* (Montpelier, Vermont: Published by General G. Dodge, 1911). Edited by William A. Ellis.

[31] Details regarding T.E.G. Ransom's life may be found in the following sources: *Martyrs and Heroes of Illinois* by James Barnet (Chicago: Barnet Press, 1865); *Generals In Blue* by Ezra J. Warner (Louisiana State University Press, 1964); An anonymously authored article, "Obituary: Brigadier General T.E.G. Ransom," *United States Service Magazine* (New York, 1865) Vol. III, p. 386; *The Civil War Dictionary* by Mark M. Boatner III (New York: David McKay, 1959).

[32] *Dictionary of American Biography*, (New York: Charles Scribner's Publishers, 1930), Vol. III, Dodge, p. 349; Ransom, Vol. XV, p. 380. Also, Grenville M. Dodge, *Personal Biography of General Dodge*, a typed manuscript on file at the State Library Commission of Iowa in Des Moines.

[33] Frederick Eugene Ransom, "Recollections of an Illinois Veteran Volunteer," Sketchbook with notations, Illinois State Historical Library, Springfield.

[34] From an undated story which appeared in the *Maine Bugle* around 1900. Copy provided by Dr. Gary T. Lord of Norwich University, Northfield, Vermont.

[35] Dumas Malone, *Dictionary of American Biography*, Vol. XV, p. 380.

[36] A letter from Mrs. Margaret Ransom to General G.M. Dodge, November 9, 1864. Copy is located in the Dodge Collection, State Library Commission of Iowa, Des Moines.

[37] James Barnet, *Martyrs and Heroes of Illinois in the Great Rebellion* (Chicago: Barnet Press, 1865), p. 236.

[38] A letter from "John" in the 11th Illinois Infantry to the *Lacon Illinois Gazette*, August 2, 1861. Published August 15, 1861.

[39] *Ibid.*

[40] *Ibid.*, September 18, 1861.

[41] A letter from Fred Shaw of Lacon to the Illinois adjutant general in Springfield, April 15, 1861. On file at the Illinois State Archives with the Regimental Papers of the 11th Illinois. "...please command my services in whatever capacity you may desire...I trust that Illinois will not be backward in efficient aid to the President in this hour of trial..."

[42] A letter from Mr. R. Fay which appears in the March 5, 1862 edition of the *Lacon Illinois Gazette*.

[43] An article in the *Lacon Illinois Gazette*, January 29, 1862.

[44] Carrington diary, p. 19. *"John" of Company B recalls a typical expedition in a letter dated October 14, 1861, subsequently published on October 23, 1861 in the *Lacon Illinois Gazette*: "They (the 11th) have left this place three different times, but had 'nary' a fight...Two weeks ago they made another move--with every prospect of having a fight--accompanied by a part of the Iowa second, a

part of the 14th Illinois,....three companies of cavalry and two pieces of artillery, to Charleston, twelve miles north...When they arrived they found the place all quiet. The forces were put in motion again and went three miles out on the Charleston and Columbus turnpike, when the infantry were placed in ambush in a cornfield, and the...artillery at the turn of the road, so that at a moment's notice they could be placed in a position to sweep the road. The cavalry were sent as a decoy, but the rebels didn't bite, and after a couple hours of patient waiting they were led out of their hiding places, and all returned to this place (Bird's Point) without a fight...The cavalry stationed here have all the fun to themselves, as they often come in contact with their shot gun rivals; and the bushwackers come out second best..."

[45] Colonel Wallace's report, October 9, 1861, in the *Papers of U.S. Grant*, Volume III, p. 21.

[46] A letter from Colonel Wallace to his wife, November 20, 1861. On file with the Wallace-Dickey Collection at ISHL, Springfield. *Time and again the 11th Illinois set out after Thompson. They never caught up with the elusive Rebel who fought on until May, 1865. Colonel Wallace felt a lack of cavalry was the reason for the Union failure to seize Thompson.

[47] Report by Colonel Richard Oglesby, November 13, 1861, in the *Papers of U.S. Grant*, Volume III, p. 105.

[48] Carrington diary, p. 23.

[49] A letter from "John" in the 11th Illinois dated November 11, 1861. Appeared in the November 27, 1861 edition of the *Lacon Illinois Gazette*.

[50] *Ibid.*

[51] A letter from Lieutenant Colonel T.E.G. Ransom to Grenville Dodge, January 3. 1862. On file with the Dodge Collection in Des Moines.

[52] A letter from T.E.G. Ransom to Colonel W.H.L. Wallace, then on leave in Ottawa, Illinois. Dated October 27, 1861. On file with Wallace-Dickey Collection in Springfield, Illinois.

[53]Carrington diary, p. 22. Always with an eye for detail, this diligent observer recorded how the men of the 11th received new weapons during this period. They turned in their 1855 Harpers Ferry muskets for Enfield Muskets, .577 caliber, made in Great Britain. At this time the 11th Illinois was outfitted with gray uniforms although they wore a blue kepi and winter coat. The gray uniforms were not replaced with blue until January 1, 1862.

[54]A letter from Major G. Nevius to his brother, Henry, dated September 6, 1861. On file in a private collection.

[55]The health of the 11th Illinois was much better than most newly recruited units. The U.S. Sanitary Commission singled out the 11th and the 12th Illinois for their strict enforcement of health regulations. See, *Documents of the U.S. Sanitary Commission*, Vol. I (New York: 1866), Document Number 36, p. 35. Report covers the three months ending November 30, 1861.

[56]Newcomb. *Four Years...*, p. 22.

[57]*Ibid.*, p. 15.

[58]A letter from "John" to the *Lacon Illinois Gazette*, October 14, 1861. Published October 23, 1861.

[59]Stella S. Coatsworth, *The Loyal People of the North-West* (Chicago: Church, Goodman & Donnelley Printers, 1869) p. 79.

Chapter Three

Lost All But Honor

[1]Stella S. Coatsworth, *The Loyal People of the North-West*, p. 92.

[2]A letter from Colonel Wallace to his wife, October 13, 1861. Wallace-Dickey Collection. Despite such pleasant pastimes the devoted Wallace constantly wrote his wife and longed to return home to "the stone house in the woods with its green lawns and rustling leaves."

³Coatsworth. p. 95.

⁴*Ibid.*, p. 94. *The band of the 11th Illinois was allegedly one of the best at Bird's Point. Colonel Wallace bragged how the musicians could "knock the socks off" any other regimental band. (See October 11, 1861 letter to his wife in the Wallace-Dickey Collection, Springfield) **Lieutenant Henry H. Dean of Company D, 11th Illinois was equally proud: "We can just beat any of them on music and they know it...Every man on the Point allows we have 'right smart' music. They have kept our boys very busy...not only in our regiment but by invitations sent in by others to play...(The 11th Illinois) is the 'better officered, and better equipped and clothed than any regiment in south east Missouri, and as far as I have seen, in the state.'" See a letter from Lt. Dean to the *Rock River Democrat* in Rockford, dated October 16, 1861. Published October 29, 1861.

⁵"War Diary of Nathaniel C. Kenyon In The Civil War," Company K, 11th Illinois Infantry (an unpublished typed manuscript provided by Mrs. Howard Kenyon of Washington, D.C.), p. 1.

⁶Coatsworth. p. 96.

⁷A letter from Colonel Wallace to his wife, January 13, 1862. Wallace-Dickey Collection, Springfield. Note: The January 9, 1862 ambush, mentioned on this page, is described in detail at the beginning of Chapter 1.

⁸*Ibid.*, January 16, 1862.

⁹Charles Carleton Coffin, *The Boys of '61*, (Boston: Estes and Lauriat Publishers, 1881), p. 58.

¹⁰A letter from Major G. Nevius to his brother, February 7, 1862.

¹¹A letter from Colonel Wallace to his wife, January 28, 1862. (Wallace-Dickey Collection, Springfield)

¹²*Ibid.*, January 31, 1862.

¹³*Ibid.*

[14] An anonymous letter from "John" Company B, 11th Illinois to the *Lacon Illinois Gazette*, dated September 18, 1861. Published September 26, 1861.

[15] Mary Newcomb, *Four Years...*, p. 22.

[16] A report entitled, "The 11th at Donelson," by Captain Smith D. Atkins, Company A, 111th Illinois. Appeared in the March 20, 1862 edition of the *Freeport Bulletin*.

[17] Isabell Wallace, *Life and Letters...*, p. 153.

[18] Mary Newcomb, *Four Years...*, p. 25.

[19] Carrington diary, p. 33.

[20] Mary Newcomb, *Four Years...*, p. 26.

[21] Isabell Wallace, *Life and Letters...*, p. 155.

[22] Carrington diary, p. 33.

[23] Isabell Wallace, p. 155.

[24] Carrington diary, p. 34.

[25] A report by Captain Atkins, March 20, 1862, *Freeport Bulletin*.

[26] *Ibid.*

[27] *Ibid.*

[28] *Ibid.*

[29] Dr. Thomas M. Eddy, *The Patriotism of Illinois*, p. 375.

[30] A letter from Editor C.K. Judson of the *Freeport Journal*, dated October 1, 1861 and addressed to Governor Richard Yates of Illinois. The letter charged the 11th was "discouraged and disheartened" because of conditions at the point. (letter on file with the Regimental Papers at the Illinois State Archives.)

[31] A report by Captain Atkins, March 20, 1862.

[32] Carrington diary, p. 37.

[33] A letter from Private John W. Reading, Company F, 11th Illinois, dated February 20, 1862. Published in the March 12, 1862 edition of the *Grundy County Weekly Herald* in Illinois. His description is fairly accurate except that the Rebel breastworks were closer to three miles in length rather than six.

[34] *Ibid.*

[35] A report by Captain Atkins, March 20, 1862. *After the first Rebel attack was repulsed, Private George D. Carrington gaped at the sight of dead men in the snow. They were from Company K, 11th Illinois: "This was the first time we had stood in line of battle and faced death. I looked at those men. They lay on the snow just as they had fallen. Were they dead? Yes! I could hardly realize it. They were so still. The wind scarcely moved the capes of their coats. They were so motionless...Yes, these men were dead. What a feeling crept over me." (See Carrington diary, p. 38.)

[36] A report by a reporter from the *Louisville Journal* which appeared in the March 8, 1862 edition of the *Ottawa Republican* in Illinois.

[37] A report by Captain Atkins, March 20, 1862.

[38] A letter from Colonel T.E.G. Ransom to Grenville Dodge, March 12, 1862. A part of the Dodge Collection at the Iowa State Library Commission in Des Moines. Ransom left his command at Donelson for only five minutes to have his wound dressed.

[39] Carrington diary, p. 39.

[40] *Ibid.*

[41] *Fort Henry and Fort Donelson Campaigns*, compiled documents concerning these battles, (Fort Leavenworth: The General Service Schools, 1923), p. 823. Extracted from Colonel W.H.L. Wallace's official report as brigade commander.

[42] James J. Hamilton, *The Battle of Fort Donelson* (New York: Thomas Yoseloff and Co., 1968), p. 222.

[43] A letter from Lt. James Churchill to his parents, dated April 10, 1862. The text can be found on page 840 in the *Fort Henry and Fort Donelson Campaigns*, previously cited.

[44] "Civil War Experiences of Henry 'Soldier' Uptmor," Company K, 11th Illinois Infantry. Unpublished manuscript on file at the Illinois State Historical Library, Springfield.

[45] Carrington diary, p. 40.

[46] Ransom's report, *Official Records*, Ser. 1, Vol. VII, p. 199. *Colonel Ransom described Color Sergeant Hubert A. McCaleb's heroism at Donelson in a letter dated February 25, 1863 at Lake Providence, La. The sergeant underwent a long convalescence after the Donelson fight but returned to serve as a lieutenant in the 11th. Eventually McCaleb was promoted Colonel of a U.S. Colored Infantry Regiment. Well over six feet tall, he was a hard-looking man with almost saturnine features. (The letter is in the Regimental File at the Illinois State Archives.)

[47] A report by Captain Atkins, March 20, 1862.

[48] A letter from Lt. James Churchill, April 10, 1862, previously cited.

[49] A.W. Gore quoted in a story which appeared in the March 5, 1862 edition of the *Lacon Illinois Gazette*.

[50] Lt. Blackstone quoted in a story which appeared in the March 12, 1862 edition of the *Lacon Illinois Gazette*.

[51] Private Charles Crane quoted in the *Lacon Illinois Gazette*, March 5, 1862. *Mrs. Margie Bearss was very skeptical regarding the accuracy of the reports by Lt. Blackstone and Private Crane. She points out there wasn't any Texas cavalry in the battle. Furthermore, she finds these accounts implausible: "A man on foot badly wounded, kills three cavalry men. Now I ask you!" The reader is cautioned to take these stories with a "grain of salt." The claims can't be substantiated but neither can they be refuted.

[52] Carrington diary, p. 41.

[53] A report by Captain Atkins, March 20, 1862.

[54] *Ibid.*

[55] A letter from Lt. James Churchill, April 10, 1862, previously cited.

[56] *Ibid.*

[57] *Ibid.*

[58] Isabel Wallace, *Life and Letters...*, p. 162.

[59] A report by Captain Atkins, March 20, 1862.

[60] Isabell Wallace, *Life and Letters...*, p. 167. *LTC Ransom was especially protective of his men's reputation won so dearly at Ft. Donelson. Illustrative of the fact is a letter, dated March 20, 1862 at Savannah, Tenn., from Ransom to James Doane of Morris, brother to Lt. George Doane of the 11th Illinois. Reprinted in the April 2, 1862 edition of the *Morris Grundy County Weekly*, the letter was both a clarification and a challenge: "I need not tell you of my surprise and indignation when I learned that the unavoidable absence of Lt. Doane from the battle of Ft. Donelson, had given rise to remarks, which evil disposed persons had taken advantage of to pass reflections upon the courage of your brother...I ordered him to remain (at Ft. Henry), though he pleaded with me to go...It is but justice to him for me to say that in ten months intimate intercourse with him...at all times have I found him prompt to duty, and cool and collected in danger...I can only add, any miserable attempt to cast a shadow upon his fair name, will re-act upon the authors, and be promptly resented ...by his fellow officers, and by none sooner than
   Truly Yours
   T.E.G. Ransom
   LTC, comd'g 11th Ill.

Chapter Four

Hideous Night

[1] News article, *Chicago Tribune*, dated February 18, 1862. Also see the February 21, 1862 edition headlined: "Gallantry of the 11th Illinois."

[2] Dr. Thomas M. Eddy, *Patriotism of Illinois*. Also, William F. Fox, *Regimental Losses In The American Civil War*, (Albany: Albany Publishing, 1889). Inevitably there are discrepancies in the various casualty figures. In this case all sources are fairly in agreement. The "one in five" killed statement is based on Fox's figure divided into the 500 "actively engaged" that Ransom reported at Donelson.

[3] News article, *Lacon Illinois Gazette*, March 5, 1862. A reprint of a *Chicago Times* story dated February 17, 1862. *Another excellent account of the battle's aftermath was provided by William H. Hutton of the 20th Illinois, a unit which fought on the immediate left flank of the 11th. His description was published in the March 15, 1862 edition of the *Ottawa Republican*.

[4] Uptmor diary, p. 4.

[5] Carrington diary, p. 43.

[6] Mary Newcomb, *Four Years...*, p. 30.

[7] *Ibid.*, p. 32.

[8] *Ibid.*, p. 30.

[9] *Ibid.*, p. 36.

[10] Hapeman diary, Feb. 16, 1862. (ISHL, Springfield)

[11] Harvey M. Parker, *Proceedings of the Re-union of the 11th Illinois Infantry*, (Ottawa: Osman and Hapeman Publishers, October 27, 1875), p. 66. Also see, Mary Newcomb, *Four Years...*, p. 38.

[12] News article, *Ottawa Free Trader*, March 8, 1862. Also see April 2, 1862 edition of the *Lacon Illinois Gazette*.

[13] *Ibid.* *On March 12, 1862, Colonel Ransom of the 11th voiced identical remarks to Grenville Dodge: "You will readily see that damn bad generalship was shown by somebody, in leaving the 1st and 2nd brigades unsupported to fight 15,000 men but I must not criticize my superiors." (letter in Dodge Collection)

[14] Isabell Wallace, *Life and Letters...*, p. 164.

[15] A letter from Captain Dickey to the *Ottawa Free Trader*, March 11, 1862. Published March 15, 1862.

[16] *Ibid.*

[17] Maud E. Uschold, *This Is The Place*, (Lacon: Published by the Marshall County Historical Society, Vol. 4 of the Heritage Sampler Series, January, 1968), p. 22-35.

[18] News article in the *Lacon Illinois Gazette*, March 12, 1862.

[19] Isabell Wallace, *Life and Letters...*, p. 171.

[20] Maud E. Uschold, *This Is The Place*.

[21] News article in the *Lacon Illinois Gazette*, March 12, 1862.

[22] *Ibid.* *Mrs. Margie Bearss, a fine editor, questions the authenticity of Vernay's bravado: "Sounds like an afterthought or what he wished he'd said. You really don't taunt armed captors. Some hot-headed Rebel would have blown his head off...Chances are, he (Vernay), like the rest of the Yanks & Rebs who were captured, kept his mouth shut. Otherwise he'd be a casualty."

[23] A letter from Colonel Ransom to the Illinois Adjutant General, April 4, 1862. On file with Regimental Papers at the Illinois State Archives.

[24] A letter from Lt. Henry Dean to the *Rock River Democrat*, March 9, 1862, on board the steamer *Silver Moon*. Published on March 15, 1862.

[25] Carrington diary, p. 46.

[26] A letter from Major G. Nevius to his brother, March 17, 1862. *The 11th was assigned to the Second Brigade of Colonel C.C. Marsh, in McClernand's First Division. The First Brigade was under Abraham M. Hare while Julius Raith commanded the Third Brigade. **General Wallace commanded the Second Division. His brigade commanders included James M. Tuttle, John McArthur, and Thomas W. Sweeny.

[27] Mary Newcomb, *Four Years...*, p. 40.

[28] Isabell Wallace, *Life and Letters...*, p. 186.

[29] Warner Whipple, "Recollections of a Soldier," an unpublished monograph dated April 7, 1861. Provided by Mrs. Warner Whipple of Waltham, Ill.

[30] Carrington diary, p. 48.

[31] News article in the *Ottawa Free Trader*, April 19, 1862.

[32] James Wilson, *Sketches of Illinois Officers*, p. 33.

[33] Carrington diary, p. 48.

[34] Ransom's report, *Official Records*, Ser. 1, Vol. X, Pt. 1, p. 137.

[35] Carrington diary, p. 48.

[36] Wiley Sword, *Shiloh: Bloody April*, (New York: William Morrow and Company, Inc., 1974), p. 310-315.

[37] Carrington diary, p. 48.

[38] *Ibid.*, p. 49.

[39] Ransom's report, *Official Records*, previously cited.

[40] A letter from Colonel Ransom to Grenville Dodge, April 17, 1862. (The Dodge Collection).

[41] *Ibid.*

[42] McClernand's report, *Official Records*, Ser. 1, Vol. X, Pt. 1, p. 117.

[43] A letter from Ransom to Dodge, April 17, 1862, previously cited.

[44] J.P. Thompson, "Brigadier General T.E.G. Ransom," *Hours at Home*, p. 478.

[45] A news article in the *Freeport Journal*, May 4. 1864.

⁴⁶Ransom's report, *Official Records*, previously cited.

⁴⁷James Wilson, *Sketches...*, previously cited.

⁴⁸A letter from Lt. Henry H. Dean to the *Rock River Democrat*, April 8, 1862. Published on April 29, 1862.

⁴⁹*Ibid.*

⁵⁰*Ibid.*

⁵¹*Ibid.* *Shiloh's ferocity can be measured by the fact that C.C. Marsh's brigade suffered a 33 per cent casualty rate with 571 killed, wounded or missing out of 1,514 men engaged. On April 7, the command buried 437 dead rebels and 115 of its own, all lying within the immediate area. Dead horses, mules and 1,363 abandoned rifles and other arms were also littering the field. (See Marsh's report, *Official Records*, Ser. 1, Vol. X, Pt. 1, p. 136.)

⁵²Report by General McClernand to General U.S. Grant, dated April 24, 1862. Original included in the McClernand Collection at the Illinois State Historical Library, Springfield.

⁵³George Mason, editor, *Illinois At Shiloh* (Report of the Shiloh Battlefield Commission, 1909), p. 39.

⁵⁴E.L. Hobart, "The Truth About Shiloh" (Copy on file at Newberry Library, Chicago, 1890), p. 31.

⁵⁵News article, the *Ottawa Free Trader*, April 12, 1862.

⁵⁶A letter from Lt. Cyrus Dickey to a brother, dated April 10, 1862 (Wallace-Dickey Collection, Springfield).

⁵⁷Isabell Wallace, *Life and Letters...*, p. 187.

⁵⁸Uptmor diary, p. 5.

⁵⁹Carrington diary, p. 50.

⁶⁰Hapeman diary, April 7, and April 8, 1862.

⁶¹An anonymous letter from an Illinois soldier to the *Rock River Democrat*, published September 2, 1862.

⁶²A letter by Lt. Dean, April 8, 1862, previously cited.

⁶³*Ibid.*

⁶⁴Isabell Wallace, *Life and letters...*, p. 199.

⁶⁵Z. Coleman, "A Discourse On The Death of Gen'l W.H.L. Wallace," delivered April 13, 1862 at the Ottawa Baptist Church. Copy on file at the Chicago Historical Society.

⁶⁶Carl Sandburg, *Abraham Lincoln: The War Years* (New York: Harcourt, Brace, 1939), V. III, p. 521.

Chapter Five

A Thousand Ties of Affection

¹Mary Newcomb, *Four Years...*, p. 43.

²A letter from Ransom to Grenville Dodge, dated April 17, 1862. (Dodge Collection).

³*Ibid.*, April 13, 1862.

⁴News clipping, *Toledo Blade*, dated June 11, 1881. On file with Carrington papers at the Chicago Historical Society Library.

⁵A letter from Ransom to Grenville Dodge, April 17, 1862.

⁶*Ibid.* *Ransom's dislike for "political officers," whether warranted or not, extended to his own command in the case of Captain Smith D. Atkins of Company A. After Donelson, this officer resigned his commission pleading ill health. A few weeks later the men in the 11th learned, to their great surprise, that Atkins had been appointed major of their regiment by the Illinois Adjutant General. Ransom's reaction was instantaneous and emphatic. He charged that Atkins had not been on active duty but for two months in the year since the 11th first mustered, and claimed the officer "is not competent to command a Company, much less a Regt. Out of respect for my command and myself, I can only say if, under these circumstances, Capt. Atkins is appointed Major of this

Regt., I shall tender my resignation at once and will be followed in this step by Lt. Col. Nevius and the officers of the line..." (See Ransom letter dated April 19, 1862 on file with the Regimental Papers in the Illinois State Archives) Ironically, Smith D. Atkins had resigned his commission on April 17, 1862. On September 4, 1862, he was named Colonel of the 92nd Illinois Infantry. Later he commanded Federal mounted forces in the Carolinas and was breveted Major General in January, 1865.

[7] Carrington diary, p. 54.

[8] News Article, *Ottawa Republican*, May 17, 1862.

[9] *Ibid.*

[10] Carrington diary, p. 61.

[11] *Proceedings of the First Reunion of the Eleventh Regiment*, p. 71, previously cited.

[12] A letter from Colonel Nevius to his brother, May 6, 1862.

[13] *Ibid.*

[14] *Ibid.*

[15] Hapeman diary, July, 1862.

[16] *Ibid.*

[17] Carrington diary, p. 58.

[18] A letter from Lt. Henry Dean to the *Rock River Democrat*, dated June 10, 1862. Published June 24, 1862.

[19] A letter from Colonel Nevius to his brother, June 9, 1862.

[20] *Ibid.*

[21] *Ibid.*

[22] Special Order Number Three dated June 21, 1862 at Jackson, Tenn. On file in the Regimental Order Book of the 11th Illinois in the National Archives.

²³*Ibid.*, July 5 and July 9, 1862 entries in the Regimental Order Book.

²⁴A letter from Colonel Nevius to the Illinois adjutant general, dated September 18, 1862. On file with Regimental Papers at the Illinois State Archives.

²⁵Ransom's report, *Official Records*, Ser. 1, Vol. X, Pt. 1, p. 138.

²⁶A letter from Colonel Nevius to the Illinois adjutant general, dated May 2, 1863. Regimental Papers, State Archives.

²⁷A report in the Regimental Papers of the 11th Illinois, in the National Archives, gives a rundown on casualties. Dated October 15, 1862, Ransom listed 103 killed in battle, 55 prisoners, and 145 wounded and discharged. This constitutes a 37 percent casualty figure based on a strength of 800 as recorded at Bird's Point. This includes 12.8 percent killed.

²⁸General John Logan's report, *Official Records*, Ser. 1, Vol. XVII, Pt. 11, p. 115.

²⁹Nevius Report, July 2, 1862 in the Regimental Letter Book in the National Archives.

³⁰General Order 13 by Colonel C.C. Marsh, dated July 28, 1862 and recorded in the Regimental Letter Book of the 11th, at the National Archives.

³¹News article, August 19, 1862 in the *Rock River Democrat*. Based on a *Chicago Times* story filed August 5, 1862.

³²Gebhardt, *The 11th Illinois...*, p. 105. *Not only did the 11th fail to recruit anywhere near the numbers needed, they lost one of their most promising young officers--Lt. Douglas Hapeman who had commanded Company H at Donelson and Shiloh. Acting as regimental adjutant, he left Cairo in August to recruit in his home town of Ottawa. Instead, he was offered the Lieutenant Colonelcy of the newly formed 104th Illinois Infantry. Colonel Ransom approved Hapeman's transfer with grace even though he must have regretted losing such a fine officer. "None know how well you deserve this smile of fortune and none can feel more gratified that you have received it than myself...," Ransom wrote to

young Hapeman. "I trust, my dear friend, that you will not forget the old and sacred associations that cling to the name of 'the Eleventh...' Remember that wherever you go, our eyes are upon you; we shall ever watch your career with pride and confidence. We expect much from you and know We shall not be disappointed." (See, Stephen J. Adolphson, "Our Little Colonel: Doug Hapeman," in the *Lincoln Herald*, spring, 1973.) **Hapeman was captured and spent many months in Rebel prisons following the battle of Hartsville, Tenn. After his exchange, he led the 104th at Chickamauga, Missionary Ridge and on the march through Georgia. In 1898, he was awarded the Medal of Honor for valor at Peach Tree Creek, Georgia, July 20, 1864.

[33] *Ibid.*, p. 103. *Ransom was still the official commander of the Eleventh during this period. Within a span of weeks, he served as Inspector General and Chief of Staff for General John McClernand, commanded the post at Cairo, and then commanded at Paducah, Kentucky. (See Ransom's report of service at the National Archives.)

[34] A letter from Ransom to Grenville Dodge, August 14, 1862. (Dodge Collection)

[35] *Ibid.*

[36] Carrington diary, p. 71.

[37] A letter from Lt. Henry Dean to the *Rock River Democrat*, August 31, 1862. Published September 9, 1862.

[38] *Ibid.*

[39] *Ibid.*

[40] A letter from Colonel Nevius to his brother, dated September 12, 1862.

[41] Carrington diary, pp. 72, 73.

[42] *Ibid.*

[43] A letter from Ransom to Grenville Dodge, September 21, 1862. (Dodge Collection)

[44] Carrington diary, p. 73.

[45] *Ibid.*

[46] A letter from Ransom to Dodge, September 21, 1862, previously cited.

[47] A letter from Colonel Nevius to his brother, September 12, 1862. *In early November, 1862, Ransom once again struck Woodward's command near Garrettsburg, Ky., but the 11th was absent from the action having been left behind at Hopkinsville, Ky., about 15 miles back. They camped in front of the Court House and were treated well by the populace. The notation in Company C's morning report, read: "The 11th was never treated better...This is a white town." Ransom's clash with Woodward netted him 16 dead Rebels, 40 wounded and 25 captured, according to Major General Grant who called the Garrettsburg skirmish "a great success." Grant had earlier remarked on Ransom and his command: "Colonel Ransom, an excellent officer, has a splendid set of men..." (See, *The Papers of U.S. Grant*, Vol. 6, p. 296, and p. 423.)

[48] News article, *Centralia Sentinel*, December 3, 1863. Reprint of a *Chicago Journal* story.

[49] Carrington diary, p. 78. *The 11th had been briefly assigned the Third Brigade, First Division, Reserve Corps. **Carrington also mentions Ransom's promotion to Brigadier as occurring in November. This was not official until March 10, 1863, even though Ransom commanded the Brigade long before that.

[50] Uptmor diary, p. 9.

[51] Carrington diary, p. 80.

[52] *Ibid.*, p. 81.

[53] *Ibid.*

[54] A letter from Lt. Henry Dean to the *Rock River Democrat*, December 6, 1862. Published December 17, 1862.

[55] Carrington diary, p. 84.

[56] A letter from Colonel Nevius to his brother, December 4, 1862.

[57] A letter from Lt. Henry Dean to the Rock River Democrat, December 6, 1862. Published December 17, 1862.

[58] *Ibid.*

[59] News article, the *Lacon Illinois Gazette*, January 14, 1863. Reprint of a *Chicago Tribune* story headlined, "The Facts as Seen By An Eye Witness," dated December 22, 1862.

[60] An anonymous letter from a soldier of the 109th Illinois to the *Jonesboro Gazette*, January 22, 1863. Published February 7, 1863. *Dr. J.G. DuPree, an officer with the First Mississippi Cavalry, gives an excellent description of the raid on Holly Springs. The account is in the journal of the Mississippi Historical Society, Vol. IV, p. 49-61. "The women of Holly Springs, many of them still in their nightgowns, and with their dishevelled hair floating in the winter wind, clapped their hands with joy and shouted encouragement to the raiders. This scene was indescribable, with Federals running, Confederates yelling, tents and buildings burning, torches flaming, guns popping, sabres clanking, negroes and abolitionists begging for mercy...."

[61] Carrington diary, p. 85.

[62] *Ibid.*

[63] A letter from Colonel Nevius to his brother, dated January 6, 1863.

Chapter Six

Blaze of Musketry

[1] Carrington diary, p. 90. *Young's Point was a very unhappy place for Private William E. Holden of Company E, 11th Illinois. The soldier spent a few days as prisoner of the rebels, and was released. Officers in the 11th suspected something "fishy" about the affair--enough for a court martial. Holden's record was not in his favor. Allegedly, he had been insubordinate to Lt.

Samuel Deane of Company B during a fatigue detail at Moscow, Tenn. Holden, it was said, had told that officer: "He would go when he was ready. Also, that there would be a day coming when he would be a free man and he would be God-damned if he would not make him (Lt. Deane) smell Hell!" This incident was certainly a factor when Holden was found guilty of "unnecessarily being taken prisoner by the rebels and paroled." His sentence was harsh but typical of the punishment prevalent in the service of the time. Holden was to be confined through the war's duration at hard labor; "wearing a ball weighing 24 pounds attached to his left leg by a log chain four feet in length; that he be marked indelibly with indelible ink on the left hip with the letter D...and at the expiration of his term...have his head shaved and drummed out of service." February 1, 1864. (As noted in the Company E Order Book of the 11th Illinois in the National Archives)

[2] A letter from Colonel Nevius to his brother, February 15, 1863.

[3] Carrington diary, p. 93.

[4] A letter from Colonel Nevius to his brother, February 15, 1863.

[5] Warner Whipple, "Recollections of a Soldier...," previously cited.

[6] Carrington diary, p. 95.

[7] Ransom's report, recorded in the Company C, 11th Illinois Order Book, February 12, 1863. (Regimental Papers, the National Archives)

[8] Kenyon diary, p. 6, previously cited.

[9] *Ibid.*, p. 8.

[10] *Ibid.*, p. 9.

[11] *Ibid.*, p. 10.

[12] *Ibid.*, p. 12.

[13] *Ibid.*

[14] *Ibid.*, p. 15.

[15] *Ibid.*, p. 17.

[16] *Ibid.*, p. 18.

[17] *Ibid.*, p. 22.

[18] *Ibid.*

[19] *Ibid.*, p. 23.

[20] *Ibid.*, p. 24.

[21] G. Dodge, *Norwich University; Her History...*, previously cited, p. 25.

[22] A letter from Mrs. M.M. Ransom to Dr. Simpson, December 12, 1862. On file in Lt. Frederick Eugene Ransom's records jacket, National Archives.

[23] A letter from Colonel Nevius to Fred A. Horsman of Rockford, Ill., dated February 3, 1863. Published in the *Rockford Register* on March 7, 1863.

[24] News article, *Chicago Times*, dated February 2, 1862. Includes denial by James Evans of the 109th Illinois. *A vivid impression of how one man in the 109th thought and acted is included in the court martial file of Private John C. Shore of Company F, 109th. The hearing was held May 4, 1863 in Cincinnati, Ohio, where the deserter was captured. Warden H. Thompson testified how the AWOL soldier led a mob which rescued two deserters from the Provost Marshall in Anna, Illinois. "You d--d abolitionist son of a bitch," Shore allegedly shouted at Thompson who was serving as a deputy. "He stepped up to me, and pulled his pistol round, and said; 'I am a deserter, take me to Cairo.' He [Shore] hollered for a rope, said: 'Let us get a rope.'" Shore was found guilty and sentenced to be shot. The punishment was later reduced to hard labor at Sandusky, Ohio for the war's duration. Shore's blind mother had written Lincoln pleading for mercy. (Records pertaining to the case are still on file at the National Archives.)

[25] Carrington diary, p. 99.

[26] A letter from Colonel Nevius to Fred A. Horseman of Rockford, February 3, 1863. Previously cited.

[27] A letter from Colonel Nevius to his brother, April 22, 1865.

[28] *Ibid.*

[29] Capt. George W. Kennard's report, *Official Records*, Ser. 1, Vol. XXIV, p. 568. Dated April 23, 1863.

[30] William E. Strong, "The Campaign Against Vicksburg," *Military Essays and Recollections*, Vol. VII (Chicago: Published by the Military Order of the Loyal Legion, 1894), p. 313.

[31] *Ibid.*

[32] Ransom's Special Order Number 23, dated April 25, 1863 at Millikin's Bend, La. In the Regimental Papers of the 11th, National Archives.

[33] Ransom's report, *Official Records*, Ser. 1, Vol. XXIV, Pt. II, p. 296.

[34] A letter from Colonel Nevius to his brother, April 22, 1863.

[35] Carrington diary, p. 101.

[36] *Ibid.*, p. 103.

[37] Uptmor diary, p. 12.

[38] Joseph Stockton, *War Diary of Brevet Brigadier General Joseph Stockton*, (Published in Chicago by his son John, 1910), p. 14.

[39] Carrington diary, p. 104.

[40] *Ibid.*

[41] U.S. Grant, *Personal Memoirs of U.S. Grant*, Vol. I, (New York: Charles Webster and Company, 1885), p. 527 and 579.

[42] Ransom's report, *Official Records*, previously cited, p. 296.

[43] Carrington diary, p. 107.

[44] *Ibid.*

[45] Ransom's report, *Official Records*, previously cited, p. 296.

[46] Uptmor diary, p. 13.

[47] J. Stockton, *War Diary...*, p. 16, previously cited.

[48] Carrington diary, p. 108.

[49] *Ibid.*

[50] Ransom's report, *Official Records*, previously cited, p. 296.

[51] Carrington diary, p. 109.

[52] Anonymous letter from a soldier in the 11th Illinois to the *Rock River Democrat*, published June 10, 1863.

[53] *Ibid.*

[54] Uptmor diary, p. 13.

[55] A letter from Frederick Hardten to Frank Whipple, dated January 8, 1884. Original provided by the family of Warner Whipple of Waltham, Illinois.

[56] Prof. Thomas Eddy, *Patriotism of Illinois*, p. 469. Previously cited.

[57] *Ibid.*

[58] J. Thompson, "Brigadier General...Ransom," *Hours at Home*, p. 480, previously cited.

[59] Chaplain R.L. Howard, *History of the 124th Regiment*, (Springfield: Printed by H.W. Bokker, 1880), p. 107.

[60]*Ibid.*, p. 108.

[61]Ransom's report, *Official Records*, previously cited, p. 296.

[62]Anonymous letter published on June 10, 1863 in the *Rock River Democrat*, previously cited.

Chapter Seven

Lightning In The Evening Sky

[1]Uptmor diary, p. 13.

[2]Carrington diary, p. 111. *Joseph Stockton of the 72nd Illinois was a part of Ransom's brigade that day. His diary entry for May 22 reads: "Up we started and rushed ahead with a yell, and were greeted with a most wonderous volley. Our colors were planted about fifteen feet from the ditch, but could not go forward; the fire was too severe, men could not live...we were ordered back to camp. What a night! Such a night I never spent before! About dusk there was quite a panic, but fortunately it was checked. The stench was horrible... I cannot go into the details of the charge, but it was horrible, bloody work. Our loss in twenty minutes was one hundred and ten killed and wounded. Such was the 22nd of May, 1863." **Ransom's Second Brigade included the 11th Illinois, and the 95th Illinois. The 11th suffered the least with 53 casualties recorded on May 22. The 95th Illinois was punished more than any other regiment in the brigade, having taken 161 casualties on that date. ***Cpt. George McKee of Company C, 11th Illinois recalled the firing on May 22 as "terrific." His company took seven casualties including one man, Jacob Keller, whose right arm was shot off. McKee had been hit at Shiloh and was wounded once again at Vicksburg on May 22: "I am wounded in the forehead, but not so bad as to leave the field. My head feels like it had a dozen aches in it, but it will not be serious. I don't think it will make a scar if it heals up well..." A letter to his father, dated May 23, 1863. Published on June 4, 1863 in the *Centralia Sentinel*.

[3]Proceedings of the First Reunion of the Eleventh Regiment, p. 76, previously cited.

[4] A letter from James H. Coates to the mother of the late Colonel Nevius, dated November 13, 1863. From an undated copy of the *Rockford Register.*

[5] J.P. Thompson, *Hours at Home,* p. 481, previously cited.

[6] *Ibid.*

[7] A letter from Captain Cyrus Dickey to his sister, Ann Wallace, dated May 29, 1863. (Wallace-Dickey Collection, Springfield)

[8] Carrington diary, p. 111.

[9] *Ibid.*

[10] *Ibid.,* p. 124.

[11] A letter from the surgeon of the 11th Illinois in the rear of Vicksburg, dated June 7, 1863. Published in the *Ottawa Free Trader* on June 27, 1863.

[12] *Ibid.*

[13] A letter from Captain Dickey to his sister, dated June 28, 1863. (Wallace-Dickey Collection, Springfield)

[14] *Ibid.*

[15] Carrington diary, p. 113.

[16] *Ibid.,* p. 117.

[17] A letter from Captain Dickey to his sister, June 17, 1863. (Wallace-Dickey Collection, Springfield)

[18] *Ibid.,* May 29, 1863.

[19] Carrington diary, p. 122. *Carrington was promoted to corporal in late June, 1863.

[20] A letter from Surgeon Hunt, June 7, 1863, previously cited.

[21] News Article in the June 1, 1863 edition of the *Chicago Tribune*, based on a dispatch from Vicksburg dated May 22, 1863.

[22] *Ibid.*, June 6, 1863.

[23] *Ibid.*, July 2, 1863.

[24] An address by General William T. Sherman delivered June 20, 1884 in St. Louis. Printed in *The Reveille*, Vol. IV, No. 1, October, 1884 at Northfield, Vt. Copy at Norwich University.

[25] A letter by Lt. Robert Jehu of Company C, 11th Illinois, June, 1863. Published in the *Centralia Sentinel* on July 16, 1863.

[26] Account recorded by Kenyon's son, Howard Kenyon in June, 1921. Copy provided by Mrs. Howard Kenyon of Washington, D.C.

[27] Carrington diary, p. 118.

[28] News article, *Chicago Tribune*, July 2, 1863. Based on story filed June 22, 1863 at Vicksburg by a correspondent.

[29] Carrington diary, p. 122.

[30] *Ibid.*

[31] A letter from Lt. Jehu, June, 1863, previously cited.

[32] J.P. Thompson, *Hours at Home*, previously cited.

[33] A letter from Lt. E.P. Thomas of Company G, 11th Illinois, July 7, 1863. Published on July 25, 1863 in the *Rockford Register*.

[34] A letter from Private John W. Reading of the 11th Illinois, July 5, 1863. Published in the *Grundy County Herald* on July 22, 1863.

[35] Uptmor diary, p. 17.

[36] J.P. Thompson, *Hours at Home*, previously cited.

[37] A letter from Lt. Thomas, July 7, 1863, previously cited.

[38] Carrington diary, p. 128.

[39] A Rebel's letter dated March 23, 1863 and found by Private Smith of Company C, 11th Illinois. Published on July 23, 1863 in the *Centralia Sentinel*.

[40] *Ibid.*

[41] McPherson's report, *Official Records*, Ser. 1, Vol. XXIV, Pt. III, p. 521.

[42] Elizabeth Dunbar Murray, *My Mother Used To Say*, (Boston: Christopher Publishing, 1959), p. 170.

[43] *Ibid.*, p. 183.

[44] Ransom's report, *Official Records*, Ser. 1, Vol. XXIV, Pt. II, p. 680.

[45] Dumas Malone, *Dictionary of American Biography*, previously cited.

[46] Ransom's report, *Official Records*, previously cited.

[47] A letter from Frank Whipple of Company H, 11th Illinois, August 23, 1863. Part of a collection in the possession of Mrs. Warner Whipple of Waltham, Illinois. *On September 6, 1863, Whipple wrote home once again: "...best fixed that we ever have been. We are encamped in a beautiful grove just on the outskirts of the city. The Church bells are now tolling for divine services. One would not think by the appearance that there was such a war going on and we were in the very heart of the enemy's country but so it is...."

[48] A letter from Theodore Copple of Company C, 11th Illinois, dated September 5, 1863. Published in the *Centralia Sentinel* on September 24, 1863.

[49] News article, published in the August 6, 1863 edition of the *Centralia Sentinel*. *The 11th experienced a quiet time at Natchez. The closest thing to action occurred in early september when mounted Rebel raiders pounced on a pontoon train detachment on the other side of the river. Yank horse soldiers from the

19th Wisconsin and 1st Kansas took up the chase with infantry from the 11th Illinois trailing far behind as support. "They followed the Rebels up some fifteen or twenty miles, and had an important skirmish with them. We (the 11th) found five dead bodies that our men had killed..." See an anonymous letter from a soldier of the 11th Illinois, published September 29, 1863 in the *Rockford Register*.

[50] *Ibid.*

[51] Elizabeth D. Murray, *My Mother...*, p. 183, previously cited.

[52] *Ibid.*, p. 171.

[53] *Ibid.*, p. 173.

[54] A letter from Samuel C. Copple of Company C, 11th Illinois, dated July 24, 1863 at Natchez. Published August 20, 1863 in the *Centralia Sentinel*.

[55] *Ibid.*

[56] A letter from Lt. Robert Jehu, Company C, 11th Illinois, dated June 1, 1863. Published in the *Centralia Sentinel* on July 16, 1863.

[57] A letter from Private Jacob Copple Company C, 11th Illinois, August 27, 1863. Published in the *Centralia Sentinel* on October 1, 1863.

[58] Isabell Wallace, *Life and Letters...*, p. 122, previously cited.

[59] Bowie Letter, *Official Records*, Ser. 1, Vol. XXX, Pt. III, p. 25.

Chapter Eight

Dying Is No Easy Thing

¹Ransom's report, *Official Records*, Ser. 1, Vol. XXVI, Pt. 1, p. 426.

²*Ibid.*, p. 427.

³General C.C. Washburn's reports, *Official Records*, Ser. 1, Vol. XXVI, Pt. 1, p. 420. *General Ransom landed on Mustang Island with 13th and 15th Maine Infantry, two companies of the 20th Iowa Infantry, the First Engineers, Corps d'Afrique, and two howitzers. The 34th Iowa Infantry and additional artillery joined Ransom a few days later.

⁴A letter to the *Lacon Illinois Gazette* from Lt. John M. Shields, dated February 2, 1864. Published on February 24, 1864. Also mentions how Ft. Esperanza was a "fine fort to look at" until the "Lincoln Minions" bombarded it from 1,000 yards out with rifled cannon.

⁵*Ibid.* *Lt. Shields remarked how the flag had been stored "in some lonely garret during the dark days of the rebellion" but now flew in "pristine glory" above Ransom's camp.

⁶Mark M. Boatner III, *The Civil War Dictionary*, p. 42, previously quoted. Also see, *The Dictionary of American Biography*, p. 577.

⁷Ransom, *Official Records*, Ser. 1, Vol. XXXIV, Pt. 11, p. 614.

⁸Boatner, *The Civil War Dictionary*, P. 685, previously cited.

⁹Lt. W.H. Bentley, *History of the 77th Illinois Volunteer Infantry* (Peoria: 1883), p. 248.

¹⁰J.P. Thompson, *Hours at Home*, p. 481, previously cited.

¹¹Lt. W.H. Bentley, *History of the 77th Illinois...*, p. 247, previously cited.

[12] A letter to Ella Gilson in Illinois from General Ransom, dated March 26, 1864 at Alexandria, La. Copy provided by descendant.

[13] *Ibid.*

[14] *Ibid.*

[15] *The Red River Expedition*, extracts from hearings before the Joint Committee on the Conduct of the War, the U.S. Congress, 1863-66 (Mellwood, N.Y.: Kraus Reprint Company, 1977), Admiral Porter's testimony, p. 270.

[16] *Ibid.*, p. 11, Banks's testimony.

[17] *Ibid.*, p. 57, Lee's testimony.

[18] Ludwell H. Johnson, *Red River Campaign: Politics and Cotton In The Civil War* (Baltimore: John Hopkins Press, 1958), p. 113.

[19] William H. Heath, "Battle of Pleasant Hill, Louisiana," in the *Annals of Iowa*, Vol. VII, Number 7, Des Moines, Iowa, October, 1906, p. 518.

[20] Ransom's report in *The Red River Expedition*, p. 36, previously cited.

[21] *Ibid*, p. 37.

[22] *Ibid.*

[23] *Ibid.*

[24] William H. Heath, "Battle of Pleasant Hill, Louisiana," p. 518, previously cited.

[25] A letter from Lieutenant Joseph D. Tredway to Judge T. Lyle Dickey of Ottawa, Illinois, April 11, 1864. (Wallace-Dickey Collection, Springfield)

[26] Lt. W.H. Bentley, *History of the 77th Illinois...*, p. 251, previously cited. *Many officers present at the engagement report-

ed how General Ransom objected to initiating a battle at that time and place. Lt. Bentley wrote that, when Banks ordered the move forward, Ransom said: "That will finish me."

[27] J.P. Thompson, *Hours at Home*, p. 480, previously cited.

[28] Ransom, *The Red River Expedition*, p. 39, previously cited.

[29] A letter from Lt. Henry Roe to his brother, Robert, in Chicago, dated May 4, 1864. Original on file at the Chicago Historical Society Museum Library.

[30] A letter from C.H. Dickenson of the Chicago Mercantile Battery, dated April 11, 1864. Extracted from an undated copy of the *Chicago Evening Journal*.

[31] Ludwell H. Johnson, *Red River Campaign...*, p. 140, previously cited.

[32] "Diary of Lemuel Burke, Co. K, 119th Illinois Infantry," a typed copy provided by Mrs. June Slater of LaSalle, Illinois.

[33] William H. Heath, "Battle of Pleasant Hill, Louisiana," p. 519, previously cited.

[34] A letter from Lt. Tredway to Judge Dickey, April 11, 1864, previously cited.

[35] Anonymous author, "Obituary: Brigadier General T.E.G. Ransom," in *The United States Service Magazine* (New York: Vol. III, 1865), p. 388.

[36] William H. Heath, "Battle of Pleasant Hill, Louisiana," p. 520, previously cited.

[37] *Ibid.*

[38] Burke diary, previously cited.

[39] News article, *The Chicago Evening Journal*, April 19, 1864. *Other stories, varying in detail and accuracy, were carried by the *Baton Rouge Weekly Gazette and Comet*, April 23, 1864; and

the *Chicago Evening Journal*, April 20, 1864. A fine series of accounts may be found in *The North Reports The Civil War* by James Andrews (University of Pittsburgh Press, 1955), p. 507.

[40] A letter from Lt. Henry Roe to a brother, May 4, 1864, previously cited. *Lt. J.M. Shields of the 77th Illinois Infantry also saw his unit pulverized at Sabine, but did not feel General Ransom was to blame. In fact, he saw the young corps commander as a victim: "The noble, brave and generous Ransom is sacrificed. May he ventillate this as he well knows how. I think he will. I hope he will." (See, *Lacon Illinois Gazette*, April 27, 1864)

[41] Isabell Wallace, *Life and Letters*, p. 125, previously cited.

[42] News article, *The Ottawa Free Trader*, May 21, 1864. Also see article April 23, 1864 and Cyrus Dickey obituary on the same date.

[43] Undated Chicago news clipping preserved by Mrs. Gladys Todd of Scotch Plains, New Jersey. Her mother, Ella Gilson, was a first cousin to General Ransom.

[44] News article, the Burlington, Vermont *Free Press*. The story is datelined, Fair Haven, August 11, 1908. Copy provided by Dr. Gary Lord of Norwich University.

[45] Ransom's report, *Official Records*, Ser. 1, Vol. XXXVIII, Pt. 111, p. 390.

[46] A letter from General Ransom to Grenville Dodge, dated September 13, 1864 at East Point, Georgia (Dodge Collection). *General Dodge felt he was being shunted by the high command. On October 13, 1864, General Ransom provided his friend with a candid picture of the situation: "I expected the evidence of feeling that your letters evince, relative to the depriving you of your command, and assure you that there is but one expression here in regard to it, and that is unqualified disapproval of your treatment. I do not think General Howard is responsible for it, any more than he allowed the change to be made. Sherman shows no friendship for you and has said that he has made you no promises...I hope my dear 'Ocean' you will remain in the service, though I know you have good cause for retiring. I don't for a moment think any officer superior...The change that has been made was not for personal reasons at all, I am sure, and is only the result of the cold-blooded

military expediency that controls all things in this army. Grant or McPherson would, of course, never have done it; but Sherman does not care a fig for any man, you well know..." (Dodge Collection)

[47] J.P. Thompson, *Hours at Home*, p. 480, previously cited.

[48] *Ibid.*

[49] A letter from Lt. Joseph D. Tredway of the 23rd Wisconsin, a member of Ransom's staff at his death. Typed copy of the undated letter provided by Mrs. Gladys Todd of Scotch Plains, N.J. Original on file at the Norwich Historical Society in Vermont.

[50] *Ibid.* *Ransom and the 11th Illinois were almost synonymous terms. On May 7, 1864, the *Rockford Register* noted: "The 11th Illinois Volunteers have an enviable reputation where Western troops are known, and no man has contributed more to this renown than B.G. Ransom."

[51] Ellis, William, *Norwich University; Her History...*, p. 493, previously cited.

[52] A letter from Lt. Joseph D. Tredway, previously cited.

[53] *Ibid.*

[54] *Ibid.*

[55] Report of Service (June 18, 1864) by General Ransom and a supplement to that report written by Lt. Joseph D. Tredway. On file at the National Archives along with some correspondence pertaining to Ransom directed to the Adjutant General. One item, dated March 2, 1863, quotes Judge T. Lyle Dickey, saying: "Other men shine but Ransom blazes!" Many prominent individuals are on record advocating Ransom's promotion including Grant, McClernand, Governor Richard Yates, Governor Richard Oglesby, the mayor of Chicago, members of the Chicago Board of Trade, and prominent Wisconsin citizens. *U.S. Grant said the late General T.E.G. Ransom was "my best fighting man!" See, *The United States Service Magazine* (New York: Vol. III, 1865), p. 388. **Grant's faith in Ransom was demonstrated on January 18, 1864 when he recommended that the 29-year-old soldier be put in charge of the Cavalry Bureau. Grant went on record to say Ransom was, "as

fine an officer for the place as can be found in the service." (See, *Official Records*, Ser. 1, Vol. XXXII, Pt. 11, p. 130. ***Ransom was a popular leader among the ranks of the 77th Illinois who fought under his command during the tragic Red River expedition. On file at the Illinois State Historical Library is a poem written by "Billy R.M." of the 77th entitled "Sabine Cross Roads." It reads, in part:

> With General Ransom in command,
> we did not fear to go,
> And meet the Reb Dick Taylor,
> And charge upon the foe...
>
> To meet such heavy forces,
> And no relief at hand,
> It seemed to us bad management,
> By those in high command.
>
> But Gen. Ransom true and brave,
> would never disobey,
> when ordered front with his command,
> He boldly led the way...
>
> Great praise to Gen. Ransom,
> He did command our corps,
> To gain the day and save his men,
> No Gen. could do more...

[56] A letter from Thomas E.G. Ransom to relatives after the death of his Uncle George Gilson in Chicago, dated October 7, 1856. Copy provided by Mrs. Gladys Todd whose mother was a first cousin to Thomas.

[57] Ransom's obituary, the *Chicago Times*, November 8, 1864.

[58] *Ibid.* *Strangely, there is almost no surviving correspondence to indicate the reaction of the 11th Illinois upon Ransom's demise. One eulogy did appear in the *Lacon Illinois Gazette* on January 25, 1865. It was signed only "Orion" and dated December 20, 1864 from New Orleans. This may well have been written by a man from the 11th. Most certainly it was composed by a man familiar with the fallen soldier. The piece was entitled, "Eulogy On The Lamented Ransom." "But the mother will whisper to her

cherub boy the name of Ransom, and bid him be like him. She will tell him how his voice never faltered to speak the truth. But that voice is hushed. She will tell him that the arm never failed to strike the enemies of his country. But that arm is palsied in death. She will tell him of the daring glance of that eagle eye. But that eye is closed. No more can it beam with love on a friend or with defiance on the foe." **One of General Ransom's most enthusiastic supporters was Major General O.O. Howard who commanded the Army of the Tennessee. His General Field Orders, No. 21, issued on November 1, 1864, read, in part: "General Ransom was much beloved by all who knew him, and this army has lost one of its most useful officers and brightest ornaments. His noble record is too familiar to need recounting here...He showed himself an officer of the highest order of merit, as also a man of pure and elevated character. It is with a feeling of deep sorrow at our loss that I refer to this young man, so full of promise, so enthusiastic in his country's cause, so untiring in his exertions to thwart the wicked men who have raised their hands against us; but he has done well his part, and like so many other of our comrades who have worked with us, he has gone peacefully to the haven of rest. We will cherish his bright memory, and strive to attain his irreproachable character." (See, *Official Records*, Ser. 1, Vol. 39, Pt. 1, p. 733.) ***On November 1, 1864, a certain Colonel Spencer wrote Grenville Dodge from Rome, Ga.: "Poor Ransom! He died the 29th...It is a great loss, as he was one of the best men I have ever met..." (Dodge Collection) ****The First Division, 14th Army Corps, was on the march on the road that fronted the house in which General Ransom lay dying. Ironically, the column included the 104th Illinois Infantry commanded by Colonel Douglas Hapeman--a friend of Ransom who had served with the 11th at Donelson and Shiloh. It seems likely that the officer would have taken the opportunity to visit Ramsom's death bed, but no evidence exists to confirm this supposition. First Division Commander, General William Passmore Carlin, was one of the last to speak with the ailing Ransom. Also, we know that the 104th Illinois was aware that the Illinois General was near death based on the October 29, 1864 diary entry by Captain Moses Osman of Company A, 104th Illinois: "...we got within about 4 miles of Rome, when an officer came riding down along the line and requested that the troops might pass a certain house, a short distance ahead, as quietly as possible, that Gen. Ransom was lying there at the point of death. The word was passed along the ranks, and the dark column moved by in almost deep silence..." (See, *Ottawa Free Trader*, November 26, 1864)

Chapter Nine

Don't Scare A God Damn!

[1] F. Eugene Ransom, "Recollections of an Illinois Veteran Volunteer," previously cited.

[2] A letter from Frank Whipple of Company H, 11th Illinois, March 16, 1862. Original in the possession of Mrs. Warner Whipple of Waltham, Illinois.

[3] *Ibid.*, August 23, 1863.

[4] Parkinson Obituary, the *Centralia Sentinel*, August 13, 1863: "It is not so much on the battle field that the soldier is tested as on the dreary...march, the lonely, silent and dangerous picket duty..."

[5] Carrington diary, p. 97, 98.

[6] *Ibid.*, p. 139.

[7] *Ibid.*, p. 141, 143.

[8] *Ibid.*, p. 140.

[9] Uptmor diary, p. 18.

[10] Margie Bearrs, *The Yazoo Expedition*, Chapter One, "Prelude to Yazoo City's Bloodiest Fighting," typed monograph provided by the author.

[11] *Ibid.*

[12] *Ibid.*

[13] Edward M. Main, *The Story of the Marches, Battles and Incidents of the Third United States Colored Cavalry* (New York: Negro University Press, 1908), p. 95.

[14] Coates's report, *Official Records*, Ser. 1, Vol. XXXII, Pt. 1, p. 315.

[15] *Ibid.*, p. 35.

[16] *Ibid.*

[17] Margie Bearrs, *The Yazoo Expedition*, previously cited.

[18] Coates's report, *Official Records*, p. 315.

[19] Margie Bearrs, *The Yazoo Expedition*, previously cited.

[20] Coates's report, *Official Records*, p. 316.

[21] A letter from Colonel F.E. Peebles of the 8th Louisiana Infantry (African Descent), dated March 21, 1864. Published in the *Rockford Register*, April 2, 1864.

[22] Edward M. Main, *Third United States Colored Cavalry...*, p. 97, previously cited.

[23] *Ibid.*

[24] Coates's report, *Official Records*, p. 317.

[25] Edward M. Main, *Third United States Colored Cavalry...*, p. 100, previously cited.

[26] Captain Owen's report, *Official Records (Naval)*, Vol. XXV, p. 735.

[27] Coates's report, *Official Records*, p. 318.

[28] Margie Bearrs, *The Yazoo Expedition*, previously cited.

[29] Edward M. Main, *Third United States Colored Cavalry...*, p. 112, previously cited.

[30] Margie Bearrs, *The Yazoo Expedition*, previously cited.

[31] Edward M. Main, *Third United States Colored Cavalry...*, p. 106.

[32] *Ibid.*

[33] *Ibid.*

[34] *Ibid.*

[35] Coates's report, *Official Records*, p. 323.

[36] Coates's battle report as it appears in the *Regimental Letter Book* of the 11th Illinois on file at the National Archives.

[37] A letter from Colonel F.E. Peebles, March 21, 1864, previously cited.

[38] Coates's report, *Official Records*, p. 319.

[39] Surrender Demand of Brigadier General L.S. Ross, C.S.A., *Official Records*, Ser. 1, Vol. XXXII, Pt. II, p. 326.

[40] Coates's reply, *Official Records*, p. 327.

[41] Anonymous letter from a soldier in the 11th Illinois, dated March 22, 1864. Appeared in the March 29, 1864 edition of the *Rockford Register*.

[42] Carrington diary, p. 150.

[43] Edward M. Main, *Third United States Colored Cavalry...*, p. 119, previously cited.

[44] Anonymous letter, March 22, 1864, *Rockford Register*, previously cited.

[45] Edward M. Main, *Third United States Colored Cavalry...*, p. 120, previously cited.

[46] Uptmor diary, p. 21.

[47] Coates's report, *Official Records*, p. 324.

[48] McKee Parlay, *Official Records*, p. 327.

[49] *Ibid.*

[50] Uptmor diary, p. 22.

[51] General Ross's response, *Official Records*, p. 328.

[52] Uptmor diary, p. 22.

[53] Coates's report, *Official Records*, p. 325.

[54] Edward M. Main, *Third United States Colored Cavalry...*, p. 122, previously cited.

[55] A letter from Major George McKee, dated March 10, 1864. Published in the *Centralia Sentinel* on March 17, 1864.

[56] A letter from Colonel F.E. Peebles, March 21, 1864, previously cited.

[57] *Ibid.*

[58] Anonymous letter, March 22, 1864, *Rockford Register*, previously cited. *Colonel Peebles, in his March 21, 1864 letter to the *Rockford Register*, gave an excellent portrait of the Yazoo City community: "The dwellings were mostly closed, as was every store and public building, except the Court House, which told more plainly than words how ruthless is war. All the doors were thrown open, the floors were strewn with paper, some of it dating as far back as 1839; the county records were thrown here and there about the rooms--everything betokened desolation. A printing office, I passed by, was broken open, and the same chaos reigned there. The side-walks, made of brick, were torn up. Now and then a solitary female was seen on the street, and the most of them wore the sable badge, doubtless for loved ones, lost in the rebel army. After hearing so much of rebel conscription, I was unprepared to see so many able-bodied men as were left there. They seemed to have nothing to do, but walked listlessly back and forth, or congregated in the street corners..." **The Confederate general at Yazoo City, who threatened massacre, was a distinguished Texas Indian fighter, an associate of Sam Houston, and a future governor of the Lone Star state. Lawrence Sullivan Ross had fought Comanches as a Texas Ranger before the war. After Appomattox, he accumulated property and wealth on his plantation on the Brazos. He served as governor from 1887 until 1891 and was president of Texas A.S.M. College until his death in 1898. ***Union and Confederate accounts of the Yazoo City action are at loggerheads. Both sides claimed a victory; both claimed to inflict heavy casualties on the enemy. Brigadier General L.S. Ross claimed the withdrawl from the town was a planned maneuver based on his decision that nothing more could be gained from

continuing the struggle. He claims McKee's sally from the redoubt did not rout the Ninth Texas during this movement in contradiction to Union reports. (See, *Official Records*, Ser. 1, Vol. XXXII, Pt. 1, p. 387). ****Another interesting resume of the battle is found in the report filed by Thomas McElroy, Acting Master, commanding the gunboat U.S.S. *Petrel*. Indicative of the nature of the struggle is McElroy's assertion that his howitzer crew, fighting ashore, expended 250 shells during the melee in the town's streets. "The crew at one time was driven from the gun, they not having sufficient support to hold it, but the soldiers seeing the crew driven, rallied, charged on the rebels and retook it, losing three men in the charge, and wounding James Stoddard of the *Marmora*....(See *Official Records (Naval)*, Ser. I, Vol. 26, p. 14.)

Chapter Ten

Each In His Own Heart Wondering

[1] Mark M. Boatner III, *The Civil War Dictionary*, p. 522, previously cited. See also Eddy's *The Patriotism of Illinois*, Warner's *Generals in Blue*, and the *Dictionary of American Biography*.

[2] Edwin C. Bearss, "McArthur's May Expedition Against The Mississippi Central Railroad," in the *Journal of Mississippi*, Vol. 28, No. 1, p. 1

[3] *Ibid.*

[4] *Ibid.*, p. 4.

[5] Carrington diary, p. 160.

[6] *Ibid.*, p. 161.

[7] *Ibid.*, p. 160.

[8] Edwin C. Bearss, "McArthur's May Expedition...," p. 9, previously cited.

[9] Carrington diary, p. 162.

[10] *Ibid.*, p. 163.

[11] *Ibid.*

[12] Carrington diary, p. 163-64.

[13] *Ibid.*

[14] *Ibid.*, p. 165.

[15] McArthur's report, *Official Records*, Ser. 1, Vol. XXXIX, Pt. 1, p. 6.

[16] *Ibid.*

[17] A letter from Colonel Coates, dated June 2, 1864. In Lt. Frederick Eugene Ransom's records at the National Archives.

[18] F.E. Ransom, "Recollections of an Illinois Veteran Volunteer," previously cited.

[19] Endorsement by Colonel Coates to Ransom's resignation, dated June 16, 1864. In Ransom's records, National Archives.

[20] A letter from General Ransom to Grenville Dodge, October 13, 1864. (Dodge Collection)

[21] News article, December 17, 1868 edition of the *Chicago Tribune*.

[22] Edwin C. Bearss, "The Tupelo Campaign," a monograph published by the National Park Service on May 15, 1969, p. 157.

[23] *Ibid.*

[24] A letter from R.W.H. of the 46th Illinois Infantry, dated July 11, 1864. Published in the *Freeport Journal* on August 3, 1864.

[25] General Slocum's report, *Official Records*, Ser. 1, Vol. XXXIX, Pt. 1, p. 242.

[26] Special Order Number 22, dated October 22, 1862 at Paducah, Ky. In the Regimental Order Book of the 11th Illinois on file at the National Archives.

[27] Carrington diary, p. 184. *At about this time, the regiment turned in their Enfield rifles for the modern Springfield rifle, model 1863.

[28] Edwin C. Bearss, "The Tupelo Campaign," p. 166-67, previously cited.

[29] Ibid.

[30] Uptmor diary, p. 24.

[31] Edwin C. Bearss, "The Tupelo Campaign," p. 169, previously cited.

[32] Uptmor diary, p. 24.

[33] Chaplain R.L. Howard, History of the 124th Regiment..., p. 236, previously cited.

[34] Lieutenant Colonel John J. Jones's report, Official Records, Ser. 1, Vol. XXXIX, Pt. 1, p. 244. (46th Illinois officer)

[35] Uptmor diary, p. 25.

[36] Jones's report, Official Records, p. 244, previously cited.

[37] General Slocum's report, Official Records, p. 242, previously cited. *The 11th Illinois took 22 casualties during the Jackson raid including five dead and three missing. Private Uptmor claimed all the dead were slain during the rear guard action on July 7. The Rebels' charge was spearheaded by the 2nd Regiment of Mississippi State Cavalry under Colonel W.W. Lowry.

[38] Carrington diary, p. 184.

[39] Edwin C. Bearss, "The Tupelo Campaign," p. 174, previously cited.

[40] An anonymous letter from the 11th Illinois, dated July 10, 1864. Published in the Jonesboro Gazette on July 23, 1864.

[41] An anonymous letter from the 11th Illinois, dated July 20, 1864. Published in the August 6, 1864 edition of the Jonesboro Gazette.

⁴²Carrington diary, p. 176.

⁴³William A. Pitkin, "Michael K. Lawler's Ordeal With The 18th Illinois," in the *Journal of the Illinois State Historical Society*, Vol. 58, 1965. *This is very sympathetic to Lawler.

⁴⁴Court Martial Transcripts of Colonel M.K. Lawler, Dec. 18, 1861. On file at the National Archives.

⁴⁵*Ibid.*

⁴⁶*Ibid.*

⁴⁷*Ibid.*

⁴⁸*Ibid.*

⁴⁹Uptmor diary, p. 26.

⁵⁰*Ibid.*

⁵¹Carrington diary, p. 181.

⁵²*Ibid.*

⁵³Uptmor diary, p. 27.

⁵⁴*Ibid.*

⁵⁵Carrington diary, p. 195.

⁵⁶An anonymous letter from the 11th Illinois, dated October 22, 1864. Published in the *Jonesboro Gazette* on October 29, 1864.

⁵⁷A letter by Colonel Coates, dated December 6, 1864. On file with the Regimental Papers of the 11th Illinois at the National Archives.

⁵⁸Anonymous letter, October 22, 1864, *Jonesboro Gazette*, previously cited.

⁵⁹Carrington diary, p. 194. *George D. Carrington was promoted 2nd Lieutenant on December 4, 1864.

[60] J.P. Thompson, *Hours at Home*, p. 480, previously cited.

[61] Carrington diary, p. 198-99.

[62] *Ibid.*, p. 202.

[63] *Ibid.*, p. 205.

[64] *Ibid.*

Chapter Eleven

The Spirit of Killing

[1] General Canby's report, *Official Records*, Ser. 1, Vol. XLIX, Pt. 1, p. 91.

[2] Mark M. Boatner III, *The Civil War Dictionary*, p. 558, previously cited.

[3] Warner Whipple, "Recollections of a Soldier," a monograph, previously cited.

[4] *Ibid.*

[5] A letter from Sergeant Frank Whipple, dated February 26, 1865, from a private collection.

[6] A letter from the Bureau of Industry, National Rights League, dated February 6, 1865. On file with the Regimental Papers of the 11th at the National Archives.

[7] A letter from Captain Rankin, AAG, Headquarters First Division, 13th Army Corps, March 14, 1865. Regimental Papers, National Archives.

[8] A letter from Colonel Coates, dated February 16, 1865. Regimental Papers, National Archives.

[9] B.L. Roberson, "Valor On The Eastern Shore: The Mobile Campaign of 1865," a monograph on file at the Chicago Public Library, Special Collections Division, (Mobile: 1965), p. 2.

[10]*Ibid.*, p. 4.

[11]Carrington diary, p. 185.

[12]Colonel James Coates's report, *Official Records*, Ser. 1, Vol. XLIX, Pt. 1, p. 181. *The 11th Illinois was now attached to the Second Brigade, First Division, 13th Army Corps. The brigade commander was Brigadier General Elias S. Dennis. This New York state native had started the war with the 30th Illinois. He was no stranger to the 11th having been in actual field command during the July 4, 1864 raid on Jackson, Mississippi. The division commander was Brigadier General James Clifford Veatch, an Indiana lawyer and office holder. He had originally enlisted with the 25th Indiana Infantry, and commanded a brigade during some of the most bitter fighting at Shiloh.

[13]A letter from Samuel M. Howard of the 28th Illinois Infantry, dated February 26, 1903, in *The Truth About Shiloh* by E.L. Hobart, previously cited, p. 24.

[14]General Dennis's report, *Official Records*, Ser. 1, Vol. XLIX, Pt. 1, p. 174.

[15]Carrington diary, p. 217.

[16]*Ibid.*, p. 218.

[17]B.L. Roberson, "Valor On The Eastern Shore..." previously cited, p. 15.

[18]Mark M. Boatner III, *The Civil War Dictionary*, p. 341, previously cited. *Gibson was instrumental in the founding of Tulane University after the war.

[19]Major General C.C. Andrews, *History of the Campaign of Mobile*, (New York: D. Van Nostrand Publishers, 1867), p. 48.

[20]B.L. Roberson, "Valor On The Eastern Shore...", p. 28, previously cited.

[21]Carrington diary, p. 219.

[22]*Ibid.*

²³B.L. Roberson, "Valor On The Eastern Shore...", p. 23, previously cited.

²⁴Carrington diary, p. 219.

²⁵*Ibid.*, p. 220.

²⁶*Ibid.*

²⁷A conversation with Aaron Gunn, the elderly son of Moses Gunn. The veteran survived the war to become a Baptist clergyman in LaSalle. He lived well into the 1930's.

²⁸General Canby's report, *Official Records*, Ser. 1, Vol. XLIX, Pt. 1, p. 95.

²⁹Mark M. Boatner III, *The Civil War Dictionary*, p. 482, previously cited.

³⁰B.L. Roberson, "Valor On The Eastern Shore...," p. 30, previously cited.

³¹L.F. Hubbard, "Minnesota In The Campaign of Mobile, 1865," in *Collections of the Minnesota Historical Society* (St. Paul: Published by the Society, December, 1908), p. 628.

³²Charles B. Johnson, *Muskets and Medicine or Army life in the Sixties*, (Philadelphia: Davis Co., 1917), p. 218.

³³*Ibid.*, p. 217.

³⁴General Canby's report, *Official Records*, Ser. 1, Vol. XLIX, Pt. 1, p. 96.

³⁵B.L. Roberson, "Valor On The Eastern Shore...," p. 30, previously cited.

³⁶Carrington diary, p. 224.

³⁷*Ibid.*

³⁸C.C. Andrews, *History of the Campaign of Mobile*, p. 211 and 224, previously cited.

[39] Max L. Heyman, Jr., *Prudent Soldier, A Biography of Major General C.R.S. Canby,* (Glendale, California: Arthur H. Clark Publishers, 1959), p. 223-229. *The author explains in detail the delays which cost the Union Army two months and probably made Mobile's eventual capture strategically superfluous.

[40] An anonymous letter from a soldier in the 11th Illinois, dated April 11, 1865. Published on April 29, 1865 in the *Rockford Register.*

[41] Carrington diary, p. 225.

[42] Anonymous letter, April 11, 1865, published in the *Rockford Register,* previously cited.

[43] Report by Colonel Josiah A. Sheetz, 8th Illinois Infantry, *Official Records,* Ser. 1, Vol. XLIX, Pt. 1, p. 175.

[44] Carrington diary, p. 226-227.

[45] A letter from R.W.H. of the 46th Illinois, dated April 14, 1865. Published in the *Freeport Journal* on May 3, 1865.

[46] *Ibid.*

[47] General Canby's report, *Official Records,* Ser. 1, Vol. XLIX, Pt. 1, p. 99.

[48] Carrington diary, p. 228.

[49] *Ibid.,* p. 229.

[50] *Ibid.,* p. 230.

[51] Captain Howard N. Kenyon, *American Kenyons,* (Rutland: The Tuttle Company, 1935), p. 233.

[52] A letter from William Duncan, dated May 22, 1865 at Syracuse, N.Y. Part of the Kenyon materials provided by Mrs. Howard Kenyon of Washington, D.C.

[53] Report by Captain James G. Patton, 33rd Missouri Infantry, *Official Records,* Ser. 1, Vol. XLIX, Pt. 1, p. 566.

[54] E.L. Hobart, *The Truth About Shiloh*, p. 34, previously cited. *The only copy of this work, known to this writer, is to be found in the Newberry Library in Chicago.

[55] Carrington diary, p. 235.

[56] *Ibid.*

[57] Captain Patton's report, *Official Records*, Ser. 1, Vol. XLIX, Pt. 1, p. 567.

[58] Carrington diary, p. 236. *The 11th Illinois did not move directly back to the state capitol at Springfield for demobilization. Instead, they travelled by steamboat to Alexandria, Louisiana, on the Red River where they served as occupation troops. They soon learned that the regiment would be sent home in two installments. Men whose enlistments expired prior to October 1, 1865 were to be discharged in late July while the remainder served out their terms in the 8th and 46th Illinois Regiments. Of the 496 men who were discharged in July, the great majority were from the 109th Illinois plus some drafted men. Eighty-four veterans of the original 11th and 150 draftees and substitutes had to wait out their time with the 8th and 46th Illinois stationed at Grand Ecore and Shreveport, Louisiana. Lieutenant Carrington of Co. B., 11th went home with the first contingent which was discharged on July 21, 1865 at Camp Butler in Springfield. He was the only soldier left from the original company organized by the late Captain Fred Shaw in April, 1861. Less lucky, for once, was Sergeant Major Frank Whipple of Company H. He expressed his anger at the mustering out procedure in a bitter letter home dated July 25, 1865 at Liberty Springs, Louisiana. "The Regt., in which we have served for 4 years, is out of the service, I suppose by this time, at least the organization known as the 11th Ill. Regt. The men that gave that Regt. a good name (if it ever had one) are all still in the Service transferred like a set of criminals that were worthy of nothing better. This transaction will long be remembered by the men of the 11th. The 109th--a lot of deserters, a Regt. that had disgraced the state--go home on our credit...There are plenty who would shoot him (Gen. E.R.S. Canby) as quick as a dog!"

Sources

Books and Periodicals

Adolphson, Steven J., "Our Little Colonel: Douglas Hapeman," *Lincoln Herald*, Vol. 75 (Spring, 1973), 18.

Andrews, C.C., *History of the Campaign of Mobile*, New York: D. Vann Nostrand Publishers, 1867.

Andrews, J. Cutter, *The North Reports the Civil War*, Pittsburgh: University of Pittsburgh Press, 1955.

Angle, Paul M. and Miers, Earl S., *Tragic Years, 1860-1865*, New York: Simon and Shuster Publishers, 1960.

Anonymous, "Obituary: Brigadier General T. E. G. Ransom," *United States Service Magazine*, Vol. III (April, 1865), 386.

Barnet, James, *Martyrs and Heroes of Illinois*, Chicago: Barnet Publishers, 1865.

Baskin, O.L., *History of Grundy County Illinois*, Chicago: Baskin and Co., 1882.

Battles and Leaders of the Civil War, New York: Thomas Yoseloff, Inc., 1956.

Bearss, Edwin, "Fort Henry," *Civil War Times Illustrated*, IV (November, 1965), 9.

Bearss, Margie, *The Yazoo Expedition*, Chapter One, "Prelude to Yazoo City's Bloodiest Fighting," 1969.

Belisle, John G., *History of Sabine Parish, Louisiana*, Manny, Louisiana: Sabine Bannes Press, 1912.

Bentley, W.H., *History of the 77th Illinois Volunteer Infantry*, Peoria: E. Hine Printer, 1883.

Boatner, Mark M. III, *The Civil War Dictionary*, New York: David McKay Co., Inc., 1959.

Brockett, L.P., *The Camp, The Battle Field, and The Hospital*, Chicago: National Publishing Co., 1892.

Burton, William L., *Descriptive Bibliography of Civil War Manuscripts in Illinois*, Evanston, Illinois: Northwestern University Press, 1966.

Cadwallader, Syvanus, *Three Years With Grant*, New York: Alfred A. Knopf, 1955.

Calkins, William W., *The History of the One Hundred and Fourth Regiment of Illinois Volunteer Infantry*, Chicago: Donahue and Henneberry Printers, 1895.

Catton, Bruce, *Grant Moves South*, Boston: Little, Brown and Company, 1960.

Centennial Commission of Illinois, *Civil War Medal of Honor Winners from Illinois*, Springfield: Centennial Commission of Illinois, 1962.

Church, Charles A., *Historical Encyclopedia of Illinois and History of Winnebago County*, Chicago: Munsell Publishers, 1916.

Coatsworth, Stella S., *The Loyal People of the North-West*, Chicago: Church, Goodman & Donnelley Printers, 1869.

Coffin, Charles Carleton, *The Boys of '61, or Heroes of the Rank and File*, Boston: Estes and Lauriat Publishers, 1881.

Coleman, Z., "A Discourse On The Death of Gen'l W.H.L. Wallace," Copy of the April 13, 1862 sermon on file at the Chicago Historical Society Library.

Company A. Veterans, *First Re-union of Company A, 11th Illinois Infantry, September 3, 1885*, Freeport: Adrian Times Press, 1885.

Decision in Mississippi, Jackson: Mississippi Commission on the War Between the States, 1962.

Dornbush, Charles E., *Regimental Publications and Personal Narrations of the Civil War: A Checklist*, New York: New York Public Library, 1961.

Drury, John, *Old Illinois Houses*, Springfield: Illinois State Historical Society, 1948.

Dufour, Charles L., *The Mexican War, A Compact History 1846-48*, New York: Hawthorn Books, Inc., 1968.

DuPree, J.G., "The Holly Springs Raid" in the *Mississippi Historical Society Journal*, Vol. IV, 49.

Eddy, Thomas M., *The Patriotism of Illinois*, Chicago: Clark and Co., 1866.

Ellis, William A. (Editor), *Norwich University, 1819-1911: Her History, Her Graduates, Her Roll of Honor*, Montpelier, Vermont: Capital City Press, 1911.

Ewer, James Kendall, *The Third Massachusetts Cavalry in the War for the Union*, Maplewood, Mass.: W.G.J. Perry Publishers, 1903.

Feldhake, Hilda E. (Editor), *Effingham County Illinois Past and Present*, Effingham: Published by the Effingham Regional Historical Society, 1968.

Foote, Shelby, *The Civil War, A Narrative*, New York: Random House Publishers, 1958.

Force, Manning F., *From Fort Henry to Corinth*, New York: C. Scribner's Sons, 1881.

Fox, William F., *Regimental Losses in the American Civil War*, Albany, New York: Albany Publishing, 1889.

Fremont, John C., "The War In Missouri," *Battles and Leaders of the Civil War*, New York: Thomas Yoseloff, Inc., 1956.

Fulwider, Addison L., *History of Stephenson County, Illinois*, Chicago, S.J. Clarke Co., 1910.

Gebhardt, Carl Dean, *The Eleventh Illinois Infantry Regiment in the Civil War*, Thesis on file at Western Illinois University, Macomb, 1968.

General Service Schools, "Fort Henry and Fort Donelson Campaigns", Fort Leavenworth, Kansas: General Service Schools, 1923.

Grant, Ulysses S., *Personal Memoirs*, New York: Charles L. Webster and Company, 1885.

Hamilton, James J., *The Battle of Fort Donelson*, New York: Thomas Yoseloff and Co., 1968.

Harrington, Fred H., *Fighting Politician, Major General N.P. Banks*, Philadelphia: University of Pennsylvania Press, 1948.

Heath, William H., "Battle of Pleasant Hill, Louisiana" in the *Annals of Iowa*, Vol. VII, No. 7 (October, 1906), 518.

Heyman, Max L. Jr., *Prudent Soldier, A Biography of Major General E.R.S. Canby*, Glendale, California: Arthur H. Clark Publishers, 1959.

Hicken, Victor, *Illinois in the Civil War*, Urbana, Ill.: University of Illinois Press, 1966.

Hobart, E.L., "The Truth About Shiloh", undated pamphlet at the Newberry Library in Chicago.

Horn, Stanley F., *The Army of Tennessee: A Military History*, Indianapolis: Bobbs-Merrill Co., 1941.

Howard, Chaplain R.L., *History of the 124th Regiment Illinois Infantry Volunteers*, Springfield: H.W. Rokker, 1880.

Howard, Oliver O., *Autobiography of Oliver Otis Howard*, New York: Baker and Taylor Co., 1907.

Hubbard, L.F., "Minnesota In The Campaign of Mobile, 1865," in *Collections of the Minnesota Historical Society*, St. Paul: Published by the Society, December, 1908, p. 628.

Illinois Adjutant General, *Report of the Adjutant General of the State of Illinois*, 8 Vols., Springfield: Phillips Brothers, 1900.

Johnson, Charles B., *Muskets and Medicine, Or Army Life in the Sixties*, Philadelphia: F.A. Davis Co., 1917.

Johnson, Ludwell H., *Red River Campaign: Politics and Cotton in the Civil War*, Baltimore: John Hopkins Press, 1958.

Jones, Thomas B., *Complete History of the 46th Regiment, Illinois Volunteer Infantry*, Freeport, Ill., 1907.

Journal of Mississippi, Vol. 28, Number 1.

Koch, Charles R., *Illinois at Vicksburg*, reprinted by an act of the 45th General Assembly of Illinois, Illinois-Vicksburg Park Commission, Chicago: Blakely Printing Co., 1908.

Lewis, Lloyd, *Sherman, Fighting Prophet*, New York: Harcourt, Brace and Co., 1932.

Livermore, Mary A., *My Story of The War: A Woman's Narrative*, Hartford, Conn.: A.D. Worthington Co., 1889.

Logan, Mary S., *Reminiscences of a Soldier's Wife*, New York: Charles Scribner's Sons, 1913.

Main, Edward M., *The Story of the Marches, Battles and Incidents of the Third United States Colored Cavalry*, New York: Negro Universities Press, 1908.

Malone, Dumas, *Dictionary of American Biography*, New York: Charles Scribner's Publishers, 1930.

Mason, George, *Illinois at Shiloh*, Chicago: M.A. Donohue and Company, 1905.

McElroy, John, *The Struggle For Missouri*, Washington: National Tribune Co., 1909.

Miller, Francis T., *The Photographic History of the Civil War*, New York: Thomas Yoseloff Co., 1957.

Monaghan, Jay, *Civil War On The Western Border, 1854-1865*, Boston: Little, Brown and Co., 1955.

Murray, Elizabeth D., *My Mother Used To Say*, Boston: Christopher Publishing, 1959.

Nevins, Allan; Robertson, James I; and Wiley, Bell I., *Civil War Books, A Critical Bibliography*, Baton Rouge: Louisiana State University Press, 1967.

Newcomb, Mary A., *Four Years of Personal Reminiscences of the War*, Chicago: H.S. Mills and Co., 1893.

O'Byrne, Michael, *History of LaSalle County Illinois*, Chicago: Lewis Publishing, 1924.

Parker, Harvey M., *Proceedings of the Re-union of the 11th Illinois Infantry, October 27, 1875 at Ottawa, Illinois*, Ottawa: Osman and Hapeman Printers, 1875.

Parks, George E., "Story of the 109th Illinois Volunteer Infantry Regiment," in the *Journal of the Illinois Historical Society* (Summer, 1963).

Pitkin, William A., "Michael K. Lawler's Ordeal With The 18th Illinois," in the *Journal of the Illinois State Historical Society*, Vol. 58, 1965.

Pullen, John J., *The Twentieth Maine: A Volunteer Regiment in the Civil War*, Philadelphia: Lippincott Co., 1957.

Reed, D.W., *The Battle of Shiloh and the Organizations Engaged*, Washington, D.C.: U.S. Government Printing Office, 1903.

Roberson, B.L., "Valor On The Eastern Shore: The Mobile Campaign of 1865." A typed monograph dated 1965 at Mobile. On file in the Special Collections Division of the Chicago Public Library.

Rose, Victor M., *Ross' Texas Brigade*, Louisville: Louisville Courier-Journal, 1881.

Sandburg, Carl, *Abraham Lincoln: The War Years*, 4 Vols. New York: Harcourt, Brace and Company, 1939.

Schley, Winfield Scott, *Forty Five Years Under The Flag*, New York: D. Appleton and Co., 1904.

Sherman, William T., *Memoirs of General William T. Sherman*, New York: D. Appleton and Co., 1875.

Simon, John Y., *The Papers of U.S. Grant*, Carbondale, Ill.: Southern Illinois University Press, 1970.

Slocum, Charles E., *Life and Services of Major General Henry Warner Slocum*, Toledo: Slocum Publishing Co., 1913.

Stockton, Joseph., *War Diary (1862-65) of Brevet Brigadier General Joseph Stockton*, Chicago: Printed by John T. Stockton, October, 1910.

Strong, William E., "The Campaign Against Vicksburg" in *Military Essays and Recollections*, Vol. VII, Chicago: Military Order of the Loyal Legion.

Swamp Fox of the Confederacy, Tuscaloosa: Confederate Publishing Company, 1956.

Sword, Wiley, *Shiloh: Bloody April*, New York: William Morrow and Company, 1974.

Tennessee Historical Quarterly, Vol. XXI (March, June, 1962), Numbers 1 and 2.

Thompson, J.P., "Brigadier General T.E.G. Ransom" in *Hours At Home*, V-I, (October, 1865), 478.

The Tupelo Campaign. Monograph published by the National Park Service, May 15, 1969.

U.S. Congress, *Red River Expedition*, Extracts from the hearings of the Joint Committee on the Conduct of the War, 1863-66, Millwood, N.Y.: Kraus Reprint Co., 1977.

U.S. Government, *Documents of the U.S. Sanitary Commission*, New York: 1866.

United States War Department, *The War of the Rebellion: A Compilation of the Official Records of the Union and Confederate Armies*, 70 Vols. Washington, D.C.: U.S. Government Printing Office, 1880-1901.

Uschold, Maud E., *This Is The Place*, Lacon, Illinois: Marshall County Historical Society, 1968.

Van Metier, Alice, "Southern Sympathizers in Illinois During the Civil War", unpublished thesis, University of Maryland, 1947.

Veterans Committee, *The Story of the Fifty-Fifth Regiment Illinois Volunteer Infantry in the Civil War*, 1887.

Wallace, Isabel, *The Life and Letters of General W.H.L. Wallace*, Chicago: R.R. Donnelly Publishers, 1909.

Wallace, Lew, "The Capture of Fort Donelson" in *Battles and Leaders of the Civil War*, New York: Thomas Yoseloff, Inc., 1956.

Warner, Ezra J., *Generals in Blue*, Baton Rouge: Louisiana State University Press, 1964.

Wiley, Bell D., *The Life of Billy Yank*, Indianapolis and New York: Bobbs-Merrill Co., 1952.

Wilson, James Grant, *Sketches of Illinois Officers*, James Barnet Publishers, 1862.

Williams, Thomas H., *Hayes of the Twenty Third; the Civil War Volunteer Officer*, New York: Knopf, 1965.

Wyeth, John A., "Lieutenant-Colonel Forrest at Ft. Donelson," in *Harper's New Monthly Magazine*, Vol. XCVIII (February, 1899), 339.

Manuscripts and Other Unpublished Material

Adams, Lemuel, "A letter describing the Charleston skirmish," Illinois State Historical Library, Springfield. Adams was an officer in the 22nd Illinois Infantry.

Billy, R.M., "Sabine Cross Roads," a copy of an unpublished poem by a veteran of the 77th Illinois Infantry. Illinois State Historical Library, Springfield.

Burke, Lemuel, "Diary of Lemuel Burke, Co. K, 119th Illinois Infantry," a typed copy provided by Mrs. June Slater of LaSalle, Illinois.

Carrington, George D., "Diary of George D. Carrington, Company B, 11th Illinois Infantry," manuscript, Chicago Historical Society Library.

Carrington, George D., Jr., "Brief Notes On The Life of George Dodd Carrington," a typed monograph at the Chicago Historical Society Library.

DeWolf, Dzora, "A.L. Swap in the Civil War," typed manuscript at the Illinois State Historical Library, Springfield.

Dodge, Grenville M., "Personal Biography of General Dodge," a typed manuscript at the State Library Commission, Des Moines, Iowa.

Hapeman, Douglas, "Civil War Diaries and Correspondence of Douglas Hapeman," Illinois State Historical Library, Springfield. He served with Co. H., 11th Illinois Infantry.

Kenyon, Nathanuel C., "War Diary and Correspondence of N.C. Kenyon, Company K., 11th Illinois Infantry," copy provided by Mrs. Howard Kenyon of Washington, D.C.

Letters From General Ransom to General Grenville Dodge, 1861-1864, on file with the Dodge Collection, Iowa State Library Commission, Des Moines.

McClernand, John A., "General John A. McClernand Collection," assorted letters, reports and other documents. Illinois State Historical Library, Springfield.

Nevius, Garrett L., "Letters to Henry Nevius in Lodi, New York, 1861-1863," copies provided by Winfield Nevius of Pleasantville, New York.

Ransom, Frederick Eugene, "Recollections of an Illinois Veteran Volunteer," an Order Book originally belonging to General T.E.G. Ransom, his brother, but mainly containing sketches and notations by F.E. Ransom, 1875-1876. Eugene was a member of Company E, 11th Illinois Infantry.

Ransom, Thomas E.G., "A letter dated March 26, 1864 during the Red River campaign," original provided by Mrs. Gladys Todd of Scotch Plains, New Jersey.

"Report of Service, June 17, 1864, and a supplemental report by Lt. J.D. Tredway, November 14, 1864," the National Archives, Washington, D.C.

Regimental Records of the 11th Illinois. Orders, muster rolls, correspondence and related items. Illinois State Archives, Springfield.

Regimental Records, including Letter Book, Order Book, and various reports and correspondence. The National Archives, Washington, D.C.

Roe, Henry, "A letter dealing with Sabine Crossroads, dated May 4, 1864." The author was an officer in the Chicago Merchantile Battery. Original on file at the Chicago Historical Society Library.

Taylor, John B., "Diary of Private, John B. Taylor, 1861-1863," Stephenson County Historical Society Museum, Freeport, Illinois. He served with Company A., 11th Illinois Infantry.

Tredway, Joseph D., "A letter explaining the particulars of General Ransom's death," undated copy provided by Mrs. Gladys Todd of Scotch Plains, New Jersey.

Tyler, James Monroe, "Civil War Diary of Private James M. Tyler," the State Historical Society of Wisconsin, Madison. He served with the 14th Wisconsin Infantry which was a part of Ransom's Brigade during the Vicksburg Campaign.

Uptmor, Henry, "Civil War Experiences of Henry 'Soldier' Uptmor," typed manuscript, a translation from the original German. Illinois State Historical Library, Springfield. He was a member of Co. K., 11th Infantry.

U.S. Government, "Court Martial Records of Colonel M.K. Lawler of the 18th Illinois, convened December 18, 1861 by Brigadier General John McClernand," original transcript on file at the National Archives.

Wallace, "The Wallace-Dickey Collection," assorted letters and documents pertaining to W.H.L. Wallace, Ann Wallace, Judge T. Lyle Dickey, Cyrus Dickey, and other family members. Illinois State Historical Library, Springfield.

Wallace, Ann, "A photo album dated December, 1862 containing carte-de-visites of the officers of the 11th Illinois Infantry," Chicago Public Library, Special Collections Division.

Whipple, Frank, "Letters of Frank Whipple to his family in Illinois, 1862-65," originals supplied by Mrs. Warner Whipple of Waltam, Illinois.

Whipple, Warner, "Recollections of a Soldier," a typed monograph relating the Civil War yarns of Frank Whipple, Company H, 11th Illinois. Provided by Mrs. Warner Whipple of Waltham, Illinois.

Newspapers (1861-1865)

More than seventy letters from soldiers serving in the 11th Illinois were reprinted in the pages of many of these newspapers. They provided a vast amount of information supplemented by numerous news articles dealing with the Eleventh.

Baton Rouge Weekly Gazette and Comet

Centralia Sentinel

Chicago Evening Journal

Chicago Times

Chicago Tribune

Freeport Bulletin

Freeport Journal

Grundy County Weekly (Morris, Illinois)

Jonesboro Gazette

Lacon Illinois Gazette

Louisville Journal

Maine Bugle

New York Times

Ottawa Free Trader

Ottawa Republican

The Reveille (Northfield, Vermont)

Rockford Register

Rockford Rock River Democrat

Toledo Blade (Ohio)

Vermont Free Press

This index references all people listed in the text.

----, Jack 161 John 34-36 42-44 48 Ocean 104 Rosie 161
ADAMS, Lemuel 37 Lt 38 W Wirt 223 Wert 226
ALEXANDER, W D 29
ALLEN, Pvt 82
ANDERSON, Bloody Bill 27
ANDREWS, C C 243
ARMSTRONG, William 70
ARNOLD, Benedict 38
ATKINS, 62 68 Capt 61-63 65 67 73 74 77 Smith D 19 61
BANKHEAD, 91
BANKS, 171 172 174-176 182 183 Gen 170 171 174-176 179-181 184 N P 183 Nathaniel P 167 Nathaniel Prentiss 170
BEAUREGARD, P G T 99
BEDDO, Ira 96
BENTLEY, Lt 173 W H 172 178
BERGE, 62
BERING, Maj 178
BERRYHILL, John 190
BIRD, 22 28 31 Col 28 John 28 Lt 6 12 13 15 18-21 24 28 29 31 33 Robert 6
BLACKSTONE, 72 B F 72 Capt 218 Lt 119
BLAIR, 145 Frank 187
BOLTON, 227
BOWIE, A T 167
BOWMAN, 184
BRADY, Mathew 185
BRAGG, Pvt 122
BRANSON, Sgt 97
BUEL, 104
BUELL, 88 100 Don Carlos 88 98
BURKE, Lemuel 180 182
BURROW, 91 92
BUTLER, 44 Benjamin 171
CAIN, James 156
CAMERON, 179 180 R A 172 Simon 28
CANBY, 222 238 247 252 E R S 222 241 Edward Richard Sprigg 237 Gen 240 247 249-251 Maj Gen 240
CARRINGTON, 15 33 47 64 105 117 119 121-123 139 140 142 144 150 152 154 156 157 161 196 217-219 Corporal 157 158 161 Edwin 4 George 217 227 George D 1 4 234 Lt 234 235 242 245 247 248 250 252-255 257 Pvt 2 5 11 15 23 28 33 46 47 49 59 60 64 65 68 70 73 81 87 90-93 99 100 104 106 107 110 118 121 125 127 129 136 139

CARRINGTON (continued) 141 143 146 147 149 150 Sgt 195 216 228 231 232
CARTER, Henry H 92 134
CHURCHILL, 71 75 76 James 69 71 74 Lt 75
CLEBURNE, Patrick 186
COATES, 148 198-207 209-213 215 216 224 226 Capt 89 91-93 Col 148 158 197-202 205 206 210 219 221 223 224 235 239 240 242 244 253 254 James 83 89 112 197 233 James H 15 147 216 239 241 257 Jas H 208 Lt-col 147 148 Maj 123
COATSWORTH, Mrs 51 53 54 Stella 51 Surgeon 54
COBB, 94
COFFIN, Charles 56 Charles Carleton 55
COLLIER, Dr 82
COLMAN, A 101 Rev 101
CONLEY, Pvt 46 Thomas 46
COOK, 209 Jeremiah 202 Jeremiah B 198 Maj 205 209 210
COPPLE, Jacob 166 Samuel C 165 Theodore 163
CORSE, Gen 188
CRANDELL, Col 213 F M 207
CRANE, 72 Charles 72
DAVIS, Jeff 5 37
DEAN, 96 117 124 Capt 123 Henry 95 100 110 117 122 136 194 Henry H 87 Lt 100
DEANE, 85 Samuel B 85 195
DENNIS, Elias 231 Elias S 223 242
DEWITT, Pvt 100
DICKEY, 154 178 Ann 10 Capt 152 153 166 170 177 184 Cyrus 84 97 115 149 152

DICKEY (continued) 181 184 Judge 10 Lt 84 97 Lyle 8 T Lyle 8 10 57 184
DICKINSON, C H 179
DICKMAN, 229 Robert 229
DOANNE, Capt 190 244 246 Dory 190 George 190 241 244 245
DODGE, 40 104 105 187 Gen 104 105 116 221 Grenville 40 103 185 186
DORNBLAZER, 226 B 216 Col 223
DOUGHERTY, Col 37 38 Henry 37 48
DOUGLAS, 10 Senator 6 Stephen A 130 Steven 5
DRUM, Adjutant 39
DUDLEY, 177 Col 176
DUNCAN, William 255
ELLET, 167
ELLSBURY, H S 71
ELLSWORTH, 18 Elmer 6 17 32
EMORY, 180 Gen 182 W H 180
FARRAGUT, David 238
FELLOWS, S M 9
FIELD, Lt 103 Silas 92
FILLER, 23 29 Joseph W 23 Lt Commander 24
FLOOD, 116
FLOYD, Gen 81 131
FOOTE, Admiral 64 Andw H 64
FORREST, 70 71 74 116 131 134 205 222 227 232 Gen 205 Jeoffrey 204 Nathan Bedford 69 197
FORT, Greenbury 5 Lt 5 6
FRANKLIN, Gen 179 182 William B 175
FREMONT, 36 43 44 Gen 36 43 John C 35 44 Maj-gen 35
GARRISON, William Lloyd 194

GHOLSON, 224 Gen 226 227 Samuel 223
GIBSON, Gen 245 250 Randall Lee 243
GILSON, Ella 41 173 174 Frances 41 173 George 40 41 173
GOODWIN, H E 13
GORE, 72 A W 71 Pvt 71
GRANT, 57 58 65 87 88 96 98 99 103-105 120 121 124 127 135 137-140 142 143 146 147 151 154 160 187 Gen 56 73 79 99 105 106 126 154 222 230 U S 3 36 48 53 84 141 162 229
GREAT, Pathfinder 36
GREEN, Billy 73
GREENFIELD, 41 Margaret 41
GUNN, Moses 246 Pvt 246
HALLECK, 104 222 Gen 111 Henry 106 229 Henry W 104
HAMILTON, H 13
HANSON, 69 70
HAPEMAN, 109 Doug 17 83 92 100 103 Lt 83 91 109
HARDIN, 9 Col 10 James 9
HARDTEN, Frederick 144
HARE, Abraham M 91 93
HAWKINS, 247 Gen 253
HEATH, 182 William H 180
HENRY, Martin 14 Pvt 15
HESSE, Alex 68
HICKS, Jeff 161
HINDMAN, Charles 150
HISE, A W 13
HODGSON, 94
HOOD, 188 John Bell 185-187
HOOKER, Gen 185 Joe 222
HORSMAN, Fred A 136
HOTCHKISS, Charles 15
HOWARD, Gen 187 Oliver Otis 41 185 R L 145
HUBBARD, L F 248

HULL, Adjutant 134
HUNT, 154 Oliver G 151 Surgeon 151 154
HUNTER, Col 37 David 44
HURD, J S 209
HURLBURT, Steven A 239
HURLBUT, 93 97
INDIAN, John 156
INGERSOLL, Capt 212 Orton 211
JACKSON, Andrew 9 Andy 204 Gen 204 William H 202
JAMES, 27
JEHU, Lt 156 157 Robert 155 166 213
JOHNSTON, 88 89 222 Albert Sidney 88 99 Joe 121 140 250 Joseph 149 Joseph E 237
JONES, Col 227 John 226
KARPPI, 13
KASSON, 116
KENYON, 132-135 Lt 131 156 Lt Col 255 Nathaniel 156 244 Nathaniel C 54 131
KINNARD, George 138
LAFLORE, Col 204
LANDRAM, 176 177 178 180 Col 176 Gen 175 W J 172
LAWLER, 228-231 Gen 228 M K 141 Mike 228
LAWRENCE, Artemas 39 Mr 39
LEE, 158 222 A L 175 Albert L 175 Robert 250 Robert E 251 Stephen D 186
LEFLORE, Greenwood 204
LEITH, Joe 134
LEWIS, 218 T N 223 227
LIDDEL, Saint John R 247
LIDDELL, Gen 252
LIEBER, Maj 176
LINCOLN, 10 11 17 44 45 125 255 Abraham 5 8 101 Pres 43 44 116 171 234

LINDSAY, R H 245
LINDSEY, Lt-col 178
LOGAN, 67 68 157 159 161 Black Jack 186 Col 80 Gen 115 158 186 John 113 John A 67 106 109
LOWE, Col 118 119 W W 117
LYON, J D 152
MABRY, Col 210
MADDON, Jim 76
MAIN, Capt 204 Ed 209 Edward 201 203 Maj 203 204 213
MALONE, Dumas 41
MARSH, 91 92 94 C C 89 105 114 Col 91
MATTHEWS, Pvt 59 Wade 50 58 82
MAURY, D H 240 Dabney 243 Gen 249
MAXIMILLIAN, 255
MCALLISTER, 91 92 96
MCARTHUR, 62 200 207 215 217-220 223 Gen 152 200 205 215 219 John 121 155 215
MCCALEB, Color Sgt 70
MCCLELLAN, 44 234 Gen 84 George B 16 53
MCCLERNAND, 61 62 67 84 94 96 106 158 Gen 60 69 79 80 94 95 105-107 114 John 57 229
MCDOWELL, Gen 20
MCELHAINY, Sam 210
MCELROY, John 30 Lt 211
MCKEE, 164 198 208 211-214 George 163 197 Maj 163 199 209-211
MCNEAL, Rev 5
MCPHERSON, James 152 James B 155 164
MILLER, Paul 199
MOORE, S F 223

MORAN, Terrence 14
MORGAN, John Hunt 119
NEVIUS, 68 87 108 109-114 118 120 142 144 147 148 Capt 2 16 17-19 Col 107 110-113 123 125 129 136 137 139 146 Garrett 6 32 56 107 241 Henry 111 Lt-col 128 Maj 49 67 68 88 92 95 Will 2 107 108
NEWCOMB, Charles 82 Mary 16 19 50 57-59 81 82 89 Mother 51 82 Mrs 50 59 60 Nurse 50 59
NIM, 177
OGLESBY, 47 48 61 62 Richard 47
OLIVER, W S 138
ORMSBY, Dr 190
OSBAND, Col 205 Embury D 203
OSMAN, 83 84 William 83 184
OWEN, Capt 202 205 Elias K 197
PARKINSON, William D 195
PATTON, James G 256
PECK, Warren 195
PEEBLES, Col 213 F E 198 200 Lt Col 206
PEMBERTON, 141 Gen 141 158 John C 140
PERCZEL, N 2
PICKENY, Prof 9
PIERCE, Franklin 39
PILLOW, Gen 49 81
POLK, James K 8
POND, 96
PORTER, 174 Admiral 183 David 171
PRENTISS, Ben 16 96 Gen 24 133
QUANTRILL, William 27
RANSOM, 23 28 38 41 42 47-49 51 62 63 65 66 69 70 72

RANSOM (continued)
 73 76 79 83 84 87 91-95
 103 104-107 112 117-119
 121 128 138 140-146 148
 149 150 152 155 162-165
 167 170 174-182 184-191
 193 241 255 Amasa 39 Brig
 Gen 220 Col 36 37 39 58
 66-68 70 83 87 107-109
 116 119 121 Dunbar 39 40
 134 220 Eugene 134 135
 194 208 220 221 F E 220
 Frederick Eugene 41 134
 221 Gen 135 138 140 143
 145 148 149 152 154-158
 160 170 172 173 178-181
 183 184 185 188 189 221
 234 George 38 Green 41
 174 Joseph 38 Lt-col 46 Maj
 24 28 30 Margaret 41 42
 135 185 Matthew 38 T E
 165 T E G 41 42 115 121
 130 163 169 171 234 240
 Thomas 23 39-42 134 221
 Thomas Edwin Greenfield
 38 191 Truman 38 39
 Truman B 38
RAWSON, 184
READING, John 65 John W 64
 159
RICHARDSON, Robert V 206
ROBINSON, Charles 14 Pvt 15
ROCKWOOD, N L 27
RODAN, 2
ROE, Henry 178 183
ROGERS, Lt 211
ROSE, Capt 19 112
ROSS, 203 204 Gen 210 211 L
 S 212 Lawrence 199 211
 Sull 199 202 206 207
ROUSE, Mrs 46
ROUTH, John 167 Mr 167
RYDER, W H 42
SCANLON, Lt 229

SHAW, 45 85 Capt 14 45 76
 Fred 4 85 Frederick 45
 George B 208
SHERIDAN, 232 255 Phil 185
 221
SHERMAN, 90 91 186-189 197
 199 202 206 222 Gen 185
 189 222 Uncle Billy 222 W T
 250 Wm T 121 196 William
 Tecumseh 155 Willie 189
SHIELDS, J 165 James M 170
 Mary 162 Mrs 162 164 165
 167
SHUBNER, 27
SIMPSON, Dr 135
SLOCUM, 187 221-228 Gen
 223 Henry W 186 Henry
 Warner 221
SMITH, 73 182 A J 175 180
 182 243 250 251 C F 73 76
 89 Gen 183 251 Kirby 162
 255 M A 161 Sooy 197 205
 W Sooy 197
STARLING, Col 144
STEELE, Frederick 171 247
STENGER, 218
STOCKTON, Joseph 140 Lt-col
 143
STRONG, William K 116
SWANK, 1
SWAP, A L 12
SWEENY, Sgt 71
SWITZER, John M 253
TAYLOR, 10 62 69 77 175 177
 180 Benjamin 120 Dick 174
 Gen 175 176 Richard 170
 240 Zachary 9 170
THATCHER, H K 244
THOMAS, Adjutant Gen 194 E
 P 158 160 Hattie 158 160
THOMPSON, 30 54 Capt 257
 Charles H 256 J P 188 Jeff
 1 30 46 47 57
TILGHMAN, Lloyd 60

TREDWAY, 177 J D 181 189
   Joseph D 177 Lt 184 190
TRENDALL, Isaac 200
UPTMOR, 70 160 225 226 231
   Henry 69 80 98 140 147
   159 196 224 241 Pvt 121
   142 144 201 210-212 227
   230
VANDORN, 125 126 Earl 124
VANLANDINGHAM, Clement
   136
VEATCH, 94 C 93
VERNAY, David 86 James 85
   86 131 James D 138 Sgt 86
VINCENT, Washington 200
VORE, Capt 227 H C 198 199
   208 216 223 Lt 223
WADDELL, 112 113 Capt 95
   112 Lloyd 91 95 112 163
   Maj 152 154
WALKER, Eugene 209
WALLACE, 8-11 14 17 21 23
   24 27-30 34-36 38 44 46 51
   54 55 57 59 61 63 67 69 73
   74 83 84 89 90 92 101 148
   229 230 Ann 8 11 23 55 56
   58 84 86 89 98 101 115 149
   153 166 181 Col 7 12 14-16
   19 23 24 27 29 32 34-36 46

WALLACE (continued)
   47 49 50 54-60 69 76 77 83
   148 229 Gen 83 89 97 99
   101 184 Isabell 11 Lew 73-
   75 99 101 Lt 9 Martin R M
   97 Mathew 58 Mrs 17 89 W
   H L 83 96 97 104 215 229
   240 Will 7 10 85 89 97
   William Henry Lamb 7
WASHBURN, Cadwallader C
   169 170
WEIS, George 80 George
   Gerard 80
WHARTON, 96
WHEATON, Lloyd 253
WHIPPLE, Frank 90 129 144
   194 199 238 241 Pvt 163
   Sgt 199 238 239 Warner
   129
WHITFIELD, 73
WILSON, Capt 199
WINSTON, Maj 184
WIRZ, Col 131 Henry 131
WOOD, Col 207 208 S A M 91
WOODWARD, Thomas G 119
WRIGHT, Col 143
YATES, Gov 5 Richard 3
ZERRUSEN, Karl 80 81

www.ingramcontent.com/pod-product-compliance
Lightning Source LLC
Chambersburg PA
CBHW071953220426
43662CB00009B/1105